A Teacher's Guide to Including Students with Disabilities in General Physical Education

Second Edition

A Teacher's Guide to Including Students with Disabilities in General Physical Education

Second Edition

by

Martin E. Block, Ph.D.
Kinesiology Program, Curry School of Education
University of Virginia, Charlottesville

·PAUL·H·
BROOKES
PUBLISHING Co.

Baltimore • London • Toronto • Sydney

Paul H. Brookes Publishing Co.
Post Office Box 10624
Baltimore, Maryland 21285-0624

www.brookespublishing.com

Typeset by Eastern Composition, Binghamton, New York.
Manufactured in the United States of America by
Hamilton Printing Company, Rensselaer, New York.

All of the case studies in this book are composites of the author's actual experiences. In all instances, names have been changed; in some instances, identifying details have been altered to protect confidentiality.

Permission is gratefully acknowledged to use the drawings appearing in this publication courtesy of Martha Perske.

Purchasers of *A Teacher's Guide to Including Students with Disabilities in General Physical Education, Second Edition,* are granted permission to photocopy the blank forms appearing in this publication. Photocopying privileges are for educational purposes only; none of the forms may be reproduced to generate revenue for any program or individual. Photocopies must be made from an original book.

Library of Congress Cataloging-in-Publication Data

Block, Martin E., 1958–
  A teacher's guide to including students with disabilities in general physical
  education / by Martin E. Block.—2nd ed.
    p. cm.
    Includes bibliographical references (p.) and index.
    ISBN 1-55766-463-3
    1. Physical education for handicapped persons. 2. Mainstreaming in
  education. I. Title.
  GV445.B56 2000
  371.9'04486—dc21

                                             00-034288

British Library Cataloguing in Publication data are available from the British Library.

Contents

About the Author

Martin E. Block, Ph.D., Associate Professor with the Kinesiology Program in the Curry School of Education, 202 Emmet Street South, University of Virginia, Charlottesville, VA 22904-4407, has been the co-director of the Adapted Physical Education Program at the University of Virginia in Charlottesville since 1992. Previously, he was an adapted physical education specialist for Prince William County Public Schools in Virginia and the Ivymount School, a private school for children with disabilities, in Maryland. Dr. Block has conducted numerous workshops around the country for physical educators, special educators, therapists, and paraprofessionals on how to better include children with disabilities in general physical education, and he has co-authored more than 40 articles on adapted physical education. He also has served as Chair of the Adapted Physical Activity Council and Motor Development Academy for the American Alliance of Health, Physical Education, Recreation, and Dance. Dr. Block's current research interests focus on improving in-service training to practicing physical educators as well as studying the perceptions of inclusive physical education by students with and without disabilities, general and adapted physical educators, parents, and administrators.

The Contributors

Phillip Conatser, Ph.D., Associate Professor, Slippery Rock University, Slippery Rock, Pennsylvania 16057, has taught individuals with disabilities since 1983.

Ron French, Ed.D., Professor, Texas Women's University, Pioneer Hall 208D, Post Office Box 425647, Denton, Texas 76204, teaches in the area of special physical education and is especially interested in the application of behavior management techniques to improve the performance and learning of students with disabilities.

Lisa Silliman-French, Ph.D., Adapted Physical Education Coordinator, Denton Independent School District, 1117 Riney Road, Denton, Texas 76207, is also a visiting professor at Texas Women's University, supervising and instructing undergraduate and graduate students in the kinesiology department.

Preface

The most noticeable change in this second edition is the use of the word *general* rather than *regular* in the book's title, in recognition of the negative effects of labeling and stigmatization that once resulted when students were separated into "regular" and "special" education classes. Today, the trend is toward including students with disabilities in typical, *general* classrooms with the supports and accommodations they need. In addition, I have updated extensively the first five chapters of the text. Chapter 1 updates the concept of what constitutes a quality physical education program. Chapter 2 reviews the history of inclusion and then clearly defines the key characteristics of inclusion. Chapter 3 revisits collaborative teaming and provides new information on the importance of communication among professionals. In addition to providing the preparation model and assessment tools designed for this model that were presented in the first edition, Chapters 4 and 5 provide new information and assessment tools to determine who qualifies for physical education and to complete the individualized education program (IEP) process. Chapters 6, 7, and 8 have been expanded and provide detailed information, models, and examples of how to implement instructional, curricular, and game modifications to facilitate inclusion.

Four new chapters that are based on feedback from colleagues and professionals in the field have also been added. Chapter 9 examines the importance of encouraging and facilitating the social acceptance of children with disabilities in general physical education, emphasizing what the general physical educator can do to create a welcoming environment as well as how physical educators can prepare children without disabilities for inclusion. Chapter 10 examines the important issue of safety when including children with disabilities. This chapter first focuses on some basic legal issues, then on more practical ways to create the safest possible environment for both children with and without disabilities. Chapter 11 presents information on coping with children who display behavior problems in general physical education. This chapter, which is co-authored by Ron French and Lisa Silliman-French, two of the leaders in behavior management, introduces a simple, step-by-step model for creating a behavior plan that focuses on examining the underlying causes of inappropriate behavior. In addition, Chapter 11 provides detailed information on ways to increase positive behavior and decrease inappropriate behavior. Finally, Chapter 12, co-authored by Phillip Conatser, a leader in adapted aquatics, provides practical information on how to include children with disabilities in general aquatics programs. Information presented applies the preparation model outlined in Chapter 4 to aquatics programs. Chapter 12 also contains information on safety considerations and adapted equipment.

When I wrote the first edition of this book, *A Teacher's Guide to Including Students with Disabilities in Regular Physical Education*, I advocated the placement of virtually *all* children with disabilities in general physical education programs (Block, 1994; Block & Krebs, 1992). In retrospect, I now realize that inclusion may be difficult for some children with disabilities and for many individual schools. Some children need a quieter, smaller environment than can be found in the general physical education classroom. I also realize now that some general physical education teachers have difficulty meaningfully including children with disabilities. Efforts should continue to be made to provide these teachers with information and ideas; in the meantime, however, students with disabilities who are in these programs may be better served in different, more appropriate physical education environments.

Despite my belief that inclusive general physical education may not benefit *every* child with disabilities, I still advocate inclusion in general physical education for *most* children with disabilities. I continue to be a strong believer in making placement decisions based on the least restrictive environment (LRE) tenet in the Individuals with Disabilities Education Act (IDEA) Amendments of 1997 (PL 105-17), which states that

> To the maximum extent appropriate, children with disabilities...are educated with children who are not disabled, and special classes, separate schooling, or other removal of children with disabilities from the regular educational environment occurs only when the nature or severity of the disability of a child is such that education in regular classes with the use of supplementary aids and services cannot be achieved satisfactorily.

With appropriate supplementary aids and services, most children with disabilities *can* be included in general physical education alongside children without disabilities. In fact, I know that many children with disabilities who are not currently placed in general physical education can and should be placed in this environment if given proper support.

I also still hope that with proper training and support, the vast majority of general physical educators will find including children with disabilities to be relatively easy and very rewarding. Even the most resistant general physical education teachers can learn simple modifications that make general physical education more inviting, appropriate, and successful for children with disabilities. As advocates of quality physical education for all children, we just have to keep holding in-services, writing papers, and offering our support to these teachers. Attitudes can change, and when attitudes change, behavior changes follow!

It is this latter hope that has compelled me to write this second edition. I hope this revised text continues to help the dedicated general and adapted physical educators who want to do what is right for their students with disabilities. Moreover, I hope this book inspires those physical educators who clearly are struggling with the realities of including students with disabilities in their programs.

Acknowledgments

I would like to thank several people for their assistance in the development and completion of this second edition. First, I would like to thank my wife, Vickie, for keeping me grounded and reminding me to make this book practical for real teachers. Our informal chats about what was "doable in the real world" were extremely helpful throughout this process. Second, I would like to thank my two daughters, Samantha and Jessica, for simply being who they are—loving, wonderful girls who are the true joy in my life! It was easy to leave my work at the office knowing that they would be home waiting for me.

I would like to thank my father, Herbert Block, for his support throughout this effort. He has always been a positive influence on my life, and his encouragement when I was getting bogged down with various aspects of the book was extremely helpful. It is wonderful having someone you can call at the spur of the moment to get a little boost and shot of confidence. My father served that role extraordinarily well.

Special thanks goes to all of the parents, teachers, and children who contributed their personal thoughts to the introductions of each chapter. These are the people who experience inclusion every day and help me understand what is important. Also, special thanks to Martha Perske for allowing me to use her beautiful illustrations throughout the book. These pictures show better than words what can happen when inclusion is done well!

Thanks go to Drs. Ron French and Lisa Silliman-French for co-writing the behavior management chapter and Dr. Phillip Conatser for co-writing the aquatics chapter. Ron, Lisa, and Phillip are leaders in the field of adapted physical education, and I am truly honored that they wrote these chapters.

Thanks goes to the staff at Paul H. Brookes Publishing Co. for guiding me through the process of revising this text. In particular, thanks to Lisa Benson who never pushed me too hard when I was having trouble getting started but who also kept in contact to make sure I stayed on track. Also, special thanks to Maura Cooney and Kristine Dorman for their expert editing and for making sure I kept to my deadlines. I really would not have been able to complete this second edition without their support. As I noted in my first edition, I really feel honored that my book is part of the Brookes family of wonderful books on inclusion and special education.

Finally, thanks goes to all of the children with and without disabilities, my graduate students, practicing physical education teachers, and higher education colleagues from around the country who have talked to me about inclusion in general physical education. I have learned so much by watching and talking to children here in Virginia. They have been my best teachers! I also have learned so much by traveling to places such as Missoula, Montana; Rochester, New York; Birmingham, Alabama; and Houston, Texas, and talking frankly and openly with physical educators. They have shared with me their concerns about inclusion, and I have tried to include these concerns and solutions to these concerns throughout the text. I have had wonderful conversations with colleagues such as Claudine Sherrill, David Beaver, Paul Jansma, Jim Rich, Julian Stein, Ron French, Lisa Silliman-French, Katie Stanton, Fiona Conner Kuntz, Lauren Lieberman, Ron Davis, Tim Davis, Bill Vogler, Pat DiRocco, Phillip Conatser, Luke Kelly, and John Dunn, just to name a few. They have provided me with new ideas and ways of thinking that, in turn, have shaped my current views on inclusion.

1

What Is Physical Education?

THERE IS A CHILD INVOLVED

Mainstream, self-contain, integrate, include
How's the wind blow, what's the mood?
General ed., special ed., adapted or not,
Teachers everywhere are put on the spot.
Lighter balls, larger goals, and shorter distances too,
The menu's so large; no one's sure what to do.

These concerns each could be solved
If we'd only remember,

THERE IS A CHILD INVOLVED

Baseball, basketball, floor hockey too,
Do I have to adapt all of them for you?
Why can't you watch, maybe keep score?
Then the "regulars" will get to play more.
Gross motor, fine motor, wheelchairs and walkers,
And all those fancy augmentative talkers.
I went to college to learn how to teach,
But no one told me, there'd be so many to reach.

Relax, take a breath, for this too can be resolved
If we'd only remember,

THERE IS A CHILD INVOLVED

Frustrated kids who just want the chance
To score a goal, or join in a dance.
They can't quite catch, or keep up the pace,
And seem to get lost in the midst of a race.
But you need not lower the ceiling
For those who stumble and fall,
Just adapt and level the field
For one and for all.

So what's to be done, what's the goal to be?
It's plain, it's simple, just teach PE

And remember. . .

THERE IS A CHILD INVOLVED

Michael Marsallo, principal

To the memory of my mother, Helen Block. With every passing year I realize more and more how she continues to inspire me and influence my work. She was the most positive, caring person I have ever known and think I ever will know, and she touched so many people through her volunteer work at a center for children with cerebral palsy in New York and her braille for the blind in Maryland. I can only hope that I have as positive an influence on the people I meet and teach as she had on me.

A Teacher's Guide to Including Students with Disabilities in General Physical Education

Second Edition

Madison is an active, 10-year-old fourth-grade student who arrives at Northwood Elementary School each day with a smile on her face. She has cerebral palsy, which requires her to use a walker for mobility. Madison participates in general physical education three times per week with Mrs. Martin, a general physical education teacher (there is no adapted physical education specialist in this school district). Madison and all of the other students at Northwood love physical education because of the way Mrs. Martin runs her program. What makes Mrs. Martin's physical education program so special?

First, Madison and the other students know ahead of time what they will be doing in physical education each day and how each day's activities fit into Mrs. Martin's units or "themes." Some themes revolve around learning one specific skill such as throwing overhand or jumping rope; other themes revolve around learning multiple skills and concepts that relate to a specific topic such as dancing, gymnastics, physical fitness, or a sport. Each theme lasts for about 2–4 weeks, depending on the number of skills within that theme and the skill level of the students. Themes that are particularly important (e.g., physical fitness) or themes that have skills that are difficult to master (e.g., overhand throw) are often revisited throughout the year. In addition to practicing specific skills during physical education, students are encouraged to practice skills within a theme at home. Using themes allows Mrs. Martin to help her students focus on specific skills for a concentrated amount of time.

Second, regardless of the particular theme, Mrs. Martin makes sure each student knows on which skills or parts of skills to work and how to work on them. Rather than hold all students to the same standard, however, Mrs. Martin makes sure each student has individualized goals within each skill or concept that he or she can work toward based on his or her abilities. For example, during a recent throwing unit, some students worked on following through; some worked on fully extending their arm back; and others, who already had mastered the specific components of the throw, worked on throwing for distance and accuracy. Madison worked on throwing while standing in her walker using a special throwing pattern that she and Mrs. Martin devised just for Madison. Furthermore, Mrs. Martin always provides lots of choices of activities for the students to practice and equipment for them to use to reinforce their skills. For example, during a throwing unit, Mrs. Martin offered activity choices that included throwing at a parachute, throwing over a large cardboard box, throwing into a curtain, and throwing against the wall. In addition, students were allowed to choose what types of objects they wanted to throw (e.g., paper balls, yarn balls, koosh balls, bean bags) as well as how far away they would stand from the target at each station. This way, each student had a chance to be successful and challenged at his or her own level. (Madison prefers the bean bags because she is better able to grip them.)

Third, Mrs. Martin finds a way to make sure all the students always are active and engaged in fun activities. Students never have to stand around and wait for their turn. Each student has his or her own piece of equipment (unless he or she is involved in partner or group work), and the gymnasium is set up so that there is a lot of space for all of the students to participate at the same time in a safe manner. Also, Mrs. Martin tries to have the students play many games that reinforce a particular skill theme. However, she never plays traditional sports following regulation rules (e.g., softball, volleyball) because they often exclude many students, leaving them standing around without turns. She also does not play elimination games in which students have to sit out for extended periods of time. For example, during a basketball unit, Mrs. Martin had the students play tag games while dribbling a basketball, keep-away games to reinforce passing and catching, and a two-person relay race in which the students threw a ball toward a target on the wall to reinforce shooting. Madison's classmates often tag her during the dribble tag games; however, all she has to do is reach down and touch her toes three times to get back into the game. She never has to sit out.

Fourth, Mrs. Martin uses a variety of teaching styles to keep the students interested, to encourage active learning and cognitive development, and to promote interaction with peers and teamwork. For example, during a fitness theme, Mrs. Martin had the students do cooperative push-ups. Students were placed into groups of fives and were told to determine how many push-ups they could do as a team. Some students did modified push-ups, whereas other students did regular push-ups. (Madison is very strong in her upper body, so she did regular push-ups!) Then, the total for the group was added. Each day during the unit, the cooperative teams tried to beat their total number of push-ups from the previous day. During a typical unit, Mrs. Martin often uses cooperative learning as well as other unique teaching styles such as reciprocal teaching (i.e., peer tutoring), student designed activities, task sheets, and guided discovery.

Across town, Jared attends fourth grade at Squirrel Ridge Elementary School. Jared is just as bright-eyed and active as Madison. Jared has cerebral palsy, too, and, like Madison, requires the use of a walker. However, whereas Madison and her peers at Northwood love physical education, Jared and a lot of other students at Squirrel Ridge hate it because of the way Mrs. Hanover, the physical education specialist, runs her program. Unlike Mrs. Martin, Mrs. Hanover does not teach in themes. Rather, she usually decides what to teach when she arrives at school each morning. Sometimes students do something different each day of the week, whereas other times they do the same thing for up to 2 months! Students never really know what they will be doing in physical education from day to day. During a cold spell in January, Mrs. Hanover had all of her classes (kindergarten through fifth grade) play dodge ball every day. Although Jared likes to play dodging and fleeing games, he is often an easy target and one of the first students to be eliminated.

Mrs. Hanover also does not believe in adapting physical education for each student. All students are expected to meet the one standard she has created, which often is designed for students of average ability. Students with less skill as well as students with disabilities, such as Jared, often fail in physical education and get frustrated. By the time these students reach the fourth and fifth grades, they spend most of their time in physical education avoiding participation rather than learning new skills. On the other end of the spectrum, skilled students are often bored because activities are too easy for them. Often, these students develop problem behaviors; they use equipment inappropriately or goof off to get attention.

Similar to Mrs. Martin, Mrs. Hanover likes to have her students play games to reinforce skills. However, Mrs. Hanover feels that there is only one way to play games—the regulation way. During softball units, there are 10 students in the field standing and watching, 9 students behind home plate standing and watching, and 1 student up at the plate getting ready to hit. Many students only get one turn to bat and never even touch the ball in the field. Yet, if you asked Mrs. Hanover what skills she was working on with the students, she would say throwing, catching, and striking! When a student finally does get a turn at bat, he or she has to use a regulation softball bat (the one Mrs. Hanover uses when she plays in a summer league) and try to hit a pitched ball. It doesn't matter that the bat is too heavy for most of the students or that most of them cannot consistently hit a pitched ball. Jared, in fact, has never successfully hit a pitched ball during Mrs. Hanover's class.

Finally, Mrs. Hanover has only one way of teaching. Although she has read about cooperative learning and other ways of presenting information to the students, she believes that she will not have enough control over the students if she uses these alternative methods. Consequently, she uses the same teaching style during physical education class that she uses when she coaches—direct instruction that usually involves a brief demonstration followed by the students waiting in line to take a turn to practice the skill. Unfortunately, many of the students (including Jared, who also has a slight visual impairment) do not learn by watching Mrs. Hanover demonstrate, and they certainly do not get enough practice trials with feedback when they get only one or two turns.

What type of physical education program do you conduct? Is it like Mrs. Martin's program—carefully planned, comprehensive, and designed to meet each student's needs? Do you make an effort to really teach your students skills and concepts? Do students receive numerous opportunities to practice activities at which they can be successful? Or, is your program more like Mrs. Hanover's— more or less thrown together at the spur of the moment? Do you teach your students as if they all possess the same abilities and learning styles? Do you rarely modify games to promote students' active involvement and success?

Before you can provide an appropriate program for students with disabilities who are included in your general physical education class, you must develop a quality general physical education program. The purpose of this chapter is to review what quality physical education is and what it encompasses as well as the legal basis for physical education services as outlined in select federal legislations. Specifically, the first part of this chapter outlines the characteristics and benefits of a quality physical education program. The second part of the chapter provides legal definitions of physical education and the provision of physical education as outlined in the Individuals with Disabilities Education Act (IDEA) of 1990 (PL 101–476) and the IDEA amendments of 1997 (PL 105–17) including a detailed analysis of the key components that make up a comprehensive physical education program. The third part of the chapter discusses the concept of developmentally appropriate practices in physical education. Finally, a definition of adapted physical education is provided.

What Is Quality Physical Education?

Sherrill (1998) noted that physical education should be considered an "academic subject," such as math or reading, that is instructional with a planned sequence of activities. If physical education is to be regarded as an "academic subject," then physical educators must provide a high-quality program. Simply "rolling out the ball" and supervising a volleyball game between two teams consisting of 20 students each is not quality physical education!

So, what is quality physical education? The Council on Physical Education for Children (COPEC) provided the following statement regarding quality physical education:

> The Council on Physical Education for Children (COPEC) of the National Association for Sport and Physical Education (NASPE), the nation's largest professional association of children's physical education teachers, believes that quality, daily physical education

should be available to all children. Quality physical education is both developmentally and instructionally suitable for the specific children being served. Developmentally appropriate practices in physical education are those which recognize children's changing capacities to move and those which promote change. A developmentally appropriate physical education program accommodates a variety of individual characteristics such as developmental status, previous movement experiences, fitness and skill levels, body size, and age. Instructionally appropriate physical education incorporates the best known practices, derived from both research and experiences with teaching children, into a program that maximizes opportunities for learning and success for all children. The outcome of a developmentally and instructionally appropriate program of physical education is an individual who is "physically educated." (COPEC, 1992, p. 3)

In addition, COPEC defined a physically educated person as follows:

1. HAS learned the skills necessary to perform a variety of physical activities
2. IS physically fit
3. DOES participate regularly in physical activity
4. KNOWS the implications of and the benefits from involvement in physical activities
5. VALUES physical activity and its contributions to a healthful lifestyle (p. 3)

Finally, Graham, Holt/Hale, and Parker outlined six key points regarding quality physical education:

1. Physical education *should not* be recess!
2. Physical education *should not* simply be a time to provide planning time for classroom teachers!
3. Physical education *should not* just be a "fun" time for students to expend excess energy that is built up from sitting in a classroom!
4. Physical education *should* be a developmentally appropriate educational experience designed to provide immediate and lifelong benefits—important benefits that are typically only taught in physical education classes.
5. Physical education curricula and instruction *should* emphasize enjoyable participation in physical activity and "help students develop the knowledge, attitudes, motor skills, behavioral skills, and confidence needed to adopt and maintain physically active lifestyles" (United States Department of Health and Human Services, 1996, p. 205).
6. Physical education *should* be an experience that guides youngsters in the process of becoming physically active for a lifetime. (1998, p. 4)

When examined, it is clear that quality physical education requires thoughtful planning on the part of the physical education teacher. It requires an in-depth knowledge of each student's developmental status and learning style and constant monitoring in order to adapt the program as each student changes.

Benefits of Quality Physical Education

Quality physical education during a student's school years often results in physically educated adults who maintain an active lifestyle. Physically active people derive the following benefits, as noted by the Surgeon General's (USDHHS, 1996) report:

1. Significant health benefits can be obtained by including a moderate amount of physical activity (e.g., 30 minutes of brisk walking or raking leaves, 15 minutes of running, 45 minutes of volleyball) on most, if not all, days of the

week. Through a modest increase in daily activity, most Americans can improve their health and quality of life (p. 4).

2. Additional health benefits can be gained through greater amounts of physical activity. People who can maintain a regular regimen of activity that is of longer duration or more vigorous intensity are likely to derive greater benefit (p. 4).

3. Physical activity reduces the risk of premature mortality in general, and of coronary heart disease, hypertension, colon cancer, and diabetes mellitus in particular. Physical activity also improves mental health and is important for the health of muscles, bones, and joints (p. 4).

4. Consistent influences on physical activity patterns among adults and young people include confidence in one's ability to engage in regular physical activity (e.g., self-efficacy), enjoyment of physical activity, support from others, positive beliefs concerning the benefits of physical activity, and lack of perceived barriers to physical activity (p. 249).

5. Physical activity appears to improve health-related quality of life by enhancing psychological well-being and by improving physical functioning in people compromised by poor health (p. 8).

Additional benefits of *quality* physical education programs include 1) the development of a variety of motor skills and abilities related to lifetime leisure skills; 2) improved understanding of the importance of maintaining a healthy lifestyle throughout life; 3) improved understanding and appreciation of the human body and how it can move; 4) improved knowledge of rules, strategies, and behaviors of particular games and sports; and 5) improved self-confidence and self-worth as they relate to physical education and recreational activities (Graham et al., 1998; NASPE, 1992; Sherrill, 1998) (see NASPE's detailed definition of a physically educated person in Table 1.1).

The previously listed benefits of physical education are even more important for students with disabilities than for students without disabilities. Many students with disabilities have more free time than their peers without disabilities (e.g., in the past, students with disabilities have had limited opportunities to participate in after-school clubs or community programs) (Datillo, 1991; Schleien, Ray, & Green, 1997). Most individuals with disabilities, however, have limited recreation skills, which greatly restricts their abilities to participate in community activities and interact with peers who do not have disabilities. Extra free time coupled with limited recreation skills often lead to a sedentary lifestyle that in turn can lead to health and social problems (Schleien et al., 1997). Quality physical education programs can help students with disabilities acquire critical lifetime leisure skills including appropriate behaviors and an appreciation for continued participation in active recreational pursuits.

Legal Definition of Physical Education

Physical education services, specially designed if necessary, must be made available to *every* student with a disability who receives a free and appropriate public education (Block & Burke, 1999). Physical education has been required since 1975, when PL 94-142, the Education for All Handicapped Children Act (EHA) (Federal Register, 1977), was enacted. It has remained an essential part of special education services through the many reauthorizations of PL 94-142, including PL 101-476 in 1990 and the most recent reauthorization, PL 105-17, in 1997 (see

Table 1.1. National Association for Sport and Physical Education (NASPE) definition of a physically educated person

The Physically Educated Person:

HAS learned the skills necessary to perform a variety of physical activities

1. . . . moves using concepts of body awareness, space awareness, effort and relationship.
2. . . . demonstrates competence in a variety of manipulative, locomotor and non-locomotor skills.
3. . . . demonstrates competence in combinations of manipulative, locomotor and non-locomotor skills performed individually and with others.
4. . . . demonstrates competence in many different forms of physical activity.
5. . . . demonstrates proficiency in a few forms of physical activity.
6. . . . has learned how to learn new skills.

IS physically fit

7. . . . assesses, achieves and maintains physical fitness.
8. . . . designs safe, personal fitness programs in accordance with principles of training and conditioning.

DOES participate regularly in physical activity

9. . . . participates in health enhancing physical activity at least three times a week.
10. . . . selects and regularly participates in lifetime physical activities.

KNOWS the implications of and the benefits from involvement in physical activities

11. . . . identifies the benefits, costs and obligations associated with regular participation in physical activity.
12. . . . recognizes the risk and safety factors associated with regular participation in physical activity.
13. . . . applies concepts and principles to the development of motor skills.
14. . . . understands that wellness involves more than being physically fit.
15. . . . knows the rules, strategies and appropriate behaviors for selected physical activities.
16. . . . recognizes that participation in physical activity can lead to multi-cultural and international understanding.
17. . . . understands that physical activity provides the opportunity for enjoyment, self-expression and communication.

VALUES physical activity and its contributions to a healthful lifestyle

18. . . . appreciates the relationships with others that result from participation in physical activity.
19. . . . respects the role that regular physical activity plays in the pursuit of life-long health and well-being.
20. . . . cherishes the feelings that result from regular participation in physical activity.

Reprinted from *Outcomes of Quality Physical Education Programs* with permission from the National Association for Sport and Physical Education (NASPE), 1900 Association Drive, Reston, VA 20191-1599.

Table 1.2 for a brief chronology of IDEA). Not only did legislators define physical education, but physical education was considered so important that they made it the only curricular area that was specifically placed within the definition of special education:

> The term special education means specially designed instruction, at no cost to parents, to meet unique needs of a child with a disability including—
>
> (A) instruction conducted in the classroom, in the home, in hospitals and institutions, and in other settings; and
>
> (B) instruction in PHYSICAL EDUCATION (emphasis added) (IDEA Amendments of 1997, PL 105–17, 20 U.S.C. §§ 1400 et seq.[25]).

Unfortunately, many parents, professionals, and administrators are unfamiliar with the physical education requirements in the law, and students with disabilities continue to be excluded from physical education or to receive inappro-

Table 1.2. Chronology of Individuals with Disabilities Education Act (IDEA) Amendments of 1997 (PL 105-17)

Year	Act	Description
1975	PL 94-142 Education for All Handicapped Children Act (EHA)	Landmark legislation that required free and appropriate public education, including physical education, for all eligible children ages 3–21. EHA is known as Part B in the current Individuals with Disabilities Education Act (IDEA).
1983	PL 98-189 EHA Amendments of 1983	Increased funding and provided *incentives* for states to develop and implement an early intervention system to serve children with disabilities from birth to age 5. States were not mandated to provide services to children birth to age 3 at this point.
1986	PL 99-457 EHA Amendments of 1986	*Required* states to provide services to eligible preschoolers ages 3–5 years or lose federal funding. Also, Part H of 99-457 (still referred to Part H in IDEA) commissioned funds to states to develop and implement a comprehensive, multidisciplinary, interagency program of early intervention services for infants and toddlers with disabilities (birth to age 2) and their families.
1990	PL 101-476 Individuals with Disabilities Education Act (IDEA) of 1990	Renamed EHA to Individuals with Disabilities Education Act (IDEA). All references to *handicap* in previous law are replaced with term *disability*. Major changes include new definitions of attention-deficit/hyperactivity disorder and traumatic brain injury and the creation of a new eligibility category for autism. Reemphasized least restrictive environment with focus on training general education personnel and the use of assistive technology. Added new term, *transition services*, which emphasizes a coordinated effort to help students ages 16 and older (14 for students with severe disabilities) acquire skills needed to move from school to postschool activities. As such, social services, recreation therapy, and rehabilitation counseling reemphasized.
1997	PL 105-17 IDEA Amendments of 1997	Greater focus on parental rights and participation in process. Greater emphasis on least restrictive environment (LRE) and justification of placement in settings other than regular education. Require general educator to participate in all IEP meetings.

[handwritten annotations: "What is locally county convention?", "Starts with age 15"]

priate physical education services (Chandler & Greene, 1995; Jansma & Decker, 1990). Because lawmakers feared that the requirements would be unnoticed or neglected by parents, professionals, and administrators, they placed the following comments into the rules and regulations of the original law:

> Special education as set forth in the Committee bill includes instruction in physical education, which is provided as a matter of course to all non-handicapped children enrolled in public elementary and secondary schools. The Committee is concerned that although these services are available to and required of all children in our school systems, they are often viewed as a luxury for handicapped children . . . The Committee . . . specifically included physical education in the definition of special education to make clear that the Committee expects such services, specially designed where necessary, to be provided as an integral part of the education program of every handicapped child. (Federal Register, August 23, 1977, p. 42489)

IDEA defined physical education services as follows:

> (a) **General:** Physical education services, specifically designed as necessary, must be made available to every handicapped child receiving a free appropriate public education. (Federal Register, August 23, 1977, p. 42489)

This statement reinforces the notion that all students with disabilities must receive some form of physical education. Many school districts have placed physical education on their individualized education program (IEP) forms (typically in the form of an area to check whether the student receives general or adapted physical education) to emphasize that each student must receive some form of physical education services.

> (b) **Regular physical education:** Each handicapped child must be afforded the opportunity to participate in the regular physical education program available to non-handicapped children unless:
>
> (1) the child is enrolled full time in a separate facility; or
>
> (2) the child needs specially designed physical education, as prescribed in the child's individualized education program. (Federal Register, August 23, 1977, p. 42489).

Many students with disabilities can receive a safe, successful, and meaningful physical education experience in general physical education and do not need any special goals or objectives for physical education on their IEPs (Bateman, 1996). However, for some students to be successful in general physical education, they need modifications to the curriculum, equipment, and/or instruction. These modifications might include an interpreter for a student who is deaf, a beep ball for a student who is blind, a peer tutor for a student with mental retardation, or a teacher assistant for a student who has autism. These accommodations, determined by each student's specific needs, should be noted on the student's IEP (Bateman, 1996; Block & Burke, 1999).

> (c) **Special physical education:** If specially designed physical education is prescribed in a child's individualized education program, the public agency responsible for the education of that child shall provide the services directly, or make arrangements for it to be provided through other public or private programs. (Federal Register, August 23, 1977, p. 42489).

If assessment reveals that a student with a disability needs special physical education, the student's IEP team should develop individualized goals and objectives for physical education and write the goals into the student's IEP (Bateman, 1996; Block & Burke, 1999). For example, a 10-year-old student with cerebral palsy needs to learn how to walk using a special gait trainer. Because this is a unique goal designed for this particular student, the goal, along with incremental short-term objectives, should be written into this student's IEP.

It is important to note that qualifying a student for special physical education and developing IEP objectives does not necessarily mean that a student will be pulled out into a separate adapted physical education program. Many students with disabilities can work on their unique IEP goals and objectives within the general physical education environment. For example, the student who uses the gait trainer can practice walking while the other students run laps during warm-ups or play tagging and fleeing games or games that require running such as basketball and soccer. For safety purposes, the student might require a peer or an assistant's aid, but he or she should be able to work on his or her unique goals while interacting with peers without disabilities.

> (d) **Education in separate facilities:** The public agency responsible for the education of a handicapped child who is enrolled in a separate facility shall insure that the child receives appropriate physical education services in compliance with paragraphs (a) and (c) of this section. (Federal Register, August 23, 1977, p. 42489)

This means that a student with a disability who is educated in a separate facility, such as a school for the deaf, must still receive physical education services that are specially designed if necessary (Bateman, 1996).

Clearly, lawmakers define physical education as an important, *direct service* that should be a part of every student's educational program. Contrast this with the law's stipulation regarding *related services* such as physical, occupational, and recreation therapy:

> . . . "related services" means transportation and such developmental, corrective, and other supportive services as are required to assist a handicapped child benefit from special education (Federal Register, August 23, 1977, p. 42479).

These related services are provided only to those students who need extra support to benefit from special education. Because physical education is included in the definition of special education and related services are provided to assist students who need extra support to benefit from special education, related services can be viewed as support given to students to help them benefit from physical education! All students should receive physical education services, whereas only those students who need extra support to benefit from special education require related services. Related services (including physical, occupational, or recreation therapy) *cannot* be considered a substitute for the physical education requirement; nor can recess, unstructured free time, or training in sedentary recreational activities (e.g., board and card games) be considered appropriate substitutes for physical education services (Block & Burke, 1999; Sherrill, 1998).

Components of Physical Education

Although it is clear that physical education should be viewed as an important part of a student's overall education program, what exactly is physical education? Physical education is further defined in IDEA as

> The development of physical and motor fitness, fundamental motor skills and patterns, and skills in aquatics, dance, and individual and group games and sports (including intramural and lifetime sports). The term includes special physical education, adapted physical education, movement education, and motor development. (Federal Register, August 23, 1977, p. 42480)

The following provides a more detailed examination of each component contained within the definition of physical education.

Physical and motor fitness refers to the development of both health-related and skill-related fitness. Health-related fitness focuses on factors pertaining to a healthy lifestyle and the prevention of disease related to a sedentary lifestyle (Graham et al., 1998; Hastad & Lacy, 1989; Pangrazi, 1998). Pangrazi (1998) provided the following definitions of the specific components of health-related fitness:

- *Cardiovascular endurance (aerobic endurance):* Ability of the heart, blood vessels, and the respiratory system to deliver oxygen efficiently over an extended period of time. Moving (e.g., riding a bike, walking, jogging) without stopping for extended periods of time retains or increases cardiovascular efficiency.

- *Body composition:* Refers to the division of total body weight into two components: fat weight and lean weight. A fit person has a relatively low percentage of body fat. Performing aerobic and strength activities in addition to following a reasonable diet will help retain or decrease percentage of body fat.

- *Flexibility:* Range of motion of the musculature (i.e., muscles, tendons, and ligaments). Flexibility is joint specific and, therefore, must be measured at several joints. Stretching activities help musculature retain or increase elasticity.

- *Muscular strength:* Ability of muscles to exert force (e.g., to lift heavy objects). Lifting weights or other objects that are heavier than those lifted during typical daily activities increases muscular strength.

- *Muscular endurance:* Ability of muscles to exert force over an extended period of time. Lifting weights or heavy objects repeatedly retains or increases muscular endurance.

Skill-related fitness refers to specific fitness components associated with successful performance in specific motor activities and sports (Graham et al., 1998; Hastad & Lacy, 1989; Pangrazi, 1998). Hastad and Lacy (1989, p. 248) provided the following definitions of the specific components of skill-related fitness:

- *Agility:* Ability to rapidly and accurately change the position of the body in space. Examples of agility include quickly changing positions in wrestling or avoiding a tackler in football.

- *Balance:* Maintenance of equilibrium while stationary (static balance) or moving (dynamic balance). Examples of static balance include performing a headstand or maintaining balance while swinging a golf club; examples of dynamic balance include walking a balance beam or running in a football game without falling.

- *Coordination:* Ability to simultaneously perform multiple motor tasks smoothly and accurately. Hitting a tennis ball, using a smooth throwing pattern when pitching a ball, or dribbling a soccer ball are examples of athletic skills that require coordination.

- *Power:* Ability to transfer energy explosively into force. The standing long jump, the shot put, or kicking a soccer ball are all examples of skills that require power.

- *Speed:* Ability to perform a movement in a short period of time. Running to first base or dribbling a ball quickly down a basketball court are examples of activities that require speed.

- *Reaction time:* Difference between the stimulation (seeing, hearing, feeling something) and the response (moving) to the stimulation. A sprinter's response to the starting gun or a racquetball player's reaction to a hard-hit ball are examples of activities that require short reaction times.

Fundamental motor skills and patterns refer to the development of basic motor skills that form the foundation for more advanced, specific movements used in individual and team sports and activities (Gabbard, 2000; Gallahue & Ozmun, 1998; Graham et al., 1998; Pangrazi, 1998). Each fundamental motor skill has a distinct pattern or structure that defines the movement. Fundamental movement patterns are usually divided into locomotor and manipulative patterns. Locomotor patterns are movements used by individuals to travel from one place to another, whereas manipulative patterns are movements used to propel objects away from the body or to receive objects. Tables 1.3 and 1.4 provide more detailed descriptions of the most common fundamental locomotor and manipulative patterns as described by Gallahue and Ozmun (1998) and Graham et al. (1998).

Aquatics refers to activities conducted in the water and includes 1) swimming, which involves moving independently in the water using various strokes; 2) water exercises, which are used to develop health-related fitness; and 3) hydrotherapy, which involves using the water environment to work on specific therapeutic goals such as walking, relaxing, or maintaining/increasing range of motion (Lepore, Gayle, & Stevens, 1998; Priest, 1990).

Rhythm and dance refers to the ability to repeat an action or movement with regularity and in time to a particular pattern (Kirchner & Fishburne, 1998). Rhythm involves three major components: 1) tempo (speed), 2) pattern (even or uneven beats), and 3) accent (emphasis) (Kirchner & Firshburne, 1998). Dance refers to a combination of movements and rhythm in which movement qualities and components along with rhythmic movements are purposefully integrated into a progression with a beginning, middle, and end (Krebs, 1990). Dance can in-

Table 1.3.   Descriptions of fundamental locomotor patterns

Walking	Standing upright with eyes forward, swing one leg forward while swinging the opposite arm forward; then swing the other leg forward and the other arm forward.
Running	Standing upright with eyes forward, bend arms at elbow. Push off and swing one leg forward while swinging opposite arm forward. Then swing the other leg forward and the other arm forward.
Jumping	Standing upright with eyes forward and feet shoulder width apart, bend legs at knee and bring both arms behind body. Simultaneously, lean forward, swing arms forward, and forcefully straighten out legs.
Galloping	Standing upright with eyes forward, start with one leg forward in front of the other. Slide the back leg toward the front leg, and then step forward with the front leg. Pump arms either together or in alternating pattern.
Hopping	Stand upright with one leg bent so that the foot is off the ground. Bend the support leg at the knee and bring both arms back behind the body. Simultaneously lean forward, swing arms forward, and forcefully straighten out support leg.
Skipping	Alternate hopping on one foot, then stepping onto the other foot, and then hopping with that foot. Movement is a hop-step on one foot followed by a hop-step on opposite foot.

Locomotor patterns also can include pushing a manual wheelchair/controlling an electric wheelchair.

Table 1.4. Descriptions of fundamental manipulative patterns

Throwing	Propelling a small ball away from body using one hand. Skillful throwing is initiated by a forward step with opposite leg, followed by hip and trunk rotation, and concluded with a whipping arm action.
Catching	Receiving and controlling a ball that is tossed or kicked to the student. Skillful catching is noted by extending arms to meet the ball, retracting hands upon contact with ball, and using hands to catch ball rather than trapping ball against body.
Striking (bat)	Propelling a ball away from body by hitting ball with a long-handled implement. Skillful, two-handed striking consists of stepping forward followed by quick hip, trunk, and arm rotation; swinging horizontally; and whipping arms forward in a forceful follow-through.
Striking (racquet)	Propelling ball away from body by hitting ball with a racquet. Skillful, one-handed striking consists of stepping forward followed by quick hip, trunk, and arm rotation; swinging horizontally; and whipping arm forward in a forceful follow-through.
Kicking	Propelling ball away from body by using foot to impart force on ball. Skillful kicking consists of planting support leg next to ball, bringing kicking leg back by flexing knee, forcefully swinging leg forward to contact ball, then continuing to swing leg forward in forceful follow-through.
Punting	Propelling ball away from body using foot to impart force on ball. Punting is different than kicking in that the ball is held and then dropped by the child, and the ball is kicked before it touches the ground.

clude anything from basic rhythmic activities and action songs for young students to traditional dances (e.g., ballroom, folk, square), aerobic dances, and modern dances (i.e., creative dance) for older students and adults (Graham et al., 1998; Krebs, 1990).

Individual sports include culturally popular sports that involve one player or teams consisting of no more than two players each. Popular individual sports in America are listed in Table 1.5. Potential activities within each individual sport include practicing skills as well as playing lead-up (simplified or modified forms of traditional sports that help students acquire game skills and concepts), recreational, or competitive games. In addition, many of the sports listed in Table 1.5 are considered lifetime leisure activities because they can be played by individuals across the life span.

Team sports include culturally popular sports that involve three or more players per side. Popular team sports in America are listed in Table 1.6. As is the case

Table 1.5. Popular individual sports

Archery	Gymnastics	Scuba diving
Badminton	Hiking	Shooting
Boccie	Horseback riding	Skiing
Bowling	Horseshoes	Swimming
Cycling	Hunting	Table tennis
Croquet	Ice skating	Tennis
Fencing	Martial arts	Track and field
Darts	Racquetball	Water skiing
Golf	Rollerskating	Weight training

Table 1.6. Popular team sports

Basketball	Football	Softball
Baseball	Lacrosse	Team handball
Field hockey	Rugby	Volleyball
Floor hockey	Soccer	

with individual sports, activities in each team sport can include practicing skills as well as playing lead-up, modified, recreational, or competitive games. It is interesting to note that some team sports (e.g., football, baseball) are not considered lifetime leisure activities because most individuals do not participate in these activities after middle age. However, team sports such as volleyball and softball are often played by older adults and, therefore, should be considered lifetime leisure activities.

Objectives of Physical Education

The components of physical education help define the types of activities that should be included in a comprehensive physical education program. However, presenting activities without purpose or focus is not what physical education is about. Good physical education programs use specific activities to promote more global physical education objectives that facilitate psychomotor (motor and fitness performance), cognitive (intellectual skills), and affective (feelings, opinions, attitudes, beliefs, values, interests, and desires) development (Sherrill, 1998). Pangrazi and Dauer (1992) outlined several physical education objectives that, when taken together, define the purpose of physical education. These objectives include the following:

1. *A physical education program should help each child become competent in a wide variety of body management and physical skills.* These skills include 1) body management (ability to move the body through various circumstances and environments), 2) rhythmic skills (ability to move with a certain regularity or timing), 3) fundamental skills (locomotor and manipulative patterns), and 4) specialized skills (individual and team sports).

2. *A physical education program should provide all children with the opportunity to develop and maintain a level of health-related physical fitness commensurate with individual needs. Allied to this objective is giving children an understanding of how to develop and maintain an adequate fitness level throughout life.* Not only should students be exposed to activities that promote health-related fitness, they also should learn how to develop and maintain physical fitness throughout their lives. For example, all students, including students with disabilities, should learn how to perform activities that promote cardiovascular efficiency such as jogging at a steady speed, brisk walking, riding a bicycle, or pushing a wheelchair. Students also should learn how to regulate the intensity (how to get heart rate up to a training level), duration (how long to exercise to gain cardiovascular benefits), and frequency (how often to exercise to gain cardiovascular benefits) of their exercise.

3. *Each child should enjoy a broad experience in movement activities, leading to an understanding of movement and the underlying principles involved.* This objective refers to the need for students to participate and train in a variety of movement activities, which enables them to learn not only how to move, but how to become skill-

ful movers and apply various movement patterns to different environments. For example, students with disabilities should not only learn the most skillful way to throw and catch; they also should learn how to use these basic skills in a variety of situations, including lead-up and traditional sports such as softball or basketball.

4.   *The physical education environment should allow children to acquire desirable social standards and ethical concepts.* Social objectives that can be enhanced in physical education include cooperation, appropriate levels of competition, tolerance for varying abilities, and general good citizenship and fair play. Situations can be set up in which cooperation and teamwork are required or in which one team loses and team members learn how to be "good sports."

5.   *Each child should develop a desirable self-concept through relevant physical education experiences.* Self-concept refers to how a student feels about his or her ability. Part of self-concept is associated with physical abilities and physical fitness. Success in physical education can promote positive self-concepts in students who have difficulty in other aspects of school. Thus, physical education programs should be success-based by modifying activities to meet the needs of each student based on his or her unique abilities. For example, a shooting station in basketball might allow students to shoot at baskets set at different heights, use balls of assorted sizes, or shoot from various distances.

6.   *Through physical education, each child should acquire personal values that encourage living a full and productive life.* This includes opportunities that promote enjoyment in participating in physical activities, a healthy lifestyle and stress reduction, and an attempt to do one's best in all activities. Again, developing a success-based program in which students learn skills that are geared to meet their individual needs will promote student enjoyment and enhance the likelihood that the students will want to continue to participate in physical activity throughout their lives.

7.   *Through physical education, children must acquire knowledge of safety skills and habits and develop an awareness of safety with respect to themselves and others.* Students should learn good safety habits that can prevent serious injury, such as wearing protective gear, using a buddy system in the water, and warming up prior to participation in an activity.

8.   *Through physical education, children should learn physical skills that allow them to participate in and derive enjoyment from wholesome recreational activities throughout their lifetimes.* Ideally, upon graduation from high school, students should have competency in at least two or three lifetime recreational activities in which they can participate throughout their adult years. Some of these recreation competencies would include activities that promote health-related fitness, such as aerobic dancing, weight training, or swimming. This is perhaps the most important objective of physical education for all students, including students with disabilities—to help them acquire the skills they need to participate in lifetime leisure skills as independently and successfully as possible.

Developmentally Appropriate
Programming in Physical Education

Physical education comprises several different components designed to promote certain global objectives (e.g., to be physically educated), and it is important that all students receive training in each of these components if the objectives are to be achieved. However, should young students learn how to play team sports or participate in intricate dances? Should older students and young adults participate in simple rhythm activities and activities that promote fundamental motor skill development? The answer is no. Students should be exposed to each of the above physical education components, but these components should be presented across the student's life span. The term *developmentally appropriate* refers to activities that are geared to a student's developmental status, previous movement experiences, fitness and skill level, body size, and age (COPEC, 1992). Developmentally appropriate practices suggest that programming as well as instruction should be different for preschool-age students compared with elementary-age students compared with secondary-age students. Wessel and Kelly (1986) outlined major content areas for general physical education activities, broken down by grade level (Table 1.7). Note that younger students are presented with activities that promote development of motor skills and movement competencies, whereas older students learn to apply these skills and competencies to culturally popular sports and lifetime leisure/fitness activities.

Most physical educators understand which activities are appropriate for younger students and which are appropriate for older students. However, this understanding is often lost when it comes to students with disabilities. Oftentimes, physical educators present activities based on a student's developmental rather than chronological age. Unfortunately, such an approach may mean that students with disabilities graduate from school with only a smattering of developmental skills, such as the ability to throw a ball or walk on a balance beam, but with no real ability to participate in lifetime leisure skills such as bowling, golf, weight training, or aerobic dancing. It is critical that students with disabilities, including students with severe disabilities, be exposed to chronological-age-appropriate activities that will lead to the development of functional skills they can use when they graduate from school (see Block, 1992, and Krebs & Block, 1992, for a more in-depth discussion of helping students acquire lifetime leisure skills).

What Is Adapted Physical Education?

As noted previously, legislators who created IDEA believed that students with disabilities could benefit from physical education and that physical education services, modified when necessary, should be a part of all students' educational programs. Although legislators realized that many students with disabilities could participate in general physical education without adaptations to the general program, they also realized that some students with disabilities would require modifications or support to safely and successfully participate in and benefit from general physical education. When students with disabilities need extra support to benefit from general physical education or when these students need a special physical education program as an alternative to general physical education, they qualify for "specially designed physical education" or *adapted physical education* (Bateman, 1996).

Definition of Adapted Physical Education

Adapted physical education is a subdiscipline of general physical education and emphasizes physical education for students with disabilities. The term *adapted physical education* generally refers to school-based programs for students ages

Table 1.7. Major content areas for general physical education by grade level

Lower elementary school (Kindergarten through third grade)	Upper elementary/middle school (Fourth through seventh grade)	High school (Eighth through twelfth grade)
Locomotor patterns • Run • Skip • Jump • Slide • Gallop • Leap • Hop • Climb	**Locomotor patterns for sports** • Locomotor patterns used in sports • Combination of two or more locomotor patterns • Locomotor patterns used in dance	**Locomotor sports** • Track events • Special sports applications • Locomotor patterns used in dance • Locomotor patterns used in leisure activities
Manipulative patterns • Throw • Catch • Kick • Strike	**Manipulative patterns for sports** • Throw • Volley • Catch • Dribble • Kick • Punt • Strike	**Ball sports** • Basketball, soccer, softball, volleyball, bowling, golf, tennis, racquetball, and so on
Body management • Body awareness • Body control • Space awareness • Effort concepts	**Body management for sports** • Gymnastics • Body management skills applied to sports	**Body management for sports** • Body management skills applied to sports
Health and fitness • Endurance, strength, and flexibility to perform locomotor and manipulative skills	**Health and fitness** • Cardiorespiratory endurance • Muscular strength and endurance • Flexibility	**Health and fitness** • Personal conditioning • Lifetime leisure exercises • Introduction to body composition concepts
Rhythms and dance • Moving to a beat • Expressing self through movement • Singing games • Applying effort concepts	**Dance** • Folk • Modern • Interpretive • Aerobic	**Dance** • Folk • Modern • Interpretive • Aerobic and social
Low-organized games • Relays and tag games • Games with partners • Games with a small group	**Lead-up games to sports** • Lead-up games to team sports	**Modified and regulation sports** • Modified sports activities • Regulation sports

From Wessel, J.A., & Kelly, L. (1986). *Achievement-based curriculum development in physical education.* Philadelphia: Lea & Febiger; adapted by permission.

3–21, whereas a more global term, *adapted physical activity,* refers to programs across the life span, including postschool programs (Sherrill, 1998). Because this book focuses on school-age students, the term *adapted physical education* will be used throughout.

Various definitions of adapted physical education have been developed since the inception of PL 94-142 in 1975 (e.g., Auxter, Pyfer, & Huettig, 1997; Sherrill, 1998; Winnick, 1991). However, the definition developed by Dunn seems to be most appropriate for this text: "Adapted physical education programs are those that have the same objectives as the general physical education program, but in which adjustments are made in the regular offerings to meet the needs and abilities of exceptional students" (1997, p. 3). Note that both general physical education and adapted physical education share the same objectives. In addition, the components of physical education as defined in IDEA should be included in a comprehensive adapted physical education program. The major difference between general and adapted physical education is that, in adapted physical education, adjustments or adaptations are made to the general offerings to ensure safe, successful, and beneficial participation (Dunn, 1997; Sherrill, 1998). Simple adaptations such as asking a peer to provide assistance, modifying the equipment and rules of games, or providing alternative activities under the guidance of a trained adapted physical education specialist do little to disrupt the learning environment while creating a productive and enjoyable physical education experience for all students.

It is important to note that adaptations, including specific therapeutic activities, often can be implemented within the general physical education environment. For example, a high school–age student with cerebral palsy who uses a wheelchair can work on special stretching exercises during general physical education while his peers perform their warm-up activities. Similarly, this student can work on individual goals such as pushing his wheelchair forward and developing the ability to play cerebral palsy soccer (an official sport of the United States Cerebral Palsy Athletic Association) while his peers practice their running and soccer skills. This student may require special equipment such as a wheelchair and a larger ball as well as extra assistance in the form of a peer tutor, volunteer, or paraeducator; however, the student can easily be accommodated in the general physical education program and still receive an appropriate, individualized program designed to meet his or her unique needs.

Although the objectives of adapted and general physical education are the same, the way in which these objectives are prioritized varies from individual to individual in adapted physical education. Thus, individualization is one of the hallmarks of adapted physical education programs. For example, although all students should work on health-related physical fitness, maintenance of low levels of health-related physical fitness might be a priority goal for a student with muscular dystrophy or cystic fibrosis, whereas such a fitness goal may be a lesser priority for physically fit students without disabilities. Similarly, motor skill development might be a priority for a student with a learning disability or cerebral palsy, whereas social/affective development might be a priority for a student with a behavior disorder.

Finally, it is important to note that adapted physical education should not be viewed as a place to which a student goes to receive special physical education or a specific person whom a student visits who provides these special services. Rather, adapted physical education is a service that can be provided in a variety of environments (including general physical education classes) and by a variety of qualified people (including, in many states, a general physical education specialist). Therefore, a student with a disability could receive adapted physical education services (individual goals and objectives for physical education) within a general physical education environment and provided by a general physical education teacher. Decisions regarding which services will be provided, where they will be provided, and who will provide them vary from state to state but generally are left up to each student's IEP team.

Who Is Qualified to Provide Physical Education Services?

Although in 1975 legislators wanted to ensure that only "qualified" individuals would provide physical education services to students with disabilities, they believed strongly that determining who was qualified to provide services to students with disabilities (including physical education services) should be left up to each state: "Qualified means that a person has met state educational agency approved or recognized certification, licensing, registration, or other comparable requirements that apply to the area in which he or she is providing special education or related services" (Federal Register, August 23, 1977, p. 42479). Unfortunately, more than 20 years after the original passage of the law, only 17 states have developed specific requirements and/or licensure for professionals who provide physical education services to students with disabilities (Kelly & Gansneder, 1998). The states that do not require any special training/licensure often certify other professionals, including general physical education teachers, special education teachers, and general classroom teachers, as "qualified" to provide physical education services to students with disabilities. Unfortunately, many of these "qualified" professionals do not have the training, knowledge, or experience to provide physical education to students with disabilities (Block & Rizzo, 1995; Chandler & Greene, 1995; National Association of State Directors of Special Education [NASDE], 1991). Consequently, a new national examination, known as the Adapted Physical Education National Standards (APENS) exam, has been devised to ensure that providers of adapted physical education are qualified. Individuals who have a baccalaureate degree in physical education, a minimum of 200 hours of practicum experiences in adapted physical education, at least one three-credit course in adapted physical education, and a valid teaching license can take the exam. Those who pass the exam become Certified Adapted Physical Educators (CAPE) (Kelly, 1998). Although it is hoped that more professionals will become CAPEs and that more states will recognize the need to hire CAPEs to provide physical education to students with disabilities, to date there are no requirements for local school districts to hire one of these certified adapted physical education professionals (NCPERID, 1995).

2

What Is Inclusion?

We are Totally Committed to:

Those who would love to compete,
But are given no appropriate opportunities;
Those who could compete;
If only the distance were shorter, the basket lower, or the equipment lighter;
Those who do not express their thoughts and feelings in the same manner as most;
Those who have difficulty processing and remembering
All of the rules and regulations given so quickly;

We are Totally Committed to:

Those who are fleet of foot;
But know not where or when to stop;
Those who are made to feel "different,"
Because of they way they walk, talk, or act;
Those who need extra practice time
To learn the most basic skills and games;

We are Totally Committed to:

Those who others "pity,"
And will not deal with;
Those we love to teach,
And those others would love for us to teach;
Those we see as just plain 'ol kids;
Despite their wheelchairs, crutches, canes, hearing aids, or glasses;

We are Totally Committed to:

Those whose parents never envision them playing baseball, basketball, soccer
And other "normal activities";
Those who hurt so much,
Yet smile so often;
Those who are so optimistic;
When those around them are so often pessimistic.

These are the adapted physical education students
That we are so Totally Committed to;
But are they different in their needs as other kids?
Do they have the right to have fun and learn in physical education?
We have a duty to remain committed to Them to ensure
That they get what they deserve –
Quality Physical Education!!!

Michael Marsallo, principal

Jessica is a third grader who has big brown eyes, two blonde pigtails, and an imp-ish smile that never seems to go away. She also has autism, which has severely affected the development of her communication and social skills. Jessica is basi-cally nonverbal; however, she has learned to communicate her wishes and wants by using gestures and signs and pointing to pictures. Although she seems to un-derstand simple verbal commands, she often needs extra cues to follow more complex directions. Jessica also tends to prefer isolated play, but she is beginning to interact occasionally with her peers.

Jessica began her education in a special school for students with autism. For the past 2 years, however, she has been attending her "home school"—the gen-eral education school attended by students without disabilities in her neighbor-hood. In addition, Jessica has been included in a general third-grade class rather than a special education class; she is considered a full member of this class rather than a visitor from another class who comes in occasionally. Jessica also rides a bus to school with her neighborhood friends and has several friends in her class with whom she sits during lunch and assemblies. These friends encourage Jessica to play with them during recess and free time in addition to the time she already spends with them. Although Jessica tends to interact with objects and peers in her environment in inappropriate ways, she is becoming more socially aware and appropriate with her peers, increasingly careful with objects in the classroom, and more compliant with some of the rules and routines of the school.

Although Jessica is included in a general education class, she is at a different level of the curriculum and, in many cases, has different goals and objectives compared with her peers without disabilities. Therefore, Jessica still requires an individualized education program (IEP) that outlines adaptations to the general curriculum, her individual goals and objectives, and accommodations to her unique learning style. Jessica and the general education teacher also receive con-sultative and direct support from an autism specialist and a part-time teacher as-sistant and through peer tutoring by classmates.

As part of her daily routine, Jessica attends general physical education with her third-grade class. During physical education, Jessica receives adaptations to the general physical education curriculum; she works on her individual goals and objectives and receives accommodations for her unique learning style and sup-port from her peers. The general physical education specialist also receives con-sultative support from the districtwide autism specialist and the adapted physical education specialist. For example, through observation and assessment, it was determined that Jessica's ball skills were significantly delayed compared to those of her peers, whereas her locomotor patterns and fitness were relatively at age level. Therefore, Jessica's physical education goals and objectives address ball skills as well as accommodations to instruction (e.g., extra cues and extra help from peers or the teacher assistant). In order to address Jessica's physical educa-tion goals, the physical education teacher modifies warm-ups 2 days per week to include games in which students can practice their throwing and catching skills. During these activities, the physical education teacher spends extra time with Jessica working on throwing and catching patterns. In addition to practice during warm-ups, Jessica is part of the "throwing club," which meets twice a week in the mornings before the school day begins to work on students' throwing and catching skills. The "throwing club," run by the physical education specialist, is designed for students with and without disabilities who, based on the results of a pretest administered at the beginning of the school year, need extra help learning to throw and catch. Finally, when ball skills are the focus of physical education activities, peers are assigned (one at a time) to help Jessica work on her ball-skill patterns. These peers have been trained by the autism specialist and adapted physical education specialist regarding how to best instruct Jessica (usually by giving additional demonstrations and physical assistance) given her unique learning style and communication skills. Not only do these peers help Jessica with ball skills, they also assist her during other physical education activities. For example, they help her stay in line during relay races, determine where to go and what to do during dance and expressive movement, and follow the rules while participating in various games and activities.

Because Jessica has been part of the general physical education class from the beginning of the year, she is perceived by her peers and the physical education specialist as a regular member of the third-grade class. Although her skills are generally lower than those of most of her classmates, her classmates do not seem to mind; they all have their own particular strengths and weaknesses. In fact, Jessica does not stand out more than any other third grader in her class because the physical educator individualized the curriculum for all students. For example, in an introductory basketball unit, students use assorted size balls, stand various distances from the basket, focus on different components of shooting, and receive levels of instruction based on their needs. Thus, the curriculum is modified for all students so that they can be successful, challenged, and meaningfully involved in the program.

Although this scenario may seem too good to be true, such programs are being implemented in many schools that have adopted an "inclusion" philosophy. When done right, inclusive education environments, such as the one described above, demonstrate that students with varying abilities (including students with severe disabilities) who are grouped together can benefit from an appropriate and challenging educational program. In addition, such programs foster more favorable attitudes and a better understanding of individual differences. But why the seemingly sudden shift from self-contained, special education programs to full inclusion? What exactly does inclusion mean? This chapter reviews the concepts of least restrictive environment (LRE), mainstreaming, the general education initiative, and inclusion. A rationale for inclusion versus segregation as well as a review of research that has demonstrated the potential success of inclusive physical education are also included in this chapter.

Evolution of Inclusion

The Early Years: Limited Access to Education

Inclusion has grown out of a long history of how our society in general and how professionals and parents in particular have viewed children with disabilities. In the beginning of the 20th century, the biggest hurdle faced by children with disabilities was a lack of any special education. Children with mild disabilities were placed in general education classes without any special support. As long as they kept up with the other students in the class and did not cause any problems, they were accepted by the teacher and their classmates. There were no special services or trained specialists to help the student with disabilities or the general education teacher (Lewis & Doorlag, 1991). If the student fell behind, caused problems, or was perceived as too disabled to benefit from education, then he or she was excluded from the public schools and sent home (Beirne-Smith, Patton, & Ittenbach, 1994; Karagiannis, Stainback, & Stainback, 1996; Sigmon, 1983). As noted by Sigmon, "almost all children who were wheelchair-bound, not toilet trained, or considered ineducable were excluded because of the problems that schooling would entail" (p. 3). The one exception was the advent of special schools for children who were deaf or blind.

Special Schools and Special Classes

From 1950 to the early 1970s, perhaps following the education example used for children who were deaf or blind, children with disabilities were educated in special schools. Initially, many of these special schools were developed privately by parents who were frustrated by the lack of special education for their children with disabilities within the public schools.

Parental interest and advocacy, as well as a new awareness of the needs and capabilities of children with disabilities, led to the development of public special schools or classes for children with disabilities. Educators reasoned that children with disabilities needed to be educated by a trained specialist in a highly structured, intense, and unique teaching environment that could not be provided within the general education classroom (Lewis & Doorlag, 1991). It was also understood, however, that children with disabilities were not wanted in general schools or classrooms and that their removal would inevitably benefit students without disabilities (Chaves, 1977). Even when special classes were housed in general education school buildings, students with disabilities (or, for that matter, the staff members who served these students) rarely became "true" members of the school. In fact, in many states children with more severe disabilities continued to be excluded from education altogether (Stainback, Stainback, & Bunch, 1989a).

These special schools had special education teachers and therapists who received specific training and used special materials, equipment, and teaching methodologies. Although such training was certainly warranted, the end result was a rather elaborate dual system of education consisting of general education on the one hand and special education on the other (Stainback, Stainback, & Bunch, 1989a). In fact, programs for children with specific types of disabilities became so specialized that separate day and residential facilities were created for children with learning disabilities, children with hearing impairments, children with visual impairments, children with mental retardation, children with emotional disturbances, and children with physical disabilities (many of these specialized schools are still in existence today).

Although the special school/special class model proliferated in the 1960s and early 1970s, many parents and educators were beginning to find fault with the system. It was becoming clear that students with disabilities were viewed as different, and "different" meant that they were excluded from being educated with students without disabilities (DuBow, 1989; Stainback et al., 1989a). Reports to Congress in the early 1970s suggested that labeling and separating students with disabilities from their peers without disabilities led to stigma, ridicule, and poor self-image (Lewis & Doorlag, 1991; Turnbull, 1990).

Educators and parents were also concerned that many students with disabilities were placed in special programs without first determining if the student could benefit from a general education placement (this practice continues today despite the LRE mandate) (Brown, 1994; Stainback et al., 1989a). Furthermore, educators believed that, given the chance, many children with disabilities, at least, would be able to participate in some of the activities of the general class, and almost all students with disabilities could benefit from contact with their typically developing peers (Lewis & Doorlag, 1991).

The *Brown v. Board of Education* ruling in 1954 suggested that "separate but equal" self-contained classrooms actually tended to be unequal (Karagiannis et al., 1996; Stainback et al., 1989a; Taylor, 1988). Testimony to Congress just prior to the enactment of IDEA suggested that special education placement often translated into being taught by the "worst" teacher in inferior facilities with limited educational materials. Finally, educators and parents were concerned about the "terminal aspects of special education" (Turnbull, 1990, p. 150). Many of the children placed in special education classrooms would spend the remainder of their education in these special programs. Few of the students were ever provided with the opportunity to move to a general education environment (Karagiannis et al., 1996; Taylor, 1988).

In addition to the problems associated with special schools and special classes, the public was experiencing a growing awareness of civil rights. The *Brown v. Board of Education* (1954) decision as well as the Civil Rights Act of 1964 led to an examination of the practice of separating children with disabilities from the mainstream of public education (Beirne-Smith et al., 1994; Stainback et al., 1989a). Lawsuits in Pennsylvania (Pennsylvania Association for Retarded Citizens [PARC] v. Commonwealth of Pennsylvania, 1971) and the District of Columbia (Mills v. D.C. Board of Education, 1972) established the rights of children with disabilities within these jurisdictions to a free and appropriate education.

Federal Intervention: IDEA and Least Restrictive Environment

Out of this dissatisfaction with special education and the realization that students with disabilities could benefit from increased interactions with students without disabilities, the Federal Government enacted the Education for All Handicapped Children Act in 1975. Now renamed as the Individuals with Disabilities Education Act (IDEA), this landmark legislation guarantees individuals with disabilities the right to a free and appropriate public education. Included in this legislation is a provision designed to ensure that children with disabilities have increased opportunities to interact with their peers without disabilities in general education classrooms. Termed *least restrictive environment (LRE)* in IDEA (20 U.S.C. 1412 [5][B]), the provision directs public agencies:

(1) To the maximum extent appropriate, children with disabilities, including children in public or private institutions or other care facilities, are educated with children who are not disabled; and

(2) That special classes, separate schooling, or other removal of children with disabilities from the regular educational environment occurs only when the nature or severity of the disability is such that education in regular classes with the use of supplementary aids and services cannot be achieved satisfactorily.

This passage suggests that the LRE for students with disabilities is one that, whenever possible, is the same environment in which students without disabilities receive their education. Clearly, lawmakers advocated placing students with disabilities in general schools and general classrooms (including general physical education) whenever possible (Aufsesser, 1991; Taylor, 1988; Turnbull, 1990). This passage also suggests that appropriate placement of students with disabilities into general environments may necessitate the use of supplementary aids, support, and services. Without such support, the student may fail in the general environment. In other words, it might not be the environment that is inappropriate but rather the support that is given to a student within that environment (Block & Krebs, 1992).

Although segregated placement is not prohibited under the law, school districts are required to clearly demonstrate that a child with a disability placed in a separate environment cannot be satisfactorily educated within the general environment, even with supplementary aids and services (Arnold & Dodge, 1994; Hollis & Gallegos, 1993; Lipton, 1994; Maloney, 1994; Osborne, 1996). Lawmakers who enacted EHA and IDEA wanted to prevent the unnecessary placement of children with disabilities in separate programs. Lawmakers considered the practice of simply placing students in separate programs based on a label or preplacement evaluation a violation of the intent of the act (Bateman & Chad, 1995; Lipton, 1994; Maloney, 1994; Osborne, 1996).

However, placement options other than the general education classroom for children with disabilities are still required under the law. Lawmakers made this clear when they added a statement regarding a "continuum of alternative placements":

(a) Each public agency shall ensure that a continuum of alternative placements is available to meet the needs of children with disabilities for special education and related services.

(b) The continuum . . . must—

(1) Include the alternative placements listed in the definition of special education (instruction in regular classes, special classes, special schools, home instruction, and instruction in hospitals and institutions); and

(2) Make provisions for supplementary services (such as resource room or itinerant instruction) to be provided in conjunction with regular class placement (Federal Register, September 29, 1992, p. 44823).

An example of a continuum of placement options for physical education can be found in Table 2.1. Note that, by strict definition of the law, school districts should offer these or similar options for physical education placement because not all children with disabilities within a district can be accommodated within only one or two of these options. For example, a child with cerebral palsy who is in the hospital for surgery cannot receive physical education within the general environment.

Although the continuum of placement provision is important, it should be read within the context that it was written. Recall that data presented in the early 1970s showed that more than half of the students with disabilities in the United States were in educational programs that were deemed inappropriate for their needs, and an estimated 1 million children with disabilities were excluded entirely from the public school system. Prior to 1975, many children with disabilities still resided at home, in residential facilities, or in hospitals. The few day programs that were available for students with disabilities usually were separate from public school buildings (e.g., in churches or rented office spaces). In most cases, these residential facilities, hospitals, and day programs did not provide any systematic educational programs (Brown, 1994; Stainback et al., 1989a). Rather, these children were essentially "warehoused"; their basic needs were taken care of but their educational and social needs were not. As noted by Turnbull (1990), this dual system of education had a variety of effects, one of which was the denial of educational opportunities for children with disabilities.

Because of this denial of educational opportunities for children with disabilities, lawmakers made a clear statement that, regardless of where a child with a disability resides or the level of severity of his or her disability, he or she still must

Table 2.1. Sample of continuum of placement options for physical education

- Full-time GPE teacher, no support needed
- Full-time GPE teacher, accommodations needed (e.g., interpreter, adapted equipment, special instructions)
- APE provided within the GPE environment (student has unique goals and objectives as well as the need for special accommodations, but they these goals and accommodations can be carried out within the GPE environment)
- APE provided within the GPE environment, direct support from APE specialist (APE specialist comes into GPE to help student work on his or her unique goals and objectives and with special accommodations)
- APE provided part time within GPE and part time in special APE class
- APE provided full time in special APE class in regular school building
- APE provided full time in special APE class in special school
- APE provided full time in special APE class either homebound, in hospital, or in a treatment facility

APE=adapted physical education; GPE=general physical education.

receive education commensurate with his or her individual abilities and needs. Thus, children who did not attend traditional school programs but rather stayed at home, resided in residential facilities or hospitals, or participated in day programs were guaranteed free, appropriate public education under the law (Turnbull, 1990). It was never the intent of lawmakers for these separate placements to become an option for the placement of students with disabilities unless "the IEP of a child with a disability requires some other arrangement" (Federal Register, September 29, 1992, p. 44823). Lawmakers appeared to favor having students with disabilities educated alongside their peers without disabilities whenever appropriate. It seems unlikely that they meant for the continuum statement to serve as a justification for placement in these separate environments (Taylor, 1988; Turnbull, 1990).

In summary, the educational environment and LRE statements in the federal laws were created by Congress as a reaction to inappropriate special education practices at the time. These statements showed Congress's strong preference that children with and without disabilities should be educated together to the maximum extent possible. In addition, LRE brought attention to the notion that most children with disabilities could receive an appropriate education within the general education environment if provided with supplementary services and aids. The "continuum of alternative placements" presented by lawmakers was meant to ensure that students already placed in these more restrictive environments would receive appropriate educational programs. Finally, the law clearly notes that all placement decisions need to be made on an individual basis.

Mainstreaming

Administrators and educators in 1975 were faced with the dilemma of implementing the provisions and mandates of IDEA, including LRE. It was clear that lawmakers wanted as many children with disabilities as possible to be educated alongside students without disabilities. How to provide special education within the general environment, however, was never really made clear. Slowly, students with disabilities were moved from special schools to special classes within general schools. Additional efforts were made to integrate children with disabilities into general education classes and general school activities when it was deemed appropriate. Determining when to place children with disabilities into general education programs and how to support these children within special programs was confusing to many professionals. In an effort to provide some direction as to how to implement LRE, the Council for Exceptional Children (CEC, 1975) coined the term *mainstreaming* to describe the process of placing students with disabilities into general education classes with appropriate support services as determined by the student's IEP. The CEC defined mainstreaming in terms of basic themes relative to what it is and what it is not. According to the CEC, mainstreaming is

1. Providing the most appropriate education for each student in the least restrictive environment

2. Placing students based on assessed educational needs rather than clinical labels

3. Providing support services to general educators so they could effectively serve children with disabilities in the general environment

4. Uniting general and special education to help students with disabilities have equal educational opportunities

The CEC noted that mainstreaming is not

1. Wholesale return of all exceptional children to general classes

2. Permitting children with special needs to remain in general classes without the support services they needed

3. Ignoring the need of some children for a more specialized program that could be provided in the general education program (CEC, 1975, p. 174)

Despite these guidelines, mainstreaming developed into the unsuccessful "dumping" of students with disabilities into general education classes without support, including general physical education classes (DePaepe, 1984; Grosse, 1991; Lavay & Depaepe, 1987). In contrast to what the CEC suggested, children with disabilities who were mainstreamed into general education classes (including general physical education classes) were asked to follow the same curricular content, use the same materials and instruction, and follow the same pace as the other students in the class. Not surprisingly, many children with disabilities failed in these environments. The term mainstreaming has been misused so much that it is no longer recommended by the CEC.

Regular Education Initiative

Despite the setback with mainstreaming, more and more children with disabilities began to receive some or all of their education in general education environments. In addition, research in the 1970s and 1980s began to show that special class placements were somewhat ineffective in educating students with disabilities (e.g., Semmel, Gottlieb, & Robinson, 1979; Wang & Baker, 1986; Wang, Peverly, & Randolph, 1984). For example, Wang, Reynolds, and Walberg (1987) suggested that traditional "pull-out" programs were limited for a variety of reasons, including 1) the system for classifying students with disabilities was not educationally sound, 2) there was virtually no evidence suggesting that students with disabilities were making any educational gains simply based on special education placement, and 3) special class placement promoted isolation and stigmatization.

In 1986, Madeleine Will (then Assistant Secretary for the Office of Special Education and Rehabilitative Services, U.S. Department of Special Education) called for a *Regular Education Initiative (REI)*. In her article, "Educating students with learning problems: A shared responsibility," Will argued that the dual system of separate special and general education was not effective for students with mild disabilities. Will suggested several changes to the dual system, all of which were designed to appropriately serve students with disabilities in general education. She proposed the following: 1) increased instructional time; 2) empowerment of principals to control all programs and resources at the building level; 3) provision of support systems for general education teachers; and 4) the use of new approaches such as curriculum-based assessment, cooperative learning, and personalized curricula. Proponents of REI encouraged the scaling back of traditional special education classrooms in favor of a new merger between special and general education. Interestingly, these sentiments were voiced by Dunn (1968) nearly 20 years earlier when he questioned the efficacy of placing students with mental retardation requiring intermittent support in special classes.

Although Will originally targeted students with mild disabilities, some advocates argued that students with severe disabilities also should receive their education in the general classrooms (e.g., Snell, 1988; Snell & Eichner, 1989; Stainback & Stainback, 1990; Taylor, 1988). They noted that students with severe disabilities could learn important life skills in the general environment without interfering with the program for students without disabilities. In addition, heterogeneous grouping actually enriched the experiences of both students with and without disabilities (Stainback & Stainback, 1990). Although it was initially argued from a philosophical/moral point of view, research began to support including students with severe disabilities in general education (e.g., Chadsey-Rusch, 1990; Condon, York, & Heal, 1986; Peck, Donaldson, & Pezzoli, 1990).

Inclusion

Inclusion is an outgrowth of the regular education initiative of the 1980s and is basically used to describe the philosophy of merging special and general education (Lipsky & Gartner, 1987; O'Brien, Forest, Snow, & Hasburg, 1989; Stainback & Stainback, 1987, 1985; Stainback et al., 1989b; Taylor, 1988). The term has been used to reflect a philosophy in which all students, regardless of abilities or disabilities, are educated within the same environment—an environment in which each child's individual needs are met (Downing, 1996; Karagiannis et al., 1996; Stainback & Stainback, 1990; Stainback et al., 1989a). The philosophy of inclusion is perhaps best summed up by the following statement: "Although some children, especially those with severe and multiple disabilities, may have unique ways of learning, separating them from others who learn in a different way is unnecessary and could prevent them from achieving their full potential" (Downing, 1996, p. xii). It also is important to note that an inclusion philosophy goes beyond simply physically placing a child in a general education classroom (Block, 1998; Bricker, 1995; Brown et al., 1989; Downing, 1996; Ferguson, 1995; Snell, 1991; Stainback & Stainback, 1990). As noted by Stainback and Stainback, "An inclusive school is a place where everyone belongs, is accepted, supports, and is supported by his or her peers and other members of the school community in the course of having his or her educational needs met" (1990, p. 3).

Embedded within this definition is the understanding that children with disabilities will still receive an individually determined, appropriate program with supplementary services and supports to meet their unique needs (Block, 1994c; Stainback & Stainback, 1990, 1991). However, these services are provided to the child with a disability within the general education environment (Downing,

1996). In terms of physical education services, this means that individually deter-mined goals and objectives and accommodations are provided within the general physical education environment by staff members who are trained to provide these services (e.g., adapted physical education specialist, trained general physi-cal education specialist, trained teacher assistant, or trained peer tutor) rather than outside of the classroom by taking the child to special services (Block, 1994c). This notion of bringing services to the general education environment provides continual opportunities for the child with disabilities to interact with, learn from, and form friendships with peers while still ensuring that the child re-ceives an appropriate, individualized program (Downing, 1996; Stainback & Stainback, 1990, 1991).

Another critical tenet of the inclusion philosophy is that children with dis-abilities are the responsibility of both general and special education staff members (Downing, 1996; Giangreco, 1997; Givner & Haager, 1995; Sailor, Gee, & Kara-soff, 1993; Stainback & Stainback, 1990). Unlike traditional self-contained pro-grams in which the special education teacher (with the support of related services personnel) was solely responsible for a child's education, in inclusive environ-ments all school staff members are responsible for ensuring that each child's edu-cational program is carried out appropriately (Downing, 1996; Sailor et al., 1993; Stainback & Stainback, 1990, 1991). The notion of "he's not my responsibility" has no place in properly implemented inclusive environments. It is unreasonable, however, to expect the resources, knowledge base, and personnel that are avail-able in general education to serve the needs of children with and without disabil-ities (Stainback & Stainback, 1991). Yet, it also is clear that special education re-sources and personnel cannot serve all of the needs of children with disabilities. The inclusion philosophy suggests that only through the merger of the resources, knowledge, and talents of general and special education teachers can both chil-dren with and without disabilities receive a comprehensive, appropriate educa-tion (Lipsky & Gartner, 1998; Sailor et al., 1993; Stainback & Stainback, 1991). Continual support and training for the general education teacher is required to make such a merged system work. In addition, the use of various co-teaching arrangements (i.e., the general and special education teachers dividing and shar-ing class instruction) is an effective way to facilitate inclusion (Lipsky & Gartner, 1998). For example, Block and Zeman (1996) noted the effectiveness of having the adapted physical education specialist go into the general physical education class, work with both students with and without disabilities, and co-teach various aspects of the general physical education lesson. Lipsky and Gartner (1998) and Sherrill (1998) have also advocated these coteaching arrangements.

Note that providing services within general education does not necessarily mean that all services for a particular child will always take place within the gen-eral education environment (Block, 1994a; Brown et al., 1991; Lipsky & Gartner, 1998; Sailor et al., 1993). For limited periods of time during the school day, a child with a disability (or any other child in the class) can receive instruction (sometimes using specialized equipment) in specialized environments outside of the general education classroom. For example, a high school student with men-tal retardation requiring extensive support, with the support of a teacher assis-tant, may need extra time in the locker room to get dressed and to go back to class. This student may leave general physical education 10 minutes early so he can work on these functional dressing skills. However, this student is still per-ceived as a member of the general physical education class just like other chil-dren without disabilities (Block, 1994a; Lipsky & Gartner, 1998).

Rationale for Inclusion

As stated previously, students with disabilities have traditionally been viewed as fundamentally different from students without disabilities, resulting in a rather elaborate dual system of education, with general education on the one hand and special education on the other (Stainback et al., 1989b). Recently, Lipsky and Gartner (1998); Rainforth, York, and Macdonald (1992); Snell and Eichner (1989); Stainback and Stainback (1991); Stainback et al. (1989b); and Will (1986), to name a few, have advocated for an inclusive environment for students with disabilities. For example, Stainback et al. outlined a rationale for a single educational system for all students that included the following key points:

1. *Instructional needs of all students vary from individual to individual.* A student with disabilities should be viewed as just another student whose instructional needs need to be individualized to optimize learning. Individualization can be implemented in an inclusive environment as easily as in a segregated environment. For example, most physical education classes are composed of students with varying motor abilities, levels of physical fitness, and knowledge of the rules and strategies of games. Good physical educators present activities in such a way that every student's needs are accommodated.

2. *A dual system is inefficient since there is inevitably competition and duplication of services.* Much of what takes place in segregated environments takes place in general environments. The majority of activities presented in general physical education programs are the exact same activities that are presented in specialized adapted physical education programs. For example, most elementary-age students in general physical education work on the development of fundamental motor patterns, perceptual motor skills, physical fitness, and simple rhythms and games. These same activities are appropriate for elementary-age students with disabilities. Similarly, high school–age students work on individual and team sports, including lifetime leisure sports and physical fitness. Again, adapted physical education programs designed for high school–age students work on the exact same activities! In a dual system, two professionals often are teaching the same activities at the same time, which causes conflicts with gym time and equipment. It is more logical and cost-effective to include students with disabilities in the general program with the necessary modifications to ensure their success.

3. *Dual systems foster inappropriate attitudes.* Students with disabilities, especially students who spend most of their time separated from their peers without disabilities, are viewed as "special" and different by general education teachers and peers (e.g., Voeltz, 1980, 1982). Teachers assume that educational programs that take place in special education must be extraordinary. That is, special education staff members often are viewed as "exceptional" people who have different skills and abilities compared with general education staff and who use different equipment and materials with their students who have disabilities (i.e., equipment and materials that take years of special training to master). Similarly, students with disabilities often are viewed as more "different" than similar to students without disabilities in that they learn differently and have different interests than students without disabilities. In fact, most students with disabilities are more similar to than different from their peers without disabilities. They likely enjoy watching the same television shows, listening to the same music, cheering for the same sports teams, and participating in the same recreational activities as their peers without disabilities and dislike cleaning their rooms and do-

ing their homework. Unfortunately, teachers and peers who are not exposed to students with disabilities may view them as different—people who should be pitied, teased, or feared. By teaching students with and without disabilities together, educators learn that teaching students with disabilities is not that different from teaching typical students. Similarly, peers without disabilities quickly learn that students with disabilities are more similar to themselves than they are different (Forest & Lusthaus, 1989; Stainback, Stainback, & Bunch, 1989b).

Benefits of Inclusion

In addition to the rationale for merging general and special education, there are benefits available in inclusive environments that are not available in segregated environments. Snell and Eichner (1989) and Stainback and Stainback (1985, 1990) outlined several benefits of including students with disabilities in general education programs (see Table 2.2).

Specific Philosophies that Support Inclusion

Inclusion should not be confused with early attempts to mainstream. Mainstreaming tended to place students with disabilities into general education without support. In addition, students often were expected to follow the same curriculum as students without disabilities. Inclusion philosophies suggest that each student's unique educational needs be met through adaptations to the curriculum and with the provision of supports. The following sections, adapted from Stainback and Stainback (1990), outline some of the key philosophies regarding inclusion.

Adapt the Curriculum

One of the greatest misconceptions of inclusion is that all students must somehow fit into the existing curriculum. In many cases, the curriculum used in the general class is not appropriate for students with disabilities. In such cases, the curriculum must somehow be adapted to meet the unique educational objectives and learning needs of the student. For example, an elementary student with cerebral palsy may have difficulty performing activities in a typical tumbling/gymnastics unit. This student still could work on balance skills, rolls, and movement concepts, but he or she should work on these skills in a different manner than his or her peers. This child might, for example, work on simple sitting balance while his or her peers work on more complex sitting balances such as a v-sit (i.e., make a "v" with your body so that your legs and arms are up in the air and only your bottom rests on the floor). While other students work on forward and backward rolls, this student might work on independently rolling from his or her stomach to back and then getting into a standing position. Note how all students work on the same basic physical education objective (movement control) and learn together within the same general physical education activity (tumbling unit), but some students are evaluated using different curriculum objectives.

In some cases, the curriculum may not seem to match the needs of a particular student at all. In such cases, parts of the curriculum might be presented at different times for individual students. For example, a middle school student who is blind may not need to work on lacrosse, an activity found in many physical education curriculums in the mid-Atlantic and northeastern part of the United States. This student might be given opportunities to feel the equipment and learn

Table 2.2. Benefits of inclusion

For students with disabilities:
- Opportunity to learn social skills in inclusive, more natural environments (learn with natural cues and consequences; no need to learn to generalize to inclusive environments later in life)
- More stimulating, motivating environment (e.g., the halls of a general junior high school, the cafeteria, the recess yard, the bus loading area. Dress, conversations, and social exchanges are characteristic of students' ages and locations)
- Learn appropriate skills (e.g., refrain from stigmatizing behavior, appropriate greetings, wearing age-appropriate clothes)
- Availability of age-appropriate role models without disabilities
- Students can participate in a variety of school activities suited to their chronological ages (e.g., recess, lunch, assemblies, music, art, athletic events).
- Potential for new friendships with peers
- Parents, special education teachers, and other special education staff are also included into general schools and thus have new experiences and relationships and are less isolated.

For professional staff and students without disabilities:
- Special education teachers (as well as adapted physical educators) tend to have higher expectations for their students with disabilities when the students are placed in integrated environments.
- Special education teachers learn what is appropriate for children without disabilities.
- When guided by adults, attitudes of students without disabilities toward students with disabilities improve (e.g., fewer fears, stares, and negative comments; less teasing).
- When guided by adults, students without disabilities learn to appreciate individual differences (e.g., see the positive in everyone, find strengths and weaknesses in everyone).
- Students without disabilities experience a change in perspective: Having acne or getting a "C" on a test is not as devastating when students see a person with disabilities working as hard as he can just to keep his head up and eyes focused.
- Future parents of children with disabilities, taxpayers, teachers, and doctors learn to face people with disabilities with greater personal knowledge and optimism and less prejudice.

Adapted from Snell & Eichner (1989) and Stainback & Stainback (1985, 1990).

the rules of lacrosse; but during most of the lacrosse unit, this student might work on the softball/beep-baseball skills of throwing, striking with a bat, and retrieving beep balls. Softball is part of the middle school curriculum, but it is offered at a different time of year. Still, the basic skills of lacrosse are catching with a lacrosse stick, tossing with a lacrosse stick, and advancing the ball by tossing or running. Softball also includes skills such as catching (with hands), tossing (throwing), and advancing the ball (striking). Thus, this student works on similar educational objectives but in a way that is more beneficial to him. In addition, this student can work on these skills within the general physical education class. (See Chapters 6 and 7 for more information on adapting the curriculum.)

Integrate Personnel and Resources

A misconception of inclusion is that students with disabilities will be "dumped" into general education programs without support. As noted previously, the inclusion philosophy directs supports to follow the student into the mainstream. Supports include specialized equipment and instruction and personnel such as volunteers, teacher assistants, and education specialists. In fact, support that would have been given to the student when he or she was in a segregated program should follow the student into the inclusive environment. For example, the student in the previous example who is blind should have beep-balls and sound devices in any activity that uses balls. Such equipment can be obtained for free from various associations serving people who are blind (the student's vision therapist can assist the general physical educator in procuring this equipment). In addition, the student's orientation and mobility specialist might come into general physical education once or twice a week to assist the student in moving around the physical education environment. Other students might have special equipment such as walkers, gait trainers, mats, or bolsters that should be brought to general physical education. If these students had peer tutors or teacher assistants assisting them in segregated physical education, then these supports should be provided for them in the inclusive environment.

Utilize Natural Proportions

One of the reasons why early attempts at mainstreaming in physical education often failed was that entire special education classes (often up to 10 students) were placed in one general physical education class. Such a situation was doomed for failure right from the start because no physical educator could adequately meet the needs of all students without disabilities plus another 10 students with unique needs. Inclusion philosophy suggests that students with disabilities be placed following the principle of *natural proportions*. Natural proportions basically means that the typical distribution of people with and without disabilities should be maintained when placing students in general classes. Incidence of disability suggests that perhaps 10%–15% of the school-age population has some type of disability, the greatest number of students having high-incidence disabilities such as learning disabilities, emotional disabilities, and mental retardation and fewer students having low-incidence disabilities such as cerebral palsy, hearing impairments, or visual impairments. Such numbers translate to two to three students with disabilities (usually mild disabilities) being placed in each class, with an occasional class having a student with a low-incidence type of disability. Therefore, only two to three students with disabilities should be placed in any one physical education class at a time. Such a situation is much more manageable for the general physical educator, especially when students with severe disabilities come to physical education with extra support personnel.

Research on Inclusion in Physical Education

Although there is limited research on the effects of including children with disabilities in general physical education, research suggests that including children with disabilities in general physical education can be effective. For example, St. Clair (1995) showed that an inclusive environment could actually be more effective for the development of gross motor skills than a segregated environment. Using the Test of Gross Motor Development (Ulrich, 1995), St. Clair compared the motor performance of 20 children who were deaf and had secondary impairments. Eleven of these twenty children participated in general physical education with classmates who had hearing impairments, whereas the remaining nine students participated with their peers who had multiple disabilities in a special, self-contained, adapted physical education class. Results showed that children who were included in the general physical education program (for deaf children) demonstrated significantly greater improvements in gross motor development compared with those children who received physical education in a self-contained, adapted program.

Many researchers have focused on the use of peer tutors to promote successful inclusion (Houston-Wilson, Dunn, van der Mars, & McCubbin, 1997; Lieberman, 1996; Murata, 1995). For example, Houston-Wilson and her colleagues examined the effects of trained versus untrained peer tutors on the ability of children with developmental disabilities who were included in general physical education to perform critical components of fundamental motor patterns. Results showed that trained peer tutors were effective in assisting children with disabilities to improve their motor performance, whereas untrained peer tutors were not. Similarly, Lieberman (1996) and Murata (1995) found that trained peer tutors could significantly improve academic learning time in physical education (ALT-PE) for children with disabilities.

But, what of the claims that including children with disabilities in general physical education will have a negative effect on children without disabilities? Limited research suggests that these fears are unfounded. For example, Block and Zeman (1996); Lieberman (1996); Murata (1995); and Vogler, van der Mars, Cusimano, and Darst (1990) found that including children with disabilities in general physical education did not have a negative effect on the physical education program for children without disabilities. Specifically, including children with disabilities did not negatively affect ALT-PE (Lieberman, 1996; Murata, 1995; Vogler et al., 1990) or skill improvement (Block & Zeman, 1996) for children without disabilities. Furthermore, Block and Zeman (1996) found that inclusion in physical education promoted better attitudes in children without disabilities toward inclusive physical education in general and toward modifications of the general physical education curriculum to accommodate children with disabilities.

Appendix

Position on Inclusion and Physical Education

The following represents the National Association of Sport and Physical Education (NASPE) and the American Association for Active Lifestyles and Fitness (AAALF) position on inclusion in physical education:

- No student should have to earn his or her way into physical education. In other words, inclusion in physical education means that all students, including students with disabilities, start in regular physical education. Ultimately, it is the school's responsibility to justify why a student with disabilities should be removed from regular physical education. It is possible in some cases that a student with disabilities starts in an alternative placement before ever being placed in regular physical education. However, it should be emphasized that such placement policy should be the exception, not the rule. Demonstrating that the student will fail in regular education even with support without first placing the student in regular physical education can be very difficult and has not been supported by recent court decisions.

- It is understood that many students with disabilities will have unique learning and motor needs. This includes students who might: (a) need modified instruction while in physical education, (b) need to work on different goals while in physical education, and/or (c) derive different benefits from physical education. However, most of these unique needs can be met within regular physical education. For example, a student with mental retardation might need extra directions, but these usually can be provided by the physical educator within typical physical education instruction. A student who uses a wheelchair can work on such individual prescribed skill as improving upper body strength and pushing his/her wheelchair with increased speed and accuracy during many physical education activities. And finally, a student who is blind may benefit from the interaction and support of peers during physical education that motivated him/her to try new skills such as independently walking from the locker room to the gymnasium, running laps with assistance, and learning the rules of various team sports.

- It is fully anticipated that many students with disabilities will need support to be successful in regular physical education. Support can vary from monthly meetings with an adapted physical educator to specialized equipment to a full-time teacher assistant. Exact supports should be determined for each student by the Individual Education Program/Individual Family Service Plan (IEP/ IFSP) team including input from the regular physical educator. Removing a student with disabilities from regular physical education because of a documented lack of educational benefit or because the student is extremely

Reprinted from *Including Students with Disabilities in Physical Education* (1995) with permission from the American Association for Active Lifestyles and Fitness (AAALF) and the National Association for Sport and Physical Education (NASPE), 1900 Association Drive, Reston, VA 20191-1599.

disruptive to peers should be discussed only after attempts have been made to provide necessary supports to the student within regular physical education.

- It also is anticipated that many physical educators will need support. As above, support will vary from informal consultations with an adapted physical educator to more formal in-services and training, to possibly team teaching with a trained adapted physical educator. The exact types of support needed will, in large part, be determined by the physical educator's training and attitude as well as the characteristics of the student with disabilities. Whenever possible, support in the form of training should be provided before the student with disabilities is placed in regular physical education. In addition, on-going training while the student is in regular physical education should be available to physical education personnel.

- While most students with disabilities should start in regular physical education, it is possible that regular physical education may not be an appropriate placement. If it is determined that a student with disabilities is not benefiting from regular physical education, is disruptive to other students or is posing a severe safety risk, then the amount of support the student and the regular physical educator receives should be reviewed. Perhaps more support would alleviate any problems the student and regular physical educator are having. Support can be in the form of: (a) consultation with a special educator, adapted physical educator, parent, and/or related service personnel, or (b) direct service from a peer tutor, volunteer, teacher assistant, special educator, adapted physical educator, or related service provider.

- If it is determined that the student still is not receiving any benefit from regular physical education, continues to be disruptive to other students in the class, or continues to pose a severe safety risk, then an alternative placement should be explored. Ideally, this placement would include some time in regular physical education with support and some time in an alternative physical education placement. There should be on-going evaluation to determine if the alternative placement is effective for this student and if there are any opportunities when the student can participate in regular physical education, even if such participation is for a day, a week, or a unit. For example, a student with osteogenesis imperfecta (brittle bones) might benefit from a rhythms unit but then need an alternative setting during a ball skills unit. Similarly, a high school–age student with mental retardation might spend three days a week in the community learning how to use a local fitness center and two days a week in regular physical education working on skills needed to participate in selected team sports in community leagues and Special Olympics.

- Placement in physical education never should be solely for social development, nor is it appropriate for students with disabilities to only have passive roles such as score keeper. While there are many opportunities for social interactions in physical education, the major purpose of physical education is to help students become active, efficient, and healthy movers. Physical education goals as defined in IDEA–Part B include the development of gross motor skills, development of fundamental motor patterns, development of health-related physical fitness, and development of skills needed to participate in lifetime leisure pursuits including individual and team sports.

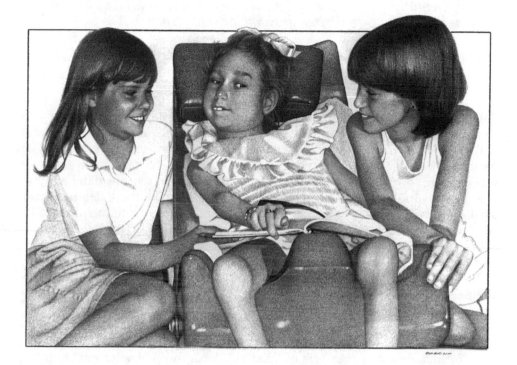

A Team Approach
to Inclusion

> *"I have found including students with disabilities into a regular pre-school environment to be just as challenging as it is at the other educational levels....I am...responsible for servicing preschool students with special needs in their "natural environments"....Typically, this preschool environment is "activity-based" and is the perfect opportunity for a young child to work on critical gross motor goals and objectives by embedding them within the daily routine. Because skills are taught within the child's daily routine, they are reinforcing, meaningful, developmentally appropriate and motivating to the child....The environment is set up to elicit desired gross motor skill responses."*
>
> Marnie Young, adapted physical education specialist

Caleb is a tenth grader at Cedar Ridge High School. He enjoys hiking, fishing, and camping with his family, and he enjoys going to football and basketball games with his friends. He is on track to graduate with his classmates in 3 years, and he has already started looking at colleges and universities. Because Caleb's mother was exposed to rubella during her pregnancy with Caleb, Caleb is blind and has hearing impairments and cerebral palsy. Despite his disabilities, Caleb has managed quite well over the years, and he does not ask for or want anyone's pity. However, he realizes that he needs help in certain situations. Physical education is one of his greatest challenges. Mr. Klein, Caleb's physical education teacher, was apprehensive when Caleb began school at Cedar Ridge last year. After all, what could a student who is blind and has hearing impairments and physical disabilities do in physical education? However, after meeting Caleb and talking to Caleb's middle school physical education teacher, he was a little less nervous. Still, he knew he would need help if he was going to provide a safe, meaningful program for Caleb.

Fortunately, many members of Caleb's IEP team were available to help Mr. Klein. Caleb's vision teacher and his orientation and mobility specialist explained Caleb's vision to Mr. Klein and demonstrated how Caleb is able to get around using a cane. They also explained that Caleb can learn quite well in physical education if Mr. Klein or a peer provides hand-over-hand assistance. Caleb's audiologist explained Caleb's hearing and effective ways to communicate with him. By standing in the front of the room and wearing hearing aids, Caleb can pick up most verbal cues quite well; if the students are spread out across the gym or are playing on the upper field, then a peer can repeat directions to Caleb. Caleb's physical therapist explained that Caleb's cerebral palsy is fairly mild and confined to his legs but that it is necessary for Caleb to stretch every day to allow for full function and to prevent contractures. The physical therapist showed Mr. Klein some simple stretches with which Caleb is familiar, and she explained how these stretches would benefit the other students in tenth-grade physical education and can be included in a general warm-up. With the initial support of these specialists and through their continued consultative support, Mr. Klein now provides a very appropriate physical education program for Caleb. Caleb's work ethic and sense of humor have made him one of Mr. Klein's favorite students!

A variety of professionals are routinely involved in the development and implementation of a student's individualized education program (IEP). Although some school districts may not employ all of the professionals described above, all school districts should have access to these professionals at least for a collaborative consultation. Together, all personnel who work with a student with disabilities (including the general physical educator) are members of the student's *collaborative team* (Rainforth & York-Barr, 1997). These professionals can be invaluable resources to general and adapted physical educators who are attempting to include students with disabilities into general physical education. This chapter defines a collaborative team and lists the key professionals who should be part of this team. In addition, specific references of how team members can facilitate inclusion in physical education are provided, and the importance of communication in collaborative teaming is discussed.

Collaborative Teaming

All students with disabilities are required to have an IEP that specifies all aspects of their educational program in writing. The concept of an IEP was specifically developed to guarantee that students receive all of the necessary services and the best education possible. Many professionals are involved in the development and implementation of a student's IEP. In fact, the Individuals with Disabilities Education Act of 1990 (IDEA), PL 101-476, and the Individuals with Disabilities Education Act Amendments of 1997, PL 105-17, mandate that a student's IEP be developed by a team that includes the student (when appropriate); the student's parents, teachers, and therapists; and a representative from the local education agency (PL 105-17, Sec. 1401, 20). Although IEP teams are designed to encourage teamwork and interactions among team members, some team members choose to work in isolation from other professionals (Craig, Haggardt, & Hull, 1999). In noncollaborative models, students may be "pulled out" for therapy or for adapted physical education a few times per week. Unfortunately, such a pull-out model does not allow the specialist to learn about the general education environment, and it makes it difficult for specialists to show other team members how to use their therapy skills to support the student in general education (Craig et al., 1999). For example, an adapted physical education specialist might work with a student who uses a wheelchair to teach him how to get up and down curbs; however, he does not share this information with the general physical education teacher, parents, or other professionals who work with this student. Furthermore, there are no curbs without curb cuts in the student's neighborhood, and there is only one curb without a curb cut (which the student never needs to go up or down) around the school. Such an isolationist approach often leads to inappropriate programming and limits the carryover and generalization of important skills.

Fortunately, most professionals are not interested in working in isolation but are interested in working cooperatively and collaboratively with other professionals during the development and implementation of a student's IEP. Such a team approach invariably maximizes the overall development of a student with disabilities. In addition, sharing expertise and resources among many professionals provides greater problem-solving abilities and enables all individuals involved in the student's educational program to utilize recommended teaching practices (Craig et al., 1999; Rainforth & York-Barr, 1997). In addition, unlike traditional IEP teams, collaborative teams meet on a regular basis to continually interact, plan, and modify a student's educational program. For example, a collaborative team that meets twice a month is stumped on how to help a student with severe autism communicate with her parents, friends, and teachers. Consequently, the speech-language therapist shares with the other team members the picture board she uses with the student and shows them ways that they can create their own picture boards to help this student communicate. At a future collaborative team meeting, the team will discuss the initial results of the new picture board program and if it should be continued, changed in some way, or dropped.

It should be noted that administrators usually do not require the formation of collaborative teams. Thus, a team approach will only work if team members have a strong commitment to work together and to share information and ideas with the goal of helping the student achieve maximum development. Most professionals will be interested in working collaboratively on the student's IEP. This is particularly true for general physical educators, who often need the expertise of others to develop and implement individualized physical education programs for their students with disabilities.

Collaborative Teams Defined

Rainforth, York, and Macdonald (1992) coined the term *collaborative teamwork* to refer to the sharing of information and responsibilities among team members. Rainforth and her colleagues noted that the term was developed as a hybrid of the *transdisciplinary model* and the *integrated therapy model*. In the transdisciplinary model, parents and professionals share information and techniques that previously had been the exclusive domain of individual disciplines. Professional boundaries (e.g., physical therapy is the only discipline that can work on gross motor goals, speech is the only discipline that can work on language goals) are removed so that each team member is committed to promoting the student's overall functional independence and participation in age-appropriate activities and routines (Craig et al., 1999). For example, physical therapists could share information on positioning that could help a student in the classroom, and the speech-language therapist could show the physical therapist how to work on language development while she conducts her physical therapy. Unfortunately, the transdisciplinary model often resulted in teachers or paraeducators conducting therapy in isolated, nonfunctional ways. For example, a paraeducator may have learned how to perform range-of-motion exercises on a student with cerebral palsy, but he conducts the program away from the student's peers while they work on another activity. In the integrated therapy model, therapy is conducted within functional contexts (Craig et al., 1999). For example, speaking in sentences could be practiced and encouraged during lunch, recess, physical education, and other natural contexts. The collaborative model combines the transdisciplinary and integrated therapy models and focuses on team members' sharing information and working together to provide students with disabilities with the necessary educational and therapeutic services within functional activities (Craig et al., 1999). Therefore, the same paraeducator who learned how to perform range-of-motion exercises might perform these exercises during warm-ups in general physical education. In addition, the student remains with the group while range of motion is performed. Consequently, specialists (including the adapted physical educator) spend more time in general education environments (including general physical education) than in isolated environments. Characteristics of collaborative teamwork, as outlined by Rainforth and York-Barr (1997), can be found in Table 3.1. Note how equal participation, shared responsibility, and the utilization of functional environments are critical aspects of the collaborative teamwork model.

The collaborative teamwork model allows team members to integrate their programs into the student's daily life routines (Craig et al., 1999). In addition,

Table 3.1.   Characteristics of collaborative teamwork

1. Equal participation in the collaborative teamwork process by family members and the educational service providers on the educational team
2. Equal participation by all disciplines that are needed for students to achieve their individualized educational goals
3. Consensus decision making regarding priority educational goals and objectives related to all areas of student functioning at school, at home, and in the community
4. Consensus decision making about the type and amount of support required from related services personnel
5. Attention to motor, communication, and other embedded skills and needs throughout the educational program and in direct relation to accomplishing priority educational goals
6. Infusion of knowledge and skills from different disciplines into the design of educational methods and interventions
7. Role release to enable team members who are involved most directly and frequently with students to develop the confidence and competence necessary to facilitate active learning and effective participation in the educational program
8. Collaborative problem solving and shared responsibility for students learning across all aspects of the educational program

From Rainforth, B., & York-Barr, J. (1997). *Collaborative teams for students with severe disabilities: Integrating therapy and educational services* (p. 23). Baltimore: Paul H. Brookes Publishing Co.; reprinted by permission.

team members are encouraged to work together to help students in various environments. For example, a speech-language therapist along with a student's parents may accompany a student to a local YMCA to work on the student's ability to communicate with the YMCA staff. Parents and family members are particularly important because they can practice physical education skills at home or take their child to local recreation facilities to follow up on community-based recreation training.

As noted previously in the story about Caleb, team members also can be of tremendous assistance to the general physical educator. For example, the student's orientation and mobility specialist can accompany a student with visual disabilities, such as Caleb, to general physical education for the first few weeks of school to help orient him to the gym and to help the general physical educator determine appropriate rule and equipment modifications; or an adapted physical educator can coteach with the general physical educator to ensure that all students, including students with disabilities, receive as individualized a program as possible.

Physical Education Inclusion Team

In terms of physical education, a subset of the collaborative team is the *physical education inclusion team* (PEIT). Generally speaking, the PEIT is comprised of all collaborative team members who can contribute to the successful development and implementation of the physical education portion of the student's IEP. It is important to note that the PEIT does not have to meet at a special time. Rather, meetings can take place during regular collaborative team meetings when physical education concerns are addressed. In many cases, the special education teacher who is in charge of the collaborative team meeting will allow the general physical educator to voice his or her concerns first because the general physical educator often has to get back to the gym (meetings often are held after school when the physical educator has coaching responsibilities). In addition to formal

PEIT meetings, ongoing discussion among PEIT members should continue on a regular basis via e-mail, telephone, and notes. For example, during a particular collaborative team meeting, the general physical educator notes that Caleb's class will be working on a gymnastics unit, and he is not sure if it is appropriate to include Caleb in gymnastics activities. The team reviews Caleb's IEP and notes that gymnastics activities are not a prioritized goal for Caleb. Consequently, the team members decide that Caleb can participate with his peers during warm-ups. After warm-ups, on Tuesdays and Thursdays, Caleb will work on setting up a tent provided by his parents (one of Caleb's goals is hiking/camping) in a corner of the gym with several of his peers; then, on Monday, Wednesday, and Friday he will go hiking around the school perimeter with the orientation and mobility specialist and several peers.

Meeting with the Physical Education Integration Team

The PEIT's portion of the collaborative team meeting should be organized with one or two team members (usually the adapted and/or general physical educators) serving as the team leader(s). The team leader takes responsibility for leading this portion of the meeting, soliciting information from key members, documenting decisions that were made during the meeting, and keeping all team members informed (via telephone calls or memos) about pertinent information. Although it may be difficult for all team members to get together for ongoing team meetings, it is imperative that all key team members, particularly the general physical educator, attend at least one preplanning meeting prior to the inclusion of the student with disabilities in general physical education. In fact, the general physical educator can attend just the PEIT portion of the collaborative team meeting if time constraints are a problem.

One important part of the PEIT meeting is for team members to introduce themselves and to offer their assistance to the general physical educator. Most general physical educators are not part of the "special education loop"; therefore, they might not know who the various specialists are or be familiar with their roles. One way of introducing team members to the general physical educator (as well as to each other) is to utilize the concept of *role release* (Woodruff & McGonigel, 1988). Role release is a systematic way for team members to share ideas about their disciplines and to begin to work collaboratively to develop and implement the best possible program for a student with disabilities. Team members basically train other team members in their various disciplines (Craig et al., 1999). Role release in introductory meetings should include the following:

1. *Role extension:* Team members begin to acquire knowledge about each others' disciplines (e.g., team members describe their roles in the student's educational program).

2. *Role enrichment:* Team members begin to share information about basic practices (team members share their best-teaching practices related to a particular student).

3. *Role expansion:* Team members exchange best-teaching practices across disciplines (team members explain how other team members can utilize these best teaching practices in their environments).

Role release in future meetings should include the following:

1. *Role exchange:* Team members begin to implement teaching techniques from other disciplines.

2. *Role support:* Team members give each other support as team members assume the roles of other disciplines.

By the end of the first meeting, the general physical educator should feel that he or she has resources that can answer specific questions about the student's physical education program. In addition, the general physical educator should have a greater understanding of the student's overall educational program (not just physical education) and how he or she can assist other team members in meeting educational goals.

A great deal of information should be presented at the initial collaborative team meeting so that team members can make informed decisions regarding the development of the student's individualized physical education program and strategies for inclusion. Various team members will be able to provide different aspects of the needed information. For example, vision teachers can provide information about a student's visual abilities, physical therapists can provide information regarding a student's motor abilities and physical fitness, the general physical educator can provide information pertaining to the general physical education curriculum and class format, and the student and his or her parents can provide information about the student's likes and dislikes. Figure 3.1 summarizes key information and the team members who are most likely able to provide this information.

Although future team meetings are important and should be planned, some members may not be able to attend meetings on a regular basis. In such cases, the team leader should request in advance information from those team members to share with the team. For example, if the general physical educator cannot attend a meeting, he or she can provide information to the team leader regarding the student's progress, whether modifications and teaching approaches have been effective, and what the next physical education unit will include. Similarly, the student's physical therapist can communicate to the group via e-mail, telephone, or memo any physical changes in the student that may affect his physical education program. Team members also should feel comfortable contacting each other if they have specific questions regarding the student's physical education program. For example, a student's vision therapist may contact the general physical educator to detail changes in the student's vision, or the physical educator may want to contact the student's social worker to determine if changes in the home have had any impact on the student's recent behavior problems. Although formal team meetings provide the best means for discussing issues regarding the student's program, the most important point is that team members feel comfortable communicating with each other whenever the need arises.

An Example of a PEIT Meeting

Sarah is a 13-year-old student who will attend sixth grade at a local middle school in the fall. Sarah enjoys holding and throwing various-size balls, pushing her wheelchair in different directions, being pushed fast by her peers, bowling, listening to music, and being around her peers without disabilities. Sarah has severe, spastic hemiplegic cerebral palsy, mental retardation requiring extensive support, and vision and speech impairments in addition to a seizure disorder, which is controlled by medication. The PEIT for Sarah includes the following team members: Sarah's parents; the special education teacher; the physical, occupational, speech, and vision therapists; the school nurse; and the adapted and general physical educators. The adapted physical educator serves as the team leader (see Figures 3.2 and 3.3 for examples of a team meeting agenda and a team meeting minutes form).

Information regarding the student:	P/S	SE	MD	PT	OT	VT	ST	PY	PE	APE
• Student's specific disability with emphasis on how this disability will affect his or her abilities in general physical education	X	X	X	X	X	X	X		X	
• Medical and health information regarding the student, particularly as it relates to contraindicated activities	X	X	X	X						
• Behaviors of student, including which behaviors to expect, what generally causes behavior outbursts, and which behavior program already is in place	X	X						X		
• Communication abilities of student, including how the student communicates, how well the student understands verbal directions, and how to best communicate with the student	X	X					X			
• Special equipment (if any) used by the student and whether this equipment will be brought into general physical education	X			X	X	X				
• Personal hygiene skills of student including locker room skills, ability to dress and undress, and ability to take a shower and perform personal grooming skills	X	X		X	X					
• Motor skills including general information regarding physical fitness, fundamental motor skills, and perceptual motor abilities	X			X	X					

A Teacher's Guide to Including Students with Disabilities in General Physical Education, by Martin E. Block, copyright ©2000 Paul H. Brookes Publishing Co.   (continued)

Figure 3.1. Information and team members who can provide information. (Key: P/S=parent and/or student, SE=special education teacher, MD=physician, PT=physical therapist, OT=occupational therapist, VT=vision therapist, ST=speech-language therapist, PY=psychologist, PE=general physical educator, APE=adapted physical educator.)

Figure 3.1. *(continued)*

	P/S	SE	MD	PT	OT	VT	ST	PY	PE	APE
• Specific information regarding recreation activities that are available in the student's community or neighborhood	X								X	X
• Interests of student and student's parents, particularly as the student reaches high school and begins to develop interests in particular lifetime leisure skills and sports (including sports for persons with disabilities	X									
• Special sports opportunities such as Special Olympics, wheelchair sports, and so on	X									X
• Specific goals developed for student that are not directly related to physical education but which can be worked on in the physical education environment	X	X	X	X	X	X	X	X	X	X
Activities that take place in general physical education:										
• How long is a typical physical education class, and how is the period broken down (e.g., 10 minutes for locker room, 25 minutes for activity)?									X	
• What is the daily routine that usually takes place during general physical education (e.g., warm-up activities, skill stations)?									X	
• What is the typical teaching style (movement education, direct teaching, highly structured)?									X	
• What are the minimal skills needed in the locker room?									X	

A Teacher's Guide to Including Students with Disabilities in General Physical Education, by Martin E. Block, copyright ©2000 Paul H. Brookes Publishing Co.

Team Meeting Agenda

Team meeting for: _____ Date: _____ Time: _____

Location of meeting: _____

Facilitator: _____ Recorder: _____

Agenda items and description	Outcomes desired	Time

A Teacher's Guide to Including Students with Disabilities in General Physical Education
by Martin E. Block, copyright ©2000 Paul H. Brookes Publishing Co.

Figure 3.2.   A form to record PEIT meeting agenda. (From Rainforth, B., York, J., & Macdonald, C. [1992]. *Collaborative teams for students with severe disabilities: Integrating therapy and educational services* [p. 272]. Baltimore: Paul H. Brookes Publishing Co.; reprinted by permission.)

Team Meeting Minutes

Team meeting for: _____ Date: _____

Start time: _____ Finish time: _____

Participants: _____

_____

Facilitator: _____ Recorder: _____

Priority sequence	Agenda items and key points	Follow-up needed: Who? What? When?
1. 2.	Anecdote: Follow-up:	

Next meeting

Date/time: _____ Location: _____

Facilitator: _____ Recorder: _____

Agenda items: _____

A Teacher's Guide to Including Students with Disabilities in General Physical Education
by Martin E. Block, copyright ©2000 Paul H. Brookes Publishing Co.

Figure 3.3. A form to record PEIT meeting minutes. (From Rainforth, B., York, J., & Macdonald, C. [1992]. *Collaborative teams for students with severe disabilities: Integrating therapy and educational services* [p. 273]. Baltimore: Paul H. Brookes Publishing Co.; reprinted by permission.)

During previous PEIT meetings, the team developed a plan for Sarah that includes the following long-term goals: 1) push wheelchair with direction, 2) acquire skills needed to participate in bowling using a ramp, 3) swim using a flotation device, 4) play miniature golf using a ramp, 5) independently participate in aerobic dance, and 6) partially participate in modified games of basketball and softball. The adapted and general physical educators review the progress Sarah has made toward these goals. For example, Sarah and her peers have just completed a unit on softball. Sarah learned how to hold the bat using one hand and hit a ball off a tee so that it traveled 5 feet in the air. In addition, she can push her wheelchair down the first base line (with verbal cueing) a distance of 10 feet in 30 seconds, which is a tremendous improvement from the previous month.

Other team members ask the general and adapted physical educators specific questions regarding their specialties. For example, the speech-language therapist notes that Sarah's ability to communicate using the picture board that is taped to her lap tray is improving; she wants to know if Sarah is using the board during physical education. The general physical educator notes that he has seen Sarah use her picture board several times to communicate with him and with her peers. Similarly, the vision and physical therapists discuss changes they have seen in Sarah over the past month and query the general and adapted physical educators as to similar changes they might have seen. On Fridays, Sarah goes with the adapted physical educator and several of her peers without disabilities to the local YMCA to swim and then to the local bowling alley to bowl. The adapted physical educator reviews the progress she has made on these IEP goals. He notes that Sarah can now push the ball down the ramp without any additional verbal cues. In addition, he notes that she will take her wallet out of her purse and give the checkout person a dollar for her shoe rental following a verbal cue. Sarah also points to the picture of a shoe on her picture board following a verbal cue (the speech-language therapist was thrilled to hear this). The occupational therapist who assists Sarah at the bowling alley notes that Sarah is gaining much more control of her good hand, and she is able to take things out of her purse and wallet independently within 30 seconds of a verbal command (this was one of the occupational therapist's goals). Although Sarah really enjoys swimming using a flotation device, she has not made any notable gains during the past month. In addition, Sarah is continuing to work on her dressing and undressing skills. The team comments that Sarah should continue with her bowling and swimming program on Fridays.

The general physical educator then reviews the next unit, which is track and field. He briefly explains the activities that will take place during this unit and then asks team members for suggestions for Sarah. The physical therapist notes that Sarah should continue to work on her wheelchair mobility skills. In addition, she shows the general physical educator some new stretches for Sarah's upper body, which Sarah can do during warm-ups with the help of her teacher assistant. The adapted physical educator suggests that Sarah train for specific Special Olympics wheelchair events so that she can culminate her training with an actual track event. The team meeting concludes with the team leader reviewing Sarah's program and noting on the minutes any actions that should take place by the next meeting. The next meeting is set for the first countywide in-service day (approximately 6 weeks away), at which time the team will discuss how well Sarah's program is going. Team members are expected to provide brief, written evaluations of Sarah's progress on her physical education goals (responsibility of general and adapted physical educator) as well as related goals. For example, the speech-language therapist will come into a general physical education class to evaluate Sarah's functional use of the picture board. The adapted physical educator reminds team members that they should feel free to contact each other if they need more information in the interim.

Collaborative Team Members

A variety of professionals can be involved on a student's collaborative team. Although each team member has specific responsibilities, the collaborative model suggests that each member assist other professionals in carrying out their responsibilities. The following describes the specific responsibilities of each of the collaborative team members and ways that they can assist the general and adapted physical educators in successfully including the student with disabilities into general physical education.

Student with Disabilities

Many researchers believe that, in addition to his or her parents, the student with disabilities is the most important member of the collaborative team; therefore, he or she should be included on the team whenever possible. Who else knows more about the student's abilities, interests, and needs than the student him- or herself? Also, a student with disabilities who is included in the process of developing his or her educational program is more likely to be committed and motivated to work on specific program goals. After all, this really is the student's team and meeting, and the team is really in place to discuss the student's present and future (CEC, 1999)! Also, participation is the first step in helping the student learn how to be his or her own best advocate.

Levels and types of participation will vary from student to student depending on his or her age, disabilities, and ability to communicate and participate in the meeting. For example, an elementary-age student with spina bifida might attend a PEIT meeting to discuss alternative ways she might participate in warm-up activities when the class is doing locomotor patterns. Similarly, a high school–age student who is blind can choose a cardiovascular training program (e.g., aerobic dancing, using the stair climber, riding a stationary bike, walking the track) that meets his interests. Again, students who are given choices tend to be motivated learners. Even students with severe disabilities can be included in team meetings, even if they only stay long enough to meet team members at the beginning of the meeting and then go back to class. In addition, having the student with a disability present at team meetings helps the team focus more on the student's needs rather than their own schedules and problems.

If a student with a disability is going to attend a collaborative team meeting, then someone should talk to him or her ahead of time about who will be attending the meeting, what will be discussed, questions he or she may be asked by team members, and what information he or she can share with the team (CEC, 1999). Also, team members should realize that the student will not be able to understand everything; therefore, they need to be careful to use terminology that the student understands. For nonverbal students, interests and abilities can be shared with the group via videotapes or portfolios.

Parents

Parents and caregivers are often overlooked resources in the education of students with disabilities despite the fact that by law they should play an integral part in the development of a student's IEP. In fact, the IDEA Amendments of

1997 have strengthened the role of parents by noting that the parents' concerns, as well as the information they provide about their child, must be considered when developing and reviewing the IEP. In addition, the IDEA Amendments of 1997 require one or both parents of a student with a disability to be present at each IEP meeting or, at least, given the chance to participate (CEC, 1999). However, parental participation on the collaborative team is more than just a legal mandate; it is critical for developing an appropriate IEP. Parents usually know more practical information about their child than any professional. In addition, parents often have developed successful management and training techniques at home that can be useful in the classroom and in physical education. For example, parents may have techniques for positioning a student so that he or she can get dressed quickly, which could be important in the locker room.

Parents should also be encouraged to share their goals and expectations for their child as well as their personal recreation interests so that the physical educator can gear the adapted physical education program to meet the unique needs of the family. It is much easier to get support from home when parents are included in the decision process. For example, if a family enjoys playing tennis and going hiking during weekend leisure time, then it would make sense to target these skills for a middle school student with a disability. These skills likely will be practiced at home and, when mastered, can help the student participate more successfully in a fun family activity. Parents should be present at their child's IEP meeting, but if they are unable to attend, Figure 3.4 is a simple form that can be sent home to them to get their input regarding what the family likes to do for recreation and what physical education goals they would like targeted for the child. This information can then be shared with the collaborative team during the IEP meeting.

Adapted Physical Education Professionals

As noted in Chapter 1, IDEA and the IDEA Amendments of 1997 require physical education for students with disabilities to be administered by a qualified professional—ideally, an *adapted physical education* (APE) *professional*—who meets certain state requirements and competencies (Kelly, 1991; NCPERID, 1995). Qualified APE professionals usually have a master's degree in adapted physical education, extensive practical experience working with students with disabilities, and considerable knowledge of disabilities and physical education. One way to ensure that a school district is getting a qualified APE professional is to hire a Certified Adapted Physical Educator (CAPE). CAPEs are licensed physical education specialists who have documented practical experience and training in adapted physical education and who have successfully passed the Adapted Physical Education National Standards (APENS) exam (Kelly, 1995).

The major role of APE professionals is to assist in the identification and remediation of physical education–related problems of individuals with disabilities (Kelly, 1995; Sherrill, 1998). Specific services provided by the APE professionals include assessing the person with disabilities, planning programs, writing individualized physical education programs and participating in IEP meetings, implementing habilitative programs for students with disabilities, consulting with general physical educators and parents, providing fitness and leisure counseling, and advocating for the student in physical education and sports (McCubbin, Jansma, & Houston-Wilson, 1993; Sherrill, 1998). Although most APE professionals work directly with students with disabilities, particularly students with more severe disabilities, they often also act as consultants (Block & Conatser, 1999; NCPERID, 1995; Sherrill, 1998). In this role, the APE professional helps others (typically the

Parent's Physical Education Interest Form

1. What do you do as a family for recreation (e.g., play tennis, go for walks, go swimming)? _____

    _____

    _____

    _____

2. What activities do you see other children in your neighborhood participate in that you think your child would enjoy (e.g., bike riding, soccer, t-ball, rollerblading)?

    _____

    _____

    _____

    _____

3. What community-based recreation program does your child participate in or would you like to see your child participate in (e.g., t-ball, soccer, Special Olympics or other special sports program)? _____

    _____

    _____

    _____

    _____

4. Do you have any fitness concerns for your child that you would like to have addressed during physical education (e.g., upper-body strength, flexibility, endurance, body weight)? _____

    _____

    _____

    _____

    _____

5. What specific activities or tasks, other than those that you listed above, would you like your child to work on during physical education (i.e., what would be your dream physical education program)? _____

    _____

    _____

    _____

    _____

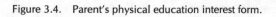

Figure 3.4.   Parent's physical education interest form.

general physical educator and parents) work more successfully with students with disabilities (Block & Conatser, 1999).

Unfortunately, less than 20 states have any type of special requirements for APE professionals other than a general physical education teaching license. Therefore, many school districts employ APE professionals who do not have any specialized training, experience, or knowledge regarding students with disabilities but who have a genuine interest in working as an APE professional (Winnick, 1995). Even worse, many smaller school districts do not have anyone on their staff who is designated as the school district APE professional. One has to question whether students with disabilities in these districts receive an individualized physical education program as required in IDEA.

If a school system has an APE professional, the APE professional should be the PEIT coordinator. The APE professional can assist the general physical educator in including students with disabilities into general physical education in a variety of ways. First, the APE professional can take all the information provided by the other team members, including specific information regarding the student's physical and motor skills, and present it to the general physical education specialist in a way that is meaningful and practical. Second, the APE professional can provide specific information to the general physical education specialist regarding ways to modify physical education activities so as to safely and successfully include the student with disabilities. This can be accomplished through counseling sessions, team teaching, or written modifications to lesson plans (Block & Conatser, 1999; Sherrill, 1998). The APE professional knows more than the other team members about the ways in which specific types of disabilities affect physical education; therefore, he or she is a critical member of the team.

General Physical Education Professional

General physical education (GPE) professionals are specifically trained and licensed to teach physical education to students without disabilities. Although, in the past, these professionals were asked only to work with students without disabilities, changing legislation and roles now require these professionals to work with all students who enter their gymnasium, including students with disabilities (Winnick, 1995). Many enjoy their new role and quickly become acclimated to working with students who have disabilities, whereas others are more resistant to change. In either case, GPE professionals should be included and welcomed to the collaborative team because they can provide critical information pertaining to general physical education that no other team member can provide. For example, GPE professionals will know more about what happens during general physical education than any other team member. He or she also will have a great deal of knowledge regarding the components of physical education (e.g., physical fitness, fundamental motor skills, individual and team sports, games). In addition, he or she will have direct information regarding the behaviors and attitude of the student with disabilities in general physical education. Perhaps of greatest importance, however, the GPE professional will know the units that will be taught during the year, the teaching approach that will be used, the equipment that will be available, the number of students who are in each class, and the pace and dynamics of the class (CEC, 1999).

It is important to remember that most GPE professionals have had very little training or experience working with students who have disabilities and, therefore, may be apprehensive about including a student with disabilities in their general program (Chandler & Greene, 1995; Janney, Snell, Beers, & Raynes,

1995). Most GPE professionals have taken only one survey course in adapted physical education during their formal training and have had very little practical experience working with students who have disabilities. It is the responsibility of all team members to make the GPE professional feel as comfortable as possible with the notion of inclusion. However, it is the GPE professional's responsibility to have an open mind about inclusion, provide opportunities for interaction between students with and without disabilities, and be a role model to students by accepting the student with disabilities and respecting his or her individual differences (Block, 1999a).

According to the IDEA Amendments of 1997, a general educator must be included on the IEP team if the student is or may be taking part in any general education environment. This does not necessarily mean that the GPE professional needs to attend every IEP meeting for every student in his or her building who has a disability. However, this does mean that the special education teacher should invite the GPE professional to IEP meetings and seek his or her input into physical education programming for students with disabilities.

Special Education Teacher

The special education teacher is the primary advocate and program planner for the student with disabilities (CEC, 1999; Stainback & Stainback, 1985). His or her role is to develop and assist in the implementation of the student's IEP, including initiation and organization of inclusive activities. In addition, the special education teacher's job is to coordinate all support and related services a student may need to benefit from special education (Stainback & Stainback, 1985). The special education teacher will know more about the student with disabilities than any other team member, with the possible exception of the student's parents. The special education teacher has access to information that could facilitate a student's inclusion into general physical education. This information includes a record of the student's developmental history and health and medical background, as well as knowledge of the student's behaviors and behavior plans, communication and cognitive skills, self-help skills, learning style, successful teaching techniques, and likes and dislikes (CEC, 1999). In addition, as coordinator of all of the student's services, he or she can quickly communicate information to other team members. The special education teacher can also assist in training peer tutors and paraeducators who may work in the general physical education environment.

Principal

The principal is responsible for everything that takes place in his or her school, including physical education programs and programs for students with disabilities. Therefore, although he or she may not be directly involved in program planning or implementation, the building principal has a vested interest in the success of an inclusive physical education environment. Principals who support inclusive physical education can have a direct impact on the attitudes of general physical education staff members who may be leery of implementing the program. In addition, principals can help team members gain important resources such as extra support, special equipment, and gym time. Finally, the principal can also act as a go-between to other administrators such as directors of physical education or special education at a school-system level.

School Nurse

The school nurse is an invaluable resource to the team regarding the health and medical status of the student with disabilities. School nurses are mainly responsible for 1) diagnosing and treating minor injuries and illnesses, 2) handling medical emergencies and contacting other emergency personnel, and 3) monitoring and administering prescription medications. In some schools, nurses are also responsible for specific health care procedures such as suctioning a student's tracheotomy (i.e., hole in throat used for breathing); facilitating postural drainage for students whose lungs fill with fluid (e.g., students with cystic fibrosis); providing clean, intermittent catheterization to help students who do not have bladder control (e.g., some students with spina bifida); and administering tube feedings to students who cannot receive adequate nutrition through oral feeding (e.g., students with severe gastrointestinal problems). Because the school nurse has direct access to the student's parents and physicians, he or she can act as a link between the student's parents or physicians and the school. For example, if a question arises as to the effects of vigorous exercise on a seizure disorder, the school nurse can quickly contact the student's parents or physicians to get an immediate answer. The school nurse should act as a consultant to the team, and team members should feel free to contact the nurse if they have any questions regarding a particular student's health or medical state (Winnick, 1995). For example, the nurse should be consulted before a student with a seizure disorder is involved in activities such as swimming or gymnastics or when a student with allergy-induced asthma is supposed to go outside for physical education.

Physical Therapist

A physical therapist specializes in disorders of gross motor development (i.e., movements that involve large muscles of the body); he or she utilizes various techniques to relieve pain and discomfort, prevent deformity and further disability, restore or maintain functioning, and improve strength and motor skill performance (Hanft & Place, 1996; Sherrill, 1998). Physical therapists also work in the area of daily living activities (e.g., moving around the school building, dressing, sitting properly) and architectural barriers. Techniques include therapeutic exercise; developmental therapy; and the use of assistive devices such as gait trainers, walkers, braces, canes, crutches, and wheelchairs. The type of therapy depends on the goals that have been set by the IEP team (Hanft & Place, 1996; Sherrill, 1998). In most states, a PT must have a written referral from the student's physician (usually an orthopedic surgeon) before he or she can provide therapy to students with disabilities. The physician provides a diagnosis, goals to be accomplished, and instructions regarding precautions and contraindications.

The physical therapist will know more about the student's physical condition than any other team member. As such, he or she should be included in decisions regarding contraindicated activities or positions, selection of motor skills for training, positioning and limb use for optimum functioning, and modifications to equipment or game rules. For example, if a student who is learning to walk with a walker is placed in a third-grade general physical education class, the physical therapist can provide information regarding which warm-up activities are appropriate or inappropriate; how to modify appropriate warm-up activities and which alternative warm-ups could be used when scheduled warm-ups are inappropriate; how far and how fast the student should be expected to walk; the student's aerobic capacity, strength, and flexibility; and how to modify activities in general physical education.

Occupational Therapist

According to IDEA, occupational therapists utilize various techniques to 1) improve, develop, and/or restore functions impaired or lost through illness, injury, or deprivation; 2) improve ability to perform tasks for independent functioning when functions are impaired or lost; and 3) prevent, through early intervention, initial or further impairment or loss of function (Federal Register, August 23, 1977, p. 42479). One of the major focuses of occupational therapists is to assist people in performing activities of daily living (ADL) as independently as possible through training or adapted equipment. Another major focus, particularly with students with disabilities, is the presentation of sensorimotor integration activities designed to help students fully utilize and integrate vestibular information (i.e., information from the inner ear that tells the person where his or her head is in relation to gravity), tactile information (i.e., sense of touch and feedback from touch sensors on the skin), and visual information (Kimble, Ball, & Jansma, 1999). The OT can be an important resource on the team regarding a student's abilities (and possible adaptations to suit the student's abilities) in 1) self-help and personal hygiene skills needed in the locker room prior to and after a physical education class; 2) fine motor skills, fundamental manipulative skills, and sport-specific manipulative skills; and 3) skills related to sensory integration such as static and dynamic balance, tactile awareness, and proprioception.

Recreation Therapist

According to the IDEA Amendments of 1997, the primary responsibilities of recreation therapists include 1) assessment of leisure function, 2) therapeutic recreation services, 3) recreation programs in schools and community agencies, and 4) leisure education (Federal Register, August 23, 1977, p. 42479). Basically, recreation services are used to improve functional abilities, enhance well-being and facilitate independence, teach or enhance recreation skills and attitudes that can be used throughout life, and promote health and growth through leisure and recreation experiences (National Therapeutic Recreation Society, 1995). Recreation therapy includes an array of programs such as music, art, dance, drama, horticulture, camping, and sports and fitness. Regardless of the type of recreation program selected, recreation therapy utilizes a student's existing skills and interests as well as facilitates new skills for daily living and leisure functioning (Schleien, Ray, & Green, 1997). Recreation therapy is provided by trained and licensed professionals who, like physical therapists, must obtain a physician's referral before they can provide therapy to students with disabilities. For this reason, recreation therapy is more common in children's hospitals and rehabilitation centers than it is in public schools.

Recreation therapists can provide the team with suggestions for adaptations for performing recreation/leisure programs and information regarding recreation/leisure assessment and availability of community recreation facilities. This information can be particularly important to the physical educator who helps the student with disabilities transition from a school-based physical education program to a postschool recreation program. Recreation therapy professionals also often have a good understanding of how well the student is dealing emotionally with his or her disability.

Speech-Language Therapist

The primary role of the speech-language therapist is defined in IDEA as

Identification of students with speech or language disorders, diagnosis and appraisal of specific speech or language disorders, referral for medical or other professional attention necessary for the habilitation of speech or language disorders, provision of speech and language services for the habilitation or prevention of communicative disorders, counseling and guidance of parents, children, and teachers regarding speech or language disorders. (Federal Register, August 23, 1977, p. 42480)

Speech-language therapists can assist team members in understanding a particular student's receptive and expressive language abilities. For example, speech-language therapists can explain to staff members and peers how best to communicate with certain students. Some students might understand verbal cues and simple demonstrations, whereas other students might require communication through sign language or physical assistance. Similarly, speech-language therapists can explain to team members as well as peers how particular students communicate. Expressive language can include speech, sign language, communication boards, and electronic devices such as Canon communicators or speech synthesizers. Knowing how to best present information to students, as well as understanding how a student might express his or her desires, is extremely important for successful inclusion in physical education.

Audiologist

Audiologists are trained professionals who work with students who are hearing impaired. The major role of the audiologist is to determine the extent of a student's hearing loss and hearing abilities and recommend special augmentative hearing devices such as hearing aids. In addition, audiologists often consult with speech-language therapists to determine a particular student's potential for speech and language development. An audiologist can assist the general physical educator by explaining a student's hearing loss and specifying his or her residual hearing abilities. In collaboration with the speech-language therapist, the audiologist can then recommend ways to communicate with a student who has a hearing impairment. For example, an audiologist might suggest that a student who is in general physical education and has a severe hearing loss may need to have verbal directions repeated by a peer or have demonstrations to supplement verbal commands. In addition, the audiologist can explain safety precautions for this student, such as avoiding contact to the ear while the student is wearing hearing aids and removing the hearing aids before swimming.

Vision Specialist

Vision specialists (also called vision teachers) are certified, trained professionals who have specialized training in meeting the educational needs of students with visual impairments (Brasher & Holbrook, 1996). The major goal of vision teachers is to help students with visual impairments become as functional and independent as possible given their limited visual abilities. For students with low vision, specific goals include learning orientation and mobility skills that are necessary to move about in various school and community environments and adapted techniques for classwork such as reading large print and using felt-tip markers, a magnifying glass, and computers. For students who have very limited vision or who are blind, goals include orientation and mobility skills such as using a cane and a sighted guide and learning adapted techniques for classwork such as braille and computers.

Other areas that vision teachers work on with students who have visual impairments include 1) encouraging movement and introducing toys that are visually or tactually interesting, 2) stimulating the use of all senses, 3) teaching prereading skills such as tracking and finger positioning, 4) teaching braille reading, and 5) helping with daily living skills such as eating and dressing (Brasher & Holbrook, 1996).

Vision teachers work very closely with other professionals; they are some students' primary teachers. Vision teachers' expertise on particular students as well as general adaptations for students with visual impairments can be invaluable for adapted and general physical educators. For example, the vision teacher can teach the general physical educator and peers without disabilities how to make the student with a visual impairment feel more comfortable in the gym environment, appropriately interact with the student, and assist the student. Vision teachers can also provide ideas for adapted equipment, safety precautions, and rule modifications such as guide ropes for running, beep-balls for softball, and tandem bike riding. Many vision teachers have easy access to adapted equipment such as beep-balls and balls with bells, whereas others are knowledgeable about special sports programs designed for people with visual impairments such as the United States Association for Blind Athletes (USABA).

Orientation and Mobility Specialist

Orientation and mobility specialists (also called O&M teachers or travel instructors) are certified teachers who have received specialized training in teaching students and adults with visual impairments how to travel in a variety of environments safely and efficiently (Brasher & Holbrook, 1996). Initially, the orientation and mobility specialist works with students on general space awareness and directionality, including things such as over, under, left, and right. As the student progresses, training moves to more specific travel skills, including traveling within a room (e.g., in the classroom or on the playground) and traveling between rooms (e.g., traveling from the classroom to the gym). Depending on the student's visual and cognitive abilities, the O&M specialist might have students use a sighted guide, a cane, or, as they get older, a dog. O&M specialists can be an invaluable aid to physical education. First, the O&M specialist can help the student learn how to independently move from the classroom to the gym. Second, the O&M specialist can help orient the student to the locker room, pool area, gymnasium, and any other physical education environments. Third, the O&M specialist can help the physical educator look for dangerous areas in the gym, show the physical educator how to help a student with a vision impairment move more safely in the gym, and give the physical educator ideas for adapting equipment and rules.

Paraeducator

Paraeducators (also known as paraprofessionals, educational aides, instructional assistants, teacher assistants, and individualized learning assistants) are hired to assist teachers (including general physical educators) in implementing a student's IEP. Paraeducators work under the supervision of a teacher or other professional (including the general physical educator) who is responsible for the overall management of the class, creation and implementation of the IEP, and assessment of the student's progress (Doyle, 1997). In inclusive environments, the paraeducator often is the person who has the most one-to-one contact with the student with disabilities.

Paraeducators range greatly in their background and training from certified special education teachers to people with high school degrees who have virtually no prior experience working with students with disabilities. In addition, paraeducators are utilized differently by various teachers. Some paraeducators are only responsible for noninstructional responsibilities such as clerical work (e.g., making copies, tallying a lunch count, taking attendance); monitoring students in the hallway, at lunch, or on the playground; setting up the classroom for the teacher; or providing specific personal care such as toileting, dressing, feeding, and repositioning (Doyle, 1997). Others have more instructional responsibilities such as observing, recording, and charting a student's behavior and academic progress, assisting in full classroom instruction; assisting with individualized instruction for particular students; tutoring small groups of students; implementing and reinforcing teacher-developed lessons; contributing ideas and suggestions regarding a student or a group of students; and participating in team meetings (Doyle, 1997).

Regardless of the exact role of paraeducators, their close contact with the student with disabilities enables them to provide unique insight into the needs, peculiarities, and interests of the student. Therefore, paraeducators can provide valuable information to the team regarding a student's behaviors at certain times during the day, communication skills, likes and dislikes, preferred positions, and effective adaptations and activities. In many programs, the paraeducator will accompany the student with disabilities into physical education, so that he or she will not only know about the student but also how the student reacts to physical education activities. It is important, however, to note that paraeducators *are not* responsible for the initial design and development of instructional procedures for students with disabilities in physical education, assessment, or decision making (Doyle, 1997). Although the paraeducator can be included in the process, the general physical educator should be responsible for developing lesson plans and then training the paraeducator on how to implement these plans. In addition, the general physical educator must be prepared to provide the paraeducator with some directions regarding 1) the plan for the day, 2) which peers should be encouraged to work with the student with a disability, 3) which modifications and adapted equipment to anticipate for certain activities, 4) which activities might be inappropriate, and 5) how to help the student work on specific skills and be part of the group. The paraeducator is there because the student with a disability cannot be independently included in physical education; he or she is not there to develop and then implement an individualized adapted physical education program for the student while the general physical educator works with the other students in the class!

Communication: The Key to Collaborative Teaming

Collaborative teaming is really nothing more than a simple exchange of ideas. Dougherty (1995) noted that collaboration is a human relationship and, as such, needs to be handled with a personal touch. He suggested that *how* team members communicate with each other often is more important than *what* they are communicating. Critical to successful collaborative teaming is each team member's ability to 1) express ideas, 2) articulate requests clearly and in a nonthreatening way, 3) elicit information from others, and 4) listen to how others feel (Gutkin & Curtis, 1982; Hanft & Place, 1996; Kurpius & Rozecki, 1993). Unfortunately, communication is such a difficult process that misunderstanding and miscommunication frequently occur during collaboration (Heron & Harris, 1993). The following section outlines key aspects of effective communication in collaborative teaming.

Establishing and Maintaining Effective Communication

Because so much of collaboration revolves around communication, it is critical for team members to understand how to establish and maintain effective communication. Heron and Harris (1993) suggested that, in order to establish open channels of communication, team members must first gain acceptance from each other and work to minimize resistance and manage conflict.

Gaining Acceptance   Gaining acceptance and establishing rapport among team members is extremely important (Hanft & Place, 1996; Pedron & Evans, 1990). Collaborative teaming is much easier if positive relationships are established from the very beginning of the process. Hanft and Place (1996) noted that all collaboration should start with the explicit goal of establishing positive relationships among team members that can be built through effective interpersonal and communication skills. Important aspects of gaining acceptance include genuineness (conveying sincerity), positive regard (treating others with respect), empathy (understanding the other's perspective), and congruence (establishing a common ground to converse and share thoughts and feelings honestly) (Heron & Harris, 1993; Kurpius & Rozecki, 1993).

Minimizing Resistance   Related to gaining acceptance is anticipating and dealing with resistance. Establishing trust in and genuineness to the interests of other team members and the student is perhaps the best way to overcome resistance (Gutkin & Curtis, 1982; Kurpius & Rozecki, 1993; Margolis & McCabe, 1988). Margolis and McCabe provided the following suggestions for creating trust:

1. Provide complete and unhurried attention.
2. Keep your word.
3. Listen to understand rather than to challenge.
4. Respond to requests for assistance in a timely manner.
5. Use easily understood language (i.e., avoid jargon).
6. Share expertise without dominating the discussion.
7. Use active listening techniques.
8. If resistance persists, use a problem-solving technique to determine how to address it.

Managing Conflict   Regardless of best efforts in interpersonal and communication skills, conflicts will arise. Most communications that occur during collaborative teaming are negotiations and conflict resolution (Hanft & Place, 1996). Conflict can arise for many reasons and can affect the teaming process both favorably and unfavorably (Gutkin & Curtis, 1982). Heron and Harris (1993) suggested five strategies to deal with conflict:

1. Withdraw if neither the goal nor the relationship is important (e.g., general physical education teacher is not going to change, and the student with disabilities is reasonably accommodated).
2. Force the issue, and use all your energy to accomplish the task if it is important but the relationship is not (e.g., student is in danger or the program is completely unacceptable and your relationship with a team member is short term).
3. Smooth things over if you want to be liked and accepted and if the relationship is more important than the task (e.g., a student with disabilities is being reasonably accommodated; you want to maintain a good relationship with the adapted physical educator, and you know she will be getting more of your students in the future).

4. Compromise if the task and the relationship are important but time is limited (e.g., develop reasonable accommodations for a student with spina bifida to participate in a basketball unit that starts next week, knowing that with more time you might have suggested other accommodations).

5. Confront the situation if the task and the relationship are equally important (e.g., take time to really problem-solve how a student's unique goals and objectives can be embedded within the general physical education curriculum).

Note that confrontation in teaming is viewed as a problem-solving technique to resolve conflicts among team members (Gutkin & Curtis, 1982; Heron & Harris, 1993). As long as confrontation avoids emotional reactions such as hostility or anger, then the confrontation is a positive way for both parties to agree on a course of action.

If a team member becomes angry, Margolis and Fiorelli (1987) suggested the following:

1. Maintain composure.

2. Listen carefully and empathetically.

3. Encourage the team member to identify and share the reasons for his or her anger and fully release the anger.

4. Resist attempts to invalidate the information that has been shared.

5. Note areas of agreement.

6. Move slowly from problem perception to problem definition.

7. Help the team member maintain self-respect.

The goal is to defuse the situation, maintain a relationship with the team member, and get back to solving the problem at hand. Team members need to realize that each team member has had unique experiences, and learning how to understand and value these differences in experience is critical for successful communication (Johnston & Wayda, 1994; Kraus & Curtis, 1986).

Practicing Good Listening Skills

Table 3.2 provides a list, developed by West and Cannon (1989), of the critical interpersonal and communication skills needed for effective collaboration. Of these skills, listening behaviors including nonverbal listening skills have been reported to be the most critical (Gutkin & Curtis, 1982; Kurpius & Rozecki, 1993). Communication involves more than just presenting information and asking questions (Johnston & Wayda, 1994). In fact, one of the most important communication skills in collaborative teaming is being a good listener (Covey, 1989; Gutkin & Curtis, 1982). If a team member cannot first fully understand other team members and their unique situations, then it will be impossible to discuss an appropriate solution. If a team member does not feel understood, then even if information given to him or her is informative and interesting, it will not help him or her with his or her unique situation. Thus, no influence or change will take place.

Although most team members understand the need to be a good listener, many team members forget to listen. Covey (1989) suggested that listening with the intent to fully understand often is threatening or unnatural because trying to fully understand someone else's perspective may cause you to change your own perspectives or values system. In addition, team members may not be good listeners because of the natural tendency to first be understood. Many people's first

Table 3.2.   Interpersonal qualities and communication skills needed for consultation

Interpersonal qualities	Communication skills
Caring	Listening
Respectful	Acknowledging
Empathetic	Paraphrasing
Congruent	Reflecting
Open	Clarifying
Positive self-concept	Elaborating
Enthusiastic attitude	Summarizing
Willingness to learn from others	Grasp overt meaning
Calm	Grasp covert meaning
Stress free	Interpret nonverbal communication
Risk-taker	Interview effectively
Flexible	Providing feedback
Resilient	Brainstorming
Manage conflict and confrontation	Nonjudgmental responding
Manage time	Developing action plan

From West, J.F., Idol, L., & Cannon, G.S. (1989). *Collaboration in the schools: An inservice and pre-service curriculum for teachers, support staff, and administrators* (pp. 277–278). Austin, TX: PRO-ED; reprinted by permission.

reaction to another person talking is to listen with the intent to speak. For example, many team members might listen to the general physical education teacher's concerns not so much to truly understand his or her concerns, but rather to jump in at the first opportunity to give an opinion or solution. If team members are waiting to speak, then they are not fully listening. Kurpius and Rozecki (1993) suggested some other common barriers to listening, which include 1) a tendency to judge or evaluate a team member's statements, 2) inattention or apathy, 3) asking questions prematurely, 4) feeling the need to define and solve the problem quickly, and 5) pursuing one's own agenda regardless of the team member's needs. Unfortunately, a team member instinctively recognizes half-hearted attempts at listening, and this creates feelings of mistrust.

Collaborative teaming is more than one team member simply giving advice to another team member. Advising does not consider the other team member's reference. This is often the case when one team member tries to fix another team member's problem by telling him or her what to do (Hanft & Place, 1996). In contrast, true collaborative teaming incorporates the perspectives of each team member. Solutions are reached as a team, which empowers and elevates each team member in the decision-making process. As each team member takes ownership of the decision-making process, his or her self-esteem is enhanced as the solution becomes resolved and he or she becomes aware of his or her own resources and establishes an increased sense of confidence.

To be a better listener, Kurpius and Rozecki (1993) suggested the following two responses: clarification and reflection. Clarification refers to asking questions in such a way as to help the team member focus more clearly on a situation. It also is a way to get the team member to talk about and elaborate on specific problems. Gutkin and Curtis (1982) noted that open-ended questions rather than *yes/no* questions encourage team members to clarify their points of view. For example, a question aimed at a GPE teacher such as, "What did you mean when you said that including this student in GPE is not working right now?" encourages the GPE teacher to clarify his or her statements.

Reflection refers to team members listening to each other and then trying to rephrase the information. For example, a GPE teacher talks about the problems she is having with two students with behavior problems who are "driving [her] crazy." After listening for several minutes and helping the GPE teacher clarify key points, team members help the GPE teacher reflect by saying, "It sounds as if you are really frustrated that these two boys were placed in your class without your prior knowledge and without any support from the special education staff." Note how reflection not only rephrases what a team member said but also includes that team member's feelings and emotions. Reflecting on a team member's feelings helps him or her focus his or her energies on identifying and resolving the targeted problem (Gutkin & Curtis, 1982).

Listening requires more than picking up key words. When a team member talks, other team members need to pay close attention to body language, emotions, and tone (Gutkin & Curtis, 1982). For example, a general physical education teacher says, "I'm really all right with my situation." This phrase can be said and expressed in various ways, each way communicating a completely different meaning. Therefore, team members need to listen with their ears, eyes, and heart as well as respond clearly, specifically, and contextually from within that team member's frame of reference. If complete attention is given to that team member, then other team members will be able to better understand the full message. Team members also need to convey through their body language their true interest in listening and understanding the other team members. Nonverbal communication can be just as important as verbal communication (Johnston & Wayda, 1994). Miscommunication often results from nonverbal factors such as facial expressions, vocal intonations, body postures and movement, and use of space. Although it is usually unintentional, a team member's nonverbal behaviors can convey lack of interest or concern, lack of genuineness, and/or a general sense of discomfort with other team members (Heron & Harris, 1993).

To summarize, the importance of communication in collaborative teaming cannot be understated. Effective communication allows for free flow of information among team members. Ineffective communication leads to misunderstandings and conflicts. Team members' abilities to be open, listen with the intent to understand, and reduce conflict will inspire openness and trust and increase the overall effectiveness of collaborative teaming.

4

Planning for Inclusion
in Physical Education

The more I learned about autism, the more I understood the body–mind connection. I saw tangible improvements in my son Michael from the adapted physical education program at the special needs preschool he attended. Adapted physical education made a big difference in helping it all come together for Michael. Michael is now fully included in general physical education, and we as his parents continue to put an emphasis on gross motor activities and consider it to be the single most useful therapy. At 10 years old, Michael plays in the regular leagues for soccer, baseball, and basketball and is one rank below brown belt in karate!

Jane Krobuth, parent

Lee is a 15-year-old student with severe cerebral palsy and mental retardation requiring extensive support who will be attending Jefferson High School in the fall. The physical education staff members at Jefferson have attended several in-services regarding inclusion and have been given specific information about Lee. Also, in the spring, they had an opportunity to observe Lee in the general education classroom and in physical education at Washington Middle School. In addition, Lee's adapted physical education specialist and his parents met with the physical education staff at Jefferson High School to outline which activities they would like to see Lee participate in during his high school years.

This is the first time that the physical education staff at Jefferson have had to include a student with such severe disabilities in their general physical education program. They have successfully included students with learning disabilities, mental retardation requiring intermittent support, and even a student who was deaf; however, Lee presents a completely different problem. In which activities can Lee participate? What parts of the high school curriculum are appropriate for Lee, and what parts are inappropriate? What adaptations and supports will Lee need to be safely, successfully, and meaningfully included in general physical education? The physical education staff at Jefferson have many questions regarding how to include him. How can these staff members make an informed decision regarding Lee's program? The physical education staff need a systematic way to develop a program for Lee so he can work on the goals specified in his individualized education program (IEP) within the general physical education environment.

Students with disabilities can receive an individualized, appropriate physical education program within the general physical education environment. However, the physical education inclusion team (PEIT) must address several issues prior to placing a student with disabilities in general physical education. For example, which students with disabilities actually require adapted physical education services? What goals should be prioritized for each student? Which goals can be incorporated into the general physical education program? What modifications will be necessary? What in-service training should be provided to the general physical educator, paraprofessionals, and peers? Successful placement of students with disabilities into general physical education involves much more than just placing the student into the general environment. This chapter outlines a systematic approach to including students with disabilities into general physical education. The focus of this approach is on making critical decisions utilizing an *ecological approach* to programming and preparing personnel *prior to* the student's inclusion. Program planning should first determine *what* to teach the student (goals and objectives) before decisions can be made regarding where to work on these objectives (placement), how to work on these objectives (modifications), or who should work on these objectives (support). In fact, the Individuals with Disabilities Education Act (IDEA) of 1990 (PL 101-476) and the IDEA Amendments of 1997 (PL 105-17) require that IEP goals and objectives be developed prior to making decisions regarding placement, teaching, and staffing (Bateman, 1996; Council for Exceptional Children, 1999; Sherrill, 1998).

Determining Who Qualifies for Adapted Physical Education Services

As noted in Chapter 2, all students with disabilities are required to receive physical education services; however, not all students with disabilities automatically qualify for adapted physical education services (Block & Burke, 1999). Therefore, the first programmatic question that should be answered is *who* qualifies for adapted physical education services? As mandated in IDEA and the IDEA Amendments of 1997, the decision as to who qualifies for adapted physical education should be made by the student's IEP team. Furthermore, decisions should not be based on a label, services received by other students in the district, or availability of services. For example, not all students who are labeled as being *orthopedically impaired* who use wheelchairs would necessarily qualify for adapted physical education services. Some students who use wheelchairs are very capable and athletic and require only minor modifications to be successful in general physical education. However, it would be wrong not to provide adapted physical education to a student with a learning disability who has significant motor and behavior problems simply because no other student with a learning disability receives adapted physical education services. Again, the key is making decisions on a case-by-case basis using formal and informal observations and examining the student's present level of performance in a variety of areas, including

- *Motor skills and abilities:* Norm- and criterion-referenced motor development and motor ability tests such as a school-district–approved physical education curriculum or assessment tool (e.g., Test of Gross Motor Development [Ulrich, 1995], Peabody Developmental Motor Scales [Folio & DuBose, 1974], Bruininks-Oseretsky Test of Motor Proficiency [Bruininks, 1978])

- *Physical fitness:* Norm- and criterion-referenced physical fitness tests (e.g., school-district–approved physical education curriculum or assessment tool, President's Council on Physical Fitness Test [President's Council on Physical Fitness and Sports, 1991], Fitnessgram [Cooper Institute for Aerobics Research, 1992])

- *Perceptual/sensory motor skills:* Criterion-referenced perceptual motor tests (self-made tests)

- *General physical education:* Informal and formal observations to determine student's ability to participate successfully in general physical education

- *Behaviors:* Informal and formal observations to determine student's behaviors in general physical education, degree to which the student understands what is going on, and the way or ways that the student's behavior affects others in the class

Based on information obtained from these formal and informal assessments and observations, the IEP team then needs to decide whether the student with a disability is significantly behind his or her peers with regard to physical education. Although the determination of what constitutes "significantly behind his or her peers" can certainly be debated, in general, this means that a student with a disability falls at least 1 year below the norm (2 years below for high school students) in motor and/or fitness testing *and* has significant problems in general physical education. "Significant problems in physical education" refers to a student who is not making expected improvement on motor, fitness, and/or behavioral goals while participating in general physical education. If the team determines that the student is significantly behind his or her peers and has significant problems in general physical education, then the student likely qualifies for adapted physical education services, and the team should continue with program planning. However, if the team determines these criteria have not been met, then the student does not qualify for adapted physical education services.

In addition to qualifying or not qualifying a student for adapted physical education services, there is another decision the team can make. Some students with disabilities who do not qualify for adapted physical education services might benefit from some accommodations in order to be successful in general physical education. Accommodations include extra support such as a teacher assistant or modifications to instruction, equipment, and/or activities. Again, based on assessment information, the team decides if and what accommodations are required for a particular student; then, these accommodations should be noted on the student's IEP (Bateman, 1996; Sherrill, 1998). For example, a student with a behavior-problem might need a teacher assistant to accompany him or her to general physical education; a student who is deaf may need an interpreter; a student who is blind may need to have written material translated into braille; and a student with mental retardation may need the teacher to repeat instructions or have a peer assist him or her to understand where to go and what to do. Again, accommodations are made on a case-by-case basis to ensure that each student's individual needs are met.

An Ecological Approach to Planning

Once the IEP team determines that a student qualifies for adapted physical education services, they must decide which skills to teach the student, how to embed the skills in general physical education, what modifications will be required, which staff members will teach the skills, and what training these staff members will need. There are many models to program planning, but the two most common in adapted physical education are the ecological (also known as top-down or functional) approach and the developmental or bottom-up approach (Auxter, Pyfer, & Huettig, 1997; Block & Block, 1999; Kelly et al.,1991; Sherrill, 1998).

Ecological Approach

The ecological approach to program planning reflects the interactions between the individual student and the environment in which he or she will function (Rainforth & York-Barr, 1997). In the case of physical education, an ecologically referenced program focuses on the student's abilities and interests in relation to the skills the student will need to be successful in his or her present environment (e.g., physical education, playground skills, activities seen in the student's neighborhood) as well as the skills the student will need to be successful in future environments (e.g., community-based recreation). Once the student's abilities and interests have been determined, team members develop an individualized plan that includes all the skills, activities, and environments that are most important to that student (Rainforth & York-Barr, 1997).

The ecological approach is considered a top-down model, in which planning begins by envisioning where the student will be upon graduation from the program and what skills the student will need to be successful in his or her future environment (Auxter et al., 1997; Kelly et al., 1991; Rainforth & York-Barr, 1997). For example, top-down goals for a middle school or high school student reflect individually selected fitness and recreation activities in which the student can participate independently upon graduation from school (e.g., using a local health club, going to a local driving range, shooting baskets in the driveway of the group home, developing skills needed to play on a community softball or bowling team). For preschool and elementary school students, the top of the plan would reflect goals in two areas: First, the team would design goals to help prepare the student for his or her next school placement such as kindergarten physical education for a preschool student and middle school physical education for an elementary-age student. Second, the team would establish goals to help the student participate in age-appropriate neighborhood activities and community recreation programs such as learning how to ride a tricycle/bicycle, rollerblade, play on playground equipment, or play on a community sports team or league (e.g., baseball, basketball, soccer).

Again, the key to the ecological model is deciding what future activities the student would likely enjoy and be successful in and, then, deciding what skills the student will need to be successful in those activities. Assessment take places after top-down goals have been established and is referenced directly to these top-down goals (Kelly et al., 1991). To illustrate, a fourth-grade student with Down syndrome would have goals that reflect individually selected skills needed to be successful in general fourth-grade physical education; middle school physical education (future PE placement); and intramural, neighborhood, and community-based sport/recreation programs in which the student will participate in the present and when he or she graduates from school. For example, if the team anticipates that this student is going to play on a community soccer team, then the team assesses those skills that the student will need to play soccer (e.g., dribbling, shooting, trapping, passing, running, following rules, understanding strategies). Information from such an assessment leads to programming that is directly related to skills the student will need to be successful.

Developmental Approach

Contrast this approach to a developmental model or bottom-up approach, in which activities are based on the scope and sequence of typical development of young students. It is believed that lower-level developmental skills are prerequisites for the development of higher level skills (Auxter et al., 1997; Block, 1992; Block & Block, 1999; Brown et al., 1979; Kelly et al., 1991; Sherrill, 1998). However, these lower level, prerequisite developmental skills are often targeted without regard to their relevance to skills required for the student's success in current and future physical education and recreation environments. For example, balancing on one foot is a prerequisite for hopping, and hopping is a prerequisite to skipping. Therefore, in a bottom-up approach, skipping would not be taught until the student has mastered balancing on one foot and hopping on one foot. However, in the ecological model, one would question whether balancing on one foot, hopping, or skipping are skills that are relevant to the individualized pre-scribed program plan for a particular student. If skills are not relevant (e.g., skills are not needed to help a student acquire the skills needed to play t-ball), then they would not be targeted for instruction.

Another difference between the ecological and developmental models is that, in the developmental model, assessment takes place prior to the develop-ment of goals and objectives. For example, a student is first assessed using a de-velopmental test, such as the Peabody Developmental Scales (Folio & DuBose, 1974) or Bayley Developmental Scales (Bayley, 1993), or a norm-referenced test, such as the President's Council on Physical Fitness Test (President's Council on Physical Fitness and Sports, 1991) or the Bruininks-Oseretsky Test of Motor Pro-ficiency (Bruininks, 1978). Results from these tests are then used to determine a student's approximate developmental age or percentile rank compared with other students his or her age as well as specific skills on which the student should work. Then, teachers and therapists develop program goals based on the stu-dent's assessment results to move the student up the developmental scale or im-prove his or her percentile ranking. For example, a student who jumped only 24" when being tested using the Peabody Developmental Motor Scales would be en-couraged to jump 30"; a student who cannot yet balance on one foot while being tested using the Bruininks-Oseretsky Test of Motor Proficiency would practice one-foot balance activities; and a student who scored below the 20th percentile on sit-up performance on a fitness test would practice sit-ups. Note how these ac-tivities, although related to the student's present level of performance, are not necessarily relevant to skills the student will need to be successful in his or her current or future life circumstances. Does it matter that the student is in the 20th percentile in sit-ups or can only jump forward 24 inches? Will these problems in performance affect the student's success in general physical education, on the playground, in the neighborhood, or in community recreation?

Another problem with the developmental approach is the amount of time it takes students with severe disabilities to achieve developmental goals (if they are able to achieve them at all) (Block, 1992; Block & Block, 1999; Brown et al., 1979; Kelly et al., 1991). Many students with physical disabilities such as cerebral palsy will never be able to balance on one foot, jump on two feet, or walk along a balance beam. Even if they could master some of the developmental goals, it could take years of training and practice; focusing on developmental goals leaves little time for the student to practice and learn ecologically relevant, functional skills that will help him or her be successful in general physical education and in community recreation (Block, 1992; Brown et al., 1979). If a student can achieve developmental skills and these developmental skills *can* be related to success in general physical education and community recreation, then it makes sense to target these skills for instruction. However, if these skills cannot be achieved in a reasonable time frame and/or cannot be shown to be ecologically relevant to the student, then these skills should not be taught.

An Ecological Approach to Including Students with Disabilities in General Physical Education

The following model utilizes the ecological approach to program planning (see Table 4.1). The focus is on 1) identifying the ecologically relevant functional goals and objectives on which a student should work, 2) deciding how these goals and objectives can be embedded within general physical education activities, 3) de-

Table 4.1. Ecological model for including children with disabilities in general physical education (GPE)

Determine what to teach.
- Develop a long-term plan and prioritize long-term goals.
- Determine student's present level of performance.
- Develop short-term instructional objectives.

Analyze the GPE curriculum.
- Which GPE activities match the student's IEP?
- Which GPE activities do not match the student's IEP but still seem important for the student?
- Which GPE activities are inappropriate for a particular student?
- What is the general physical educator's teaching style?

Determine modifications needed in GPE.
- How often will the student receive instruction?
- Where will the student receive instruction?
- How will the student be prepared for instruction?
- What instructional modifications are needed to elicit desired performance?
- What curricular adaptations will be used to enhance performance?
- How will performance be assessed?

Determine supports needed by student with disability in GPE.
- Who will provide the support?
- What type of support will be provided?
- How often will support be provided?

Prepare general physical educator.
- Discuss the amount of support that will be provided.
- Discuss the availability of consultation with APE and special education teachers.
- Explain what general physical educator's responsibility is for the entire class, not just the special student.
- Explain that general physical educator's workload should not be increased.

Prepare general education students.
- Talk to students in general about children with disabilities.
- Role-play various types of disabilities.
- Invite guest speakers with disabilities to speak in your class.
- If your school has a special class, allow students to visit the special class and meet the students.
- Talk specifically about the student who will be attending GPE (focus on student's abilities).
- Discuss ways that students without disabilities can help student with disabilities and GPE teacher.

Prepare support personnel.
- Discuss the specific student with whom they will be working.
- Discuss the student's physical education IEP.
- Discuss their responsibilities in GPE.
- Discuss who they can go to if they have questions.

termining what support the student and staff will need to implement the program, and 4) preparing staff and peers. Note how this approach actually facilitates the inclusion of students with disabilities into general physical education by carefully analyzing the general physical education environment, determining what supports a student will need to be successful in general physical education, and then preparing the support personnel.

Determine What to Teach

The first step in the planning process is to determine what to teach. What are the most critical skills a student will need to be successful in his or her present and future physical education and recreation environments? The critical skills are first defined globally in a long-term plan such as succeeding in a particular sport skill, recreation skill, or fitness skill. The long-term plan guides the entire educational program and helps the team stay focused as to what specific skills the student should have upon completion of the physical education program (Kelly et al., 1991; Wessel & Kelly, 1986). The long-term plan should be based on the activities that occur in general physical education, programs available in the student's community, and the student's unique skills and interests. For example, it does not make sense to have a long-term plan that includes swimming if there are no pools in the student's school or community. Similarly, it would be inappropriate to target volleyball for a particular student if the student has a severe disability and can only play volleyball with assistance and modifications to the game, yet the only volleyball league in the community is a high-level, competitive league in which players and coaches play regulation games without modifications. However, softball might be an appropriate activity for this student if the community softball league has different divisions including a recreation-level division in which modifications would be accepted by other players. Therefore, the student's abilities and availability of particular community recreation programs will dictate what activities make up each student's long-term plan.

There are several factors that will help determine which skills to target for a student's long-term plan: 1) the student's general strengths and weaknesses (e.g., the team will not want to target baseball for a student who is totally blind), age, and interests; 2) his or her parents' interests; 3) available recreation facilities and programs in the school and the community; 4) the time you have to teach the skills; and 5) the support that is available (see Table 4.2).

For example, a ninth-grade student with a spinal cord injury who uses a wheelchair but has good upper-body control is just coming back to school after a year of rehabilitation. He and his PEIT are deciding on goals. The following information is shared and examined by team members to facilitate planning: 1) the student's overall strengths (good upper-body strength, independent in wheelchair) and overall weaknesses (still depressed, not very motivated, cannot use legs), 2) the student's age (ready for sports, recreation, and fitness activities), 3) the student's interests (played tennis before his injury, also seems interested in weight lifting to improve his upper-body strength, does not seem interested in team sports at this point), 4) his parents' interests (parents belong to a club where they play tennis, used to go for a run together after work before their son's injury), 5) availability of community recreation programs (the community offers almost every recreational and sport activity possible in both recreational and competitive forms), 6) the time required to teach the skill (only the ninth and tenth graders take physical education, unless the student continues to take physical education as an elective in eleventh and twelfth grades), and 7) available supports (plenty available). Following some discussion, the team decides that wheelchair tennis, weight training, and wheelchair road racing would be the most motivating and relevant activities in which this student could participate.

Table 4.2. Factors to consider when prioritizing goals and objectives

General	Application to physical education
Student's strengths and weaknesses with regard to current and future needs (severity of disability)	What are the student's abilities with regard to general physical education activities and community play/recreation activities?
How much time do you have to teach skills, and what is the chance that the student will acquire the skills?	Younger students can be "exposed" to a greater variety of skills, whereas older students should begin to focus on the skills they will need to participate in specific lifetime leisure activities.
Student's interests	What recreational/sport activities does the student prefer?
Parents' interests	What recreational/sport activities do the student's parents prefer?
Peers' interests	In what activities do peers participate on the playground, in the neighborhood, and in community recreation?
What recreation facilities are available in the community?	Prioritize activities that will be available to the student in his or her community (e.g., Are there bowling alleys, recreation centers, and so on? Are they accessible?)
What equipment/transportation is available?	Does the student need special equipment (e.g., bowling ramp, flotation devices)? Is transportation to community recreation facilities available?
What support services (in terms of personnel) are available?	Who will be available to assist the student in physical education and recreation? Do you need specially trained persons to work with the student (e.g., vision therapist for a student who is blind)?

It may be more difficult to determine what sport, fitness, and recreation skills a student with severe disabilities might be interested in or able to learn. In such cases, team members might informally assess the student on a variety of age-appropriate sports and recreational activities, examining the student's interests and potential for the activity. Figure 4.1 shows an example of this type of sport/recreation sampling for Sue, a 15-year-old student with mental retardation requiring extensive support. Note the way in which traditional assessment information regarding the acquisition of motor skills, fundamental motor pattern performance, and physical fitness is embedded in the ecologically referenced assessment. Ideally, this evaluation should follow a team approach, utilizing the expertise of key members of the collaborative team. For example, the vision therapist can assist the general or adapted physical educator in assessing ball skills that require eye–hand coordination (e.g., striking, catching, dribbling, volleying), and the physical therapist can assist physical educators in assessing locomotor patterns and physical fitness related to specific sports. Based on this information, a long-term plan can be developed (see Figure 4.2).

Develop Long-Term Objectives   Once a long-term plan has been established, the next step is to write long-term goals that eventually lead to the student achieving the long-term plan. Long-term goals are part of the IEP process and describe the specific skills that a teacher expects a student to acquire in the

Present level of performance statement with reference to activities in general physical education

Tennis

Sue walks slowly in an attempt to get to balls that are hit to her, but she only can reach balls hit within 5 feet of her. She will get into a side position for a forehand and swing forcefully (no step or body rotation), but she misses more than she hits (two out of five hits are successful). She also does not grip the racket correctly. She will get into a backhand position after verbal cues and demonstrate a backhand stroke (no step or body rotation), but she only hits about one out of five balls. Also, her grip is incorrect. She has the strength to hit the ball over the net from 15 feet away, and she really seems to enjoy playing and trying to hit the ball.

Golf

Sue can hold a golf club and swing with a stiff pattern (no leg or arm bend, very little body rotation) with verbal cues. She can hit the ball off a tee with a 5 iron in three out of five trials, and the ball travels approximately 25 yards.

Soccer

Sue walks slowly and occasionally jogs to get the ball. She can kick with her toe so ball travels 10 to 15 feet. She can trap slow-moving balls that are kicked directly to her. She does not understand team concepts, and she often sits down in the middle of the field when she gets tired or bored.

Volleyball

With verbal cues, Sue can set and bump a ball that is tossed directly to her. She can serve a ball over the net from 10 feet away. She cannot hit balls in the course of a game, and she seems afraid of getting hit by the balls.

Basketball

Sue can dribble a ball several times while standing in place but not while moving forward. She can make a regulation basket from 5 feet away in one out of five trials. She will demonstrate a chest and bounce pass from 10 feet away with verbal cues, and she will catch bounce passes (not chest passes) when ball is gently passed from 10 feet away. She does not understand team concepts and prefers to wander around the court.

Softball

Sue can hit a softball off a tee (not pitched) so ball travels 15 to 20 feet. With verbal cues, she will jog to first base as well as the other bases, although she often needs to point her in the right direction. Sue can throw overhand (no stepping or body rotation) a distance of approximately 10 feet. Sue will try to bend over and pick up grounders and catch balls tossed directly to her from 10 feet away. She tends to sit down in the outfield, but she will stay more focused with verbal cues when she plays catcher.

Aerobics

Sue will try to follow the routine, but she tends to be off-beat compared to her peers. She does exert more effort in aerobics than in any other activity, but she tires easily (after 3 to 4 minutes she stands and rests). Sue has adequate flexibility and strength.

Weight training

Sue can do six different exercises on the Universal machine with verbal cues and occasional assistance for positioning. She needs assistance to set correct weight. Her strength is similar to that of her peers.

Figure 4.1.   Sample present level of performance (with regard to general physical education) for Sue, a 15-year-old student with mental retardation requiring extensive support.

Figure 4.1.   (*continued*)

Present level of performance statement from Sue's IEP reference to community-based recreation (Sue's parents took Sue to various recreation sites and reported results to her teacher)	
Tennis	*See previous assessment. Sue reiterated her interest in tennis.*
Mini-golf	*Sue could independently hold the putter and hit the ball, but she had trouble controlling the force of her putts (she hit everything really hard). Although Sue could walk the course easily, she never really seemed interested in the game; therefore, she never got excited when the ball went in the hole.*
Aerobics	*See previous assessment. Sue reiterated her interest in aerobics.*
Bowling	*Sue was able to hold a regulation ball and roll it using a regular pattern and grip. She took a few steps toward the pins for her approach, stopped, and then kind of tossed the ball down the alley. She was not very accurate, and she did not seem interested in learning how to bowl. She did not like the loud sounds of the bowling alley.*
Karate	*Sue was physically able to do all the movements, but the pace of the class was too fast for her. She did not like it when the instructor tried to physically help her, and she did not like the sounds and smells of the studio.*
Yoga	*Sue was not interested in yoga, so she was not assessed in this area.*

course of a year. For example, a long-term plan for Sue might be to play tennis upon graduation. A long-term goal for Sue might be to demonstrate the ability to hit a tennis ball using a backhand and forehand strike in a beginning-level game of doubles. Long-term goals should be based on assessment results and, in particular, a student's present level of ability in a specific activity. For example, if the PEIT is targeting tennis for Sue, they should assess her ability to grip a racket, hit a forehand and backhand, move around the court, and understand the basic rules of tennis. The team would then arrange these skills in a logical sequence of skills, from most to least important. For example, Sue's grip would be most important, then the forehand, then the backhand, then moving to get balls that have not been hit directly to her, and finally the rules of the game. So, in the first year of Sue's program, a long-term goal for tennis might be to hold the racket correctly and hit a forehand and backhand using the optimal pattern.

Develop Short-Term Objectives   Once long-term goals have been established, the next step is to write short-term instructional objectives that lead to the acquisition of the long-term goals. Short-term instructional objectives also are part of the IEP process and usually are written in anticipation of the student achieving a particular short-term objective in 2–3 months. In addition, these objectives are written in behavioral (measurable) terms so that any observer can immediately tell if the student has acquired a particular objective (see Figure 4.2 for an example). It should be noted that at this point in the process, the team is not concerned with where the student will work on the goals and objectives or how much support or special equipment the student will need. Rather, team members only are concerned that the overall plan and specific goals and objectives have been prioritized for this student and reflect his or her present level of

LONG-TERM PLAN: *Sue will demonstrate the ability to participate independently (with occasional cues from peers as needed) in recreational softball and tennis as well as participate in fitness activities at a local health club.*

Long-term goal 1: *Sue will improve her cardiorespiratory endurance.*

Short-term instructional objectives:

1. *At the University Health Club, Sue will pedal a stationary Lifecycle continuously for 20 minutes on Level 2 while maintaining an RPM level of 70, with verbal reinforcements every 5 minutes in three of four trials.*

2. *Sue will participate in an aerobics class during general physical education imitating movements as best as she can so that her heart rate (as measured by a peer) reaches 120–150 bpm for 25 minutes on 3 out of 4 days.*

Long-term goal 2: *Sue will develop the skills needed to participate in modified and regulation individual and team sports.*

Short-term instructional objectives: (specific to softball):

1. *Using a regulation softball bat with encouragement to "choke up" 2 inches (tape cue markers), Sue will hit a regulation softball off a tee so that ball rolls at least 60' (distance to first and third base) in three of four trials.*

2. *After hitting ball off tee, Sue will run to first base independently so that she arrives at first base in 7 seconds or less in three out of four trials.*

3. *Sue will play catcher during a softball game, while independently demonstrating the following behaviors in three out of four trials:*

   a. *Put on face mask.*

   b. *Find correct position behind plate.*

   c. *Squat into correct position and maintain position for duration of each pitch.*

   d. *Move glove in direction of ball when ball is pitched.*

Long-term goal 3: *When Sue plays doubles tennis at a beginner's level with her peers, she will demonstrate the ability to hit a forehand and backhand stroke so that the ball travels over the net 50% of the time.*

Short-term instructional objectives:

1. *When ball is hit within 10 feet of Sue, she will hit a backhand demonstrating the components listed below so that the ball travels over the net and into the opposing player's court in 5 out of 10 trials, 2 days in a row.*

   Components of the backhand:

   - *Display proper grip.*
   - *Stand facing opposing player.*
   - *Move to ball.*
   - *Set up in sideways position.*
   - *Bring arm back horizontally across body so that head of racquet is behind body.*
   - *Shift weight and step forward with front foot.*
   - *Bring arm forward horizontally and contact ball slightly ahead of body.*
   - *Follow through with arm and racket moving toward opposing player.*

(continued)

Figure 4.2.   Sample long-term plan, long-term goals, and short-term instructional objectives for Sue, a 15-year-old student with mental retardation requiring extensive support.

Figure 4.2.   (*continued*)

---

2. *When ball is hit within 10 feet of Sue, she will hit a forehand demonstrating the components listed below so that the ball travels over the net and into opposing player's court in 5 out of 10 trials, 2 days in a row.*

   Components of the forehand:

   • *Display proper grip.*

   • *Stand facing opposing player.*

   • *Move to ball.*

   • *Set up in sideways position.*

   • *Bring arm back horizontally away from body so that head of racket is behind body.*

   • *Shift weight and step forward with front foot.*

   • *Bring arm forward horizontally and contact ball slightly ahead of body.*

   • *Follow through with arm and racket moving toward opposing player.*

Long-term goal 4*: *Sue will develop the skills needed to participate in community-based leisure activities in integrated environments.*

   Short-term instructional objectives:

   1. *Sue will enter the University Health Club, show her ID card, locate the locker room, put her gym bag in locker, lock the locker, then locate the weight room using natural cues only (including asking Health Club staff for assistance) with 100% accuracy on 4 of 5 days.*

   2. *Sue will follow picture cards and complete a six-machine Nautilus weight-training circuit performing the exercise for each machine correctly and independently completing one set of 10–12 repetitions per machine (or asking YMCA staff for assistance) with 100% accuracy on 4 out of 5 days.*

   3. *Sue will demonstrate appropriate behavior in the locker room and weight room 100% of the time on 4 out of 5 days as noted by 1) changing clothes quickly without acting silly, 2) only saying "hi" to strangers or responding appropriately when a stranger initiates a conversation in the locker room, and 3) not acting inappropriately or talking to others while others are working out unless they initiate conversation in the weight room.*

---

*Sue participates in community-based recreation two times per week instead of general physical education.

---

performance, his or her age, the skills he or she needs in the present, and the skills he or she will need in the future.

Analyze the General Physical Education Curriculum

Once each student has been evaluated and a long-term plan, including long-term goals and short-term instructional objectives, has been established, the next step is to determine whether the student's individualized education program (IEP) matches the general curriculum. This step requires a careful analysis of the general physical education curriculum, including an analysis of the yearly plans for various grade levels, unit plans and daily lesson plans for specific activities, and the general teaching style of the general physical educator. This information can then be used to determine whether a particular student can work on his or her

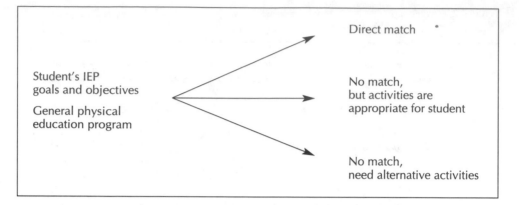

Figure 4.3.   Possible outcomes of analysis of general physical education curriculum.

individual goals in the general physical education environment or if alternative activities might be needed (i.e., which activities in general physical education directly match the student's IEP objectives, which activities somewhat match the student's IEP, which activities do not match the student's IEP and require alternative activities) (see Figure 4.3). Note that no effort is made at this point to detail specific ways to accommodate a student in the general program or to present methods to work on specific IEP goals and objectives. Such information is determined later in the process. At this point, the team should just try to get a general idea of how well the student's IEP fits into the general physical education curriculum.

   Analyze the Yearly Plan   Figure 4.4 contains a yearly plan for a typical second-grade general physical education program with initial considerations for including John, a student who is blind. Figure 4.5 contains a yearly plan for a typical tenth-grade general physical education program with initial considerations for including Sue, a student with mental retardation requiring extensive support. Note that the activities in general physical education at the lower-elementary level (kindergarten through third grade) generally match the goals and objectives for most students with disabilities. That is, most elementary-age students need some foundational skills before they can apply those skills to popular sports and recreational activities. In John's case he needs to work on understanding movement concepts and developing skillful locomotor and manipulative patterns. These goals match very nicely with the goals of the general program (even though John may need special accommodations to participate and receive instruction). Even when John's IEP goals do not directly match the goals of the other students (e.g., gymnastics, rhythms), the activities in which the general class participates are deemed beneficial to John and important enough that John's team recommended that he participate in them with his peers.

   The story is a little different for middle school and high school–age students. A quick glance at Sue's IEP in relation to the general tenth-grade curriculum reveals that she can work on her IEP goals with the general physical education class while her peers participate in the tennis unit in September, the aerobics unit in December, the weight training unit in February, and the softball unit in May. The other units do not match Sue's IEP goals; therefore, while Sue's peers participate in other units, Sue may need to participate in the alternative activities stated on her IEP. For example, while the class is playing soccer in October, Sue could go to the tennis court to work on her tennis goals with peers rotating in to assist and

September	•	Learning rules; general movement concepts
October	•	Movement concepts and locomotor patterns
November	•	Throwing and catching
December	•	Striking and kicking
January	•	Movement concepts and locomotor patterns
February	☐	Rhythms
March	☐	Tumbling
April	•	Throwing and catching
May	•	Striking and kicking
June	•	Review all skills

John's goals:

1. Understand movement concepts.
2. Develop skillful locomotor skills with a focus on running, jumping, and galloping.
3. Develop manipulative patterns with a focus on throwing, rolling, catching, and striking.

* Note movement concepts and locomotor patterns will be incorporated via warm-up activities in all units.

Figure 4.4.   Yearly physical education plan for second-grade physical education. (• = activity directly matches John's IEP goals; ☐ = activity does not directly match, but it is appropriate for John to participate; ∆= activity does not match John's IEP goals and is inappropriate for John.)

play with her. Similarly, Sue could work in the weight room with various peers in March while the rest of the class is working on field hockey and lacrosse. How-ever, Sue certainly could benefit from the endurance and stretching activities in track and field (e.g., walking around the track with peers at a vigorous pace, par-ticipating in warm-ups), so she could be included in this unit. Similarly, Sue could participate in the golf unit with her peers to see if she enjoys this activity (golf could replace tennis as a lifetime sport if Sue really enjoys it).

The important point is that inclusion does not necessarily mean that stu-dents with disabilities have to do the same activities in the same way as their peers without disabilities. Most students without disabilities can be exposed to a variety of activities in general physical education (i.e., try a lot of activities but not necessarily master anything) and still leave the program with the ability to successfully participate in two or more lifetime leisure activities. However, stu-dents with moderate to severe disabilities will only acquire critical lifetime leisure skills if training focuses intensely on these skills (Block, 1992; Brown et al., 1979; Wessel & Kelly, 1986). Therefore, decisions need to be made as to which activities will be most beneficial for the student with disabilities and which ones really will not help the student achieve his or her IEP goals.

This does not necessarily mean that a student with disabilities will require programming away from the general physical education environment. Sue cer-tainly can participate in warm-up activities with her peers during general physi-cal education. In addition, while Sue's peers are working on activities such as basketball in the gym, Sue can practice hitting a tennis ball back and forth or hit-ting a softball off a tee with a peer in the corner of the gym or in the hall. Peers without disabilities can be rotated into the station to assist and actually partici-

September	•	Tennis
October	Δ	Soccer
November	Δ	Volleyball
December	•	Wrestling (males), aerobics (females)
January	Δ	Basketball
February	•	Weight training
March	Δ	Field hockey/lacrosse
April	□	Track and field
May	•	Softball
June	□	Golf

Sue's goals:
1. Improve cardiovascular fitness.
2. Develop skills necessary to play doubles tennis at a beginner level.
3. Develop skills necessary to play softball at a beginner level.
4. Develop skills needed to participate in community-based leisure activities.

Figure 4.5. Yearly physical education plan for tenth-grade physical education. (• = activity directly matches Sue's IEP goals; □ = activity does not directly match, but it is appropriate for Sue to participate; Δ = activity does not match Sue's IEP goals and is inappropriate for Sue.)

pate with Sue so that Sue still receives the social benefits of inclusion while working on her specific IEP goals.

Analyze Specific Units   Once you have a general idea of which units are going to be taught throughout the year and when they will be taught, the next step should be to analyze each physical education unit that matches the student's program. Unit plans usually can be obtained from general physical education specialists a week or so prior to the introduction of that unit (more seasoned teachers may have their unit plans from previous years in a file for your use). Figure 4.6 contains an example of the tenth-grade softball unit plan. An analysis of the softball unit suggests that Sue can work on many of the softball skills highlighted in her IEP during this unit (with modifications as needed). In addition, Sue could easily be accommodated in the modified game that includes peers without disabilities.

Some physical education programs at the high school level focus only on the actual game and not on skills. It would be much more difficult to include Sue into such a program because her softball skills are still very weak. By analyzing the unit ahead of time (even 1 week prior to the beginning of the unit), you can begin to make decisions regarding ways for Sue to work on her goals during the unit, including the modifications Sue might need to be successful. Again, more detailed accommodations and modifications will be developed later in the process.

Analyze the Daily Lesson Plan   Finally, an analysis of a general daily lesson plan should be conducted so that you can further determine in which areas the student's IEP goals and objectives can be implemented and with which specific activities the student may have difficulty. Again, most general physical educators can quickly outline their typical daily lesson plan. Most physical education lesson plans begin with some type of warm-up activity that is followed by

WEEK 1

1. *Introduction to game*
    *   *Equipment*
    *   *Field dimensions*
    *   *Basic rules*
    *   *Basic concepts and positions*

2. *Warm-up activities*
    *   *Stretching major muscles of upper and lower body*
    *   *Strengthening abdominal, arm, and leg muscles*
    *   *Cardiovascular endurance activities (e.g., jogging around the base path)*

3. *Introduction to basic softball skills (emphasis on learning correct movements)*
    *   *Striking*
    *   *Throwing*
    *   *Fielding*
    *   *Base running*

4. *Lead-up games to work on skills*
    *   *Base running relays, hot-box, 500*
    *   *Pepper, 500*
    *   *Home run derby, spot hitting*

WEEK 2

1. *Continue warm-up activities (have students lead warm-ups)*

2. *Team concepts and team strategies*
    *   *Base running strategies; hitting ball to various places in field; hitting cut-off person*
    *   *View video of softball game that shows concepts and techniques*

3. *Continue refinement of skills*
    *   *Throw from greater distances; throw with varying force*
    *   *Field balls hit to the side; field high flies in the outfield*
    *   *Hit fast-pitched balls; hit balls in different parts of strike zone*

WEEK 3

1. *Continue warm-up activities (have students lead warm-ups)*

2. *Review of all softball skills*

3. *Introduce games:*
    *   *Play a game of 10 versus 10, with outfield players practicing throwing balls back and forth during down time and batting team practicing hitting balls off a tee behind backstop during their down time*
    *   *Play modified game of softball for students who have less skill (including typical students with limited softball skills)*

WEEK 4

1. *Continue warm-up activities (have students lead warm-ups)*

2. *Continue to review softball skills*

3. *Continue games with less instruction (both regulation and modified)*

Figure 4.6.   Sample 4-week softball unit plan.

Figure 4.6.   (continued)

Some anticipated accommodations for Sue:

1. *Have peer assist Sue during warm-ups (demonstration, an occasional physical prompt).*

2. *Have peer assist Sue as she moves from station to station and at each station as needed.*

3. *Have adapted physical educator write down activities for Sue to do at each station.*

4. *Use a smaller ball (e.g., tennis ball) for throwing and catching with mitt.*

5. *Use a lighter bat (e.g., whiffle bat) and place ball on tee for striking.*

6. *Have Sue play in outfield with peers during games or play catcher with batter's assistance.*

7. *Allow Sue to run to a shorter distance when running to first base, and allow peer to run with her around the other bases until she understands where to go.*

8. *Have Sue play in a recreational game.*

---

some type of skill activity, which is then followed by some type of game activity. In addition, physical education at the middle school and high school levels will include locker room activities (e.g., dressing, showering, grooming) immediately prior to and after each physical education class. Figure 4.7 outlines a typical daily lesson plan for a tenth-grade class with considerations for Sue.

An alternative way of determining which activities take place in a typical general physical education class is called an *ecological inventory* (Brown et al., 1979). An ecological inventory provides a detailed analysis of all the activities students without disabilities typically do during a particular situation (in this case, physical education). The analysis begins by identifying subenvironments and activities that take place within each subenvironment. This is followed by a *discrepancy analysis,* which determines how the student with disabilities currently performs each activity and provides suggestions for modifications so that the student can be more successful. Figure 4.8 provides an example of an ecological

---

1. **Locker room:** *Change into physical education uniform (approximately 5 minutes).*
2. **Squads/attendance:** *Students sit in squads while attendance is taken (2 minutes).*
3. **Warm-ups:** *Students are led by teacher in several stretching, strength, and aerobic activities (7 to 10 minutes).*
4. **Skill focus:** *Work on specific skills related to team or individual sports (as few as 5 minutes to as many as 30 minutes, depending on where class is in unit [beginning of unit focuses more on skill; end of unit focuses more on games]).*
5. **Game:** *Play lead-up and regulation games related to team or individual sports (5 to 30 minutes).*
6. **Locker room:** *Shower, groom, and put on street clothes (approximately 10 minutes).*

Note: Sue will need assistance in the locker room both prior to and following each class. The teacher assistant can assist initially, but peers who have lockers near Sue's will eventually learn how to assist her. Sue should be able to participate in warm-ups with minimal cues from peers. Sue will need modified ways to practice skills and to participate in group activities (ask APE specialist or IEP team to provide suggestions).

Figure 4.7.   General daily lesson plan for tenth-grade physical education with comments regarding Sue.

Ecological Inventory with Discrepancy Analysis

Student's name: _Jonathan Smith_   Student's birthdate: _8-10-85_   Teacher: _M. Block (APE specialist)_

Environment: _GPE - Soccer_   Dates of unit: _9/21/99 - 10/21/99_   Suggested assistant: _Steve Smith (peer tutor)_

What are the steps that a person without disabilities uses?		What assistance does the student with disabilities currently need?	What adaptations or levels of assistance might help this student?
Subenvironment: *Locker room*			
Activity 1:	Locates locker room	V	Teach student to use natural cues on walls; add arrows on walls.
Activity 2:	Enters locker room	I	None needed.
Activity 3:	Locates empty locker	V	Teach student to ID lockers without locks; color-code one locker.
Activity 4:	Takes off clothes	PP	Wear pull-on clothes; practice dressing at home; use Velcro instead of buttons.
Activity 5:	Places clothes in locker	I	None needed.
Activity 6:	Puts on exercise clothes	P	Use pull-on clothes; equip shoes with special ties; use Velcro instead of buttons.
Activity 7:	Locks locker	P	Repeated practice; perhaps longer lock; key lock might be easier than combination lock.
Subenvironment: *Gym/Attendance*			
Activity 1:	Locates gym	V	Natural cues on walls; have extra cues on walls.
Activity 2:	Finds squad and sits down	V	Teach student to ID members of squad; have squad members cue student if he appears lost.
Activity 3:	Sits quietly with squad	I	None needed.
Subenvironment: *Gym/Warm-up*			
Activity 1:	Stands up with squad	V	Have peers provide cues.
Activity 2:	Performs 10 jumping jacks	VP	Have peers provide cues; do arm jumping jacks.
Activity 3:	Performs leg stretches	VP	Have peers provide cues; have peer tutor provide physical assistance as needed.
Activity 4:	Performs 10 sit-ups	VP	Pair up with peer tutor; perform 5 sit-ups rather than 10.
Activity 5:	Performs 10 push-ups	VP	Have peers provide cues; perform modified knee push-ups.
Activity 6:	Runs continuously for 3 minutes	V	Have peers provide cues; alternate run/walk for 10 minutes.

Figure 4.8.   Sample ecological inventory with discrepancy analysis for tenth-grade physical education. (Key: I = independent; V = verbal cues or reminder; PP = partial physical assistance; P+ = physical assistance [student tries to help]; P = physical assistance [student is passive]; P− = physical assistance [student fights assistance].) (From Block, M.E. [1994]. All kids can participate in general physical education. In M.S. Moon [Ed.], *Making school and community recreation fun for everyone: Places and ways to integrate* [pp. 146–151]. Baltimore: Paul H. Brookes Publishing Co.; reprinted by permission.)

Figure 4.8. (continued)

What are the steps that a person without disabilities uses?	What assistance does the student with disabilities currently need?	What adaptations or levels of assistance might help this student?
Subenvironment: Gym/Soccer stations		
Activity 1: Locates squad and station	V	Have peers provide cues.
Activity 2: Practices shooting	VP	Shoot from closer distances; shoot at wider goal; use lighter ball.
Activity 3: Waits turn	I	None needed
Activity 4: Moves to next station	V	Have peers provide cues.
Activity 5: Passing/trapping	VP	Stand closer to peer; use deflated ball; use tape markings on foot to cue correct contact point; pass to stationary partner.
Activity 6: Waits turn	I	None needed
Activity 7: Moves to next station	V	Have peers provide cues.
Activity 8: Dribbling	VP	Dribble with deflated ball or Nerf ball; work on dribbling straight ahead without obstacles; work on walking then jogging while dribbling.
Activity 9: Waits turn	I	None needed
Activity 10: Goes back to original squads	V	Have peers provide cues.
Subenvironment: Gym/Soccer game		
Activity 1: Listens to instructions by teacher	V	Have peer tutor reexplain teacher's rules in simpler terms.
Activity 2: Puts on assigned pinnie	PP	Have peers provide assistance.
Activity 3: Goes to assigned position	V	Have peers provide cues.
Activity 4: Plays game	VP	John will play a wing fullback, and a nonskilled peer will go against him.
Activity 5: Plays game	V	Have peer tutor provide cues.
Activity 6: Watches flow of game	V	Have peer tutor provide cues.
Activity 7: Interacts with teammates	V	Have peer tutor provide cues.
Activity 8: Shakes hands with other team	PP	Have peer assist student.
Activity 9: Takes off pinnie	V	Have peers provide cues.
Activity 10: Puts pinnie away	V	Have peers provide cues.

	What are the steps that a person without disabilities uses?	What assistance does the student with disabilities currently need?	What adaptations or levels of assistance might help this student?
Subenvironment: Locker room			
Activity 1:	Locates locker room	✓	Use natural cues on wall; use additional wall cues.
Activity 2:	Enters locker room	I	None needed
Activity 3:	Locates locker	✓	Tape colored sign on locker; have peer provide cues as needed.
Activity 4:	Takes off gym clothes	PP	Have peer provide assistance as needed.
Activity 5:	Places exercise clothes in gym bag	I	None needed
Activity 6:	Gets towel, soap, shampoo	✓	Have peer tutor provide cues as needed.
Activity 7:	Locates shower	✓	Place extra sign on wall; have peer provide cues.
Activity 8:	Turns on water and modulates water temperature	PP	Practice starting with cold and gradually add hot; have peer tutor assist.
Activity 9:	Shampoos hair; washes self	EP	Start from top and work down; practice at home; have peer provide assistance.
Activity 10:	Turns off shower	EP	Step away from water, then turn off hot then cold; have peer assist as needed.
Activity 11:	Dries off	✓	Start from top and work down; practice; peer can give verbal cues as needed.
Activity 12:	Locates and uses deodorant	✓	Have peer provide cues as needed.
Activity 13:	Puts on street clothes	P	Use pull-on clothes; use special ties for shoes; have peer assist as needed.
Activity 14:	Goes to mirror and combs hair/ checks appearance: hair combed, shirt tucked in, shoes on	✓	Start from top and work down; cue in on correct feet; have peers give cues as needed.
Activity 15:	Places all personal belongings in gym bag	✓	Teach student to check area and locker; use picture cue cards; peer gives cues.
Activity 16:	Leaves locker room and goes to	✓	Use natural cues on wall; use additional wall cues; have peer tutor assist as needed.

inventory with discrepancy analysis. Although the ecological inventory is more difficult to develop compared with a simple daily lesson plan, the information provided presents much more detail regarding daily routines and potential modifications to general physical education. Special education teachers often have experience developing ecological inventories and, with the assistance of the general physical educator, can quickly develop such an inventory for the team.

One final analysis of the general curriculum should be of the particular *teaching style* an educator uses when conducting his or her program (see Mosston & Ashworth, 1994, as well as Chapter 6 for a more thorough review of teaching styles). There are many different teaching styles, but most fit into one of two basic types: *direct approaches* (teacher directed) or *indirect approaches*. In direct teaching approaches, each student performs the same basic movements under the direct guidance of the physical educator. The physical educator is responsible for most decisions. He or she tells or shows students exactly what is expected of them, how particular skills should be performed, and when and where to perform these skills. Obviously, such an approach provides tremendous control over a class while still allowing for some individualization. However, creativity and the process of discovering the best way to perform a particular skill, or "learning how to learn," is not provided in this approach. For example, a teacher who is working on the overhand throw with a second-grade class might have all of her students stand a certain distance from the wall and, on her verbal cue, shift their weight to their back feet, reach back with their throwing arms, shift their weight forward, rotate their bodies, and throw the balls at the wall. Some teachers who use this approach are quite inflexible and expect all of their students to perform a particular movement the same way, at the same time, and with the same requirements for success. Such a rigid interpretation of the direct approach is not very accommodating for a student who has a disability. However, teachers can use the direct approach and still accommodate varying abilities. For example, in the previous throwing example, the teacher could allow some students to stand closer to or farther away from the wall, give some students larger balls and other students smaller balls, or even allow a student with cerebral palsy to throw using a different pattern.

In indirect approaches, students are encouraged to discover the best way to perform certain skills by actively exploring and experimenting with equipment, rules, distances, patterns, and so on. Such an approach allows for more creative learning and encourages students to problem solve. The student is responsible for most decisions. However, it may be more difficult to control a class while using an indirect approach, learning specific skills often takes longer when compared with a direct approach, and some students may never problem-solve the movement problem in the way that you prefer (e.g., some students may never throw overhand even though you had hoped that they would discover that throwing overhand is the best way to throw a small ball for distance). Indirect instruction tends to be very accommodating to students with disabilities, particularly students with physical disabilities who are encouraged to discover the best way to perform particular movements. However, an indirect approach can be confusing to students with mental retardation, autism, and attention-deficit/hyperactivity disorder; and the freedom allowed in such programs can promote behavior problems in students with emotional disturbances.

At this point in the process you should get a feel for the teaching approach that is used in general physical education and the way in which this approach matches the unique abilities of the student with disabilities who you plan to include. Ideally, a student with disabilities should be placed in a class in which the teacher uses an approach that matches the student's learning style. Realistically, however, this may not happen. Still, general physical educators should be encouraged to teach the group of students without disabilities one way and the student with disabilities another way, if necessary. For example, a teacher might use a command approach when teaching throwing to students without disabilities, but at the same time, she can encourage a student who has cerebral palsy to explore different ways to throw to see which method is most effective given his unique movement abilities (see Chapter 6 for more detail on various teaching approaches).

Determine Modifications Needed in General Physical Education

At this point, you should know each student's present level of performance, long-term plan including long-term goals and short-term instructional objectives, and whether the student will be able to work on these goals and objectives within the general physical education program. The next step is to determine any specific modifications that will be required to implement the individual program for the student with disabilities within the general physical education environment. Rainforth et al. (1992) outlined several questions that should guide the decision-making process when determining specific instructional modifications for students with disabilities (see Table 4.3).

How Often Will Instruction Occur?   Students with disabilities may need more instruction than their peers without disabilities to learn even simple skills. Therefore, one of the first decisions that should be made in terms of modifications is how often the student with disabilities will receive instruction. For example, if elementary-age students without disabilities receive physical education two times per week, you may want to request that a student with severe disabilities receive general physical education with peers without disabilities two times per week in addition to working in a small group of students (comprising both students with and without disabilities) who need extra help on specific skills two times a week. Another possibility is working with the student one-to-one on Mondays to preview the activities that will take place during the week. You can give the student extra practice on skills and explain and practice some of the activities that will take place (see Wessel & Kelly, 1986, for a detailed description of how to determine the number of times a week a student should receive physical education).

The question of how often also can include the frequency with which an adapted physical education specialist co-teaches with the general physical educator or that particular support personnel come in and assist the student with disabilities. For example, a speech-language teacher may come to general physical

Table 4.3.   Considerations for determining a student's individual instructional program

- How often will student receive instruction?
- Where will student receive instruction?
- How will student be prepared for instruction?
- What instructional modifications are needed to elicit desired performance?
- What curricular adaptations are needed to enhance desired performance?

Adapted from Rainforth, York, & Macdonald, 1992.

education once a week to assist a student with autism in physical education activities as well as in using verbal language. Having this professional assist the student (with guidance from the general and/or adapted physical educator) may optimize the student's time in general physical education, thus giving him or her even more instruction and practice in critical skills. Similarly, the adapted physical education specialist may come into general physical education once a week to work with the student and with other students without disabilities who need extra help. Such a team approach allows the general physical educator time to work with a smaller, more-skilled group of students without disabilities while the adapted physical educator works with a smaller, less-skilled group of students (including the student with disabilities).

Where Will the Student Receive Instruction?   The second question that should be asked in determining modifications for a student with disabilities is where instruction should occur. Because the focus is on inclusion, instruction will occur in the general physical education environment in most cases. Activities that are directly related to the student's IEP goals can be modified so that the student can work on his or her goals in a safe and successful environment. Even when general physical education activities do not match the student's IEP goals, alternative activities can be presented within the general environment. For example, an elementary-age student who is working on independent walking can practice this skill (with assistance as needed) while his or her peers without disabilities work on kicking skills. In either of these cases, you should note whether specific IEP objectives (including objectives from other team members) can be embedded into the typical daily physical education routine (see Figures 4.9 and 4.10 for examples).

In other cases, general physical education may not be the most appropriate environment for particular students, and alternative environments that include interaction with peers without disabilities should be identified. Table 4.4 provides a list of factors to help determine where the student with disabilities should receive physical education. The previous example suggests one solution; a student with disabilities who needs extra physical education could receive these services in a small group that includes students without disabilities. Similarly, students with autism-like behaviors who cannot cope with the stimulating environment of a large gymnasium and 20 or more peers running around may need to begin their programs in a quieter, less-threatening environment. Such environments could include the cafeteria or a work room with one or two peers without disabilities. Gradually, the student can be included into the more stimulating general physical education environment. Finally, older students should receive part of their physical education instruction (i.e., instruction in community-based recreation) at local recreation facilities such as health clubs, bowling alleys, or recreation centers. Again, peers without disabilities can be included in these outings to make the experience more normalizing and to promote appropriate social skills. Decisions regarding how often and where to teach particular skills, like all decisions, should be student-based (i.e., determined based on what is best for the student). Factors such as age and severity of disability, availability of support personnel, and availability of transportation and recreation facilities in the community will no doubt influence the team's decision as to how often and where the student will receive community-based physical education.

One cautionary note: Other team members may wish to target physical education as a good place to work on their goals. For example, a physical therapist might ask physical education staff members to do particular stretching activities

Activity in GPE	IEP Objectives for PE (written generally)				
	Improve endurance	Improve strength	Develop tennis skills	Develop softball skills	Gain access to local YMCA
1. Walks to locker room	X				
2. Changes clothes, puts clothes in locker					X
3. Goes to squad					X
4. Sits in squad					X
5. Warm-ups	X	X			
6. Participates in skill activities (choosing stations)			X	X	
7. Participates in game	X		X	X	
8. Walks to locker	X				X
9. Showers, changes clothes					X
10. Walks to class	X	X			

Figure 4.9. Sue's IEP objectives for physical education and where they will be embedded within general physical education.

during physical education for a student with cerebral palsy; a speech-language therapist may ask physical education staff to encourage a particular student to practice answering "wh" questions (i.e., who, what, where, why); or an occupational therapist might ask physical education personnel to assign a peer to a student with spina bifida to help her in the locker room so that she can work on independent dressing and undressing skills. Although these requests are often appropriate and easily implemented by physical education staff, the particular goals of other team members should not take precedence over specific physical education goals. In addition, some special education teachers include their students with disabilities in general physical education to improve social and communication skills without regard to whether the student improves in physical education and recreation. These teachers may push to have the student with disabilities participate with his peers without disabilities in *all* general physical education activities, including activities that you as a physical educator do not feel are safe or appropriate for the student. You must help teachers understand that participating in general physical education activities just so the student can talk with his peers is not good use of the physical education period (Block & Garcia, 1995). Furthermore, by participating in all activities, even those that are not safe or appropriate, this student is missing out on necessary practice time in his targeted activities. Again, most requests are reasonable and can be easily ac-

Activity in GPE	IEP Objectives from Other Team Members (written generally)				
	Walk/move faster	Behave appropriately	Dress/ undress	Make choices	Follow one-cue directions
1. Walks to locker room	X	X			
2. Changes clothes, puts clothes in locker			X		
3. Goes to squad	X	X			
4. Sits in squad		X			X
5. Warm-ups	X	X			X
6. Participates in skill activities (choosing stations)		X		X	
7. Participates in game	X	X		X	
8. Walks to locker	X	X			
9. Showers, changes clothes		X	X		X
10. Walks to class	X	X			

Figure 4.10. Sample objectives from IEP (including IEP goals from other team members) and where they will be embedded within the general program.

commodated; but make sure all team members understand that the purpose of physical education is to teach students specific motor, fitness, sport, and recreation skills and that physical education should not be considered a dumping ground for everyone else's goals and objectives.

How Will the Student Be Prepared for Instruction?   Preparation for instruction can involve several factors. For students with physical disabilities such as cerebral palsy, preparation might include relaxation techniques, techniques to normalize muscle tone, range-of-motion activities, and positioning to facilitate active, independent movement (Rainforth & York-Barr, 1997). Physical educators can incorporate specific range-of-motion and relaxation activities into their warm-ups (either have the entire class do them or have the student with disabilities do these activities while his or her peers do other warm-ups). Such exercises can help the student demonstrate functional arm or leg use during physical education. In other situations, preparation may take place in the classroom prior to physical education class. For example, a student with a severe physical disability typically sits in a wheelchair during academic classes. Although sitting in the chair might be the best position for this student in terms of academic work such as using eye-gaze when working on the computer, sitting in a chair may not be the best position for functional arm and hand use. For physical education purposes, a better position for this student might be in a prone stander or side-lyer so that he or she will have more range of motion in his or her arms for pushing balls down a ramp (see Table 4.5 for examples of positioning decisions).

Table 4.4. Where to teach targeted skills

GPE no support	GPE support by peer/TA	APE w/in GPE setting	½ GPE; ½ pull-out APE	Full-time pull-out APE
IEP goals match GPE 85% of time	IEP goals match GPE 50%–80% of time	IEP goals match GPE 25%–50% of time	50% of IEP goals cannot be worked on	Child does not benefit at all from GPE
Safely can work on IEP goals with few to no modifications	Safely can work on IEP goals with support	Safely can work on IEP objectives with more special zec support	Safely can work on IEP goals part of the time, but GPE is unsafe part of time	GPE setting is not safe for student
Child does not affect program for peers	Child does not affect program for peers with support	Child does not affect program for peers with specialized support	Child does not affect program for peers ½ time, but does affect peers ½ time	Child is disruptive even with support or is a danger to peers
Benefits and learns from peers; enjoys being with peers	Benefits and learns from peers and enjoys being with peers if supported	Benefits and learns from peers and enjoys being with peers if given specialized support	Benefits and learns from peers and enjoys being with peers sometimes	Never benefits or learns from peers, and does not seem to enjoy peers
Setting does not cause undue anxiety in student.	Setting does not cause undue anxiety in student if student is supported.	Setting does not cause undue anxiety in student if student s given special-ized support.	Setting sometimes is OK for student but other times it can cause extreme anxiety even with support.	Setting always causes extreme anxiety for student, even with support, such that child cannot learn in setting.

APE = adapted physical education; GPE = general physical education. (Adapted by permission from class project submitted by Mel Mitchell at the University of Virginia.)

Table 4.5. Considerations in selecting positions for students with severe physical disabilities

Considerations	Activity	
	Warm-ups	Basketball skills
What positions do peers without disabilities use when they engage in the activity?	Lying down, standing, moving	Standing, moving
Which of these positions allow for easy view and access to activity materials and equipment?	Sitting more than standing	Standing more than sitting
Do the positions allow for proximity to peers?	Yes—sitting on mat with peers	Yes—stander is easy to move near peers
Do the positions promote efficient movement as needed to perform the task?	Sitting on mat allows participation in many warm-up activities.	Standing allows free movement of hands for holding/pushing.
What positions provide alternatives to overused postures and equipment?	Usually sits in chair; stretching on mat is good alternative	Usually sits in chair; stander is good alternative
If positioning equipment is required, is it unobtrusive, cosmetically acceptable, and not physically isolating?	None needed	Prone stander, while fairly obtrusive, is nicely decorated and peers are used to it.
Is the positioning equipment safe and easy to handle?	None needed	Should be placed in stander by therapist or teacher; easy to move
Is the equipment individually selected; is it modified to individual learner needs?	None needed	Fit to student by physical therapist
Is the equipment available and easily transported to natural environments?	None needed	Available from special education class
Final position	*On mat*	*Prone stander*

From Rainforth, B., York, J., & Macdonald, C. (1992). *Collaborative teams for students with severe disabilities*. Baltimore: Paul H. Brooks Publishing Co.; adapted by permission.

The student's physical therapist is the best resource for determining how to help the student warm up and what the best positions are for students with disabilities during certain activities. Therapists also can develop easy-to-follow picture cards that illustrate how to warm up and position students. In some cases, the teacher or teacher assistant can warm up the student and place him or her in particular pieces of equipment prior to physical education.

Another consideration for preparing students for instruction is how to work with students who have behavior problems or mental retardation. Some of these students may have difficulty making the transition from quiet, classroom activities to the stimulation of the gymnasium. These students may need to be reminded several times in the class prior to physical education that physical education is their next class. In addition, some students such as those with autism may need strategies to help them cope with the transition, such as using a picture schedule, being the first or last person in the gym, sitting in a smaller squad, sit-

Table 4.6.   Instructional modifications to accommodate students with disabilities in GPE

- Teaching style (direct, indirect)
- Class format and size of group (small/large group; stations/whole class instruction)
- Level of methodology (verbal cues, demonstrations, physical assistance)
- Student's method of communication (verbal, sign language, pointing to pictures)
- Starting/stopping signals (whistle, hand signals)
- Time of day when student is included (some do better in morning than afternoon)
- Duration (of instruction, expected participation, length of activities)
- Order of learning (in what order you will present material and instruction)
- Instructional setting (indoors/outdoors; part of gym/whole gym)
- Eliminate distractors (extra lighting, temperature)
- Provide structure (set organization of instruction each day)
- Level of difficulty (control complexity of instruction, presentation of information, organization)
- Levels of motivation (make setting and activities more motivating)

ting at the end of a squad, sitting and watching the first few warm-up activities, and so on. Students who have behavior problems might need extra reminders of the rules of the gymnasium and any specific consequences or reinforcements for obeying or disregarding these rules that may be presented during physical education. Such simple reminders prior to entering the gymnasium often help the student with behavior problems refocus on appropriate behaviors. A concerted effort by the classroom teacher and physical educator to make transitions smoother for students with disabilities can prevent many behavior problems.

What Instructional Modifications Are Needed?   There are many factors related to instruction that can be modified to accommodate students with disabilities in general physical education. Factors such as teaching style, length of instruction, types of cues given, and type of structure are just a few instructional factors that the teacher controls (see Table 4.6). Simple adjustments to the way in which you present various aspects of your lesson can help students with disabilities be more motivated and more successful, follow directions, and improve the quality of their practice and rate of skill development. For example, will the student respond to verbal cues or will some other form of instruction be necessary? Will the student respond to the same start/stop signal to which the other students respond, or will the student need some other signal? Can the student sit and wait his or her turn for the same length of time as the other students, or will some adjustment in length of waiting time need to be made? The team should work together to determine how instruction will be modified to meet the unique needs of students with disabilities. Chapter 6 provides additional detailed information regarding various instructional factors and how they can be used to facilitate inclusion in physical education.

What Curricular Adaptations Will Be Used to Enhance Performance?   Perhaps the greatest challenge to the physical education team is finding ways to accommodate students with disabilities who cannot perform the skill in the same way or at the same level as their peers. The goal at this level is to create adaptations that allow the student to participate and acquire skills in a safe, successful, and challenging environment. There are many ways to adapt specific situations, skills, or activities to enhance the student's performance. In some situations, adaptations might be as simple as giving a student with limited strength a lighter bat. For other students, such as those with visual impairments, a simple adaptation might involve assigning a peer to assist the student in re-

Table 4.7.   Curricular adaptations to accommodate individuals with specific limitations

Does the student have limited strength, power, or endurance?
- Lower targets.
- Reduce distance/playing field.
- Reduce weight/size of striking implements, balls, or projectiles.
- Allow student to sit or lie down while playing.
- Use deflated balls or suspended balls.
- Decrease activity time/increase rest time.
- Reduce speed of game/increase distance for students without disabilities.

Does the student have limited balance?
- Lower center of gravity.
- Keep as much of body in contact with the surface as possible.
- Widen base of support.
- Increase width of beams to be walked.
- Extend arms for balance.
- Use carpeted rather than slick surfaces.
- Teach student how to fall.
- Provide a bar to assist with stability.
- Teach student to use eyes optimally.
- Determine whether balance problems are related to health problems.

Does the student have limited coordination and accuracy?
- For catching and striking activities, use larger, lighter, softer balls.
- Decrease distance ball is thrown and reduce speed.
- For throwing activities, use smaller balls.
- In striking and kicking, use stationary ball before trying a moving ball.
- Increase the surface of the striking implement.
- Use backstop.
- Increase size of target.
- In bowling-type games, use lighter, less stable pins.
- Optimize safety.

Adapted from Sherrill, 1998.

trieving balls. Still, other students, particularly those with severe disabilities, may need special equipment such as ramps, special switches, and major modifications to the rules of the game in addition to physical assistance to successfully participate in general physical education.

Chapters 7 and 8 provide an extensive review of specific strategies for modifying the curriculum to accommodate students with disabilities in general physical education (see Tables 4.7 and 4.8 for a list of some of these strategies). Suggestions for accommodating students who have problems with fitness, balance, and coordination and for making specific modifications to traditional games and team sports are provided. The physical education inclusion team should work together to examine the student's abilities with regard to the requirements of specific skills and rules of games to determine which adaptations should be implemented. Chapter 8 provides detailed information on how to modify select individual and team sport activities for students with specific types of disabilities.

Decisions regarding which modifications to employ should be weighed against the student's age, which equipment is closest to that used by peers with-

Table 4.8.   Curricular adaptations when modifying group games and sports

- *Can you vary the purpose/goal of the game?* (e.g., some students play to learn complex strategies, others play to work on simple motor skills)
- *Can you vary the number of players?* (e.g., play small games such as two-on-two basket-ball)
- *Can you vary movement requirements?* (e.g., some students can walk while others can run; some can hit a ball off a tee while others hit a pitched ball; more-skilled students can use more complex movements while less-skilled use simpler movements)
- *Can you vary the field of play?* (e.g., set up special zones for students with less mobility; make the field narrower or wider as needed; shorten the distance for students with movement problems)
- *Can you vary the objects used?* (e.g., some students use lighter bats or larger balls; some use a lower net or basket)
- *Can you vary the level of organization?* (vary typical organizational patterns; vary where certain students stand; vary the level of structure for certain students)
- *Can you vary the limits/expectations?* (vary the number of turns each student receives; vary the rules regarding how far a student can run, hit, and so on; vary the degree to which you enforce certain rules for certain players)

Adapted from Morris & Stiehl, 1999.

out disabilities, which equipment will likely be available in the community, and so on (see Table 4.9 for sample questions that apply to physical education). For example, a seventh-grade student with mental retardation requiring extensive support is included into an introductory tennis unit. Due to limited strength and coordination, this student is given a shorter, lighter racket (racquetball racket versus tennis racket) and is allowed to hit a ball off of a tee or a ball that is gently tossed to the student by a peer. These adaptations allow the student to practice the skill and improve performance. Although this student may someday have the strength and control to use a regulation tennis racket and hit a moving ball, for now, she needs adaptations to successfully participate. In addition, these adaptations will not affect the student's ability to participate in tennis in the community later in her life.

Even students with very severe disabilities can be accommodated via adaptations to equipment and rules (see Tables 4.10 and 4.11 for examples). As with modifications regarding prompts and cues given to students, each student should be provided with the necessary adaptations to promote meaningful participation and success. Still, special equipment and changes to rules should be systematically faded away whenever possible so that students can participate in activities using the same rules and equipment as their peers without disabilities. In addition, caution should be taken when instituting adaptations that stigmatize the student or dramatically change the game for students without disabilities. For example, allowing a high school student to use a Mickey Mouse balloon as a substitute for a volleyball accentuates the differences rather than the similarities between this student and his or her peers. A better adaptation might be to have a peer catch a regulation volleyball for this student and then hold it while the student with disabilities hits it. Similarly, forcing all students to walk rather than run in a soccer game to accommodate a student who uses a walker would ruin the game for students without disabilities. A better solution would be to set up a small zone for this student in which he or she is the only player allowed to kick the ball (see Chapters 7 and 8 for more detail on modifications).

Table 4.9.   Questions for determining appropriateness of adaptations with applications for physical education

Consideration	Application to physical education
Will the adaptation increase active participation in the activity?	Lower basket or shorter distance to first base allows student to play team sports with peers.
Will it allow the student to participate in an activity that is preferred or valued by the student and his or her friends or family members?	Modifications allow student to participate in team sports, popular group games, playground activities, community sports, and so on.
Will it continue to be useful and appropriate as the student grows older and starts using other environments?	Bowling ramp can be used in regular bowling facilities; flotation devices can be used in community pools; adapted golf club can be used at local driving range.
Will it take less time to teach the student to use the adaptation than to teach the skill directly?	Use flotation devices rather than teach swimming; have student hit ball off tee rather than hit pitched ball.
Will the team have access to the technical expertise to design, construct, adjust, and repair the adaptation?	Use special switches to hit or toss balls (will physical educator be taught how to use equipment and do simple maintenance?).
Will use of the adaptation maintain or enhance related motor and communication skills?	Adapted switch promotes independent arm and hand movements; participating with peers promotes socialization and communication.

Source: York & Rainforth (1991).

Determine Supports Needed by the Student with Disabilities in General Physical Education

Although many general physical educators are quite competent and interested in including students with disabilities in their general programs, from time to time, some students will present such unique challenges that support will be necessary. York, Giangreco, Vandercook, and Macdonald (1992) noted that the need for support should not be construed as a reflection of the general physical educator's shortcomings. Rather, support should be viewed as a reminder to all team members that no one, regardless of his or her training, experience, or attitude, has the ability to meet the needs of all students who participate in inclusive physical education programs. Therefore, a key step in developing a physical education program for a student with disabilities is to determine who (if anyone) will provide assistance to the student with disabilities and the level of intensity of this support (Luckasson et al., 1992; Rainforth & York-Barr, 1997; York, Giangreco, et al., 1992).

Some students such as those with spina bifida or mental retardation requiring intermittent support may not need any special assistance, whereas students with severe learning disabilities or mental retardation requiring extensive support may need peers to give them extra cues every now and then in order to follow directions. Students with severe disabilities or those with medically fragile conditions may need a trained teacher assistant or professional to provide assistance on a regular basis. Decisions regarding what type and how much support a student receives should be determined on a case-by-case basis rather than simply by the student's disability. For example, one student with Down syndrome might

Table 4.10.   Chronological age-appropriate activities and sample modifications for elementary-age students with severe disabilities

Age-appropriate activities	Modifications
Manipulative patterns	
Throwing	Push ball down a ramp; grasp and release.
Catching	Track suspended balls; reach for balloons.
Kicking	Touch balloon on floor; push ball down ramp with foot.
Striking	Hit ball off tee; hit suspended ball.
Locomotor patterns	
Running	Have peer push student in wheelchair while student keeps head up.
Jumping/hopping	Move head up and down while being pushed in wheelchair.
Galloping/skipping	Move arms up and down while being pushed in wheelchair; use adapted mobility aids such as scooter boards and walkers.
Perceptual motor skills	
Balance skills	Prop student up on elbows; prone balance over wedge.
Body awareness	Accept tactile input; imitate simple movements.
Spatial awareness	Pull arms in when going between; duck head under.
Visual-motor coordination	Track suspended objects; touch switches.
Physical fitness skills	
Endurance	Tolerate continuous activity; move body parts repeatedly.
Strength	Use stretch bands; use isometric exercises.
Flexibility	Perform ROM activities as suggested by PT.

Reprinted, by permisssion, from M.E. Block, 1992, "What is appropriate physical education for students with profound disabilities?," *Adapted Physical Activity Quarterly, 9*(3): 197–213.

need a teacher assistant, whereas another student with Down syndrome may not need any support to be successful in general physical education. Each of these students with the same diagnosis should be viewed as an individual with unique abilities and needs. How much and what type of personal support a student will need depends on each individual student's age and medical and health concerns; the type of activities being presented; and the student's physical, cognitive, and social skills.

Determine Who Will Provide Support   Rainforth and York-Barr (1997) suggested that the first thing a team should do is to determine the primary challenges faced by an individual student in accomplishing his or her educational goals. These challenges can include general areas such as cognitive/learning, communication/interaction, physical/motor skills, sensory abilities, health, and current/future residency (York, Giangreco, et al., 1992). Next, Rainforth and York-Barr (1997) suggested that the team identify members with specific competencies who can address these challenges and provide necessary support (see Chapter 5, Table 5.3 for an example). For example, a well-behaved student with

Table 4.11. Chronological age-appropriate activities and sample modifications for middle school/high school/young adulthood

Age-appropriate activities	Modifications
Team sports	
Soccer skills	Pass/kick/shoot; push ball down ramp using foot.
Soccer game	Set up special zones; use ramp for kicking.
Volleyball skills	Track suspended balls; reach and touch balls.
Volleyball game	Have "buddy" catch ball; student has 3 seconds to touch ball.
Basketball skills	Use switch that shoots ball into small basket, keep head up and arms out on defense; push ball off tray for passing.
Basketball game	Buddy pushes student into offensive or defensive zone, ball is passed to buddy, student has 5 seconds to activate a switch that shoots his ball into small basket.
Individual sports	
Bowling	Use a ramp (play at community facility when possible).
Boccie (lawn bowling)	Same as above
Miniature golf	Push ball down ramp using mini-putter.
Golf (driving range)	Activate switch that causes ball to be hit.
Physical fitness skills	
Endurance	Move body parts during aerobic dance program.
Strength	Use stretch bands, isometrics, free weights.
Flexibility	Perform ROM activities as suggested by PT during aerobics or during warm-up activities prior to team sports.

Reprinted, by permission, from M.E. Block 1992, "What is appropriate physical education for students with profound disabilities?," *Adapted Physical Activity Quarterly, 9*(3): 197–213.

Note: In all activities, utilize the principle of partial participation to ensure that the student is successful.

mental retardation requiring limited support and no behavior or medical problems could be assisted by classmates during physical education. In fact, assisting such a student could be the responsibility of the entire class rather than of just one classmate. The physical educator might tell the class, "If you are near John and he looks confused or looks like he needs help, please assist him." Similarly, a student with muscular dystrophy may only need a classmate to retrieve balls during a throwing activity. However, the general physical educator might also want to consult with an adapted physical education specialist and physical therapist to learn more about this student's posture, fitness abilities, physical activity capabilities, and potential curricular modifications. Likewise, a student who is blind could have a peer help him move from one station to another and to participate in various activities. In addition, this student's orientation and mobility specialist could come in to general physical education on Mondays and the adapted physical education specialist could come in on Wednesdays to work with the student during general physical education and to talk to the general physical educator.

Even students with severe disabilities can be assisted by classmates during general physical education with the additional support of other professionals. For example, a student with severe spastic cerebral palsy is in a ball-skill unit in first grade. The class is broken down into stations, and this student relies on assistance from his classmates to help him at each station. At a throwing station, the student is assisted by peers who are either resting or waiting their turns. The adapted physical educator has taught these peers how to place the ball in the student's hand and position his chair so he can throw. These peers also push the student from station to station during transitions. The student's physical therapist comes to general physical education once a week, and the APE specialist comes twice a week to support this student, work on individually prescribed goals, provide information to the general physical educator, and provide information and training to the student's classmates.

Students with severe medical conditions or severe behavior problems that pose a risk to the student him- or herself and his or her classmates will require more specialized support. For example, a high school student with mental retardation requiring extensive support and who exhibits aggressive behaviors should be supported by a trained teacher assistant, special education teacher, and/or an APE specialist. Although these professionals have been trained in how to deal with the student's behaviors, they also should be trained in how to help the student acquire IEP objectives during general physical education. Similarly, a nurse might support a student with a severe medical condition in general physical education so that medical emergencies can be handled quickly and appropriately. However, although these support staff members have been trained in dealing with the student's medical condition, they should be given specific directions regarding how to help the student work on his or her IEP goals during general physical education.

Determine Type of Support Provided   Once a decision has been made as to who will provide the support, the next step is to decide the exact type of support that should be provided. There is a delicate balance between providing necessary support that facilitates inclusion, on the one hand, and too much support, on the other hand, which actually has a negative effect on inclusion (Block, 1998, 1999b; Bricker, 1995; Ferguson, 1995; York, Giangreco, et al., 1992). For example, a student with a disability has a teacher assistant who accompanies her to general physical education. When the general physical educator asks students to partner up to do sit-ups, the teacher assistant is always the partner of the student with disabilities. Although the teacher assistant means well, she actually has a negative effect on helping this student interact with her peers and be a true member of the group (Block, 1998, 1999b).

York, Giangreco, and their colleagues (1992, pp. 104–105) identified four types of support that can be applied when including students with disabilities in general physical education:

1. *Resource support:* consists of providing the general physical educator, classmates, and the student with tangible material (e.g., adapted equipment such as beep balls), financial resources (e.g., funds to provide an off-campus aquatics program), information resources (e.g., literature about community sport programs and summer camps), or human resources (teacher assistants, other professionals). York and her colleagues noted that resources alone will not ensure a successful inclusive program. Team members still must implement the prescribed inclusive program properly.

2. *Moral support:* refers to person-to-person interactions in which the support person empathetically and without judgment listens to the general physical educator share his or her concerns. Although the support person may not always agree with the general physical educator, the important part of providing moral support is to acknowledge the general physical educator's concerns.

3. *Technical support:* refers to helping the general physical educator find specific strategies, methods, approaches, ideas, and adaptations to make inclusive physical education successful. York and her colleagues noted that simply providing a teacher with a journal article is more in line with resource support than with technical support. Technical support is more of a hands-on delivery of support such as in-service training, staff development activities, on-site collaboration, peer coaching, team teaching, and demonstrations. Therefore, technical support should be highly individualized and more directly relevant to the general physical educator than resource support. Technical support may be more critical at certain times during the year, such as in the beginning of school when both the general physical educator and peers without disabilities are adjusting to having a new student with a disability in the general physical education class.

4. *Evaluation support:* refers to assisting the general physical educator in collecting information needed to monitor and adjust support services. For example, an APE specialist can provide a general physical educator with a simple observation instrument that allows him or her to more objectively determine if a student with a disability is being successfully included. Evaluation support also refers to assisting the team in determining the impact of support on classmates, family members, and other team members.

One other type of support that is very applicable to general physical education is befriending (Luckasson et al., 1992). Befriending refers to things that the general physical educator and general education classmates do to help the student with disabilities become more successful in general physical education and feel more a part of the group (Block & Brady, 1999). For example, a general physical educator can befriend a student with a disability by simply talking to and instructing the student, making an effort to modify activities to facilitate the student's inclusion, and generally acknowledging the student as a member of the class. Similarly, classmates can befriend a peer with a disability by associating and socializing with the peer, including him in their group, helping the student as needed, and generally doing whatever they can to help the student feel more welcome and part of the group (Block & Brady, 1999). Of all the various supports that can be provided, befriending may be the simplest and least expensive support, yet the most important for successful inclusion!

Determine How Often Support Should Be Provided   Another important yet difficult decision that the team must make is how often support should be provided for individual students. The AAMR defined four levels of intensity of support that vary from intermittent support (as needed) to pervasive support (virtually the entire school day) (see Table 4.12). However, the AAMR noted that decisions regarding support must be made on a case-by-case basis and should not be based only on the student's needs but also on the student's immediate environment (AAMR, 1992). In terms of physical education, factors in the student's immediate environment that may affect the amount of support provided include 1) the general physical educator's attitude toward and capacity to successfully include the student, 2) grade level of the general physical education

Table 4.12. Definitions and examples of intensities of support

Intermittent Supports provided on an "as needed" basis; characterized by episodic nature—person does not always need the support(s), or short-term supports are needed only
during life-span transitions (e.g., job loss or an acute medical crisis). Intermittent supports, when provided, may be high- or low-intensity.

Limited An intensity of supports characterized by consistency over time, time-limited but
not of an intermittent nature; may require fewer staff members and cost less than more intense levels of support (e.g., time-limited employment training or transitional supports
provided during the school-to-adult transition).

Extensive Supports characterized by regular involvement (e.g., daily) in at least some environments (e.g., work, home); supports are not time-limited (e.g., long-term support and
long-term home living support).

Pervasive Supports characterized by their constancy, high intensity; provided across environments, potential life-sustaining nature. Pervasive supports typically involve more staff
members and a greater level of intrusiveness than do extensive or time-limited supports.

From Luckasson, R., Coulter, D.L., Polloway, E.A., Reiss, S., Schalock, R.L., Snell, M.E., Spitalnik,
D.M., & Stark, J.A. (1992). *Mental retardation: Definition, classification, and systems of supports* (9th
ed.). Washington, DC: American Association on Mental Retardation; reprinted by permission.

class, 3) the nature of the general physical education curriculum (e.g., sports and
games versus skill focus), 4) the number of students without disabilities in general physical education (some programs have as many as 150 students at one
time in general physical education), and 5) the general physical education environment (inside and outside spaces and facilities). For example, a motivated, experienced general physical educator might require only consultative support by
an adapted physical education specialist once or twice a month to successfully include a second-grade student with mental retardation requiring extensive support into a general physical education class of 25 students without disabilities
that is working on throwing and catching skills. However, another general physical educator may require daily, direct support to successfully include a similarly
functioning student in a seventh-grade general physical education class of 75 students without disabilities, in which the focus of the class is playing regulation
team sports.

When making decisions regarding support, the important point is that all decisions should be made on an individual basis through a thoughtful, team process
rather than by simply assigning a peer, volunteer, or assistant to work with a student. In addition, it is extremely important that support personnel go through
some type of formal training program prior to working with specific students as
well as ongoing training so that these individuals can provide appropriate, safe
support to students with disabilities. In addition, the general and/or APE specialist should take responsibility to inform support personnel about changes to the
daily or weekly routine, when new units will start, what modifications are appropriate for particular activities, and so on. Block and Krebs (1992) described a
continuum of support to general physical education in which they detailed how
to make decisions regarding personnel who can support students with disabilities
in general physical education (see Table 4.13).

Prepare Team Members for Inclusion

The first four steps in this model allow you to determine which goals a particular
student is working on and how these goals can be met in general physical education. In addition, support personnel have been identified to help implement the

Table 4.13.   A continuum of support to general physical education

Level 1: No support needed
   1.1 Student makes necessary modifications on his or her own.
   1.2 GPE teacher makes necessary modifications for student.

Level 2: APE consultation
   2.1 No extra assistance is needed.
   2.2 Peer tutor "watches out" for student.
   2.3 Peer tutor assists student.
   2.4 Paraprofessional assists student.

Level 3: APE direct service in GPE one time per week
   3.1 Peer tutor "watches out" for student.
   3.2 Peer tutor assists student.
   3.3 Paraprofessional assists student.

Level 4: Part-time APE and part-time GPE
   4.1 Flexible schedule with reverse mainstreaming
   4.2 Fixed schedule with reverse mainstreaming

Level 5: Reverse mainstreaming in special school
   5.1 Students from special school attend general physical education in a regular school one or two times per week.
   5.2 Students without disabilities come to special school two or three times per week for reverse mainstreaming.
   5.3 Students with and without disabilities meet at community-based recreation facility and work out together.

Adapted, by permission, from M. Block & P. Krebs, 1992, "An alternative to least restrictive environments: A continuum of support to regular physical education," *Adapted Physical Activity Quarterly*, 9(2): 104.

program. At this point, you are just about ready to include the student in general physical education; however, you should first make sure that the general physical education teacher and students without disabilities feel comfortable having a student with disabilities in their general physical education class (Morreau & Eichstaedt, 1983). You should also make sure that the support staff (teacher assistants, volunteers, peer tutors) know the student with whom they will be working as well as their responsibilities to the team. One of the primary reasons why inclusion fails is that those directly involved with the program are not adequately prepared (Block, 1999b; Grosse, 1991; Lavay & DePaepe, 1987). The next three steps discuss ways to prepare key personnel for inclusion.

Prepare the General Physical Educator   The first and probably most important person to prepare is the general physical educator. The PEIT often assumes that general physical educators are receptive to inclusion and will have the skills necessary to successfully accommodate the unique needs of students with disabilities. Although some general physical educators feel comfortable having a student with disabilities in their program, many others feel threatened (Minner & Knutson, 1982; Santomier, 1985). Those who feel uncomfortable argue that they do not have the training, the student with disabilities will take too much of their time, including the student will be dangerous, students without disabilities will not accept the special student, and so on. Although these may sound like excuses, most general physical educators rarely have the in-depth training needed to successfully include students with disabilities. For example, a typical undergraduate physical education teacher preparation program includes only one course on adapted physical education, and most of these courses focus on identifying various types of disabilities rather than recommending practical suggestions for developing and implementing individual programs within the general environment.

One of the most important steps in preparing a general physical educator is to define his or her specific role. Vandercook and York (1990) described the roles of general education teachers in facilitating the inclusion of students with disabilities into their general education classes. The role they outlined can be applied to general physical educators as follows: 1) The general physical education teacher should view the student with disabilities as a member of the class rather than as a visitor; 2) the general physical educator should contribute information regarding the general physical education curriculum, instructional strategies, teaching style, management techniques, routines, and rules; 3) the general physical educator should work collaboratively with support personnel, family members, and peers in developing physical education programs and including the student with disabilities into typical physical education activities; 4) the general physical educator should provide a model of appropriate interaction and communication with the student with disabilities (i.e., set expectations for acceptance and inclusion that transfer to peers without disabilities); and 5) the general physical educator should be willing to give it a try. This last responsibility should not be taken lightly. Many physical educators absolutely refuse to allow the student to participate in general physical education, or, if they allow the student into the gym, they make no effort to appropriately include the student in activities.

For inclusion to be truly successful, the general physical education teacher must learn to feel comfortable with the notion of having students with disabilities in the general physical education environment. This can be accomplished in several ways. First and foremost, those physical educators who feel most threatened should be assured that they will receive both direct and consultative support from an adapted physical education specialist and the student's special education teacher. The adapted physical education specialist and special education teacher can assist in the development of the individual program for the student with disabilities, obtain and set up adapted equipment, and develop appropriate modifications to the general program. The special educator can also provide specific information about the student's specific skills and weaknesses, medical/health concerns, communication skills, behaviors, and likes and dislikes. In addition, general physical educators should be assured that students with disabilities, especially students with severe disabilities, will receive support through peer tutors, paraprofessionals, the special education teacher, or the adapted physical educator. The general physical educator should never be left alone with the student until he or she feels comfortable with the situation. Finally, assurance should be made that including a student with disabilities will not cause the general physical educator any additional work. In fact, others helping the general physical educator plan and implement the program for the student with disabilities might actually make his or her job easier. For example, if a teacher assistant comes into the gym with a particular student, the general physical educator could send several students who need extra practice (along with instructions for the teacher assistant) to work with the teacher assistant and the student with disabilities. This way, the general physical educator could work with a smaller group of students on specific skills and strategies.

Another method of helping the general physical educator is to provide desensitizing workshops. These workshops can change preconceived notions about people with disabilities, foster positive attitudes, and provide suggestions for modifications. Clark, French, and Henderson (1985) outlined several activities that could be used to desensitize the general physical education teacher, including 1) visits from guest lecturers who have disabilities, 2) visits to special education classes to get to know the students better, 3) videotapes on athletes with disabilities, 4) role-playing activities in which the general physical educator has to move about in a wheelchair or is blindfolded while performing typical physical education activities, 5) brainstorming sessions with team members regarding modifications for specific physical education units, 6) visits to other schools that have successfully included students with disabilities into general physical education, and 7) team teaching sessions with an adapted physical educator early in the semester to show some concrete ways of accommodating the student with disabilities. When provided prior to inclusion, these and similar activities can facilitate acceptance and confidence in general physical educators.

Finally, it is extremely important for the general physical educator to understand that his or her responsibilities are still with the entire class, not just one or two students. The general physical educator should not spend any more time with the student who has disabilities than with students without disabilities. However, the general physical educator should feel comfortable talking with, correcting, and reinforcing the student with disabilities just as he or she would talk with, correct, and reinforce students without disabilities. In addition, activities should continue to be challenging for all students, and the general program should not be compromised (see Chapters 7 and 8 for more detail). For example, skill hierarchies could be extended to accommodate students with disabilities while still providing challenging activities at the end of the hierarchy for more-skilled students (see Figure 4.11). Similarly, modifications to group activities and team sports should be made so that students with disabilities can be included. However, these modifications should not detract from the program for the students without disabilities. It is important that general physical educators understand how certain modifications to games affect the entire class, and they should strive to implement only those modifications that allow a student with disabilities to participate without drastically affecting the students without disabilities.

Prepare General Education Students   Peer acceptance can be the critical difference between successful and unsuccessful inclusion. Research suggests that many students without disabilities have positive attitudes toward including classmates with disabilities in physical education and sports activities (Block, 1995a; Block & Malloy, 1998). For example, Block and Malloy found that girls without disabilities ages 11–13 overwhelmingly accepted a student with a disability into their competitive, fast-pitch softball league. Furthermore, they were willing to allow modifications to make sure this peer was successful. Unfortunately, the initial response of many peers without disabilities may be negative just because they have had no prior experience with peers who have disabilities. Some students will be scared of students with disabilities, particularly students with physical disabilities. Others will immediately reject students with disabilities because they feel that these students will ruin their physical education program. Still others may be sympathetic toward students with disabilities and try to parent them. Although none of these responses will facilitate successful inclusion, these responses are understandable given that most students without disabilities know very little about students with disabilities. Therefore, an important part of the process of including students with disabilities is to prepare classmates.

Several authors have suggested ways in which teachers can help peers without disabilities develop a more positive attitude toward students with disabilities

Extension of Traditional Skill Station for Dribbling a Basketball

Directions: Choose present skill level for each child in class. Child should stay at this level until he or she can perform the skill in four out of five trials; then, he or she moves to the next level.

(Child's name): _____

Trial 1   Trial 2   Trial 3   Trial 4   Trial 5

1. ___ ___ ___ ___ ___ Holds ball on lap tray while student is pushed in wheelchair around gym.
2. ___ ___ ___ ___ ___ Pushes ball off lap tray.
3. ___ ___ ___ ___ ___ Drops ball to floor.
4. ___ ___ ___ ___ ___ Drops ball to floor then reaches down to touch ball before it bounces 3x.
5. ___ ___ ___ ___ ___ Drops ball to floor then reaches down to touch ball before it bounces 2x.
6. ___ ___ ___ ___ ___ Drops ball to floor then reaches down to touch ball before it bounces 1x.
7. ___ ___ ___ ___ ___ Pushes ball to floor with two hands so that ball bounces up to approximately waist height.
8. ___ ___ ___ ___ ___ Pushes ball to floor with two hands two times in succession.
9. ___ ___ ___ ___ ___ Pushes ball to floor with two hands three times in succession.
10. ___ ___ ___ ___ ___ Pushes ball to floor with one hand two times in succession.
11. ___ ___ ___ ___ ___ Pushes ball to floor with one hand three times in succession.
12. ___ ___ ___ ___ ___ Pushes ball to floor with one hand five times in succession.
13. ___ ___ ___ ___ ___ Pushes ball up and down repeatedly with one hand.
14. ___ ___ ___ ___ ___ Dribbles ball while standing still for 10 seconds.
15. ___ ___ ___ ___ ___ Dribbles ball while standing still for 20 seconds.
16. ___ ___ ___ ___ ___ Dribbles ball while walking forward slowly.
17. ___ ___ ___ ___ ___ Dribbles ball while walking forward at normal walking speed.
18. ___ ___ ___ ___ ___ Dribbles ball while walking forward quickly.
19. ___ ___ ___ ___ ___ Dribbles ball with dominant hand while jogging forward.
20. ___ ___ ___ ___ ___ Dribbles ball with dominant hand while running forward.
21. ___ ___ ___ ___ ___ Dribbles ball with nondominant hand while walking forward.
22. ___ ___ ___ ___ ___ Dribbles ball with nondominant hand while jogging forward.
23. ___ ___ ___ ___ ___ Dribbles ball with nondominant hand while running forward.
24. ___ ___ ___ ___ ___ Dribbles ball with either hand while weaving through cones.
25. ___ ___ ___ ___ ___ Dribbles ball using a crossover dribble while weaving through cones.
26. ___ ___ ___ ___ ___ Dribbles ball with either hand while moving in a variety of directions.
27. ___ ___ ___ ___ ___ Dribbles and protects ball while guarded by opponent going at full speed.

Performance Key:

+ = Student performs skill in four of five trials; +/- = Student performs skill, but not in four of five trials; - = Student does not perform skill.

A Teacher's Guide to Including Students with Disabilities in General Physical Education
by Martin E. Block, copyright ©2000 Paul H. Brookes Publishing Co.

Figure 4.11. Extension of traditional skill station for dribbling a basketball. (From Block, M.E., Provis, S., & Nelson, E. [1994]. Accommodating students with special needs in regular physical education: Extending traditional skill stations. *Palaestra, 10*(1), 32–35 (Table 1, pg 34). PALAESTRA is a publication of Challenge Publications, Ltd., Macomb, IL; adapted by permission.)

Table 4.14.   Disability awareness activities for classmates without disabilities

- Bring in guest speakers who have disabilities but who have made a name for themselves (e.g., paralympic or Special Olympics athletes from the community).
- Set up role-playing situations so that students without disabilities can experience what it is like to have a disability.
- Discuss the purpose of sport rules and how these rules can be modified to successfully include all students. Focus on the notion of "handicapping" (e.g., bowling, golf, horse racing).
- Have students fill out a questionnaire that has statements about people with disabilities. Then discuss with the group how each person in the class responded and why they responded that way.
- Lead a discussion about famous people who have disabilities and how they achieved greatness in their chosen fields despite having a disability.
- Lead a Circle of Friends discussion.
- Have children look through books, read the local newspaper, or search the Internet to find information about people with disabilities.
- Discuss with classmates the specific disabilities (and abilities) of the student who will be integrated into general physical education.

(see Table 4.14 for a list; each of these activities will be discussed in greater detail in Chapter 10) (e.g., Auxter et al., 1997; Block & Brady, 1999; Clark et al., 1985; Getskow & Konczal, 1996; Stainback & Stainback, 1985). Each disability awareness activity can be conducted by the general physical education teacher, the adapted physical education teacher, the special education teacher, the student, the student's parents, or another knowledgeable team member. For example, the vision specialist, with the help of a student who is blind, might know a great deal about visual impairments; together, they could be asked to organize activities to help peers learn what it is like to have a visual impairment. The key is helping classmates become more knowledgeable about disabilities and avoid myths and stereotypes, learn how to view people with disabilities in a positive manner, and learn specific ways to welcome and help students with disabilities who will be in their physical education classes. Classmates generally will be receptive to having a student with a disability in their physical education class if they are given information and training.

Preparation should not stop once the student enters the program. Too often, students with disabilities are ignored in physical education because their classmates do not know how to interact with or assist the students (Block & Brady, 1999). The teacher should provide ongoing encouragement to peers (through both modeling and direct suggestion) to talk to the student with disabilities, provide feedback and positive reinforcement, gently correct or redirect the student when he or she misbehaves, and ask the student if he or she needs assistance. Rather than assigning a single peer to help the student, the entire class should take responsibility for him or her. For example, if a student who has mental retardation does not know which station to go to, one of his peers can assist him. Similarly, if a student who is blind has lost the ball he was dribbling, one of his peers can retrieve it for him. Students should be continuously prompted and reinforced for interacting with the student with disabilities. As the year progresses and classmates begin to feel more comfortable with the student, interactions will become more spontaneous.

Prepare Support Personnel   One final, often neglected step is preparing support personnel who will be assisting the student with disabilities in general physical education. Support personnel, whether trained teacher assistants, peer tutors, or community volunteers, are committed to helping the student with disabilities; however, they often have no formal training or experience with working with students with disabilities or in physical education (Doyle, 1997). Although such support personnel are given some direction by the special education teacher regarding how to work with the student in general education classrooms, they are rarely given direction for working with students with disabilities in physical education. This is probably due to miscommunication between the general physical educator and the special educator. That is, the general physical educator often assumes that the special educator has briefed the support person and provided him or her with a list of physical education activities, whereas the special educator assumes that the general physical educator is guiding the support person on how to provide specific physical education activities to the student with disabilities. The result is confused and often frustrated support personnel who have no idea what they should be doing with the student with disabilities in general physical education and often make up their own physical education program.

Obviously, such a situation prevents the student from developing necessary motor, fitness, and leisure skills and can even be dangerous depending on what activities the support person chooses to attempt. For example, a student with Down syndrome might have positive atlantoaxial instability, and this student should not be allowed to participate in forward rolls during a gymnastics unit. Yet, no one has informed this student's teacher assistant of this problem, and he has been given no direction regarding what to do and what not to do by the general physical educator. Seeing other students in the class doing forward rolls during a gymnastics unit, the teacher assistant assumes that the student with Down syndrome should be doing the same activity. Such a scenario is frightening, yet this scenario and similar ones take place all too often because no one takes responsibility in preparing support personnel.

Training of support personnel should be the ongoing responsibility of all team members. This training should focus on both general information about the person's role as a support person as well as specific information regarding the student with whom he or she will be working and how he or she will facilitate the inclusion of the student into general physical education (Doyle, 1997). Some suggestions regarding information that various team members should present to support personnel include the following:

1. Provide general information (perhaps in the form of a brochure or handout) regarding the support person's role and what is expected of him or her.

2. Provide information regarding the philosophy of the program and the general goals that have been developed for all students (i.e., opportunities to interact with peers without disabilities, improved social behavior, improved communication skills, improved independence in a variety of functional skills).

3. Provide resources and key personnel who the support person can go to with questions if he or she needs help (e.g., general physical educator or adapted physical educator if he or she has questions about modifying specific physical education activities, physical therapist if he or she has specific questions regarding positioning or contraindicated activities).

4. Provide a detailed description of the student including IEP objectives, medical/health concerns, unique behaviors, likes and dislikes, who his or her special friends are, and so on.

Table 4.15.   Common paraprofessional responsibilities applying to physical education

Responsibilities	Application
Noninstructional	
Perform clerical and organizational tasks (e.g., attendance, records, lunch count).	Help with attendance; help with fitness and other testing for the child with disabilities as well as for other children in the class.
Monitor students in the hallway, on the playground, and at the bus stop.	Monitor student going to and from physical education, in the locker room, and in the gym.
Assist with supervision during meals/snacks.	Not applicable
Operate audiovisual equipment.	Operate CD player when music is playing; assist in setting up VCR and monitor when sport films are being shown; assist in videotaping children practicing motor skills.
Provide specific personal care for students.	Assist student in locker room and in rest room.
Instructional	
Observe, record, and chart student's behavioral responses to teacher demonstrations.	Observe, record, and chart student's motor and fitness skills and behaviors during physical education.
Assist with full classroom instruction.	Assist PE teacher in instructing the entire group (e.g., help supervise during warm-ups).
Assist with individualized instruction.	Provide individualized instruction such as additional cues, different equipment, or modified curricula in physical education.
Tutor individual and/or small groups.	Assist not only the student with a disability but also other children who may need assistance in PE.
Implement and reinforce teacher-developed instruction.	Implement general PE curriculum when appropriate, and implement teacher-directed alternative PE program when cued by PE teacher.
Contribute ideas and suggestions related to general instruction.	Contribute ideas related to physical education for the student with a disability as well as for other students who might be having trouble with the regular PE curriculum and instruction.
Participate in team meetings.	Discuss both the positive and negative things that are happening in PE, and share suggestions with team members including the general PE teacher.

From Doyle, M.B. (1997). *The paraprofessional's guide to the inclusive classroom* (p. 5). Baltimore: Paul H. Brookes Publishing Co.; adapted by permission.

5. Describe specific information regarding safety/emergency procedures (e.g., what to do if a student has a seizure or an asthma attack, make sure student gets water every 10 minutes).

6. Provide specific information regarding what typically happens during physical education, including the yearly outline, unit and daily lesson plans, daily routines, rules and regulations, typical teaching procedures, measurement and record-keeping procedures, and so on.

7. Provide general suggestions for modifying activities (e.g., use a balloon or suspended ball when speed and weight of ball are a concern; lower goals or targets, make them larger, or bring them closer to student for more success).

8. Provide several alternative activities when general program activities are deemed inappropriate (e.g., when a forward roll is contraindicated, the student could work on fitness goals or fundamental motor patterns; when the class is playing field hockey, the student can work on alternative striking activities that would facilitate the acquisition of lifetime leisure skills such as croquet, golf, or tennis).

9. Provide several suggestions for facilitating interactions with peers without disabilities. Table 4.15 provides a list of common paraprofessional responsibilities with regard to physical education.

5

Assessment to Facilitate
Successful Inclusion

I have observed many changes during my years as an adapted physical education specialist. Inclusion is the best change that has occurred for students with disabilities. It is wonderful to watch students working co-operatively to help each other. It has brought regular educators, parents, special educators, administrators, and the community together . . . to make this a successful experience for children. Many physical educators previously unsupportive of inclusion have developed a new attitude of "what can I do to make this a successful experience for my students"? . . .

Shirley Brodeur, adapted physical education specialist

David is a ninth grader who has a severe visual impairment. He has just moved to Jefferson County, where he will be attending Monroe High School. David did not receive physical education at his previous school because his teachers believed that the severity of his visual impairment precluded traditional physical education. Instead, David received orientation and mobility training during physical education. At Monroe, all students, even students with disabilities such as David, receive physical education in the general environment. Programs are modified and individualized as needed to ensure that each student receives a program that meets his or her unique needs. But, how does the physical education inclusion team (PEIT) decide what is appropriate to teach David and other students with varying abilities? How do team members identify David's present strengths and weaknesses, and how do they determine how to teach and modify particular skills? Once the program has been implemented, how does the PEIT determine whether David is making adequate progress toward his goals?

Chapter 4 outlines an ecological approach to develop and implement a physical education program in the general environment for students with disabilities. However, *all* programming decisions should be based on information obtained from ecologically relevant assessment data. That is, assessments should closely relate to the skills and behaviors the student needs to be successful in his or her current and future environments. In addition, assessments should be sensitive to the interests of key people in the student's life such as the student's parents and peers. Without such assessment data, programming decisions would be based on irrelevant information, "best guesses," or assumptions that in turn could result in a poor or inappropriate physical education program.

Assessment is a critical, yet often misused, part of the overall educational process. According to PL 105-17, the Individuals with Disabilities Education Act (IDEA) Amendments of 1997, part of the individualized education program (IEP) process must include an assessment of the present level of performance of each student with a disability. Assessment data can then be used by the student's collaborative team to make informed decisions regarding specific diagnoses, types

---

Note that the checklists described in this chapter are not the only tests available for determining programming decisions. These checklists are simply samples of tools designed to assist the team in making informed decisions. Assessment can also take the form of informal observations and discussions with team members. Still, formal assessments should be used whenever a programming decision is made to ensure that the student is receiving the most appropriate program possible.

and intensity of services, instructional plans, amounts and types of supports, and, ultimately, the least restrictive placement. Assessment should be an ongoing process that begins with the development of the student's IEP and continues during the implementation of the program. Unfortunately, assessment tools often are used improperly, data are misinterpreted, or decisions are made based on a specific disability label or school philosophy and not on an individual student's needs (Block, 1996; Davis, 1984; Grosse, 1991).

The purpose of this chapter is to outline assessment procedures that can facilitate the inclusion of students with disabilities in general physical education. This chapter begins with a brief review of the legal basis for assessment as outlined in the IDEA Amendments of 1997. This review is followed by an examination of traditional assessment procedures and a detailed review of an ecological approach to assessment. Finally, an example of how an ecological assessment should be conducted is presented. It should be noted here that the term *assessment* will be used synonymously with the term *evaluation*, which is used in IDEA. *Assessment* is defined rather broadly as the process of collecting and interpreting data in order to plan and implement a physical education program for students with disabilities. The term *test* is used to describe specific tools used to collect assessment information.

Legal Basis for Assessment in Physical Education

Assessment has always been a critical part of federal special education legislation. From its beginning in 1975, the Education for All Handicapped Children Act (EHA; PL 94-142) included very specific information and procedures regarding assessment in an effort to ensure that students with disabilities were 1) appropriately diagnosed, 2) provided with appropriate services, and 3) placed in the least restrictive environment. These evaluation procedures have remained basically the same through the many revisions of IDEA, including the latest reauthorization, PL 105-17. The appendix at the end of this chapter contains excerpts from the IDEA Amendments of 1997, part B (evaluations, eligibility determinations, individualized education programs, and educational placements). As you review these excerpts, note 1) the highly individualized nature of assessment and decisions, 2) the use of collaborative teams rather than one individual to do the assessment and make the decisions, and 3) the important role of parents.

When conducting a physical education assessment, a student's IEP team should adhere to each of the procedures outlined in the chapter appendix. For example, placement decisions (including the decision whether to place a student in a general physical education class or a separate physical education environment) cannot be made until a student is given a full and individual evaluation of motor needs. This evaluation should be conducted by "trained personnel" (ideally, an adapted physical educator), draw upon information from all team members, and take into account the preferences of the student and his or her parents. In addition, testing materials must be appropriate for the student's age and abilities. For example, it would be inappropriate to give an 18-year-old the Peabody Developmental Motor Scales (Folio & DeBose, 1974), which are designed for infants and children from birth to age 6 years. Similarly, it would be inappropriate to give a student who uses a wheelchair a standard physical fitness test designed for students who can walk and run. Finally, decisions regarding placement and scope of program should be based on an ecologically relevant assessment that is directly related to the student's needs, abilities, and current and future environments. Unfortunately, not all adapted physical education assessments are conducted in this manner. The following section contrasts traditional approaches to assessment in adapted physical education with ecological approaches.

Traditional Approach to Assessment in Adapted Physical Education

The way in which adapted physical education decisions are made varies among school systems. Traditional procedures for administering and using assessments can be broken down into four major steps: 1) classification, 2) development of the student's IEP, 3) placement, and 4) instruction.

Classification

Traditionally, the first step in the assessment process is to determine whether a student needs specialized physical education services. In some school districts, students qualify for adapted physical education simply because they have a particular diagnosis. For example, students who use wheelchairs usually qualify for adapted physical education because it is assumed that the goals for these students are completely different than the goals for their peers without disabilities. Conversely, students with learning disabilities often do not receive adapted physical education because it is assumed that they do not have any special motor or fitness needs. Such practices are in direct violation of the law, which specifically mandates that each student with disabilities be individually evaluated to determine whether he or she requires special physical education services (Bateman, 1996; IDEA of 1997; Osborne, 1996; see legal description in chapter appendix). More importantly, in the previous examples, no one has taken the time to assess each student's strengths and weaknesses prior to determining whether the student qualifies for adapted physical education. Many students with learning disabilities, in fact, have motor and learning problems that justify specialized physical education, whereas many students who use wheelchairs can function quite well in general physical education without any special support.

Other professionals who try to determine if a student qualifies for adapted physical education use *norm-referenced* or *standardized* tests. A standardized test compares one student's score with the scores of others who have taken the same test (Safrit, 1990; Sherrill, 1998). That is, a student's score is compared with a set of norms. Norms are established by testing a representative sample of people from a particular population. For example, for a test to be valid for students between the ages of 2 and 6, a large sample of students ages 2–6 should be tested to develop norms. These norms can then be analyzed and organized to describe scores that correspond to a certain percentage of the population. For example, a particular score on a test might represent a point at which 75% of the norm sample scored below that particular score (75th percentile). Based on these percentiles, school systems can establish minimum cutoff scores that determine who does or does not qualify for adapted physical education. Such an approach is by far the most widely used for determining whether a student should receive special services (Ulrich, 1985). In fact, many states have set criteria based on standardized test results for determining who qualifies for adapted physical education services. Sherrill (1998) noted that students in Alabama and Georgia who score below the 30th percentile on standardized tests of motor performance qualify for adapted physical education services. Sherrill herself suggested that students who consistently score below the 50th percentile should qualify for special physical education services.

The Bruininks-Oseretsky Test of Motor Proficiency (BOT; Bruininks, 1978) is a standardized, valid, norm-referenced test designed to measure specific motor abilities of students from $4\frac{1}{2}$ to $14\frac{1}{2}$ years of age. Areas evaluated include running speed and agility, balance, bilateral coordination, response speed, strength, upper-limb coordination, visual-motor coordination, and upper-limb speed and dexterity. The BOT is frequently used by adapted physical education specialists (Ulrich, 1985) to determine which students qualify for adapted physical education (see Figure 5.1 for examples of BOT items). For example, a school system might decide that a student whose total score on the BOT is below the 30th percentile qualifies for adapted physical education.

One has to question whether the information obtained from this type of test is ecologically relevant to the needs of individual students. What information does data collected from the BOT give the team that would help them determine whether a student needs adapted physical education services? Will a student who performs at the 20th percentile have difficulty in general physical education activities? Will a student who does poorly on subtest items, such as response speed or bilateral coordination, perform poorly during activities in general physical education if he or she does not receive extensive support? Does the BOT reliably predict how well a second-grade student will do in a unit that focuses on locomotor patterns or how well a middle school student will do in a softball unit?

Similarly, why does performance at or below the 20th percentile on the President's Council on Physical Fitness Test, a test that measures health-related physical fitness for students ages 6–17, qualify a student for adapted physical education services? Areas evaluated include cardiovascular endurance (1-mile run), percent body fat (skinfold), muscular strength (sit-ups and pull-ups), and flexibility (sit and reach). Does a student's performance on any or all of these tests predict how well he or she will do in general physical education? Can limited abdominal strength, as measured by sit-ups, determine whether a high school student will be unsuccessful or need modifications to engage in popular lifetime leisure activities such as softball, tennis, or golf? It is clear that the BOT and similar tests are not always a good measure of what actually takes place in general physical education; however, these types of tests are often used to make decisions regarding who qualifies for adapted physical education services.

Development of an Individualized Education Program

Once it has been determined that a student has an impairment that requires special education services, the next step is to determine the specific skills on which the student should work. The development of the student's IEP is an important process; the IEP specifies activities on which the student should focus the next year. In most cases, information taken from the classification assessment is used to develop the student's IEP. This makes the assessment tools used for classification critical. Unfortunately, in the traditional approach, the use of standardized tests forces practitioners to follow a developmental or "bottom-up" approach. In the bottom-up approach, deficiencies at the lower end of the developmental continuum become the focus of the student's physical education program without regard to the way in which these skills affect the acquisition of real-life skills (Block, 1992; Brown et al., 1979; Wessel & Kelly, 1986). In practice, IEP goals and objectives become items that a student fails on developmental tests or tests of motor abilities. For example, an IEP goal for a student who does poorly on upper-limb speed and dexterity (e.g., sorting playing cards quickly) might be to improve upper-limb response speed. Specific activities that might be targeted to improve

SUBTEST 5/Item 7

Touching Nose with Index Fingers—Eyes Closed

With eyes closed, the subject touches any part of his or her nose first with one index finger and then with the opposite index finger, as shown in Figure 26. The subject is given 90 seconds to touch the nose four consecutive times. The score is recorded as a pass or a fail.

Trials: 1

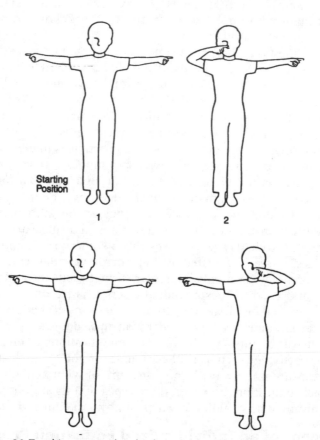

Figure 26 Touching nose with index fingers—eyes closed (Subtest 5 Item 7)

Administering and Recording

Have the subject stand facing you. Say: **Hold your arms straight out to the side. Close your hands and point with your first** (index) **fingers** (demonstrate). **Touch your nose with the tip of one of your fingers and then put your arm straight out again** (demonstrate). **Then touch your nose with the other fingertip and put that arm straight out again** (demonstrate). **Now do it with your eyes closed and your head still. Keep touching your nose until I tell you to stop. Ready, begin.**

Begin timing. If necessary, provide additional instruction. For example, remind the subject to touch the nose with the tips of the index fingers and to return one arm to an extended position before moving the other arm. Start counting as soon as the subject is moving the arms and touching the nose correctly in a continuous movement. During the trial correct the subject and start counting over if she or he:

Figure 5.1.   Select items from the Bruininks-Oseretsky Test of Motor Proficiency. (From Bruininks, R.H. [1978]. *Bruininks-Oseretsky Test of Motor Proficiency: Examiner's manual* [pp. 82-85]. Circle Pines, MN: American Guidance Service; reprinted by permission.)

a. fails to maintain continuous movements
b. fails to touch the nose with the index finger
c. fails to alternate arms
d. fails to extend arms fully after touching nose
e. moves head to meet the finger
f. opens eyes.

Allow no more than 90 seconds, including time needed for additional instruction, for the subject to touch the nose correctly four consecutive times (twice with each finger). After 90 seconds, tell the subject to stop.

On the Individual Record Form, record pass or fail.

SUBTEST 5/Item 8

Touching Thumb to Fingertips—Eyes Closed

With eyes closed, the subject touches the thumb of the preferred hand to each of the fingertips on the preferred hand, moving from the little finger to the index finger to the little finger, as shown in Figure 27. The subject is given 90 seconds to complete the task once. The score is recorded as a pass or fail.

Trials: 1

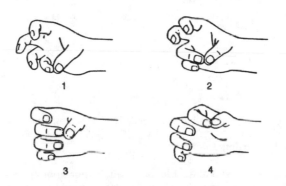

Figure 27 Touching thumb to fingertops—eyes closed (Subtest 5 Item 8)

Administering and Recording

Have the subject sit beside you at a table. Have the subject extend the preferred arm. Then say: **You are to touch your thumb to each of the fingertips on this hand. Start with your little finger and touch each fingertip in order. Then start with your first finger and touch each fingertip again as you move your thumb back to your little finger** (demonstrate). **Do this with your eyes closed until I tell you to stop. Ready, begin.**

Begin timing. If necessary provide additional instruction. During the trial correct the subject and have the subject start over if he or she:

a. fails to maintain continuous movements
b. touches any finger except the index finger more than once in succession
c. touches two fingers at the same time
d. fails to touch fingers above the first finger joint
e. opens eyes.

Figure 5.1.   (continued)

Allow no more than 90 seconds, including time needed for additional instruction, for the subject to complete the task once. After 90 seconds, tell the subject to stop.

On the Individual Record Form, record pass or fail.

SUBTEST 5/Item 9

Pivoting Thumb and Index Finger

The subject touches the tip of the right index finger to the tip of the left thumb, then pivots the hands to touch the tip of the left index finger to the tip of the right thumb. The subject continues to pivot the hands touching finger to thumb, in an upward or downward motion. See Figure 28. The subject is given 90 seconds to complete five consecutive pivots correctly. The score is recorded as a pass or fail.

Trials: 1

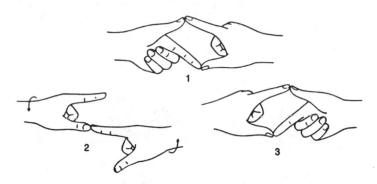

Figure 28 Pivoting thumb and index finger (Subtest 5 Item 9)

Administering and Recording

Have the subject sit beside you at a table. Say: **Touch your** (index) **finger of each hand to the thumb of your other hand** (demonstrate). **Watch how I separate one thumb and finger and move them** (demonstrate). If necessary, place the subject's thumbs and index fingers in the correct starting position. Then say: **Keep moving your thumbs and fingers this way until I tell you to stop. Ready, begin.**

Begin timing. If necessary, provide additional instruction. (For young subjects, it may be helpful to remind them of the "Eency Weency Spider" song, which uses the same action.) Start counting pivots as soon as the subject establishes a continuous motion. During the trial correct the subject and start counting over if she or he:

a. fails to maintain continuous movements
b. places the thumbs or index fingers incorrectly.

Allow no more than 90 seconds, including time needed for additional instruction, for the subject to complete five consecutive pivots correctly. After 90 seconds, tell the subject to stop.

On the Individual Record Form, record pass or fail.

response speed might include repeatedly touching his nose with his index fingers, touching his thumb to his fingertips, or pivoting his thumb and index finger. Similarly, a student who fails items #121 and #128 on the gross motor scale of the Peabody Developmental Motor Scales (Folio & DuBose, 1974) (#121: stand on tiptoes for 5 seconds with eyes open; #128: stand on one foot with hands on hips for 5 seconds) might have an IEP goal to improve static balance and a short-term instructional objective of standing on tiptoes and balancing on one foot. Although upper-limb response speed and static balance may be a problem for this student, the physical educator needs to determine whether working on these nonfunctional skills away from the rest of the class is an appropriate objective. How do these goals relate to skills the student will need to be successful in current and future physical education and recreation environments? Again, although the long-term goals may be appropriate, the short-term instructional objectives focus on nonfunctional, splinter-type skills that bear no relation to the skills a student needs to be successful in general physical education.

Placement

Once it has been determined that a student qualifies for adapted physical education services and the student has an IEP, the next step in the assessment process is to make a decision regarding the location in which the student will receive these services. The IDEA Amendments of 1997 mandate that placement decisions be based on the concept of least restrictive environment (LRE). Recall that LRE mandates that students with disabilities be educated alongside their peers without disabilities and that separate programming occur only when education in the general environment cannot be achieved satisfactorily with the use of supplementary aids and services (Bateman, 1996; Block, 1996). Placement in general education with supplementary aids and supports has been reemphasized in the IDEA Amendments of 1997. Therefore, assessment data should be used first to determine how much support a student with a disability needs in order to be successful in general physical education. Only after it has been clearly and objectively determined that the student cannot be placed successfully in general physical education can a student with disabilities be placed in an alternative physical education environment (Block, 1996; Block & Krebs, 1992; Sherrill, 1998).

In theory, information obtained from assessment data should be used to determine 1) how much support a student needs to be successful in general physical education, and 2) what alternative placement would be appropriate for the student if he or she cannot be successfully included in general physical education. In reality, placement decisions often tend to be an either-or situation: general physical education with no support or separate physical education (Jansma & Decker, 1990). Decisions tend to focus on placement options rather than on the provision of varying amounts of support to help the student be successful in general physical education (Block & Krebs, 1992). Again, a domino effect tends to occur; it begins with the use of a standardized assessment tool to determine classification, which influences IEP goals, which in turn influence placement. For example, it is difficult for a general physical educator to understand how working on upper-limb speed and dexterity (IEP goals based on results of standardized assessments) is relevant to her lessons on locomotor patterns and body awareness. In addition, there is no information regarding which modifications the student requires to be successful in general physical education. Therefore, the teacher concludes that the student should be placed in a separate adapted physical education class. The use of assessment data that are not related to the student's current and future environments often leads to inappropriate placement decisions.

Instruction

The final and perhaps most relevant aspect of assessment is how to help a student achieve the targeted goals on his or her IEP. Unfortunately, decisions at this level still will be based on the results of standardized tests, which focus on motor abilities, developmental level, and physical fitness. Again, these tests are usually conducted in such a way that they do not help the physical educator determine how to adapt instruction so that the student acquires critical physical education skills and can be successful in general physical education. For example, poor performance on sit-ups on the President's Council on Physical Fitness test does not indicate why the student is having trouble doing sit-ups or how to help this student improve his physical fitness as it relates to real-life physical education and recreation skills. Most teachers have the student practice sit-ups; but what if the student did poorly because of lack of motivation? A poorly motivated student may need a different type of instruction than a student who actually has poor abdominal strength. Similarly, how do you cue a student who has trouble with upper-limb activities? Do you just assign her extra exercises to enhance her upper-limb skills, or do you need to modify instruction? Perhaps the student would perform better if the skill was broken down into smaller steps. Maybe the student requires physical assistance, or perhaps she simply needs adapted equipment. Unfortunately, data collected from standardized assessment tools do not provide any answers regarding instruction; therefore, teachers are forced to make instructional decisions based on what they believe is best for a particular student.

An Ecological Approach to Assessment

If the traditional approach to assessment is ineffective, then what is the alternative approach? Many professionals are recommending a functional or ecologically relevant approach to assessment in which programming decisions are based on a "top-down" model (Auxter, Pyfer, & Huettig, 1997; Block, 1992; Wessel & Kelly, 1986). As described in the previous chapter, the ecological approach to programming provides a more real-world approach than the traditional approach; it emphasizes the end of the developmental continuum rather than the beginning. Thus, the first step in a top-down assessment model is to identify current and future recreation environments (top of the model) that are appropriate for each student. This is followed by an assessment to determine 1) the specific skills that a student needs to be successful in the identified recreation environments, 2) which of the needed skills a student already possesses, and 3) which of the skills a student still needs to acquire. Kelly et al. (1991) viewed this process in terms of a pyramid in which the top of the pyramid represents the ultimate goal of the program and the lower levels represent the skills needed to get to the top (see Figure 5.2).

The top-down approach forces teachers to focus on the critical skills a student needs to be successful in current and future recreation environments while eliminating less-functional items. For example, although some items on developmental tests are critical for success in recreation environments, the student might encounter later in life, many more are not functional and can be eliminated. Activities such as standing on tiptoes, walking along a circle, and skipping are items on developmental tests that rarely are related to any functional end goal in a top-down approach. These skills would not have to be taught in a top-down approach because they are not related to functional outcomes.

The ecological assessment model can be broken down into six interrelated phases, which help answer the following five real-life questions: 1) Who qualifies

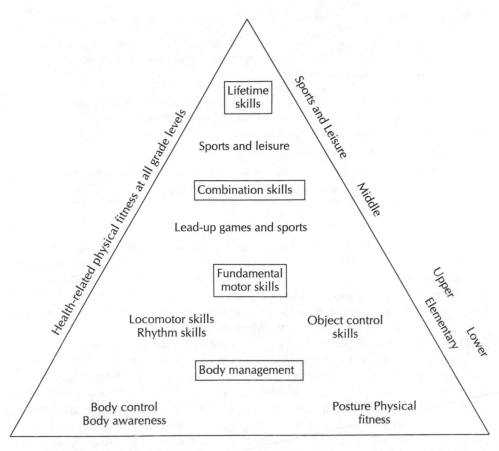

Figure 5.2.   Top-down pyramid. (From Kelly, L.E., et al. [1991]. *Achievement-based curriculum: Teaching manual.* Charlottesville: University of Virginia; reprinted by permission.)

for APE services, 2) what skills should we teach (i.e., long-term plan and goals and objectives), 3) how should these skills be taught (instructional planning), 4) where should these skills be taught (placement decisions), 5) how much support is needed and who should provide support (how well were the skills taught [ongoing evaluation]) (see Table 5.1)?

Phase 1: Who Qualifies for APE Services?

As was the case with traditional assessment, the first step in the ecological approach to assessment is to determine who qualifies for APE services. However, in the ecological approach, assessment is directly tied to real-life skills that a student needs in order to be successful in general physical education and community-based recreation. Ecologically relevant areas for elementary physical education might include 1) the general elementary curriculum for students of the same age as the student with disabilities, 2) fitness as it relates to the student's abilities to be successful in general physical education, 3) behaviors and social skills as they relate to the student's ability to be successful in general physical education, 4) cognitive skills as they relate to the student's ability to be successful in general physical education, and 5) ability to participate in community recreational activities and recess with peers. If the student demonstrates significant impairments in one or more of these ecologically relevant general physical education areas, then the student qualifies for APE services. However, if, based on this assessment, the

Table 5.1.   Six phases of an ecological approach to assessment in adapted physical education

Phase 1	Determine *who* qualifies for adapted physical education (APE) services.
Phase 2	Determine *what* to teach. • Define top-down plan and targeted skills. • Determine student's present level of performance on targeted skills. • Develop student's IEP based on present level of performance.
Phase 3	Determine *how* to teach targeted skills.
Phase 4	Determine *where* to teach targeted skills.
Phase 5	Determine *who* will teach targeted skills (i.e., support needed to teach skill).
Phase 6	Determine *how well* targeted skills were taught (ongoing evaluation).

student appears to be successful in general physical education, then the child would not qualify for APE services. Figure 5.3 shows the results of an ecologically relevant assessment to determine whether a student qualifies for APE services. Also, Figure 5.4 provides an ecologically relevant initial observation and referral form that a school district might use to determine whether a student qualifies for APE services. Note that most of the information contained in both of these assessments can be obtained from the general physical education teacher.

The key to this phase of the assessment is to try to determine if the child actually has significant impairments that affect his or her ability to participate successfully in general physical education. Because ability to participate is the key criterion, it makes sense that assessment information at this point in the process should focus on the skills and behaviors that are necessary in general physical education—the ecologically relevant part of the assessment. Contrast this with the traditional approach discussed previously, in which assessments tended to be disconnected from general physical education. In traditional assessments, a child could conceivably do very well on a traditional motor or fitness assessment tool yet do very poorly in general physical education. Conversely, Tamara in the example in Figure 5.3 shows how a student who would probably do very poorly in traditional motor and fitness tests that require locomotor and balance abilities can do quite well in general physical education without support. The important point in this phase of assessment is to try to determine whether the child actually has significant impairments that affect his or her ability to participate successfully in general physical education.

Phase 2: What Skills Should We Teach?

It is impossible to teach all skills to all students. Many students without disabilities will acquire skills quickly enough to learn a variety of lifetime leisure skills. However, students with mild disabilities will take longer to learn fewer skills compared with their peers without disabilities, and students with severe disabilities often take much longer to learn just a few skills. Therefore, it is important to target key skills on which particular students can focus (Block, 1992; Brown et al., 1979; Kelly et al., 1991).

Developing the Vision   The first phase of the assessment process defines which skills are critical in the student's present and future environments (Kelly et al., 1991; Rainforth & York-Barr, 1997). One way to begin this process is to use the Making Action Plans System (MAPS), in which team members discuss a series of questions about the child with a disability (Rainforth & York-Barr,

Name: *Tamara Jones*   **Date:** *September 14, 2000*

Date of birth: *7-15-92*   **Evaluator:** *Chandra Martin, CAPE*

Grade/class: *Second/Ms. Jacobs*

Introduction

Tamara is an 8-year-old girl who is in Ms. Jacobs second-grade class. Tamara has paraplegic, spastic cerebral palsy (i.e., affects her legs but not her arms). She independently uses a manual wheelchair for mobility. She has typical intelligence, although she does have some speech and auditory processing delays. She currently receives physical therapy once a week for 30 minutes and speech therapy twice a week for 30 minutes each session. She has been recommended for an adapted physical education evaluation by her special education teacher due to suspected delays in gross motor development.

Abilities in reference to general physical education (GPE) curriculum

The general physical education (GPE) curriculum for kindergarten through second grade focuses on mastery of body and space awareness, movement concepts, basic rhythms, and locomotor patterns in addition to an introduction to manipulative patterns and physical fitness concepts. Tamara has mastered body and space awareness concepts, movement concepts, and basic rhythms. She is unable to perform any locomotor patterns due to her disability, but she can independently move her manual wheelchair around the gym and the playground quite well. She cannot kick or punt due to her disability, but she has learned to catch and throw in her wheelchair using a modified pattern. She has good upper-body strength and flexibility, and she has very good endurance.

Behavioral, cognitive, and social abilities in reference to the GPE curriculum

Tamara is an extremely well-behaved and enthusiastic student in GPE. She really wants to please and follow directions, although the GPE teacher or a peer often has to repeat complex directions for her. She is a social child who interacts very well with her peers, and her peers seem to enjoy interacting with her.

Motor abilities with reference to recess and community-based recreation

Tamara's parents report that she is a very active participant in activities with her peers at home. She plays on a regular T-ball league with no modifications other than using her wheelchair to get from home to first. She also plays with neighborhood children without too much difficulty, again using her wheelchair rather than walking or running. Tamara's classroom teacher notes that she is able to participate in most recess activities including dodging and fleeing games, 4-square, and the swings. She cannot climb up on the playground structure independently, but that does not seem to bother her.

Recommendations

Based on this ecologically based assessment in adapted physical education, it seems that Tamara functions quite well in general physical education, in her neighborhood, and during recess. Therefore, I do not recommend APE services at this time. However, as Tamara moves to upper-elementary and middle school, she may need to be reassessed to see if she requires some form of APE services.

Figure 5.3.   Results from ecologically based qualifying assessment in adapted physical education.

1997; Vandercook, York, & Forest, 1989) (see Figure 5.5). Although such a model does not delineate which specific skills should be targeted for instruction, information from this type of assessment can be helpful in guiding the planning process.

Initial Observation and Referral Form

Child's name: _____   Evaluator: _____

School: _____   Date: _____

Use this form when first observing a child with a disability who has been referred for adapted physical education. Rate each item based on how the child compares with other children in his/her physical education class.

	Adequate	Needs improvement	Significantly inadequate	Not observed
Physical fitness				
Performs activities that require upper-body strength (e.g., push-ups, throwing, chest pass)				
Performs activities that require lower-body strength (e.g., running, hopping, kicking)				
Performs activities that require flexibility (e.g., stretching, bending, tumbling)				
Performs activities that require endurance (e.g., mile run, games that involve endurance)				
Body composition (e.g., child's weight and general appearance)				
Gross motor skills				
Performs nonlocomotor skills (e.g., twisting, turning, balance, bending)				
Moves safely around environment (e.g., dodging, space awareness, directions)				
Uses physical education equipment (e.g., balls, bats, scooters)				
Performs locomotor skills (e.g., running, jumping, galloping, hopping, skipping)				
Performs manipulative skills (e.g., throwing, catching, kicking, striking)				
Performs dance skills (e.g., rhythm, patterns, creative)				
Plays low-organized games (e.g., dodgeball, relays, tag, teacher-made games)				

Figure 5.4. Initial observation and referral form.

(*continued*)

Figure 5.4. (*continued*)

	Adequate	Needs improvement	Significantly inadequate	Not observed
Sports skills (e.g., throwing in softball, kicking in soccer, volleyball serve, hitting a tennis ball)				
Plays organized sports (e.g., basketball, soccer)				
Transition to and from physical education Enters without interruption				
Sits in assigned area				
Stops playing with equipment when asked				
Lines up to leave when asked				
Responding to teacher Remains quiet when teacher is talking				
Follows directions in a timely manner during warm-up				
Follows directions in a timely manner during skill focus				
Follows directions in a timely manner during games				
Accepts feedback from teacher				
Uses positive or appropriate language				
Relating to peers and equipment Works cooperatively with a partner when asked (e.g., shares, takes turns)				
Works cooperatively as a member of a group when asked				
Uses positive or appropriate comments to peers				
Seeks social interactions with peers				
Displays sportsmanship by avoiding conflict with others				
Uses equipment appropriately				

A Teacher's Guide to Including Students with Disabilities in General Physical Education
by Martin E. Block, copyright ©2000 Paul H. Brookes Publishing Co.

(*continued*)

Figure 5.4. (*continued*)

	Adequate	Needs improvement	Significantly inadequate	Not observed
Effort and self-acceptance				
Quickly begins the activity once instructed				
Continues to participate independently throughout activity				
Adapts to new tasks and changes				
Strives to succeed and is motivated to learn				
Accepts his or her own skill whether successful or improving				
Cognitive abilities				
Understands nonverbal directions				
Understands verbal directions				
Processes multistep cues				
Attends to instructions				

Comments regarding fitness or motor skills: _____

_____

Comments regarding behaviors and social or cognitive abilities: _____

_____

A Teacher's Guide to Including Students with Disabilities in General Physical Education
by Martin E. Block, copyright ©2000 Paul H. Brookes Publishing Co.

For example, parents and team members may realize that an 11-year-old boy with a learning disability and emotional problems is really having problems with self-esteem as it relates to physical education. The dreams for this student are to develop some skills in a particular sport and improve general fitness so he can feel better about himself in physical education and use his leisure time more appropriately. The nightmare for this student is that he continues to hate physical education, drops physical education as soon as he can in high school, and becomes an inactive, overweight adult.

Targeting Specific Goals   Once a vision for the student has been established, the team can focus on specific goals and objectives to help the student reach the dream and avoid the nightmare. As noted in Chapter 4, the team can begin to define some specific sports, recreational activities, or skills that the student might need to reach the dream and be successful in his or her present or future environments. One rather simple way to determine which activities are important for a particular student is to ask key people in the student's life (e.g., student him- or herself, parents, peers, people in community) what they perceive

---

Making Action Plans System (adapted for physical education planning)

1. What is_____'s history regarding motor development, recreation, and fitness?

2. Regarding physical education and recreation, what is your dream for_____?

3. What is your nightmare?

4. Who is_____with reference to physical education and recreation (what does he or she like/dislike)?

5. What are_____'s strengths, gifts, and abilities in physical education and recreation?

6. What does_____need to make the dream come true and to avoid the nightmare?

7. What would_____'s ideal day in physical education look like, and what must be done to make it happen?

8. What is our plan of action for physical education?

A Teacher's Guide to Including Students with Disabilities in General Physical Education
by Martin E. Block, copyright ©2000 Paul H. Brookes Publishing Co.

Figure 5.5.   Making Action Plans system (adapted for physical education planning). (From Falvey, M.A., Forest, M., Pearpoint, J., & Rosenberg, R.L. (1997). *All my life's a circle: Using the tools: Circus, MAPS, & PATH.* Toronto: Inclusion Press; adapted by permission.)

to be critical skills for the student (Voeltz, Wuerch, & Bockhaut, 1992). Student and parent preferences can be determined at an IEP meeting by simply asking them what they would like to see in the student's physical education program. Examining the activities in which the student's peers participate during physical education, recess, and after-school play also is a simple way of determining in which activities the student with disabilities should participate. In addition, the student's peers could be questioned either formally or informally about the recre-

---

Making Curriculum Decisions

Directions: List appropriate activities under each of the following headings. Then, scan the list, and place activities that are in more than one column under *Targeted activities.*

Student's preferences	Parents' preferences	Activities in GPE	Neighborhood activities played by peers	Community leisure activities
_____	_____	_____	_____	_____
_____	_____	_____	_____	_____
_____	_____	_____	_____	_____
_____	_____	_____	_____	_____
_____	_____	_____	_____	_____
_____	_____	_____	_____	_____

Targeted activities: 1. _____ 2. _____ 3. _____ 4. _____

A Teacher's Guide to Including Students with Disabilities in General Physical Education
by Martin E. Block, copyright ©2000 Paul H. Brookes Publishing Co.

Figure 5.6.   Form for making curriculum decisions.

ational activities they typically engage in after school. This information can then be used to determine which activities are popular for peers of the students with disabilities. Activities that are appropriate and important for students without disabilities are usually appropriate for students with disabilities (with modifications as needed to accommodate individual abilities).

Once information has been collected, it can be used to develop a list of critical activities and skills for the student. Figure 5.6 provides a simple form for making curriculum decisions that takes into account the student's, parents', and peers' preferences. These preferences, in addition to what is available in the school and community, will help shape the list of targeted activities for a particular student. Note that a student's particular abilities (or disabilities) are not the focus at this point in the assessment process. Once specific activities and skills have been defined, the student's ability to perform these skills and the necessity of modifications can be discussed.

For example, at this level of assessment, the IEP team might decide that wheelchair mobility is an appropriate alternative for a 7-year-old student who uses a wheelchair because running, jumping, leaping, skipping, and hopping are skills that are used in general physical education, and they are popular activities played by peers at home and during recess. In addition, the student's parents want her to improve her wheelchair skills. Locomotor patterns for this student might involve learning how to move her wheelchair forward, backward, around obstacles, and up and down ramps, all with increasing speed.

Other factors to consider when prioritizing goals for students with disabilities include availability of transportation and assistance as well as the possibility that the students will not acquire the skills needed to participate in the activity, even with minimal support and modifications. Helmstetter (1989) created a questionnaire to weigh these criteria when prioritizing goals for students with disabilities. To use the questionnaire, the general physical educator rates each of the activities using the 20 criteria then computes the total sum of criteria for each activity (see Figure 5.7). Activities in which the majority of the criteria are met should be high-priority activities. For example, the team targets 10 possible activities for a 13-year-old student who uses a wheelchair. Each of the 10 activities has met the first level of analysis; these are popular activities that are available to some degree in the student's school and in the community. The team then examines these 10 activities using the criteria listed in Figure 5.7 to determine which of the activities are most appropriate for this particular student. Weight training, aerobics, and swimming at a local health club; wheelchair road racing; and tennis emerge as the activities that receive the highest scores on the checklist; therefore, these activities are prioritized activities for this particular student.

Determine Student's Present Level of Performance

Once activities have been prioritized, the student's team has a reference against which to measure the student's present level of performance. Rather than assess *all* of the possible motor patterns, motor and perceptual-motor abilities, and fitness attributes for a particular student, only the critical skills and abilities directly related to the targeted activities need to be assessed. For example, the physical educator should measure throwing, catching, striking, and running skills if softball is a targeted skill. These motor skills will be measured in terms of *how well* the student performs the skill (i.e., qualitative assessment) as well as *how much* of the skill the student can do (i.e., quantitative assessment) (see Figures 5.8 and 5.9 for examples). Note that there is no need to measure kicking or skipping skills or other skills that are not related to the overall goal of the program.

As noted in Chapter 4, skills or characteristics associated with skilled performance such as physical fitness, general motor abilities, and perceptual skills also should be measured, but only as they relate to the skills under each targeted activity. The top-down pyramid pictured in Figure 5.2 shows how fitness and motor abilities are directly related to the skills at the top of the pyramid. This is an important difference between the ecological approach to assessment and traditional assessments that measure fitness, motor abilities, and perceptual-motor skills without reference to real skills.

For example, cardiovascular endurance is usually measured by having a student run or walk a certain distance in a specified time. Although this measure may be useful in determining a student's overall cardiovascular integrity, it does not indicate whether the student has adequate cardiovascular endurance to participate in real-life activities such as softball, soccer, basketball, swimming, or other targeted activities. A better measure of cardiovascular endurance for young students would be an appraisal of their ability to sustain various animal walks and locomotor patterns during the course of a physical education class. If the student needs to stop and rest after just a few locomotor patterns (e.g., following 2 minutes of exercise) and his peers do not need to rest until they have completed several locomotor patterns (e.g., following 10 minutes of exercise), then the student is functionally deficient in cardiovascular endurance.

Criteria	Activity 1	2	3	4	5	6	7	8	9	10	11	12
1. Can be used in current environments	—	—	—	—	—	—	—	—	—	—	—	—
2. Can be used in future environments	—	—	—	—	—	—	—	—	—	—	—	—
3. Can be used in four or more different environments	—	—	—	—	—	—	—	—	—	—	—	—
4. Affords daily opportunities for interaction	—	—	—	—	—	—	—	—	—	—	—	—
5. Increases student independence	—	—	—	—	—	—	—	—	—	—	—	—
6. Helps maintain student in, or promotes movement to, a least restrictive environment	—	—	—	—	—	—	—	—	—	—	—	—
7. Is chronologically age-appropriate	—	—	—	—	—	—	—	—	—	—	—	—
8. Student will acquire in 1 year the necessary skills to participate in the activity	—	—	—	—	—	—	—	—	—	—	—	—
9. Parents rate as a high priority	—	—	—	—	—	—	—	—	—	—	—	—
10. Promotes a positive view of the individual	—	—	—	—	—	—	—	—	—	—	—	—
11. Meets a medical need	—	—	—	—	—	—	—	—	—	—	—	—
12. Improves student's health or fitness	—	—	—	—	—	—	—	—	—	—	—	—
13. If able, student would select	—	—	—	—	—	—	—	—	—	—	—	—
14. Student shows positive response to activity	—	—	—	—	—	—	—	—	—	—	—	—
15. Advocacy, training, and other support can be arranged so that student can participate in the activity in the absence of educational services	—	—	—	—	—	—	—	—	—	—	—	—
16. Related services staff support selection of activity	—	—	—	—	—	—	—	—	—	—	—	—
17. Transportation is no barrier	—	—	—	—	—	—	—	—	—	—	—	—
18. Cost is no barrier	—	—	—	—	—	—	—	—	—	—	—	—
19. Staffing is no barrier	—	—	—	—	—	—	—	—	—	—	—	—
20. Environments are physically accessible	—	—	—	—	—	—	—	—	—	—	—	—
TOTAL	—	—	—	—	—	—	—	—	—	—	—	—

Figure 5.7. Checklist for prioritizing goals: twenty examples of criteria used for setting priorities for twelve activities. (Rating: 3 = strongly agree with statement, 2 = agree somewhat with statement, 1 = disagree somewhat with statement, 0 = disagree strongly with statement.) (From Helmstetter, E. [1989]. Curriculum for school-age students: The ecological model. In F. Brown & D.H. Lehr [Eds.], *Persons with profound disabilities: Issues and practices* [p. 254]. Baltimore: Paul H. Brookes Publishing Co.; adapted by permission.)

Quantitative Analysis for Skill Assessment

Class: _____   Date: _____

Age/grade: _____   Teacher: _____

School: _____

Skill: _____

Name	Catch balloon from 2 feet	Catch balloon from 4 feet	Catch 8-inch Nerf ball from 2 feet	Catch 8-inch Nerf ball from 4 feet	Catch 8-inch Nerf ball from 6 feet	Catch tennis ball from 3 feet	Catch tennis ball from 6 feet	Catch tennis ball tossed to side from 6 feet
	1	2	3	4	5	6	7	8
1.								
2.								
3.								
4.								
5.								

A Teacher's Guide to Including Students with Disabilities in General Physical Education
by Martin E. Block, copyright ©2000 Paul H. Brookes Publishing Co.

Figure 5.8.   Sample quantitative analysis of catching skills for preschool children.

For older students, a better measure of cardiovascular endurance is the amount of time the student can participate in targeted individual and team sports. Such a measure, though not standardized or norm-referenced, can still be objectively collected during the course of the semester to determine a student's progress. If, for example, a student needs to sit down and rest following 2 minutes of play in a game of soccer, improvement can be gauged by measuring how long the student stays actively engaged in the game by the end of the unit. Other fitness measures such as strength and flexibility as well as measures of motor abilities, perceptual-motor abilities, and functional motor patterns also should be measured with specific reference to how these factors relate to the skills targeted for the student (see Table 5.2 for another example of how abilities can be measured as they relate to functional skills).

Development of Student's Individualized Education Program

The student's IEP, including long-term goals and short-term instruction, can be formulated once the physical educator has targeted specific activities and assessed the student's present level of performance. Because the physical educator already has narrowed down the activities that constitute the student's program, formulating the IEP should be a fairly simple process. For example, tennis is one targeted activity for a particular student; therefore, the physical educator evaluates the student on his forehand, backhand, serve, and volleying skills. In addition, fitness skills such as strength (e.g., ability to hit the ball over the net from various distances) and flexibility (e.g., ability to demonstrate adequate range of motion in

Qualitative Analysis for Skill Assessment

Class:_____   Date: _____

Age/grade:_____   Teacher:_____

School: _____   Objective: <u>Catching a ball</u>

Scoring	Skill Level I	Skill Level II				Skill Level III	Primary Responses:
Assessment: Date: X=Achieved O=Not achieved /=Partially achieved	Three consecutive times						N=Not attending NR=No response UR=Unrelated response O=Other (specify in comments)
Reassessment: Date: X=Achieved O=Not achieved	Focuses eyes on ball	Stops ball with hands or hands and arms	Focuses eyes on ball	Extends arms in preparation to catch ball, with elbows at sides	Contacts and controls ball with hands or hands and arms after one bounce	Bends elbows to absorb force of ball	Two or more play or game activities at home or school demonstrating skill components over 6-week period	
Name	1	2	3	4	5	6	7	Comments
1								
2								
3								
4								
5								

Recommendations: Specific changes or conditions in planning for instructions, performance, or diagnostic testing procedures or standards. Please describe what worked best.

_____

_____

_____

_____

A Teacher's Guide to Including Students with Disabilities in General Physical Education
by Martin E. Block, copyright ©2000 Paul H. Brookes Publishing Co.

Figure 5.9. Sample qualitative analysis of catching skills for preschool children. (From Wessel, J.A., & Curtis-Pierce, E. [1990]. *Ballhandling activities: Meeting special needs of children.* Belmont, CA: Fearon Teacher Aids; adapted by permission.)

strokes and adequate range of motion for running and positioning legs) as well as perceptual skills such as eye–hand coordination (e.g., ability to hit stationary or moving ball at various heights, speeds, and trajectories) and balance (e.g., ability to move, stand, and hit ball without losing balance or falling) are measured (results of this student's assessment are in Figure 5.10). Based on the results of this

Table 5.2. Analysis of abilities and how those abilities affect kicking

Strength	Flexibility	Endurance	Eye-foot coordination	Balance	Coordination
Stand on one foot in backswing.	Bend leg in backswing.	Kick several balls during practice.	Accurately contact ball with foot.	Stand on one foot in backswing, contact, and follow through.	Interaction between upper and lower leg
Lift kicking leg up.	Bring leg forward to contact ball.			Contact and follow through.	Interaction between arms and legs
Forcefully move leg forward to kick ball.	Follow through.				Ability to plant foot next to ball
Keep arms out to side for balance.	Extend arms out to side for balance.				
Kick ball a certain distance.					

Forehand	*Demonstrates full range of motion in stroke. Has adequate strength to hold regulation racket. Has strength to hit ball over net into server box from 20 feet away (near baseline). Can hit ball off tee consistently, but when moving ball is tossed from 5 feet away, can hit ball in only one out of five trials. Qualitatively, student shows side orientation, brings arm back horizontally, and swings forward horizontally. Problems appear to be keeping eye on ball and timing.*
Backhand	*Demonstrates full range of motion in stroke. Has adequate strength to hold regulation racket. Has strength to hit ball over net into server box from 10 feet away (not from baseline). Can hit ball off tee consistently, but when moving ball is tossed from 5 feet away, only can hit ball in one out of ten trials. Qualitatively, student shows side orientation, brings arm back horizontally using two-hand pattern, and swings forward horizontally. Problems appear to be keeping eye on ball and timing.*
Serving	*Demonstrates full range of motion in stroke. Has adequate strength to hold regulation racket. Has strength to hit ball over net into server box from 10 feet away (not from baseline). Hits self-tossed ball in one out of ten trials. Qualitatively, student stands facing net, tosses ball by bending legs and tossing underhand with arm, brings racket up over head, and strikes into ball with good follow-through toward ground. Problem appears to be accuracy in toss, keeping eye on ball, and timing.*

Figure 5.10.   Functional assessment of tennis skills for high school–age student with Down syndrome.

assessment, long-term goals and short-term instructional objectives can be established for this student (Figure 5.11). Note how these goals and objectives are directly related to the student's overall program goal (i.e., to play a functional game of tennis). In addition, note how the goals and objectives are directly related to the student's present level of performance of tennis skills. It should be clear that the type of assessment used is critical in determining which types of IEP goals and

Long-term plan: *Sarah will develop the skills needed to play a beginner-level game of tennis with her peers.*

Long-term goal: *Sarah will demonstrate the ability to perform a functional forehand and backhand so that she can hit a ball back and forth with her instructor.*

Short-term instructional objectives:

1. *Sarah will demonstrate the ability to hit a tennis ball that is tossed to her from 5 feet away using the components of a skillful forehand so that she contacts the ball in four out of five trials and the ball travels over the net in three out of five trials.*

2. *Sarah will demonstrate the ability to hit a tennis ball that is tossed to her from 5 feet away using the components of a skillful, two-handed backhand so that she contacts the ball in four out of five trials and the ball travels over the net in three out of five trials.*

Figure 5.11.   IEP goals and objectives based on functional assessment of tennis skills.

objectives should be established. In the traditional approach, standardized tests often resulted in nonfunctional goals and objectives such as standing on one foot for increasing periods of time or doing an increased number of sit-ups; in contrast, in the ecological approach, balance and fitness skills are incorporated into functional goals and objectives (in this case, functional tennis goals).

Phase 3: How Should These Skills Be Taught?

The next decision is how to help the student achieve the goals outlined in his or her program. Again, Chapter 4 outlines several factors that the IEP team should consider when making instructional decisions. These factors include information on teaching style, class formats, and presentation of material (see Chapter 6 for more specific information about each of these instructional modifications).

Instructional Modifications   Figure 5.12 presents a checklist to guide the decision-making process regarding the implementation of instructional modifications. This checklist should be viewed as a tool to help the team and, most importantly, the general physical educator "brainstorm" and think about instructional modifications rather than as a tool that provides specific guidelines for instructional modifications. The important point in using this checklist is to understand that different students may need different types or levels of instruction to be successful in general physical education. Some students may respond to verbal cues, whereas others may require physical assistance. For example, most students stop when they hear a whistle, but a student who is deaf may need a hand signal. Students without disabilities might be motivated just because they enjoy the activity, whereas some students with autism or mental retardation might need alternative forms of motivation or reinforcements to try their best. Physical educators need to understand that not all students can be taught the same way. For inclusive physical education to be successful, physical educators need to be able to utilize a variety of instructional techniques.

Communication   As noted in Chapter 4, one of the most important questions regarding instruction is how to communicate with the student. One simple way to determine the best method for communicating with the student as well as how you can expect the student to communicate with you is to consult the student's speech-language therapist. A more ecologically valid approach (i.e., directly related to physical education) is to actually evaluate the way in which the student responds to varying types of cues in different physical education situations (e.g., large versus small group) (see Figure 5.13 for a sample checklist). This checklist can be used to determine how you will generally communicate with a particular student. For example, a combination of verbal cues and physical assistance might work best with a student who has a visual impairment. For another student who has a specific learning disability, environmental cues such as pictures or symbols on the wall or floor might prove most effective. Again, the speech-language therapist or adapted physical education specialist can assist with this process. Once you have a general idea of how to communicate with a particular student, repeat the process (informally as you internalize the various types of communication techniques) in various teaching–learning situations to make sure the student understands the cues you are giving.

How to Instruct the Student   The next question to ask, assuming that the student has delays in motor skill development and is not performing targeted skills correctly, is *how* to instruct the student. At this level, you should try to determine whether the student 1) does not know the correct components of the

Checklist to Determine Instructional Modifications for Students with Disabilities

Student's name: _____

P.E. class/teacher: _____

Who will implement modifications? (circle one)

GPE   classmates   peer tutor   teacher assistant   specialist

Instructional component	Things to consider	Selected modifications (if any) and comments
Teaching style	Command, problem solving, discovery	_____
Class format and size of group	Small/large group; stations/whole class instruction	_____
Level of methodology	Verbal cues, demonstrations, physical assistance	_____
Starting/stopping signals	Whistle, hand signals, physical assistance	_____
Time of day	Early A.M., late A.M., early P.M., late P.M.	_____
Duration of instruction	How long will student listen to instruction?	_____
Duration of expected participation	How long will student stay on task?	_____
Order of learning	What order will you present instruction?	_____
Instructional setting	Indoors/outdoors; part of gym/whole gym	_____
Eliminate distractors	Lighting, temperature, extra equipment	_____
Provide structure	Set organization of instruction each day	_____
Level of difficulty	Complexity of instructions/organization	_____
Levels of motivation	Make setting and activities more motivating	_____

A Teacher's Guide to Including Students with Disabilities in General Physical Education, by Martin E. Block, copyright ©2000 Paul H. Brookes Publishing Co.

Figure 5.12.   Checklist to determine instructional modifications for students with disabilities.

Checklist to Determine Communication Skills of Student

Directions: Instruct student in various situations (see below). Note how the student responds to each type of cue or combination of cues. You may need to repeat the various cues in different instructional situations (e.g., outside versus inside, simple skill versus more complex skill).

	Responds correctly	Delayed response (5–10 seconds)	Does not respond
Verbal cues			
Gestures			
Demonstration			
Environmental cues			
Physical assistance			

Situations in which this assessment was conducted (whether formally or informally):

_____ Inclusive physical education setting with peers without disabilities (large group)

_____ Inclusive physical education setting with small groups (five to seven students in each group)

_____ Inclusive physical education setting: one-to-one instruction

Figure 5.13. Checklist to determine communication skills of student.

skill and, therefore, just needs instruction and feedback or 2) knows the correct components of the skill but cannot perform the skill because of specific motor or sensory impairments. If the student does not know the components, instruction could be as simple as showing the student how to perform the skill through the use of verbal cues, physical assistance, demonstration, and/or environmental cues. For example, a 7-year-old student with mental retardation requiring intermittent support cannot perform a two-handed catch because she has received little instruction regarding how to perform this skill. In this case, the teacher simply may need to provide her with information regarding the correct pattern, specific instruction with corrective feedback, and time to practice the skill. Another 7-year-old student with a learning disability might not be able to perform a two-handed catch due to problems with visual-motor perception and body awareness. This student might require more than just instruction on how to catch; he might need supplemental practice and instruction to improve visual-motor perception and body awareness *in addition to* specific instruction in the components of the catch. Figure 5.14 provides a simple checklist to help you determine which type of instruction a student needs.

Adaptations to Skill Requirements For some students, breaking a skill down into smaller components may not be enough. For example, students

Checklist to Determine Type of Instruction Needed by Student			
	Yes	No	Comments
Does student appear to have typical sensory awareness?			
Does student appear to have typical body awareness?			
Does student appear to respond to specific instructional cues related to the targeted skill?			

Note: If the answer to some or all of the above questions is *no*, then the student might need to be checked for perceptual problems such as visual-motor problems or problems with body awareness (consult with other team members such as occupational therapist). If the student does have perceptual problems, he or she may need supplemental instruction to improve these impairments or require compensations to overcome these impairments.

A Teacher's Guide to Including Students with Disabilities in General Physical Education
by Martin E. Block, copyright ©2000 Paul H. Brookes Publishing Co.

Figure 5.14. Checklist to determine type of instruction needed by student.

with physical disabilities such as spinal cord injuries or cerebral palsy may not be able to perform skills in the same way as students without disabilities. Forcing them to perform the skill in the same manner as students without disabilities can lead to frustration and noncompliance. In addition, the student might not have enough time to work on other, more functional skills if he or she is required to learn a more fundamental skill using a particular pattern. In such cases, the student should be given an alternative way to perform the skill that meets his or her unique abilities. Again, this decision should be driven by assessment data. Figure 5.15 provides a simple checklist that can help guide this decision.

Caution should be taken when deciding if an alternative pattern should be introduced to a particular student. If the pattern does not give the student any advantage and perhaps even puts him or her at more of a disadvantage than the regular pattern, then it is not appropriate. For example, if a student has difficulty kicking a soccer ball due to spasticity in his legs, an alternative pattern may be to allow him to pick up the ball and throw it. However, because this student would not be allowed to use this alternative pattern in little league soccer games, this type of adaptation may not be very functional if the goal for the student is to be included in a soccer league. However, a student with severe spastic cerebral palsy could be allowed to throw backward over her head rather than forward to advance the ball a maximum distance. This student could then use this skill when playing horseshoes or lawn darts or when competing in the Indian club throw in sports programs for individuals with disabilities.

Curricular Adaptations   The next step is to determine whether the student needs some type of curricular adaptation or adapted equipment. Curricular adaptations and adapted equipment such as flotation devices or the use of a

Checklist to Determine Whether Student Needs Alternative Way to Perform Skill			
	Yes	No	Comments
Does student have a physical disability that appears to preclude typical performance?			
Is student having extreme difficulty performing the skill?			
Has the student made little to no progress over several months or years despite instruction?			
Does student seem more comfortable and motivated using different pattern?			
Will the alternative pattern still be useful (i.e., functional) in the targeted environments?			
Will the alternative pattern increase student's ability to perform skill?			

Note: If the answer to some or all of the above questions is *yes*, student may need an adapted pattern.

A Teacher's Guide to Including Students with Disabilities in General Physical Education
by Martin E. Block, copyright ©2000 Paul H. Brookes Publishing Co.

Figure 5.15.   Checklist to determine whether student needs alternative way to perform skill.

shorter racket during a tennis unit allow students to perform functional, lifetime leisure skills more independently. Still, students should be given every opportunity to learn skills without modifications or special equipment because such adaptations heighten the differences between students with and without disabilities and can be costly and difficult to transport. If a student has difficulty with a particular skill and you are considering curricular adaptations or adapted equipment, the questions in Figure 5.16 may help you make the decision. Once the decision has been made to utilize curricular adaptations or adapted equipment, checklists in Figures 5.17 and 5.18 can be used (see Chapters 7 and 8 for more details on curricular adaptations).

Note that some curricular adaptations and pieces of adapted equipment can be used temporarily to motivate or assist a student in learning a particular skill. If students are to use modifications or equipment only temporarily, you should develop a plan to quickly and easily wean the student from these adaptations. For example, arm flotation devices often are used to give young swimmers confidence in the water; however, it is easy for young swimmers to become dependent on these "floaties." It then becomes extremely difficult to wean the student

Checklist to Determine Whether Student Needs Adapted Equipment			
	Yes	No	Comments
Will adaptation(s) increase active participation in activity?			
Will adaptation(s) allow the student to participate in an activity that is preferred or valued by the student and his or her friends and family members?			
Will it take less time to teach the student to use the adaptation(s) than to teach the skill directly?			
Will the team have access to the technical expertise to design, construct, adjust, and repair the adaptation(s)?			
Will the use of the adaptation(s) maintain or enhance related motor/communication skills?			

Note: If the answer to most of the above questions is *yes*, then the student may need adapted equipment.

A Teacher's Guide to Including Students with Disabilities in General Physical Education
by Martin E. Block, copyright ©2000 Paul H. Brookes Publishing Co.

Figure 5.16.   Checklist to determine whether student needs adapted equipment.

away from the flotation devices so that he or she swims more independently. A systematic plan should be set up to gradually help the student swim without the aid of such devices.

Phase 4: Where Should These Skills Be Taught?

Once you have delineated a list of activities and skills, determined the student's present level of performance, written the IEP, and laid out plans regarding how to teach each skill, the next decision you should make is *where* to teach these skills. As noted in Chapter 4, data collection at this level involves comparing the student's targeted goals with the activities that take place in general physical education or community recreation (see Figure 5.19 for an example). Again, there likely will be plenty of overlap, in which case the student should be placed in general physical education with the necessary supports. Even if some general physical education activities appear to be different from those targeted for the student, the student's targeted activities can be taught to the student during general physical education.

For example, softball, bowling, swimming, and physical fitness are targeted activities for a particular student; however, the general physical education pro-

Curricular Adaptations to Accommodate Individuals with Specific Limitations

Does the student have limited strength?

Adaptations to consider	Selected modifications (if any) and comments
Shorten distance to project or move object.	_____
Use lighter equipment (e.g., lighter balls or bats).	_____
Use shorter striking implements.	_____
Allow student to sit or lie down while playing.	_____
Use deflated balls or suspended balls.	_____
Change requirements (e.g., a few jumps, then run).	_____

Does the student have limited speed?

Adaptations to consider	Selected modifications (if any) and comments
Shorten distance (or make it longer for others).	_____
Change locomotor pattern (allow running instead of walking).	_____
Designate "safe" areas in tag games.	_____

Does the student have limited endurance?

Adaptations to consider	Selected modifications (if any) and comments
Shorten distance.	_____
Shorten the playing field.	_____
Designate "safe" areas in tag games.	_____
Decrease activity time for student.	_____
Allow more rest periods for student.	_____
Allow student to sit while playing.	_____

Does the student have limited balance?

Adaptations to consider	Selected modifications (if any) and comments
Provide chair or bar for support.	_____
Teach balance techniques (e.g., widen base, extend arms).	_____
Increase width of beams to be walked.	_____
Use carpeted rather than slick surfaces.	_____
Teach students how to fall.	_____

A Teacher's Guide to Including Students with Disabilities in General Physical Education
by Martin E. Block, copyright ©2000 Paul H. Brookes Publishing Co.

Figure 5.17. Checklist to determine curricular adaptations to accommodate individuals with specific limitations. (Adapted from Sherrill, 1998.)

Figure 5.17.   (*continued*)

Allow student to sit during activity. _____

Place student near wall for support. _____

Allow student to hold peer's hand. _____

Does student have limited coordination and accuracy?

Adaptations to consider   **Selected modifications (if any) and comments**

Use stationary balls for kicking
or striking. _____

Decrease distance for throwing,
kicking, and shooting. _____

Make targets and goals larger. _____

Use larger balls for kicking and striking. _____

Increase surface area of the
striking implements. _____

Use backstop. _____

Use softer, slower balls for striking
and catching. _____

In bowling-type games, use lighter,
less stable pins. _____

Think of ways you can optimize safety. _____

* Remember, you can implement some or all of these modifications. Also, these modifications can be implemented for one child, for several children, or for the entire class to make the activity more challenging and success-oriented.

gram is beginning a basketball unit. The student with disabilities can work on fitness activities while the other students work on warm-up activities at the beginning of the class. While students without disabilities practice shooting skills, the student with disabilities can attempt to hit a softball that has been placed on a tee into a modified basket. While the student's peers work on dribbling and passing, the student with disabilities can practice pushing his wheelchair toward first base and throwing a ball to a peer, respectively. Although it may be more difficult to incorporate alternative activities into some general physical education units, most activities can be easily adapted.

Note that placement decisions are made for skills that are and will be needed in present and future environments; therefore, students should receive training in the environments in which these skills are and will be used. For elementary-age students, the most critical skills will take place in the general physical education classroom. As students reach middle school and high school, a greater number of skills may be more appropriately taught in the community (Brown et al., 1991; Sailor, Gee, & Karasoff, 1993). Upper-level high school students may spend 75% or more of their school day in the community learning job and community

Checklist to Determine Curricular Modifications for Group Games and Sports

Adaptations to consider

Selected modifications (if any) and comments

Can you vary the purpose or goal of the game?
(e.g., some students play to learn complex strategies,
others play to work on simple motor skills)

_____

Can you vary the number of players?
(e.g., play small games such as two-on-two basketball)

_____

Can you vary movement requirements?
(e.g., some students walk, others run; some hit a ball off a tee,
others hit a pitched ball; skilled students use more complex
movements, less-skilled students use simpler movements)

_____

Can you vary the field of play?
(e.g., designate special zones for students with less mobility;
make the field narrower or wider as needed; shorten the
distance for students with movement problems)

_____

Can you vary objects used?
(e.g., some students use lighter bats and larger balls;
some use a lower net and basket)

_____

Can you vary the level of organization?
(e.g., vary typical organizational patterns, where certain
students stand, the level of structure for certain students)

_____

Can you vary the limits/expectations?
(e.g., vary the number of turns each student receives;
the rules regarding how far a student can run, hit, and so forth;
how much you will enforce certain rules for certain players)

_____

Note: Use these suggestions to modify rules for both students with and without disabilities to make the game challenging, safe, and success-oriented.

A Teacher's Guide to Including Students with Disabilities in General Physical Education, by Martin E. Block, copyright ©2000 Paul H. Brookes Publishing Co.

Figure 5.18.   Checklist to determine curricular modifications group games and sports. (Adapted from Morris & Stiehl, 1999).

Comparison of Student's Goals to Activities in GPE

Directions: List the student's targeted goals in the left-hand column, activities that take place in general physical education or community recreation in the middle column, and how well these activities match in the column labeled *Match* (see figure legend for key). Then, provide suggestions for how the student can participate in general physical education/community recreation.

Student's goals	Activities in RPE/recreation	Match	Suggestion for placement
_____	_____	____	_____
_____	_____	____	_____
_____	_____	____	_____
_____	_____	____	_____
_____	_____	____	_____
_____	_____	____	_____
_____	_____	____	_____

Figure 5.19.   Comparison of student's goals to activities in GPE. (Key: *Match* column: + = activities directly match; +/- = activities can reasonably be modified; – = activities have no relation to student's goals and alternative activities are needed in GPE; 0 = activities have no relation to student's goals and alternative activities are needed outside GPE.)

skills (Brown et al., 1991). In terms of physical education, lifetime leisure skills may be taught in the community environment in which they eventually will be used. Therefore, if a student's program is vastly different from the program that takes place in general physical education and if this alternative program involves lifetime leisure activities, instructional training should take place in the community in which these skills will be used. Again, to promote inclusion, classmates without disabilities should be invited on these community trips to participate alongside students with disabilities.

Another factor in deciding where to teach the student is how well the student performs routines in the general physical education environment. As noted in Chapter 4, one way to analyze the regular routine and a particular student's performance on a specific routine is to do an *environmental inventory with a discrepancy analysis*. Such information can help the general and adapted physical education specialists determine what tasks the student can do independently or with support, on what tasks the student needs training, and what tasks need to be modified to meet the student's unique needs (see Figure 4.1 in Chapter 4 for an example).

Phase 5: How Much Support Is Needed and Who Should Provide Support?

The final step before actually implementing a program is to determine the amount of support a particular student will need and the person who will provide the support. Some students do quite well in general physical education with no extra support, whereas other students need support from their peers, volunteers, teacher assistants, or specialists. Again, ecologically referenced assessment data should guide this decision process. As noted by Rainforth and York-Barr (1997), collaboration is needed to determine the amount and type of support required by particular students.

Important factors that should be considered when determining the required level of support are the student's characteristics, the physical educator's and peers' characteristics, and the environment. Considered concurrently, these factors will help the team determine the best type of support to provide for the student. For example, York, Giangreco, Vandercook, and Macdonald (1992) noted that student characteristics such as particular abilities; previous experiences; and/or other aspects of their intellectual, communicative, social, physical, sensory, or health functioning are important factors to consider when determining levels of support. In addition, the student's behaviors in terms of his or her ability to follow directions, stay on task, and maintain control in a crowded, noisy environment are also important.

Related to the student's characteristics are the characteristics of the physical educator and the student's peers without disabilities. Physical educators and peers who know the student with disabilities, know how to successfully include students with disabilities, and have had previous experience with inclusion may need less support; whereas a physical educator who has limited knowledge of inclusion and is experiencing inclusion for the first time may require more support. Finally, environmental expectations, in this case physical education, will affect the amount of support a particular student will need. Figure 5.20 presents a checklist to help facilitate decisions regarding supports. Note how this form reads like a flowchart; the general physical educator in collaboration with other team members tries to determine how much support he or she would need to safely and successfully provide an appropriate, quality physical education program to the student with disabilities as well as to students without disabilities.

In making this important decision, the team should weigh factors such as personal (e.g., ability to dress for class, sit and wait for his or her turn, interact with his or her peers), physical (e.g., performing all of the physical education activities), and sensory (e.g., receiving information, following directions, locating certain places in the gymnasium) needs of the student; the comfort level and teaching style of the general physical educator; the level of structure in the class; and the general make-up and behaviors of the general physical education students.

Again, the types of supports that can be provided range from trained therapists to peers. In many cases, peer tutors and volunteers can provide support to students with mild disabilities, whereas specialists may need to provide support to students with severe disabilities (Block & Krebs, 1992) (see Table 5.3). Support provided by specialists often can be faded away so that the student responds to more natural cues in the environment with occasional support from his or her peers (Block, 1998). For example, a student with severe, spastic diplegic cerebral palsy who needs assistance to move his wheelchair might require the assistance

Checklist for Determining Supports in General Physical Education				
	Locker room	Warm-ups	Skills	Games
Can you handle having _____ in this situation without extra support?				
If *no,* could you handle situation with consultation from specialists?				
If *yes,* from which specialists would you like consultative support [see below]?				
Can you handle this situation on your own with consultative support?				
If *no,* can peers in class provide enough extra support (without drastically affecting their program) for you to handle the situation?				
If *no,* could an older peer tutor or volunteer provide enough support?				
If *no,* could a trained teacher assistant provide enough support?				
If *no,* could regular visits from a specialist provide enough support? (If yes, from which specialists would you like direct support [see key]?)				
Comments:				

A Teacher's Guide to Including Students with Disabilities in General Physical Education
by Martin E. Block, copyright © 2000 Paul H. Brookes Publishing Co.

Figure 5.20.   Checklist for determining supports in general physical education. (Key: APE = adapted physical educator [modifications to physical education]; SE = special educator [behavior management, personality, interests]; P = parent [interests, personality, behaviors, homework]; PT = physical therapist [gross motor needs, adapted equipment, positioning, contraindicated activities]; OT = occupational therapist [fine motor skills, adapted equipment]; ST = speech-language therapist [communication skills]; VT = vision therapist [visual skills, adaptations, mobility skills].)

of a physical therapist or adapted physical educator in general physical education. However, as the student's peers become more comfortable with the student, the specialist can begin to train the peers to assist the student in throwing balls, pushing his wheelchair, and performing other physical education activities. Again, there is no clear-cut way to determine the amount of support a particular student will need. The team should work together to make an informed decision based on as much information as they can collect regarding the student, the teacher and peers, and the environment.

Table 5.3.   Support personnel who can assist students with specific needs

Student challenge	Potential support personnel
Cognitive/learning processes	
Curricular/instructional adaptations or alternatives	Educator, speech-language pathologist, occupational therapist, psychologist, vision or hearing specialist, classmate, support facilitator
Organizing assignments, schedules	Educator, occupational therapist, speech-language pathologist, support facilitator
Communication/interaction	
Nonverbal communication	Speech-language pathologist, teacher, family member
Socialization with classmates	Speech-language pathologist, teacher, psychologist, classmates
Behaving in adaptive ways	Educator, psychologist, speech-language pathologist, classmates
Physical/motor	
Functional use of hands	Occupational therapist, physical therapist, family member, classmate
Mobility and transitions	Physical therapist, occupational therapist, orientation and mobility specialist, educator, family member, classmates
Posture (body alignment)	Physical therapist, occupational therapist
Fitness and physical activity	Physical therapist, physical educator, nurse
Sensory	
Vision	Vision specialist, occupational therapist, orientation and mobility specialist
Hearing	Audiologist, hearing specialist, speech-language pathologist
Health	
Eating difficulty	Occupational therapist, speech-language pathologist, physical therapist, nurse, educator
Medications	Nurse
Other health needs	Nurse
Current and future living	
Career and vocational pursuits	Vocational educator, counselor, educator
Leisure pursuits	Educator, occupational therapist, community recreation personnel
Support from home and community	Social worker, counselor, educator

From York, J., Giangreco, M.F., Vandercook, T., & Macdonald, C. (1992). Integrating support personnel in the inclusive classroom. In S. Stainback & W. Stainback (Eds.), *Curriculum considerations in inclusive classrooms: Facilitating learning for all students* (p. 108). Baltimore: Paul H. Brookes Publishing Co.; reprinted by permission.

Phase 6: How Well Were the Skills Taught (Ongoing Evaluation)?

The final phase of the assessment process is ongoing evaluation: a critical phase to evaluate whether the student is making progress toward his or her targeted goals. If he or she is not making adequate progress, then ongoing evaluation can help the physical educator determine the problem. If ongoing evaluations are not conducted or are conducted only at the end of a unit or semester, a student might work on skills in an incorrect way or receive inadequate instruction and feedback. For example, the IEP team of a high school student with Down syndrome decided that he should use a racquetball racket rather than a tennis racket during a tennis unit. The team based its initial assessment on the student's strength and ability to hold a regulation tennis racket. At the end of the first day, however, an evaluation of the student revealed that he performed very well with the racquetball racket but could not reach most balls that were hit toward him. Consequently, the student used a lighter regulation racket the next day, which enabled him to hold the racket *and* reach many more balls. If the student's team had waited until the end of the unit to evaluate the student, he would have used an inappropriate piece of equipment the entire time and would probably have had to relearn how to strike a tennis ball using a regulation tennis racket.

Ongoing evaluation should include all four of the previous phases of the assessment model. Ongoing Phase 1 evaluation (Does the student qualify for APE services?) can follow the same format as the initial eligibility evaluation. For example, the general physical education specialist can fill out the form found in Figure 5.4. Phase 2 evaluation (What skills do we teach?) can be as simple as talking with the student, his or her parents, and his or her peers to find out how they perceive the program. If they all observe that the program is going well and that the student is involved in appropriate activities, then the program has social validity. In addition to establishing whether the general program is appropriate, another important part of the evaluation process is to reevaluate the student's level of performance on his or her targeted skills. Effectiveness of modifications can be determined by measuring the student's progress toward targeted goals in his or her current placement and by asking the student's special education teacher, teacher assistant, general physical education teacher, and peers for their perceptions regarding how the student is performing in general physical education. As the student progresses and acquires new skills, changes should be made to his present level of performance, and expectations for the student's future progress should be modified. For example, a new goal (e.g., hopping) might be targeted for a student who has achieved the goal of demonstrating a consistent, skillful gallop much sooner than expected. Conversely, the goal for a student who is not making anticipated progress in his ability to demonstrate a skillful gallop might be modified to revisit the skills of stepping and sliding. Checklists similar to the ones shown in Figures 5.8 and 5.9 can be used to measure the student's qualitative and quantitative progress.

Ongoing evaluation of Phase 3 (How should these skills be taught?) can utilize the same evaluation forms as in the preassessment. Nothing needs to be noted if the student continues to require the same modifications to instruction as he or she required in the initial assessment. However, if the student has progressed to the point that fewer modifications are needed or if the IEP team determines that the student needs additional or different modifications, then this should be noted on the assessment forms.

Finally, ongoing evaluation of Phases 4 and 5 (Where should these skills be taught, and how much support is needed and who should provide support?) can be measured, again, by talking with the student, his peers, and the general physical educator. If the student is having difficulty in any area on the ecological inventory or is not making anticipated progress on tasks that have been targeted for training, he may need additional support. For example, the ecological inventory and discrepancy analysis suggested that a particular student needed a peer to help him change into his clothes for physical education. However, the student is taking much longer than expected in the locker room, and he and the peer are missing warm-up activities. Consequently, during ongoing evaluation, the student's IEP team decides to change the support person from a peer to a teacher assistant. In addition, the student arrives at physical education class 5 minutes earlier than his peers to make sure he has enough time to change into his uniform. Again, the ecological inventory described in Table 4.3 can be used to conduct ongoing evaluations.

Example of an Ecological Assessment to Facilitate Inclusion in Physical Education

The following example provides a look at an ecological approach to assessment for one student. John is a 10-year-old student who recently has moved into a new school district. He is diagnosed as having mental retardation requiring intermittent support; diplegic, spastic cerebral palsy, which severely limits movement in his legs and causes some loss of muscle control in his arms; and a seizure disorder that is controlled with medication. John uses a manual wheelchair for mobility, which he can push forward and maneuver around obstacles independently, although slowly. John communicates verbally with one- to two-word statements, and he seems to understand most simple directions. John can go to the bathroom and take care of his personal needs with minimal assistance (e.g., he needs help pulling up his pants, buttoning his shirt, and transferring into and out of his chair). John enjoys being with his peers and doing the same activities they do. He is a big baseball fan, his favorite team being the Chicago Cubs. Although John received special education services in his previous placement, he did not have any IEP goals for physical education. Members of John's collaborative team have scheduled a meeting to determine how they should proceed with his IEP. The adapted physical education specialist, in conjunction with the general physical education specialist and special education teacher, has been asked to assess John in order to make recommendations to the team regarding physical education services. The following sections describe, phase-by-phase, the assessment that the APE and GPE specialists and the special education teacher performed.

Phase 1: Does John Qualify for APE Services?

John's IEP team asked the general and adapted physical educators to comment on John's abilities in general physical education and to provide their recommendations for services. The report that these professionals generated can be found in Figure 5.21. Note how the results are directly applicable to John's abilities in general physical education. One of the results suggests that general physical education activities are becoming inappropriate for John. However, given John's excellent behavior and that he receives support from the adapted physical educator and the teacher assistant, the general and adapted physical educators believed

Name: _John Armstrong_   **Date:** _September 14, 2000_

Date of birth: _7-15-90_   **Evaluator:** _Susan Carter, CAPE_

Grade/class: _Fifth grade/Ms. Karish_

Introduction
John Armstrong is a 10-year-old boy in Ms. Karish's fifth-grade class. John has mental retardation requiring intermittent support; diplegic, spastic cerebral palsy such that he has very limited movement in his legs and some control over his arms; and a seizure disorder that is controlled with medication. John uses a manual wheelchair for mobility, and although he pushes it forward and maneuvers it around obstacles slowly, he does so independently. John communicates verbally with one- to two-word statements, and he seems to understand most simple directions. John currently receives physical therapy twice a week for 30 minutes each session and speech-language therapy once a week for 30 minutes per session. He has been recommended for an adapted physical education evaluation by his special education teacher due to suspected delays in gross motor development.

Abilities in reference to general physical education (GPE) curriculum
The GPE curriculum for third through fifth grades focuses on mastery of locomotor patterns, manipulative patterns, passing the physical fitness test, and introduction to individual and team sports and dance. John is unable to perform any locomotor patterns due to his disability, but he can independently move his manual wheelchair slowly around the gym and the playground. He cannot kick or punt due to his disability, but he has learned to catch and throw in his wheelchair using a modified pattern. He also can hit a ball off a tee using his hand. Although John has good upper-body strength, he has very limited flexibility both in his arms and, particularly, in his legs. He appears to have adequate endurance.

Behavioral, cognitive, and social abilities in reference to the GPE curriculum
John is an extremely well-behaved and enthusiastic student in GPE. He really wants to please and follow directions, although the GPE teacher or a peer often has to repeat complex directions for him. He interacts very well with his peers, and his peers seem to enjoy interacting with him. He is a very well-behaved student who tries to do what he is supposed to do.

Motor abilities with reference to recess and community-based recreation
John's parents report that John plays on the "Challenger Baseball Team," in which children with disabilities are provided with certain modifications. John's parents note that John does not play with other children in the neighborhood due to his limited mobility. John's classroom teacher notes that he is able to participate in very few recess activities independently. He seems to enjoy watching his peers play, and sometimes they let him play basketball or dodging games with them.

Recommendations
Based on this ecologically based assessment, it seems that John functions quite well in GPE, although he is significantly delayed compared with his peers. As he gets older and moves to middle school physical education, we feel that he will fall further behind. In addition, we feel that John needs to focus on a few long-term goals and learn them well rather than doing all the activities offered in GPE. Therefore, we recommend APE services for John to be carried out within GPE that focus on unique goals/objectives for John (APE specialist goes into GPE with John two times per week). John will have a teacher assistant accompany him to GPE the other day.

Figure 5.21.   Professionals' report with comments and recommendations for John.

that the most appropriate placement for John is still in general physical education, despite his severe disability.

Phase 2: What Skills Do We Teach?

Determining the Vision   Using the MAPS model, John's parents discussed their dreams and nightmares regarding physical education and recreation for John (see Figure 5.22). This helped the team focus from the top down on what John needs to be successful now and in the future. John's parents determined that they wanted John to 1) participate with his peers in general physical education whenever possible, and 2) develop some independent lifetime leisure skills. Their nightmare for John was that he would have no skills and no one to recreate with when he was older.

Determining What to Teach   The next phase of the assessment process involved determining what physical education skills to target for John. Information was collected in order to establish which activities John, his parents, his peers, and young adults in his community enjoy (see Figure 5.23). First, the adapted physical education specialist asked John what he would like to learn in physical education. Because John is a big baseball fan, he stated that he wants to learn how to play baseball. John also mentioned tennis; John's father noted that the family often plays tennis, but John watches from the sidelines because of his disability. Both John and his parents expressed that they would like John to be able to play tennis with the family on these weekly outings. Finally, John's mother stated that she would like to see John move his wheelchair faster, for longer periods of time, and with more precision around obstacles such as at the mall or grocery store.

Next, the adapted physical education specialist conducted a simple survey in John's school to determine which activities John's peers without disabilities like to do during recess and in their neighborhood after school. This information provides social validity to the potential activities that might be targeted for John. For example, if John's friends like to play softball and his IEP team chooses to target football skills, there is very little chance John will acquire the skills needed to play with his peers. The results of the survey revealed that the most popular recreational activities in John's neighborhood (other than computer games and watching television) are riding bikes; playing soccer in the fall, basketball in the winter, and softball in the summer; and going to the creek to fish and play in the water. Some of these activities could be targeted for John's physical education IEP; others were recommended to fellow team members, including John's parents, as suggestions for activities on which they might want to focus with John.

Next, the adapted physical education specialist conducted a second survey in John's community to determine which recreational activities are popular for young adults. Although John will not be graduating from school for some time, the severity of his physical and mental disabilities indicates that he will learn skills very slowly. Therefore, John's IEP team believes that some critical skills that John will need upon graduation should be targeted immediately. The survey revealed that the most popular active recreational activities in John's community include bowling, golf, tennis, aerobic dance, weightlifting, softball, soccer, hiking, biking, and swimming. With this information, John's team was able to determine which of these community-based recreation activities are realistic possibilities for John. For example, even though adult co-ed soccer is a popular sport in John's community, the program is very competitive. There is only one division, and only skilled players participate in the league. Given the current parameters, soccer is

Making Action Plans System (adapted for physical education planning)

What is John's history with regard to motor development, recreation, and fitness?

Due to his cerebral palsy, John has been delayed in motor development and fitness all his life. He will never be able to move like children without disabilities, so we are more interested in having him learn how to move within his abilities. John has always enjoyed watching sports on TV and trying to play with the family, especially tennis and baseball.

What is/are your dream(s) for John with reference to physical education and recreation?

- *To develop skills needed to be somewhat independent in an active recreational activity*
- *To interact and participate with peers in general physical education*
- *To have friends with similar recreation interests*

What is/are your nightmare(s)?

- *For John to be isolated from his peers*
- *For John to go through life without any skills necessary for him to do something with his leisure time*
- *For John to be alone as an adult with no friends*

Who is John with reference to physical education and recreation?

John is a boy who wants to be active but is limited by his disability. He really enjoys sports and being with his peers and family in physical education and recreation—even if he is only cheering others on.

What are John's strengths, gifts, and abilities with reference to physical education and recreation?

- *His enthusiasm for life*
- *His upbeat attitude about everything*
- *His love of friends and being part of the group*
- *His unique way of making others feel good about themselves*
- *His unselfishness*

What does John need to make the dream come true and avoid the nightmare?

- *Support for John in general physical education to participate successfully*
- *Support for the general physical education teacher to make modifications for John*
- *Training for peers to make sure they understand how to help and accept John*
- *Extra practice on targeted lifetime leisure skills if John is going to develop these skills*

What would John's ideal day in PE look like? What needs to be done for this to happen?

- *Participation in general physical education with peers who support, respect, and appreciate him*
- *Participation in some general physical education activities with modifications so he can be successful*
- *Time to work on his targeted skills*

What is our plan of action for physical education?

- *Define a long-term plan with targeted goals and objectives for John.*
- *Place John in general physical education to work on these goals but also to provide opportunities to interact and participate with peers.*
- *Provide extra time for John to work on his unique goals.*

Figure 5.22. Making Action Plans System questions completed for John. (Adapted from Falvey, Pearpoint, and Rosenberg, 1997.)

Making Curriculum Decisions

Directions: List appropriate activities under each of the following headings. Then scan the list, and place activities that are in more than one column under *Targeted activities*.

Student's preferences	Parents' preferences	Activities in GPE	Neighborhood activities played by peers	Community leisure activities
Baseball	Tennis	Lead-up	Bike riding	Softball
Tennis	Wheelchair	games and	Soccer	Swimming
	mobility	skills to	Basketball	Weight training
		a variety	Softball	Aerobics
		of team	Fishing	Wheelchair
		sports		mobility

Targeted activities: 1. Softball   3. Tennis

2. Wheelchair mobility   4. General fitness

Figure 5.23. Curriculum decisions for John.

not an appropriate activity for John. However, adult co-ed softball is another popular sport in John's community, and this program is large enough to have several divisions. As it turns out, Division C is specifically designed for people who are just learning to play softball or for those who just want to have fun. Such a division might be willing to let John participate, especially if John can learn some key softball skills such as batting, pushing his wheelchair toward first base, tossing a ball to a peer, and understanding the general rules and etiquette of the game. The team also determined that swimming, weight training, and aerobics could be targeted for John because these activities can be easily adapted to accommodate John's unique needs.

Based on the team's preliminary assessment, team members determined that softball, tennis, wheelchair mobility, and general fitness (strength and endurance in pushing his wheelchair) are activities that should be the main focus of John's program (see Figure 5.23). Tennis is an activity in which John and his parents are interested, and it is an activity that John can play now and when he leaves school. Softball appears to be a popular sport played by John's peers during recess and after school. Softball also is a lifetime recreational sport that likely will be available to John when he leaves school. Because John had already expressed an interest in baseball, the team determined that softball would be a motivating activity for him. Finally, wheelchair mobility, including improved strength, endurance, and control, is a skill that John's parents have targeted. Mobility skills can be worked on in a variety of physical education activities, and improved wheelchair skills will help John in both targeted physical education skills (e.g., tennis, softball) and community skills (e.g., shopping).

Determine John's Present Level of Performance   The second phase of the assessment was to determine John's present level of performance in motor skills and abilities, physical fitness, perceptual-motor abilities, and cognitive abilities. Because John's team already has targeted specific activities—namely tennis, softball, and mobility—for John, the APE specialist has a reference point from which to measure John's present level of performance. For example, skills that John will need to participate in softball include throwing, catching, striking, and wheelchair mobility. The team measured these skills both qualitatively and quantitatively. Qualitative measurement involves analyzing how John performs these skills (see Figure 5.24 for an example) and the underlying fitness and perceptual abilities needed to perform these skills (Table 5.4). Quantitative measurement might include counting the number of balls John can hit in five tries, the distance he can throw, and the rate of speed at which he can push his wheelchair from home to first base.

During the assessment, John's team noted that his wheelchair mobility skills on the softball field were limited. Although he could push his wheelchair forward slowly toward first base, he was not fast enough to be "safe" in most situations. John was able to hit the ball off a tee three out of four tries so that the ball traveled approximately 10 feet. Cognitively, John understood the general concept and rules of softball. He was able to stay on task during the entire assessment process (15 minutes), and he seemed motivated and receptive to instruction.

Note how the information obtained from these types of assessments (qualitative and quantitative) is directly applicable to the skills on which John needs to work in relation to his targeted skills and to determining ways that John's teacher might go about teaching those skills (e.g., shortening the distance to first base for John, allowing him to hit a ball off a tee, providing assistance when John is in the field to compensate for John's limited skills).

Develop John's Individualized Education Program   The team's next step was to develop John's IEP. Again, the development of the IEP should be a team approach that is based on assessment information. The bulk of the information regarding the physical education goals on John's IEP is based on the assessment of his present level of performance on the targeted skills. Figure 5.25 shows the softball portion of John's IEP. Note how the team arrived at these objectives based on the long-term vision and the targeted goals they had established for John and on his present level of performance.

Phase 3: How Should These Skills Be Taught?

During Phase 3 of the assessment, the team wanted to determine how to help John work on his goals and objectives. Data that were needed to make this decision included general information regarding possible instructional modifications as well as specific information regarding John's communication skills and whether John has any perceptual or motor problems, can perform a particular movement in the traditional way, or needs adapted equipment. Information obtained from the checklists in Figures 5.26 through 5.30 helped the physical educator determine how best to teach John. For example, the team discovered that John responds quite well to verbal cues and physical assistance but does not do well with demonstrations. Similarly, John seems to have the range of motion, strength, and perceptual skills that he needs to respond to general instructional cues. He should be able to generally perform the skill the same way his peers do, but some slight

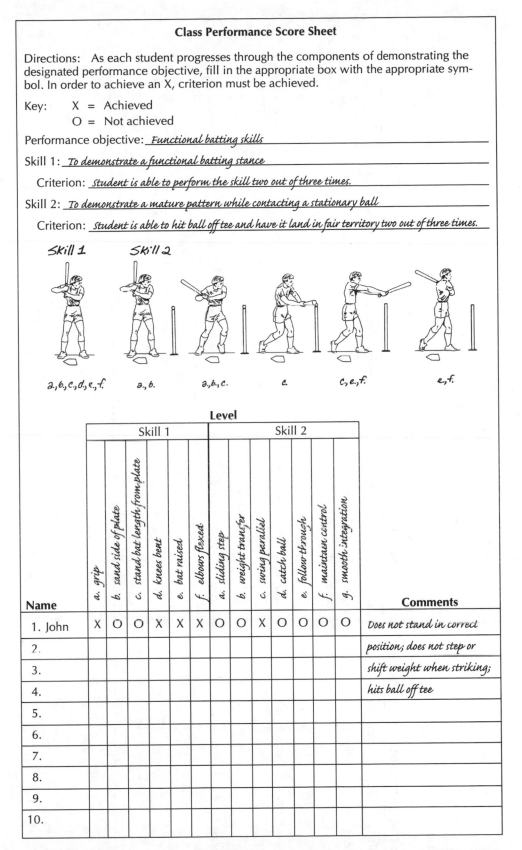

Class Performance Score Sheet

Directions: As each student progresses through the components of demonstrating the designated performance objective, fill in the appropriate box with the appropriate symbol. In order to achieve an X, criterion must be achieved.

Key: X = Achieved
       O = Not achieved

Performance objective: _Functional batting skills_

Skill 1: _To demonstrate a functional batting stance_

  Criterion: _student is able to perform the skill two out of three times._

Skill 2: _To demonstrate a mature pattern while contacting a stationary ball_

  Criterion: _student is able to hit ball off tee and have it land in fair territory two out of three times._

Skill 1   Skill 2

a., b., c., d., e., f.   a., b.   a., b., c.   c.   c., e., f.   e., f.

Level

Name	Skill 1						Skill 2							Comments
	a. grip	b. sand side of plate	c. stand bat length from plate	d. knees bent	e. bat raised	f. elbows flexed	a. sliding step	b. weight transfer	c. swing parallel	d. catch ball	e. follow-through	f. maintain control	g. smooth integration	
1. John	X	O	O	X	X	X	O	O	X	O	O	O	O	_Does not stand in correct position; does not step or shift weight when striking; hits ball off tee_
2.														
3.														
4.														
5.														
6.														
7.														
8.														
9.														
10.														

Figure 5.24. Qualitative analysis of John's softball skills. (Adapted from Wessel, J.A., & Kelly, L. [1986]. *Achievement-based curriculum development in physical education.* Philadelphia: Lea & Febiger.)

Table 5.4. Fitness, perceptual-motor, and cognitive requirements to play softball

Skills	Strength	Flexibility	Stamina	Perceptual motor	Fundamental motor	Cognitive
Batting	Hold bat.	Twist trunk. Bend and extend arms.	Stand at plate for up to 5 minutes.	See ball. Timing	Striking	Differentiate between balls and strikes.
Base running	Leg strength (arm strength if pushing wheelchair)	Bend legs and arms.	Run to first base and possibly around all bases.	Locate first base. Stay in base path.	Running	Know when to run.
Fielding	Hold mitt.	Bend and move to ball.	Stand in field for entire inning.	Locate ball when hit. Move to ball. Timing Locate person to whom to throw.	Catching Throwing ball. Know where to stand.	Know where to throw.

> **Long-term plan:** *John will demonstrate the skills needed to play in a modified game of softball with peers in school and in the community.*
>
> **Long-term goal:** *John will demonstrate functional competency in striking a pitched ball, pushing wheelchair to first base, and throwing ball to peer in practice situations.*
>
> **Short-term instructional objectives:**
>
> 1. *John will demonstrate the ability to push his wheelchair from home plate to first base that is 30 feet away (half the distance of regulation softball) in 30 seconds or in three out of four trials.*
>
> 2. *John will hit a pitched Nerf ball holding two hands on the bat and using a horizontal striking pattern that includes follow-through across body when ball is tossed slowly from 10 feet away in three out of four trials.*
>
> 3. *John will throw a ball overhand so that the ball travels a distance of 10 feet and within 1 foot to either side of peer to whom he is throwing in three out of four trials.*

Figure 5.25. Softball portion of John's IEP.

modifications—such as using a lighter bat for softball, pushing his chair to a closer base, and having a peer assist him in the field—seem appropriate. In addition, John should be encouraged to try different ways of performing each movement to determine which works best for him.

Once the team decided that John needs adaptations, Figures 5.31 and 5.32 were used to determine specific modifications. In many cases, modifications for students with disabilities are rather simple and really do not affect students without disabilities. Note that these checklists were filled out in general terms without any specific activities in mind. The team should glance over these checklists again, if not actually complete them, prior to each new physical education unit.

Phase 4: Where Should These Skills Be Taught?

The next phase of the assessment process involved determining where John should work on targeted skills. The team accomplished this by examining the curriculum for the fourth, fifth, and sixth grades at John's school. The philosophy of the physical education program at John's school is to expose students to and provide some foundational skills in a variety of individual and team sports, including lifetime leisure skills. Providing a basic foundation in a variety of activities in middle school helps students make informed choices as to which activities they want to focus on when they go to high school (high school physical education follows an elective format). Table 5.5 lists the specific activities at John's school and the time of the year that they are targeted.

A general inspection of the middle school physical education curriculum suggested to John's team that John's peers will be working on softball in the spring of the fifth grade and tennis in the fall of the sixth grade. The team determined that John should be included in these units (with necessary modifications) so that he can work on his targeted goals. However, the team needed to determine which skills John should practice when his class works on other activities. When can John be included and when might it be appropriate to remove John so

Checklist to Determine Instructional Modifications for Students with Disabilities

Student's name: _John_

P.E. class/teacher: _Mrs. Smith, 2nd period_

Who will implement modifications? (circle one)

(GPE) (Classmates) peer tutor teacher assistant specialist

Instructional component	Things to consider	Selected modifications (if any) and comments
Teaching style	Command, problem solving, discovery	_none_
Class format and size of group	Small/large group; stations/whole class instruction	_none_
Level of methodology	Verbal cues, demonstrations, physical assistance	_extra physical assistance_
Starting/stopping signals	Whistle, hand signals, physical assistance	_none_
Time of day	Early A.M., late A.M., early P.M., late P.M.	_mornings better_
Duration of instruction	How long will student listen to instruction?	_none_
Duration of expected participation	How long will student stay on task?	_give extra rest in endurance activities_
Order of learning	What order will you present instruction?	_none_
Instructional setting	Indoors/outdoors; part of gym/whole gym	_none_
Eliminate distractors	Lighting, temperature, extra equipment	_none_
Provide structure	Set organization of instruction each day	_none_
Level of difficulty	Complexity of instructions/organization	_make instruction and organization simpler_
Levels of motivation	Make setting and activities more motivating	_none_

Figure 5.26. Checklist to determine instructional modifications for John.

Checklist to Determine Communication Skills of Student

Directions: Instruct student in various situations (see below). Note how the student responds to each type of cue or combination of cues. You may need to repeat the various cues in different instructional situations (e.g., outside versus inside, simple skill versus more complex skill).

	Responds correctly	Delayed response (5–10 seconds)	Does not respond
Verbal cues	✓		
Gestures		✓	
Demonstration		✓	
Environmental cues	✓		
Physical assistance	✓		

Situations in which this assessment was conducted (whether formally or informally):

__✓__ Inclusive physical education setting with peers without disabilities (large group)

_____ Inclusive physical education setting with small groups (five to seven students in each group)

_____ Inclusive physical education setting: one-to-one instruction

---

Figure 5.27. Checklist to determine communication skills (completed for John).

that he can focus on his specific goals and objectives? Figure 5.33 summarizes the team's solutions as to how John can be included in general physical education activities. Badminton in the seventh grade is a sport similar to tennis, and, in fact, the lighter racket and birdie actually might be a useful adaptation for John. Therefore, John should probably stay in general physical education for this activity. Similarly, aerobics, weight training, and rollerskating or rollerblading are activities that can help John improve his strength, flexibility, and endurance. Weight training (i.e., improving strength and flexibility) can concentrate on the muscle groups that John uses to propel his wheelchair, and aerobics can improve John's endurance. For rollerskating or rollerblading, John can practice pushing his wheelchair following the same course his peers follow on their skates or blades. When the class goes to a local roller rink at the end of the unit, John can go along and push his wheelchair. Golf, bowling, and archery are lifetime leisure activities that are available in John's community. John might find these lifetime leisure sports enjoyable; in fact, perhaps John will find some or all of these activities so appealing that they will become targeted goals for him when he enters high school. Taking these things into consideration, the team decided that John should stay in general physical education part of the time for these activities (2 days per week) so that he can learn what they are about. On the remaining 3 days of the week, they established that he should receive specialized adapted physical education to work on his targeted goals.

Now the team needed to determine whether John should participate in soccer, volleyball, and basketball. Although these activities can be modified so that

Checklist to Determine Type of Instruction Needed by Student			
	Yes	No	Comments
Does student appear to have typical sensory awareness?	✓		*slower reaction*
Does student appear to have typical body awareness?	✓		
Does student appear to respond to specific instructional cues related to the targeted skill?	✓		*except demonstrations*

Note: If the answer to some or all of the above questions is *no*, then the student might need to be checked for perceptual problems such as visual-motor problems or problems with body awareness (consult with other team members such as occupational therapist). If the student does have perceptual problems, he or she may need supplemental instruction to improve these impairments or require compensations to overcome these impairments.

Figure 5.28.   Checklist to determine type of instruction needed by student (completed for John).

John can have a safe and successful experience, they are not high-priority goals for John. Because it is going to take John a long time to learn to master even the basic skills of tennis and softball, exposing John to other activities would take away important instructional time (Kelly et al., 1991). However, these team sports are popular with John's peers during various seasons of the year, and it would be nice if John had at least a general understanding of the skills, rules, and flow of the game. In addition, some of John's fitness and mobility goals can easily be incorporated into these sports. The team decided that John should work on tennis during the soccer unit because it is difficult to get John up to the soccer field and move his wheelchair on the grass. However, the team recommended that John participate in volleyball and basketball 2 days per week and work on his targeted skills the other 3 days per week. Although it is understood that John likely will not acquire the skills for volleyball and basketball, exposing him to these sports might be of interest to him; in addition, it would give him a chance to interact with his peers and work on his fitness and mobility skills in a different context and give him a break from focusing solely on tennis and softball. The team decided that several (five to seven) of John's peers could go with John on the days he is pulled out of general physical education These students without disabilities should not serve as peer tutors to John but should participate alongside John in his targeted activities. Different students could be picked each day to go with John and John's teacher assistant (therefore, each student would only miss one day of physical education).

Next, daily requirements in general physical education—including communication, self-help, social/emotional considerations, and motor skills—were measured. This information helped John's team determine which specific skills John will need to be safe and successful in general physical education as well as suggestions for support and accommodations that John might need. Information

Checklist to Determine Whether Student Needs Alternative Way to Perform Skill			
	Yes	No	Comments
Does student have a physical disability that appears to preclude typical performance?	✓		*John's disability affects quantitive performance*
Is student having extreme difficulty performing the skill?		✓	
Has the student made little to no progress over several months or years despite instruction?		✓	
Does student seem more comfortable and motivated using different pattern?		✓	
Will alternative pattern still be useful (i.e., functional) in the targeted environments?		✓	
Will the alternative pattern increase student's ability to perform skill?		✓	
Note: If the answer to some or all of the above questions is *yes*, student may need an adapted pattern.			

Figure 5.29. Checklist to determine whether student needs alternative way to perform skill (completed for John).

from the ecological inventory and discrepancy analysis revealed that John can follow most routines independently. For the skills with which he has difficulty, the team decided that a peer could assist John. John does have difficulty with self-help skills; therefore, he will need peer assistance changing into his physical education clothes. The occupational therapist suggested to John's parents that John wear pants with an elastic waist and pullover shirts so that he can dress faster and more independently. It does not appear that John will need more time than his peers to change into his gym clothes. The discrepancy analysis also showed that John did not have any communication problems, although a peer might have to repeat more complex directions to him. Also, John is a motivated, well-behaved learner who has no major behavior problems.

Phase 5: How Much Support Is Needed and Who Should Provide Support?

John will need some support in general physical education if he is going to be successful; however, the general physical educator and John's peers without dis-

Checklist to Determine Whether Student Needs Adapted Equipment			
	Yes	No	Comments
Will adaptation(s) increase active participation in activity?	✓		*Allows for more success*
Will adaptation(s) allow the student to participate in an activity that is preferred or valued by the student and his or her friends and family members?	✓		*Popular sport that John likes*
Will it take less time to teach the student to use the adaptation(s) than to teach the skill directly?	✓		*He may never be able to participate without some adaptations.*
Will the team have access to the technical expertise to design, construct, adjust, and repair the adaptation(s)?	✓		*Adapted physical education specialist*
Will the use of the adaptation(s) maintain or enhance related motor/communication skills?	✓		*Allow more interaction with peers and more opportunities to play in game.*
Note: If the answer to most of the above questions is *yes*, then the student may need adapted equipment.			

Figure 5.30.   Checklist to determine whether student needs adapted equipment (completed for John).

abilities feel very comfortable with John. Therefore, the team, utilizing the checklist in Figure 5.34, decided that the physical therapist and adapted physical educator could come into general physical education with John initially and provide information to the general physical educator and peers regarding how to work with John, position him, help him get dressed and undressed, practice skills, and so forth. These specialists can then monitor how well John's peers assist him and, eventually, back off and provide consultations as needed (perhaps coming in to see John and discuss his program with the general physical educator at the beginning, middle, and end of each unit).

Phase 6: How Well Were These Skills Taught (Ongoing Evaluation)?

Once the plan has been initiated, the final phase of the assessment process is ongoing evaluation. John's team realizes that ongoing evaluation is critical to determine whether John is making progress toward his targeted goals. If he is not making adequate progress, ongoing evaluation can help the IEP team quickly discover the problem. For example, John's APE teacher initially decided that a large WIFFLE ball bat was better than a regulation bat for John when he practiced striking skills; however, this bat also proved to be too heavy and too long for John. Because John plays tennis as well as softball, his lighter tennis racket was

Curricular Adaptations to Accommodate Individuals with Specific Limitations

Does the student have limited strength?

Adaptations to consider	Selected modifications (if any) and comments
Shorten distance to project or move object.	*John can be closer than peers*
Use lighter equipment (e.g., lighter balls or bats).	*Lighter, smaller bat and balls*
Use shorter striking implements.	*Cut racket/bat at handle*
Allow student to sit or lie down while playing.	*Sit in chair*
Use deflated balls or suspended balls.	*None*
Change requirements (e.g., a few jumps, then run).	*Push wheelchair*

Does the student have limited speed?

Adaptations to consider	Selected modifications (if any) and comments
Shorten distance (or make it longer for others).	*Shorter distance for John*
Change locomotor pattern (allow running instead of walking).	*Push wheelchair*
Designate "safe" areas in tag games.	*None*

Does the student have limited endurance?

Adaptations to consider	Selected modifications (if any) and comments
Shorten distance.	*Push wheelchair for time, not distance*
Shorten the playing field.	*Set up John's own "special zone"*
Designate "safe" areas in tag games.	*None*
Decrease activity time for student.	*Extra rest as needed*
Allow more rest periods for student.	*None*
Allow student to sit while playing.	*Yes*

Does the student have limited balance?

Adaptations to consider	Selected modifications (if any) and comments
Provide chair or bar for support.	*Sit in chair*
Teach balance techniques (e.g., widen base, extend arms).	*None*
Increase width of beams to be walked.	*None*
Use carpeted rather than slick surfaces.	*None*
Teach students how to fall.	*None*
Allow student to sit during activity.	*Yes*

Figure 5.31. Checklist to determine curricular adaptations to accommodate individuals with specific limitations (completed for John). (Adapted from Sherrill, 1998.)

Figure 5.31. (continued)

Place student near wall for support.	_None_
Allow student to hold peer's hand.	_None_

Does student have limited coordination and accuracy?

Adaptations to consider	Selected modifications (if any) and comments
Use stationary balls for kicking or striking.	_Yes_
Decrease distance for throwing, kicking, and shooting.	_John can stand closer_
Make targets and goals larger.	_Yes_
Use larger balls for kicking and striking.	_Yes_
Increase surface area of the striking implements.	_Yes (larger bat/racket)._
Use backstop.	_Tie string to chair for easy retrieval_
Use softer, slower balls for striking and catching.	_Nerf balls_
In bowling-type games, use lighter, less stable pins.	_Yes_
Think of ways you can optimize safety.	_Make peers aware of John; place him in skilled group that can retrieve balls_

* Remember, you can implement some or all of these modifications. Also, these modifications can be implemented for one child, for several children, or for the entire class to make the activity more challenging and success-oriented.

then used for striking in softball; this helped John to be much more successful. Similarly, John has begun to demonstrate slight rotation in his trunk when he throws the ball; therefore, his program has been adjusted so that greater rotation during throwing is a targeted skill (see Figure 5.35 for simple ongoing evaluation form).

Through ongoing evaluation, John's team discovered that John is making slower-than-expected progress on pushing his wheelchair to first base. Discussions with John, his peers, and his teachers as well as observations revealed that John has difficulty keeping his chair on the base path, which causes him to run onto the infield grass. Therefore, the IEP team modified this goal; a peer is now assigned to John to help him keep his chair straight, and extra work in physical education, in the classroom, and at home are assigned to help John push his chair with greater accuracy. Finally, it was determined that John was having difficulty getting out of his chair (even with assistance from a peer) to do push-ups and sit-ups during warm-ups. In fact, it takes John so long to get out of his chair that he never gets a chance to do these exercises. Therefore, a new modification was suggested in which John stays in his chair and works on pushing himself up out of his chair (actually, a more functional strength activity for John). Also, John now does "sit-ups" by isometrically contracting his abdominal muscles on one count and stretching his lower back by bending forward on the next count.

Checklist to Determine Curricular Modifications for Group Games and Sports

Adaptations to consider	Selected modifications (if any) and comments
Can you vary the purpose or goal of the game? (e.g., some students play to learn complex strategies, others play to work on simple motor skills)	*John will work on skill development and understanding basic rules.*
Can you vary the number of players? (e.g., play small games such as two-on-two basketball)	*Have smaller groups with John.*
Can you vary movement requirements? (e.g., some students walk, others run; some hit a ball off a tee, others hit a pitched ball; skilled students use more complex movements, less-skilled students use simpler movements)	*Hit off tee, smaller basket; push chair instead of running.*
Can you vary the field of play? (e.g., designate special zones for students with less mobility; make the field narrower or wider as needed; shorten the distance for students with movement problems)	*Set up special zone for John in basketball and soccer; shorten distance to first base.*
Can you vary objects used? (e.g., some students use lighter bats and larger balls; some use a lower net and basket)	*Use lighter equipment and larger and closer targets.*
Can you vary the level of organization? (e.g., vary typical organizational patterns, where certain students stand, the level of structure for certain students)	*John will have set position.*
Can you vary the limits/expectations? (e.g., vary the number of turns each student receives; the rules regarding how far a student can run, hit, and so forth; how much you will enforce certain rules for certain players)	*Do not enforce rules with John; John gets turn every third time in basketball.*

Note: Use these suggestions to modify rules for both students with and without disabilities to make the game challenging, safe, and success-oriented.

Figure 5.32. Checklist to determine curricular modifications for group games and sports (completed for John). (Adapted from Morris & Stiehl 1999.)

Table 5.5. GPE activities and quarter in which they are targeted in different grades

Quarter	Fifth grade	Sixth grade	Seventh grade
1st	Soccer	Tennis	Roller skating/blading
2nd	Volleyball	Aerobics	Badminton
3rd	Basketball	Weight training	Bowling
4th	Softball	Golf	Archery

Comparison of Student's Goals to Activities in GPE

Directions: List the student's targeted goals in the left-hand column, activities that take place in general physical education or community recreation in the middle column, and how well these activities match in the column labeled *Match* (see figure legend for key). Then, provide suggestions for how the student can participate in general physical education/community recreation.

Student's goals	Activities in RPE/recreation	Match	Suggestion for placement
softball	*softball*	+	*GPE*
tennis	*tennis*	+	*GPE*
fitness	*aerobics/weight training*	+	*GPE*
wheelchair mobility	*soccer*	+/−	*GPE w/modifications*
	basketball	+/−	*GPE w/modifications*
	lifetime leisure activities	0	*John can either work on his goals at another*
	(e.g. bowling, archery, golf)		*station or be exposed to these activities with peers*

Figure 5.33. Comparison of student's goals to activities in GPE completed for John. (Key: *Match* column: + = activities directly match; +/− = activities can reasonably be modified; − = activities have no relation to student's goals and alternative activities are needed in GPE; 0 = activities have no relation to student's goals and alternative activities are needed outside GPE.)

Checklist for Determining Supports in General Physical Education	Locker room	Warm-ups	Skills	Games
Can you handle having _John_ in this situation without extra support?	No	No	No	No
If *no,* could you handle situation with consultation from specialists?	Yes	Yes	Yes	Yes
If *yes,* from which specialists would you like consultative support [see below]?	APE, PT	APE, PT	APE, PT	APE, PT
Can you handle this situation on your own with consultative support?	No	No	No	No
If *no,* can peers in class provide enough extra support (without drastically affecting their program) for you to handle the situation?	probably yes	probably yes	probably yes	probably yes
If *no,* could an older peer tutor or volunteer provide enough support?				
If *no,* could a trained teacher assistant provide enough support?				
If *no,* could regular visits from a specialist provide enough support? (If yes, from which specialists would you like direct support [see key]?)	I would like this	I would like this	I would like this	I would like this

Comments: *I think if I get some ideas from the PT & APE along with help from peers, I should be able to manage with John.*

Figure 5.34. Checklist for determining supports in general physical education completed for John. (Key: APE = adapted physical educator [modifications to physical education]; SE = special educator [behavior management, personality, interests]; P = parent [interests, personality, behaviors, homework]; PT = physical therapist [gross motor needs, adapted equipment, positioning, contraindicated activities]; OT = occupational therapist [fine motor skills, adapted equipment]; ST = speech-language therapist [communication skills]; VT = vision therapist [visual skills, adaptations, mobility skills].)

	Days										
Activities	1	2	3	4	5	6	7	8	9	10	11
Hits pitched Nerf ball with WIFFLE ball bat	+/–	+/–	+/–	+/–	+	+	+	+			
Throws ball overhand 10 feet with rotation	+/–	+/–	+/–	+	+	+	+	+			
Pushes wheelchair to first base in 30 seconds	–	–	–	–	–	–	–	–			

Figure 5.35. John's ongoing progress report for softball. (Key: + = successful; – = not successful)

Appendix

Legal Description of Evaluation Procedures Outlined in PL 105-17, Part B, Section 614

(a) Evaluations and Reevaluations
(1) Initial Evaluations
(A) In General—A State educational agency, other State agency, or local educational agency shall conduct a full and individual initial evaluation, in accordance with this paragraph and subsection (b), before the initial provision of special education and related services to a child with a disability under this part.
(B) Procedures—Such initial evaluation shall consist of procedures—
(i) to determine whether a child is a child with a disability (as defined in section 602(3)); and
(ii) to determine the educational needs of such child.
(C) Parental Consent—
(i) In General—The agency proposing to conduct an initial evaluation to determine if the child qualifies as a child with a disability as defined in section 602(3)(A) or 602(3)(B) shall obtain an informed consent from the parent of such child before the evaluation is conducted. Parental consent for evaluation shall not be construed as consent for placement for receipt of special education and related services.
(ii) Refusal—If the parents of such child refuse consent for the evaluation, the agency may continue to pursue an evaluation by utilizing the mediation and due process procedures under section 615, except to the extent inconsistent with State law relating to parental consent.
(2) Reevaluations—A local educational agency shall ensure that a reevaluation of each child with a disability is conducted—
(A) if conditions warrant a reevaluation or if the child's parent or teacher requests a reevaluation, but at least once every 3 years; and
(B) in accordance with subsections (b) and (c).
(b) Evaluation Procedures—
(1) Notice—The local educational agency shall provide notice to the parents of a child with a disability, in accordance with subsections (b)(3), (b)(4), and (c) of section 615, that describes any evaluation procedures such agency proposes to conduct.
(2) Conduct of Evaluation—In conducting the evaluation, the local educational agency shall—
(A) use a variety of assessment tools and strategies to gather relevant func-

tional and developmental information, including information provided by the parent, that may assist in determining whether the child is a child with a disability and the content of the child's individualized education program, including information related to enabling the child to be involved in and progress in the general curriculum or, for preschool children, to participate in appropriate activities;

(B) not use any single procedure as the sole criterion for determining whether a child is a child with a disability or determining an appropriate educational program for the child; and

(C) use technically sound instruments that may assess the relative contribution of cognitive and behavioral factors, in addition to physical or developmental factors.

(3) Additional Requirements—Each local educational agency shall ensure that,

(A) tests and other evaluation materials used to assess a child under this section—

(i) are selected and administered so as not to be discriminatory on a racial or cultural basis; and

(ii) are provided and administered in the child's native language or other mode of communication, unless it is clearly not feasible to do so; and

(B) any standardized tests that are given to the child—

(i) have been validated for the specific purpose for which they are used;

(ii) are administered by trained and knowledgeable personnel; and

(iii) are administered in accordance with any instructions provided by the producer of such tests;

(C) the child is assessed in all areas of suspected disability; and

(D) assessment tools and strategies that provide relevant information that directly assists persons in determining the educational needs of the child are provided.

(4) Determination of Eligibility—Upon completion of administration of tests and other evaluation materials—

(A) the determination of whether the child is a child with a disability as defined in section 602(3) shall be made by a team of qualified professionals and the parent of the child in accordance with paragraph (5); and

(B) a copy of the evaluation report and the documentation of determination of eligibility will be given to the parent.

(5) Special Rule for Eligibility Determination—In making a determination of eligibility under paragraph (4)(A), a child shall not be determined to be a child with a disability if the determinant factor for such determination is lack of instruction in reading or math or limited English proficiency.

(c) Additional Requirements for Evaluations and Reevaluations—

(1) Review of Existing Evaluation Data—As part of an initial evaluation (if appropriate) and as part of any reevaluation under this section, the IEP Team described in subsection (d)(1)(B) and other qualified professionals, as appropriate, shall—

(A) review existing evaluation data on the child, including evaluations and information provided by the parents of the child, current classroom-based assessments and observations, and teacher and related services providers observation; and

(B) on the basis of that review, and input from the child's parents, identify what additional data, if any, are needed to determine—

(i) whether the child has a particular category of disability, as described in section 602(3), or, in case of a reevaluation of a child, whether the child continues to have such a disability;

(ii) the present levels of performance and educational needs of the child;

(iii) whether the child needs special education and related services, or in the case of a reevaluation of a child, whether the child continues to need special education and related services; and

(iv) whether any additions or modifications to the special education and related services are needed to enable the child to meet the measurable annual goals set out in the individualized education program of the child and to participate, as appropriate, in the general curriculum.

(2) Source of Data—The local educational agency shall administer such tests and other evaluation materials as may be needed to produce the data identified by the IEP Team under paragraph (1)(B).

(3) Parental Consent—Each local educational agency shall obtain informed parental consent, in accordance with subsection (a)(1)(C), prior to conducting any reevaluation of a child with a disability, except that such informed parent consent need not be obtained if the local educational agency can demonstrate that it had taken reasonable measures to obtain such consent and the child's parent has failed to respond.

(4) Requirements If Additional Data Are Not Needed—If the IEP Team and other qualified professionals, as appropriate, determine that no additional data are needed to determine whether the child continues to be a child with a disability, the local educational agency—

(A) shall notify the child's parents of—

(i) that determination and the reasons for it; and

(ii) the right of such parents to request an assessment to determine whether the child continues to be a child with a disability; and

(B) shall not be required to conduct such an assessment unless requested to by the child's parents.

(5) Evaluations Before Change in Eligibility—A local educational agency shall evaluate a child with a disability in accordance with this section before determining that the child is no longer a child with a disability.

6

Instructional Modifications

Inclusion works for me when I choose activities that blend the needs of all the children in class with the outcome of successful experiences. . . . I am researching and exploring teaching techniques and settings with children with developmental coordination disorder (DCD). I am finding that increased communication with them during the day in non-PE settings increases confidence, comfort and reduces withdrawal in the PE setting. I talk with these children about how they would feel more comfortable and what would help them be more successful and have more fun. . . .

Amy Seldin, general physical education specialist

Trey is a first grader who is always on the go. He never seems to be still and is constantly distracted. Physical education provides an outlet for Trey's energy, but the gym and the physical education environment create problems for Trey. For example, Trey has difficulty sitting for even 10 seconds. When he does sit, he often does not listen to instructions, so he does not know what to do. Finally, Trey is so impulsive and distracted by the gym equipment that he often needs several reminders not to touch things and to use the equipment properly. Trey's physical educator is spending a lot of time with Trey and neglecting the other first graders in her class. How can she accommodate Trey while still providing instruction to the rest of the students in the class?

Isabelle is a seventh grader with visual impairments. She is easily accommodated in all of her seventh-grade classes through the use of braille and taped lectures. However, Isabelle's physical educator has not determined how to accommodate Isabelle during general physical education. First, he does not know how to present information to Isabelle. Like many physical educators, he often depends on demonstrations to teach students new skills, but Isabelle cannot see his demonstrations. Second, he is concerned for Isabelle's safety because she cannot see objects or other students coming toward her. This physical educator does not know how to organize the class to accommodate Isabelle while still providing the other students with a quality physical education. Right now, Isabelle does warm-up activities with the rest of the class; but during the remainder of the period, she just sits off to the side and listens. What can this teacher do?

Rasheed is a tenth grader who has mental retardation requiring extensive support. He spends part of his school day in the community working on functional vocational, community, and leisure skills. For the remainder of the day, Rasheed is included in general tenth-grade classes, including general physical education. Rasheed's physical educator, however, is having difficulty communicating to Rasheed during general physical education. Rasheed does not speak or understand verbal or simple gestural cues, nor does he follow demonstrations very well. In addition, Rasheed does not know when to stop or start an activity, tires easily and often wants to sit down, and has an extremely short attention span. The general physical educator has stopped trying to instruct Rasheed; instead, she lets him run around the gym and do what he wants during general physical education. What can this physical educator do?

Students with disabilities often can be safely and successfully included in general physical education without drastically changing the program for students without disabilities or causing undue hardship for the general physical education teacher. However, the general physical educator (with support from the student's collaborative team) must be prepared to make modifications to the way that the class is organized, information is presented, and support personnel are utilized. The first step in accommodating students with disabilities in general physical education is to determine the teaching method (i.e., how to organize the class and present information). Once the teaching method has been determined, modifications can be made to accommodate students with disabilities. Instructional modifications are relatively easy to implement and can mean the difference between success and failure for students with special needs. For example, relying solely on demonstrations to teach students new skills makes it difficult to impossible for a student with a visual impairment to understand what to do in physical education. Using verbal cues in addition to physical demonstrations allows the student to be successful.

This chapter introduces a variety of instructional modifications that physical educators can use to accommodate students with disabilities in general physical education. These instructional modifications, adapted in part from Eichstaedt and Lavay (1992), Seaman and DePauw (1989), and Sherrill (1998), illustrate the way in which subtle changes in class organization and presentation of information can be implemented to better accommodate students with disabilities (see Table 6.1 for a summary). The goal of these modifications is to allow all students, including students with disabilities, to participate in a general physical education environment that is safe, challenging, and affords opportunities for success. The techniques that the general physical educator chooses to implement will depend on the particular needs of the students with disabilities, the age group with which he or she is working, the skills on which he or she is focusing, the make-up of the class, availability of equipment and facilities, availability of support personnel, and his or her own preferences. Although specific examples are provided, it is important that the teacher learn the general process of how to modify a physical education program. Once the general process of creating and implementing appropriate modifications is understood, the process can be applied to a variety of situations.

In many cases, the physical educator can modify his or her presentation to meet the unique needs of students with disabilities without changing his or her

Table 6.1. Instructional accommodations to facilitate inclusion

Class organization	Accommodations in how you present information
Teaching style	Verbal cues
Class format	Demonstrations
	Level of methodology
	Student's method of communication
	Starting and stopping signals
	Time of day
	Duration
	Order of learning
	Size and nature of group
	Instructional environment
	Eliminating distractions
	Providing structure
	Level of difficulty
	Level of motivation

presentation to the rest of the class. For example, the teacher can demonstrate a particular skill to the group and have them get started. Once the group has begun the activity, the educator can, for example, provide extra verbal cues and physical assistance to a student who has mental retardation so that the student understands the task, use a movement exploration approach when teaching body control skills and movement concepts to a first-grade class, or provide direct cues and physical assistance to a student with autism who has difficulty exploring his or her environment independently. In this way, the educator is still using his or her typical instructional approach but making subtle additions to instructions to accommodate the needs of students with disabilities.

When developing and implementing any modification, the physical educator should utilize peers and support personnel whenever possible. Chapter 3 reviews members of the collaborative team that physical educators could use as sources of support, and Chapter 4 explains ways in which these team members can help determine the types of modifications that are most appropriate for particular students. Peers and support personnel also can be used to assist the general physical educator in implementing specific modifications. Support personnel can include classmates, older peer tutors, volunteers, teacher assistants, or specialists (see Chapter 3). All of the instructional modifications outlined in this chapter (as well as the curricular modifications outlined in Chapters 7 and 8) can be implemented more effectively if support personnel are available to assist the general physical educator. Even having a parent volunteer or the school custodian come in for a few minutes to help provide more individual assistance to a student with a disability can make a tremendous difference to the student and to the general physical educator. For example, a student who is learning how to walk with a walker might need extra assistance only to prevent him or her from falling. During warm-up activities, when the class is moving about using different locomotor patterns, the parent or custodian can come into the class to assist this student. Thus, the student receives the needed one-to-one attention, leaving the general physical educator free to focus on the larger group.

Determining Whether a Modification Is Appropriate

One relatively simple way to decide which modification to use is to consider the effect that the modification will have on the student with disabilities, his or her peers, and the general physical educator. If the modification has a negative effect on any or all of these individuals, then it may not be the most appropriate modification. The following four criteria should be used whenever a particular modification is being considered for implementation. If the modification does not meet the standards set by these criteria, then an alternative modification should be investigated.

1. *Does the change allow the student with disabilities to participate successfully yet still be challenged?* Finding a balance between success and challenge can be very difficult, but it is critical for the student with disabilities. Although not providing necessary accommodations can cause a student with disabilities to be confused or to fail, providing too much support may make the activity too easy for the student or stigmatize the student, making her too different from the rest of the class. For example, a student who is blind might simply need to have a peer help her find a bucket of balls and a throwing station and then face the direction of the target in order to complete the activity independently. There is no need for the teacher or a teacher assistant or peer to then provide ongoing physical assistance to the student.

2. *Does the modification make the environment unsafe for the student with a disability or for his or her peers?* Safety should always be the top priority when determining accommodations. Often, simple instructional accommodations actually can make the environment *safer* for all students. For example, an impulsive student who gets distracted by extraneous equipment such as mats stored off to the side of the gym has been known to leave the group, climb on the mats, and then jump down before the teacher even knows he is gone. To accommodate this student (and other students who have been distracted by the stack of mats), the teacher has decided to store the mats behind a curtain on a corner of the stage that is connected to the gym. Now the student is not distracted by the mats.

3. *Does the change affect peers without disabilities?* As noted previously, some accommodations may affect the entire class; these types of modifications should be used cautiously. For example, talking very slowly and using one- to two-word sentences when talking to the entire class in order to accommodate a student with autism will not be appreciated by the students without disabilities. A better solution might be for the physical educator to talk to the class using his or her normal rate of speech and sentence structure; then, once the class has begun the activity, the physical educator, the student's teacher assistant, or a peer can provide extra verbal cues in a manner that the student can understand.

4. *Does the change cause an undue burden on the general physical education teacher?* One of the greatest concerns general physical educators have with inclusion is that accommodations will be too difficult for them to implement; yet, many modifications actually can be very *simple* to implement. For example, a student with mental retardation might not be able to understand the teacher's verbal cue to stop. One simple solution might be to have peers near the child give him an extra cue or even a hand signal to stop. This simple accommodation allows the student to be successful without causing an undue hardship on the physical education teacher.

Class Organization Accommodations

Teaching Style

Teaching style refers to the learning environment, general routine, and way in which a lesson is presented to the class. Mosston (1981) and Mosston and Ashworth (1994) described different teaching styles commonly used by physical educators (see Table 6.2 for a summary). They suggested that these various teaching styles could be arranged across a spectrum. One side of the spectrum reflects decisions made by teachers, including what to do and when, how, how long, with whom (if anyone), and with what equipment to do it. These styles are referred to as *reproductive styles* because students are supposed to reproduce or replicate a particular movement pattern. For example, students learning how to throw may each be given a yarn ball, then asked to watch the teacher throw. Students are then asked to copy the teacher's pattern. Two major advantages to reproductive teaching styles are that 1) students know exactly what they are supposed to do, and 2) teachers have more control over the class. Major disadvantages of these styles include 1) students are passive rather than active learners (they are told what they are supposed to learn rather than discovering what is important to learn), and 2) students are less likely to be creative and discover unique and different ways to solve movement problems.

Table 6.2. Mosston and Ashworth's teaching styles

Reproductive styles

Command: This style teaches the learner to do the task accurately and within a short period of time, following all of the directions given by the teacher. The essence: Immediate response to a stimulus, performance is accurate and immediate, and a previous model is replicated.

Practice/Task: This style offers the learner time to work individually and privately and provides the teacher with time to offer the learner individual and private feedback. The essence: Time is provided for the learner to do a task individually and privately, and time is available for the teacher to give feedback to all learners, individually and privately.

Reciprocal: In this style, learners work with a partner and offer feedback to the partner based on criteria prepared by the teacher. The essence: Learners work in a partner relationship, receive immediate feedback, follow criteria for performance developed by the teacher, and develop feedback and socialization skills.

Self-check: The purposes of this style are to do a task and to check one's own work. The essence: Learners do the task individually and privately and provide feedback for themselves by using criteria developed by the teacher.

Inclusion/Invitation: The purposes of this style are to learn to select a level of a task one can perform and to offer a challenge to check one's own work. The essence: The same task is designed for different degrees of difficulty; learners decide their entry point into the task and when to move to another level.

Productive styles

Guided discovery: The purpose of this style is to discover a concept by answering a sequence of questions presented by the teacher. The essence: The teacher, by asking a specific sequence of questions, systematically leads the learner to discover a predetermined target previously unknown to the learner.

Convergent discovery: Here, learners discover the solution to a problem and learn to clarify an issue and arrive at a conclusion by employing logical procedures, reasoning, and critical thinking. The essence: Teachers present the question, the intrinsic structure of the task (question) requires a single correct answer, learners engage in reasoning (and other cognitive operations) and seek to discover the single correct answer or solution.

Divergent discovery: The purpose of this style is to engage in producing (discovering) multiple responses to a single question. The essence: Learners are engaged in producing divergent responses to a single question, the intrinsic structure of the task (question) provides possible multiple responses, and the multiple responses are assessed by the possible-feasible-desirable procedures or by the verification "rules" of the given discipline.

Learner's individually designed program: The purpose of this style is to design, develop, and perform a series of tasks organized into a personal program with consultation provided by the teacher. The essence: The learner designs, develops, and performs a series of tasks organized into a personal program; the learner selects the topic, identifies the questions, collects data, discovers answers, and organizes the information; and the teacher selects the general subject matter area.

Adapted from Mosston, M., & Ashworth, S. (1994). *Teaching physical education* (4th ed., pp. 248–249). Upper Saddle River, NJ: Prentice-Hall.

On the other end of the teaching styles spectrum, students make most or all of the decisions. Teaching styles on this end of the spectrum are referred to as *productive styles* because students are supposed to produce or discover the most appropriate movement pattern to solve a particular movement problem. In some cases, there is no absolute right or wrong movement pattern, and students learn which pattern fits best with a particular situation through exploration. For example, a teacher might want her students to discover which throwing pattern is best for different situations, from bowling to playing catch with a water balloon to throwing a basketball to throwing a softball home from center field. Obviously, each situation requires a unique movement pattern that the teacher could easily share with her students; however, students who learn by actively experimenting and discovering for themselves the most appropriate patterns tend to be more invested in their learning and to retain what they have learned longer.

Some objectives in physical education can be achieved more effectively with a specific teaching style. For example, accurate replication of a precise movement pattern such as learning how to grip and swing a golf club might best be taught through various reproductive styles. In contrast, creating different types of pyramids in a gymnastics unit or developing a repertoire of locomotor patterns and movement concepts might best be taught through various productive styles. Some students will respond better to one teaching style than the other. For example, children who need more structure and direction, such as students with attention-deficit/hyperactivity disorder (ADHD) or mental retardation, do better with reproductive learning styles or reciprocal styles. Conversely, students with typical intelligence but unique movement abilities may learn to compensate for their problems by discovering for themselves the best way to move. The point is to recognize the importance of the objectives of each activity and the ways in which each student learns. Then, and only then, can the teacher choose the most appropriate teaching style.

In inclusive physical education classes, it may be necessary to use a variety of teaching styles to accommodate different students in the class. Using a variety of teaching styles can be extremely difficult; however, teachers can still employ the general principles of one particular teaching style to help a particular student while using another style for the majority of the class. For example, in the context of a command style used to teach the overhand throwing pattern, a teacher could allow a student who has cerebral palsy to explore different throwing patterns (guided discovery) that meet his unique needs. Similarly, a teacher presenting body awareness concepts to the class in a divergent style could present specific information regarding what to do and how, when, and where to do a specific action (command style) for a student with mental retardation. The key is to decide on the objective for the class as well as for individual students, determine how the class learns best as well as how individual students learn best, and then decide which teaching style will be most effective.

Class Format

Class format refers to the way in which members of a class are organized. Seaman and DePauw (1989) outlined seven class formats that are commonly used in physical education environments:

1. *One-to-one instruction:* one teacher or assistant for every student

2. *Small-group instruction:* three to ten students working together with a teacher or teacher assistant

3. *Large-group instruction:* entire class participating together as one group

4. *Mixed-group instruction:* using various class formats within one class period

5. *Peer teaching or tutoring:* using classmates or students without disabilities from other classes for teaching and assisting students with disabilities

6. *Teaching stations:* several areas through which smaller subsets of the class rotate to practice skills

7. *Self-paced independent work:* each student works on individual goals at his or her own pace by following directions on task cards or with guidance from the teacher and teacher assistants

In addition, cooperative learning and reverse mainstreaming are class formats that can facilitate inclusion in physical education. The following sections briefly review some of these class formats and how they can be used in inclusive physical education environments.

Peer Tutoring   Peer tutoring involves students helping students. Because it can be difficult for a general physical education teacher to provide individual attention to students with disabilities, peers without disabilities can be trained and then assigned to students with disabilities to provide extra instruction and support. There are three basic peer tutoring models: 1) classmates in the same class work together and provide each other with feedback (e.g., Mosston's reciprocal style), 2) classmates in the same class are assigned to help a particular classmate with a disability, and 3) older students from other classes come into a general physical education class to help a particular student with disabilities (cross-age peer tutoring) (Block, Oberweiser, & Bain, 1995; Houston-Wilson, Lieberman, Horton, & Kasser, 1997). Cross-age peer tutoring is a popular model. Some schools allow peer tutoring to count toward required community service. Other schools have peer tutoring classes in which students register for credit, go through training, and meet on a regular basis to discuss tutoring. In addition, these older peers may get involved in the tutee's life outside school by taking the tutee to high school events or out for pizza. One advantage to using older peers as tutors is that they often are more reliable and focused and can handle more responsibility than same-age classmates. In addition, some students with disabilities might behave better with an older peer than with a classmate. It may be difficult, however, to free up older students from their academic classes to come and help in physical education (see Houston-Wilson, Lieberman, et al., 1997, for more information on cross-age peer tutors).

The most cost-effective and easiest to implement method is to have same-age classmates who are already in the general physical education class provide extra instruction and support to the student with disabilities. Juggling schedules to pull students out of academic classes is not an issue, and classmates already know each other and are familiar with the routine of the general physical education class. However, using classmates as peer tutors can cause problems, too. First and foremost, one student should not be assigned to work with his or her classmate with disabilities for an entire class period. This would sacrifice the peer tutor's physical education experience. Rather, several students can be assigned to work with a student with a disability and can take turns assisting him or her. Second, using classmates as peer tutors can change the dynamics of relationships between students with and without disabilities. Peers who tutor can begin to view the student with a disability as someone who needs help rather than as a classmate (Block, 1998). This can be prevented in two ways. First, each child in the class can be partnered with another student during a classwide peer tutoring session (Block et al., 1995; Houston-Wilson, Lieberman, et al., 1997). After several minutes with one partner, students can switch and work with another partner. Second, do not assign a specific student to a student with a disability; but, rather, cue the entire class to help their fellow students who may need extra assistance. For example, a teacher might say to the class, "Practice dribbling your ball while walking forward, backward, or sideways. If a friend drops his or her ball or is having trouble, you may ask him or her if he or she needs help." This way, the child with a disability is not the only student who is targeted for assistance.

Regardless of the model used, training is critical to the success of peer tutors. Block (1995a) and Houston-Wilson et al. (1997) suggested the following topics be included in a peer tutoring training program: disability awareness; communication techniques; teaching techniques; reinforcement techniques, including how to provide specific feedback; skill analysis, including what components of a skill to look at; and ongoing data collection. Training can be formal, such as a peer tutoring or partner club (Eichstaedt & Lavay, 1992; Sutherland, 1999), or informal and part of the general physical education class. Training can take several days or can be conducted during two or three general physical education class sessions.

One way to simplify training and provide ongoing information regarding a peer tutor's responsibilities is to use task sheets. Task sheets, created by the teacher overseeing the peer tutoring, provide information to peer tutors to help them be better "teachers." They include information such as the components of the skill that the student should work on, pictures of the components, reminders of ways to communicate with the child and deal with specific behaviors, suggestions for giving feedback, and a place to record data (Block, 1995b; Houston-Wilson et al., 1997) (see Figure 6.1). Peer tutoring has been effective in various inclusive physical education environments (for examples, see Houston-Wilson, Lieberman, et al., 1997; Lieberman, 1996; and Webster, 1987).

Teaching Stations   Teaching stations are a simple and popular way to organize diverse general physical education classes. The physical educator sets up three or more places, or stations, around the gym, each one focusing on a different activity. Students are assigned to start at one of the stations, then rotate to a different station when they have completed certain activities or when the teacher signals the group to move to a new station. For example, a teacher might set up hierarchical or progressive stations at which students are placed based on their skill levels. As the students progress in skill level or master some aspect of a skill, they move up to a new station with a higher level of difficulty (Kelly et al., 1991). Alternatively, a teacher might simply assign groups of five to seven students to each of five different stations. After 3–5 minutes, the teacher signals students to stop and rotate to the next station.

Stations can be independent, unrelated activities or can revolve around a theme. For example, a teacher might set up unrelated stations that cover a variety of activities (e.g., jumping rope, throwing and catching, sit-ups and push-ups, tumbling). Or, a teacher might set up stations centered around the theme of throwing (e.g., throwing at targets, throwing to a partner, throwing into a curtain, throwing over a net) or basketball (e.g., shooting, passing and catching, dribbling, rebounding). Regardless of whether the stations are related, there should be multiple challenges at each station to accommodate the varying abilities of students in the class. For example, the teacher might set up a kicking station at which students stand at different distances from the target, use balls of miscellaneous sizes, and aim at various size targets. This way, each child who comes to the station is challenged at his or her own level yet has the opportunity to be successful. In addition, the teacher might make a list of variations to make the skill more challenging. For example, at the kicking station above, the teacher might also list challenges such as use your opposite leg, try to kick a moving ball, or try to chip the ball into the air. These variations allow students with more skills to work at the same station as students with fewer or less-developed skills.

Because stations accommodate students of different abilities, they are ideal for including students with disabilities. For example, Katie, a 12-year-old girl with severe cerebral palsy, is in a swimming class at her middle school. Some students in the class swim year-round, others can swim but need to work on stroke

Peer Tutoring Task Sheet

Student: _____ Student's goals: _____

Peer tutor: _____   _____

Directions for the peer tutor: Circle the type of prompt, reinforcement, or method of communication used with the tutee. Then watch the tutee perform the skill while you focus and comment on one component of the skill. Give the tutee a plus (+) if he or she performs the component correctly and a minus (−) if the he or she does not perform the skill component correctly. After five trials, switch roles with the tutee so that you are the tutee and your partner is the tutor.

Types of prompts	Types of reinforcements	Communication
Natural	"Good job"	Talking
Verbal	High-five	Showing how
Gestures	Pat on the back	Using pictures
Demonstration	Shooting baskets	
Partial physical assistance	Token	
Physical assistance	Food	

Skill components

1. Dominant hand above nondominant hand: ___ ___ ___ ___ ___

2. Side orientation: ___ ___ ___ ___ ___

3. Weight transfer: ___ ___ ___ ___ ___

4. Follow-through: ___ ___ ___ ___ ___

5. Other: _____ ___ ___ ___ ___ ___

A Teacher's Guide to Including Students with Disabilities in General Physical Education
by Martin E. Block, copyright ©2000 Paul H. Brookes Publishing Co.

Figure 6.1. Peer tutoring task sheet.

refinement, and others still are learning basic strokes. In order to accommodate the range of abilities in this class, the physical education teacher has set up different stations for students to work on the butterfly and breaststroke, backstroke, freestyle, or diving. The physical education teacher directly supervises the diving station while watching the other stations from afar. A lifeguard also watches the swimmers. Katie receives help from a teacher assistant. Students were pretested on the various strokes prior to being assigned to stations, so they know on which components of each stroke they are supposed to focus . The teacher assigns seven students to each station. At each station is a list of activities that includes swimming a distance in a given period of time, swimming a particular distance using a specific stroke, and swimming using a kickboard while focusing on one or two aspects of the stroke (see Figure 6.2). The students know to work independently on their own tasks, but they are also encouraged to help each other improve their strokes. For example, while resting after doing the butterfly for 25 meters in less than 2 minutes, a student watches and gives feedback to another student who is trying to gather enough courage to put his face in the water during the breaststroke. At the same station, Katie learns how to lie on her stomach and lift her head out of the water to clear an airway. A teacher assistant helps her do this task while a peer provides encouragement as he rests after his swim.

Cooperative Learning   Another class format option, *cooperative learning*, involves students working together to accomplish shared goals (Grineski, 1996; Johnson & Johnson, 1989). Students are instructed to learn the assigned information and to make sure that all members of the group master the information (at their level). For example, each student in a group must perform a specific number of push-ups for the team to reach its shared goal of 180 push-ups. One girl who is very strong and is trying to break the school record attempts 100 push-ups. Another child in the group tries to do 35 push-ups, two other students attempt to do 20 push-ups each, and a child with mental retardation tries to do 5 push-ups. In order for the team to be successful, each student must meet his or her individual goal. Team members encourage each other to reach their individual goals, which in turn helps the team reach its shared goal.

Often, individuals in the group are given specific jobs or tasks that contribute to goal attainment. Cooperative learning encourages each student to work together, help each other, and constantly evaluate each member's progress toward individual and group goals (more accountability). For example, during a gymnastics unit, a team of four members must balance so that a total of two feet, two hands, two elbows, and two knees touch the ground. The team members, including a student who is blind and has poor balance, talk together to determine the best way to solve the group challenge. After much discussion and several attempts at different patterns, the team came up with the following solution: The child who is blind stands on two feet and holds the ankles of another student, who is standing on her hands (she needs the support, or she will fall). Another student gets on his elbows and knees (feet up), and the fourth student sits on his back. The student sitting on his back then reaches over to help balance the person standing on her hands. The only way this team could be successful was for everyone to work together.

For cooperative learning to be effective, students must believe that they are positively linked to other students in their group and that each member can and must contribute to the success of the group. In addition, each group member must understand his or her role. Students with disabilities and less-skilled students could be perceived as the weak links in the group if all members believe

---

Breaststroke/Butterfly Station

Directions: Practice the challenge that matches your ability based on your pretest (see the posted pretest results if you are not sure of your level). When you have mastered a particular challenge, move to the next challenge. Help and encourage peers who are working on their challenges.

Challenges

_____ Lie on stomach, then lift head out of water. Repeat several times.

_____ Hold onto gutter and perform correct leg movements for breaststroke 20 times.

_____ Hold onto kickboard and perform correct leg movements for breaststroke 20 times.

_____ Place kickboard under stomach and practice correct arm movements for breaststroke 20 times.

_____ Place kickboard under stomach and practice correct breathing pattern for breaststroke 20 times.

_____ Place kickboard under stomach and practice correct arm and breathing pattern for breaststroke 20 times.

_____ Without kickboard, do complete breaststroke for 5 strokes.

_____ Do complete breaststroke for 10 strokes.

_____ Do complete breaststroke for length of pool.

_____ Do complete breaststroke for length of pool as fast as you can (record your time). Rest and repeat.

_____ Do complete butterfly for length of pool and back as fast as you can (record your time).

Rest and repeat (only for students on swim team).

Figure 6.2.   Breaststroke/butterfly station.

they must each perform the same task. If the group understands that each member has a unique task that maximizes his or her skills and contribution to the group goal, all students will be perceived positively. For example, a group of third graders is working on the skill of striking. The teacher divides the class into small groups of three to four students each. The cooperative task for each group is to hit 50 paper-and-yarn balls across the gym with each group member hitting each ball only once, and each student must work on one key aspect of a skillful striking pattern. Because no student can hit the ball across the gym by him- or herself, only through group cooperation can the ball get across the gym (group goal). In Group A, the skilled student begins the process by hitting a pitched ball as far as possible (pitched by one of the group members). This student is working on timing and hitting the ball up into the air. The less-skilled group member then walks to where the ball lands, picks up the ball, and places it on a batting tee; he then hits the ball forward as far as possible. This student is working on shifting weight and stepping, and the skilled student provides feedback to the less-skilled student. Finally, the tee is moved to where the ball landed, and again, the ball is placed on the tee for a student who is blind. This student is working on hitting the ball off the tee with his hand using proper preparatory position, stepping, and a level swing. Both the skilled and nonskilled students help position the student who is blind and provide him with feedback. The process is repeated until the group hits 50 balls. The group must work together to accomplish their goal, and each student must contribute in his or her own way. In addition, it benefits the group if each member improves his or her skill level. If a group member betters his or her form, then he or she can hit the ball farther and in turn help the team accomplish its goal (see Grineski, 1996, for more details on cooperative learning in physical education and Grineski, 1996, and Orlick, 1982, for excellent examples of cooperative learning activities for physical education).

Reverse Mainstreaming   In some situations, it makes sense to have a self-contained physical education class composed of only students with disabilities. Even in self-contained classrooms, however, interactions with peers without disabilities can be facilitated through a class format called *reverse mainstreaming.* In this format, several students without disabilities are included in a class of children who have disabilities. Students without disabilities do not tutor their peers with disabilities but, rather, participate in the activities alongside students with disabilities. These students without disabilities provide positive role models for students with disabilities and allow for team sports and games that require more players than there are students with disabilities. For example, once a week an adapted physical education class of seven middle school students with mental retardation requiring limited support invites seven middle school students without disabilities to participate with them in physical education class. The current unit in both adapted physical education and general physical education is soccer. In reverse mainstreaming, all of the students begin with a warm-up activity. Students without disabilities tend to use better form in stretching, thus providing a good model for their peers with mental retardation. Similarly, peers without disabilities set a good pace during warm-up laps for the students with mental retardation. Following warm-ups, a student without a disability pairs up with a peer with mental retardation to work on various soccer skills. Peers without disabilities pass the ball at a slow speed to the student with mental retardation so that the student with mental retardation can practice trapping the ball (when students with mental retardation are paired together in the adapted class, they have trouble accurately passing the ball back and forth to each other). The class culminates with a modified game of seven-on-seven soccer (which is difficult to do with a class of only seven students with disabilities). Rules are modified so that all students are challenged. Students without disabilities have to kick the ball with their opposite foot, cannot kick the ball in the air, and cannot use their hands if they are playing goalie. Because of the smaller game size and rule modifications, students with disabilities can be successful when peers without disabilities participate yet still be motivated and challenged.

Using Multiple Formats   The best format for a particular situation will vary based on numbers, attitudes, and types of students with and without disabilities; type and flexibility of the facility; and availability of resources. In most situations, a combination of the previously listed class formats is most effective. For example, a student with severe disabilities can be included in a high school physical education class during a basketball unit in which the teacher utilizes a combination of peer tutors, stations, self-paced learning, and large-group instruction. Students begin the class by following the teacher through various warm-up activities (large group). The student with severe disabilities is assisted in these warm-up activities by his physical therapist, who works on specific stretching and strengthening activities designed specifically for this student. Following warm-ups, students rotate through several basketball stations at their own pace and work on tasks geared to their individual ability levels. Students are free to choose at which station they wish to begin; but they can stay at one station for only 10 minutes, and no more than seven students can be at any one station at a time. All of the students have task cards, with a hierarchy of tasks that they move through at their own pace. In order to move to the next level on a hierarchy, the student must have another student confirm that he or she can perform the skill in four out of five trials (stations/self-paced learning). The student with severe disabilities has a task card that includes tasks at the lower end of the continuum. (Refer to Figure 6.2 for an example of different levels of challenges at a station.) In addition, peers who chose the same station as the student with disabilities are cued by the teacher to help this student as needed.

The culminating activity for the day is a game of basketball. Skilled students go with a "class leader" and learn various plays and strategies during a game of five-on-five basketball (small group). Less-skilled students including the student with severe disabilities stay with the general physical education teacher, who organizes a game of modified basketball in which the rules have been changed to accommodate the needs of all of the participants. In one version of the modified game, the defense must play a passive zone defense (i.e., they cannot steal the ball unless it is passed directly to them). In addition, every player on the offensive team must touch the ball one time before a player can shoot, and students can get points for hitting the backboard (1 point) or the rim (2 points) or for making a basket (3 points). Students who cannot shoot the ball high enough to reach a 10-foot basket can shoot at an 8-foot target on the wall, and the student with severe disabilities can score points by pushing the ball off his lap tray into a box on the floor with assistance from a peer. This general physical education class utilized a variety of class formats during one class period that allowed the teacher to accommodate the needs of all the students in her class, including a student with severe disabilities.

Accommodations in How Information Is Presented

Verbal Instructions

Verbal instructions refer to the length and complexity of commands or verbal challenges used to convey information to a class. Students with mental retardation who cannot understand complex commands or students who have hearing impairments who cannot understand verbal commands may benefit from modified instruction delivery. Seaman and DePauw (1989) suggested the following ways that instructions can be modified for students who have difficulty understanding verbal language:

1. Simplify the words used.

2. Use single-meaning words (e.g., "run to the base" rather than "go to the base").

3. Give only one (or as many as the student can process at once) command at a time.

4. Ask the student to repeat the command before he or she performs it.

5. Give the command and then demonstrate the task or physically assist student.

Although modifications are helpful for a student with a language problem, they might not be needed for the majority of students in a general physical education class; therefore, the teacher can still implement these modifications without changing the way she delivers instruction to the rest of the students. For example, a teacher might give complex verbal directions including information about abstract strategies and team concepts to the class, then ask a peer to repeat key points to the student with mental retardation. Some strategies and concepts can be demonstrated by the peer, and abstract concepts can be translated into more concrete examples or skipped altogether depending on the student's level of comprehension. Similarly, a peer can demonstrate and mimic directions to a student with a hearing impairment after the teacher presents verbal directions to the class. By using peers or other assistants to present directions to the student with disabilities, the teacher does not have to alter how he or she delivers instructions to the rest of the class.

Demonstrations

The teacher can provide a level of demonstration that is appropriate for the majority of the class while presenting extra demonstrations (or having a peer present extra demonstrations) for students with disabilities. Modifications to demonstrations can be as simple as placing students with poor vision close to the teacher while she demonstrates a skill or activity. For students with mental retardation, the teacher might need to highlight key aspects of the demonstration that other students can pick up incidentally or have a peer without disabilities repeat the demonstration several times. For example, the teacher could demonstrate the starting preparatory position, backswing, trunk rotation, and follow-through for the overhand throw to the class. For a student with mental retardation who is just learning how to throw, the teacher (or a peer) might repeat the demonstration while focusing on just one aspect of the throw (stepping with opposite foot) so that this student knows on which component he should focus.

Levels of Methodology

Often, a physical educator needs to decide whether a completely different way of communicating and instructing particular students is needed. *Levels of methodology* refer to the various methods a teacher can use to present information and communicate with a student. Some students will respond quite well to verbal cues given to the class, whereas other students may need extra verbal cues, demonstrations, or even physical assistance to understand directions and perform skills correctly.

One consideration teachers should make when instructing students is the level of cues presented, or *prompt hierarchy* (Snell & Zirpoli, 1987). Prompts are cues given to students that help them make responses that they do not or cannot make without these cues. Instructional prompts range from nonintrusive prompts, such as a student following natural cues in the environment (e.g., student sees peers stand up and run around the gym, so the student quickly stands up and runs with peers) to intrusive prompts, such as physical assistance (e.g., teacher or peer physically helps a student hold a bat and then strike a ball off a tee). (See Figure 6.3 for a list of prompts ranked from least to most intrusive.) Each type of prompt can be further broken down into levels. For example, physical assistance can vary from that in which the student passively allows the teacher to help him, that in which the student resists assistance, and that in which the student actively tries to perform movement. Although, ideally, students will follow natural prompts in the environment, many students with disabilities will need extra prompts to understand directions and instructions. For example, students with visual impairments will need verbal instruction plus physical guidance, and students with hearing impairments will need more gestural prompts and demonstrations. Students with mental retardation requiring extensive support or autism often benefit from multisensory approaches in which

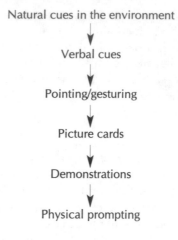

Natural cues in the environment

Verbal cues

Pointing/gesturing

Picture cards

Demonstrations

Physical prompting

Figure 6.3.   Least- to most-intrusive level of prompts.

several types of prompts are provided in sequence (e.g., verbal cue, then demonstration, then physical assistance).

Physical educators can find out from the speech-language therapist or special education teacher which level of prompt is needed for a student to understand instructions. However, most physical educators and peers will quickly discover on their own the best ways to prompt students with disabilities. For example, although the class receives verbal instructions on the day's activities, a student with mental retardation may benefit from having a peer simplify and repeat or demonstrate the teacher's verbal directions. At a skill station, some students can read directions on how to perform various skills, whereas a student with mental retardation can use picture cards. During warm-ups, a teacher assistant, with the help of a peer tutor, can physically guide a student with mental retardation requiring extensive support through the warm-ups. A teacher can give verbal instructions to the class, ask the class to begin practicing the skill, then give extra verbal instructions and physical assistance to a student who is blind. Note that in all of the previous examples, the addition of specialized instruction for one student does not necessarily have to change the way in which the teacher gives instruction to the other students.

If it is clear that a student will not be able to respond to a verbal cue or demonstration, then the physical educator or tutor should start with physical prompts or assistance so that the student will not fail at the task or be confused (Wessel & Kelly, 1986). For example, if the general physical educator knows that one of his or her students with cerebral palsy needs physical assistance to toss a ball, it makes no sense to first give the student a verbal cue, then point, then gesture, then demonstrate, then touch, and then finally physically assist the student. In going through the entire prompt hierarchy, time was wasted, and the student experienced failure for five out of six cues. However, because the ultimate goal is to have students follow natural cues whenever possible, an attempt should be made to systematically fade extra prompts during the course of the program. For example, students with mental retardation can learn to focus on natural cues in the locker room at the YMCA for locating an empty locker and to walk to the weight room independently.

Communication
with General Physical Educator

Another consideration when instructing students with disabilities is to determine ways they can communicate with the general physical educator. Many students with disabilities, like their peers without disabilities, will be able to respond using clear, concise speech. Other students, however, may speak in one- or two-word sentences, communicate with gestures or signs, communicate by pointing to pictures, or use sophisticated computer-assisted speech synthesizers or keyboards. Regardless of how a student communicates, it is important that each student's mode of communication is understood. This does not mean that the teacher necessarily has to learn sign language to communicate with a student who uses sign language; however, the teacher should discuss each student's communication skills with the speech-language therapist or special education teacher so that he or she can effectively communicate with each student who participates in the general physical education program. An inability to be understood can be frustrating for a student and, in some cases, can even lead to behavior outbursts (e.g., students with autism).

Starting and Stopping Signals

It is important to find the best way to give start and stop commands to students with disabilities. Students with hearing impairments may need hand signals and students with mental retardation requiring extensive support may need physical assistance to determine when they are supposed to start or stop an activity. The teacher can use one cue for the entire class (e.g., whistle) and provide hand signals or physical assistance to students who need extra cues. For example, the teacher could use a whistle to stop and start a soccer game for a high school class. When students without disabilities hear the whistle, they know to locate the student with a hearing impairment and raise their hands (indicating stop or start).

Time

Some students who receive medication (e.g., children with ADHD) perform or behave better once their medication has kicked in. These students might benefit from placement in an afternoon physical education class. Conversely, students who tire throughout the day (e.g., students with muscular dystrophy) might be better served in a morning physical education class. Similarly, students with allergy-induced asthma might perform better in a morning physical education class during pollen season because pollen counts are typically higher in the afternoon. Modifications to time should be made prior to the students' arrival at school (utilize the collaborative team to determine what time of day is best for students with health disorders).

Duration

Duration, or the amount of time a student will be engaged in an activity, can include number of weeks for a particular unit, number of physical education periods per week, length of time for each period, or how long the student will be engaged in each activity during physical education. For example, a student with mental retardation might need 6 weeks to reach her goals and learn a new skill, whereas students without disabilities might need only 3 weeks. Another student might benefit from physical education 5 days per week to reach his goals, whereas students without disabilities might need physical education only 3 days per week. A student with ADHD may be able to tolerate a station or activity for 1 minute, whereas her peers are expected to stay at a station for up to 5 minutes. Conversely, a student with mental retardation might need to stay at that same station for 10 minutes to receive an adequate amount of practice to learn a skill or concept.

Duration also refers to the length of time a student will stay in a game situation. A student with asthma or a heart condition who tires easily could play a game for 2 minutes, then rest on the sidelines for 2 minutes; or a teacher could allow for free substitution in soccer and basketball games so that students who tire easily can rest whenever necessary. Although many programs are locked into daily schedules, adjustments can usually be made to accommodate students with special needs. For example, a student with mental retardation has a goal of learning the skills needed to play softball. The softball unit in general physical education lasts 3 weeks, and now the class is playing volleyball. Volleyball is not one of the goals established for this student, and he has not acquired the targeted softball skills during the previous 3-week period. Although the rest of the class moves to volleyball, this student could continue to work on softball skills with a peer who already has good volleyball skills (i.e., does not need extra practice in volleyball), with another student who also needs extra work on softball, with a cross-age peer tutor, with a teacher assistant, or with a volunteer. The student can still do warm-ups with the general class and be around his peers in general physical education; he just practices different activities. Similarly, a student might work on three key skills in softball while her peers work on six skills. While the student's peers rotate through all six stations, this student can stay at each of three stations for a longer period of time to get extra practice in the three critical skills. A student with ADHD, however, might rotate through each of the six stations much faster than his peers, repeating each station two or three times so that he gets adequate practice trials without being forced to focus on one station for too long.

Order of Learning

Order of learning refers to the sequence in which the physical educator presents various aspects of a particular skill. Most teachers teach skills such as the sidearm strike in tennis by teaching the entire skill in order from first to last components (e.g., preparatory position, step, swing, follow-through). However, a student with a learning disability might need to focus on one aspect of the movement at a time, first learning the preparatory position, then to step and swing, and finally to follow through. Other students, including students with disabilities, might benefit from breaking the skill into even smaller steps or changing the order of learning.

Size and Nature of the Group

Size and nature of the group refers to the number of students who will be at one station or in a game at a time as well as the make-up of the group (similar abilities or mixed abilities). Students who have trouble working in large groups, such as students with autism, can be placed in smaller groups during station work. So that their team will not be at a disadvantage, students with mental retardation who are slower and less skilled than their peers without disabilities can be placed on a team that has more players than the opposing team. Similarly, players on the teams can be selected by the teacher so that each team has an equal number of skilled, average, and unskilled players. Players of similar ability can then be paired up against each other in the game (e.g., guarding each other in a game of soccer or basketball). The teacher should select teams so that students with lower abilities (or disabilities) are not always picked last. Also, skilled students should be encouraged to use appropriate sportsmanship during the selection process (i.e., they should not give funny looks when players with less ability are picked to be on their team).

Instructional Environment

Instructional environment refers to all aspects of the area in which the class is conducted. Factors include indoor or outdoor environment, temperature, lighting, floor surface, boundaries, markings on walls, and so forth. Most teachers cannot make major changes to their instructional environment to accommodate one or two students with special needs. However, there are some simple things a teacher can do to make an environment more accommodating for students with special needs. For example, cones or brightly colored tape can be used to accentuate boundaries for students with mental retardation or visual impairments. Carpet squares or small tumbling mats can be placed in certain areas where students with balance problems usually stand so that there will be a cushion if they fall. Carpet squares, poly spots, or hula hoops can be used to mark a student's personal space, and partitions such as tumbling mats stood up on end can be used to block off parts of the gym for students who are distracted easily.

Eliminate Distractions

It is important to create an instructional environment that is relatively free of distractions, including extraneous noises, people, or objects, so that the student can focus on instruction. Many students with ADHD or mental retardation are easily distracted and, thus, have difficulty focusing on important instructional cues. For example, balloons and cones that have been set up for a later activity might not distract most students in a class but might be extremely distracting for a student with mental retardation or ADHD. Again, the teacher should not have to make changes that negatively affect the majority of students, but there are several simple things that can be done to reduce distractions for the entire class. First, students can be positioned in such a way that they face away from distractions. For example, the teacher might position himself so that the students face the corner of the gym instead of the more distracting open area of the gym. Second, a teacher can avoid setting up equipment until right before the equipment will actually be used. Equipment can be placed at stations or around the gym but can be put in a barrel, box, or bag or covered with a tarp until it is needed. For example, balloons placed in large trash bags are much less distracting than balloons placed in clear sight of the students. Third, extraneous noises, objects, or people in the environment can be eliminated during physical education for those students who seem to be distracted easily. In many elementary schools, the gymnasium doubles as the cafeteria, and teachers and students walk through the gym/cafeteria in the morning to give the lunch count to cafeteria workers. Students with ADHD could be placed in an afternoon physical education class during which no one walks through the gym. Similarly, some gyms have stages where music or drama classes are conducted. Schedules should be established so that no other classes are in session when the student with ADHD is in physical education. Finally, teachers can help students focus on the task at hand by providing extra cues and reinforcement to the student and by making instruction more enticing. For example, using music during warm-ups can drown out the sound of noisy distractions in the environment. When the music is turned off and the environment is relatively quiet, the teacher can then give directions because her voice will be the most noticeable sound in the environment. Whistling and loud clapping are other ways to break a student's focus on one object and return his focus to the teacher.

Provide Structure or Routine

All children learn best and are most cooperative when they are familiar with class routines and expectations. Although most students can handle occasional changes to class structure or routines, change or the unexpected for children with autism, emotional disturbances, or mental retardation requiring extensive support can lead to confusion, withdrawal, misbehavior, or even self-abuse. It is important that class structure remain as constant as possible for students who are sensitive to change. Providing structure can be as easy as having students sit down on carpet squares or take two or three laps then sit against a designated wall when they first enter the gym. Even if the teacher does not have a routine for most students, it is important to establish a set routine for the student with disabilities. For example, a physical educator may lead his class through different warm-ups every day; however, he can still make sure the student with autism does the same thing every day when he enters the gymnasium (e.g., goes with the same peer to the corner of the gym and follows a certain exercise routine). By establishing a routine for this student, the student is less likely to be confused or upset, which makes the transition from the classroom to the gym much smoother. Another time when change is inevitable is when the physical educator begins a new unit.

Level of Difficulty or Complexity

Again, a teacher can vary the level of difficulty for particular students without changing the difficulty level for the class as a whole. For example, a team might play a complex zone defense in basketball; but all a student with mental retardation needs to know is to stand on a poly spot and keep his hands up. Similarly, while most students in the class work on stepping, rotating their body, and lagging their arm in the overhand throw, a student just learning how to throw can work on simply getting his arm into an overhand position. Specific examples of how to modify skills and group activities are presented in Chapters 7 and 8.

Level of Motivation

Many students without disabilities are usually intrinsically motivated to participate in physical education. Students who know they have difficulty in physical education, however, might need more encouragement. Extra encouragement can come in the form of verbal praise, extra privileges, free play, tokens, or even tangible reinforcements, such as food, for students with more severe disabilities. For example, a student with a severe emotional disturbance can be reinforced for staying engaged in a physical fitness activity for 10 minutes. Reinforcement might consist of allowing the student to do an activity he really likes for a few minutes following the fitness activity (e.g., shooting baskets, playing catch with the teacher). (See Chapter 11 for more detail regarding reinforcement.)

7

Modifying Curricula

. . .I see inclusion as an opportunity, not as a burden. . . . My heart goes out when I see many students helping our inclusion students. They truly care. . . . Inclusion works, but teachers might have to weather the storm before the sun shines through. We have an obligation to teach all students the best we know how. For me personally, inclusion brings on many new opportunities. . . . I have not always embraced these opportunities with open arms, but I can honestly say, a tear comes to my eyes when my inclusion students leave me and move on. . . .

Jeff Eaton, general physical education specialist and department chair

Ming is a second-grade student who has spina bifida. Although she uses a wheelchair in most situations, she is learning how to use leg braces and crutches. Ming is fully included in the general program at her elementary school. The general physical educator, however, is having difficulty figuring out how to best include Ming in activities; much of what takes place in second-grade physical education involves locomotor movement patterns and body control activities that Ming cannot do. In addition, the general physical educator is concerned that other students will hurt themselves if they run into Ming's wheelchair. This teacher has become so frustrated that Ming no longer receives general physical education. Rather, she receives physical therapy during this time. What can this physical educator do?

Maria is an eighth grader who has mental retardation requiring extensive support. Although she does not have any specific physical disability, she does have difficulty with activities that require strength, speed, or endurance (which includes most activities in middle school general physical education!). Maria cannot keep up with her peers in virtually any general physical education activity, including warm-ups; therefore, she works with her teacher assistant off to the side of the gym. Maria's parents are not happy with this arrangement, and they are pressuring the physical education teacher to do a better job of including Maria. How can this teacher accommodate Maria without ruining the program for students without disabilities?

Jacob is a 9-year-old student who has muscular dystrophy. Although he still is able to walk independently, he is getting progressively weaker. Jacob's third-grade class is doing a unit that includes playing tag and running relay races. Unfortunately, Jacob can no longer run, and his walk is very slow. Although the physical educator wants to accommodate Jacob's limited strength, she does not want to change the tag games or relay races so much that it negatively affects her students without disabilities. What should this teacher do?

Chapter 6 discusses modifications that can be made to class organization and information presentation. For many students, however, curricular modifications also will be necessary. *Curricular modifications* refers to any adaptation made to the general education curriculum in order to 1) prevent a mismatch between a student's skill level and the lesson content and 2) promote student success in learning targeted individualized education program (IEP) objectives and appropriate skills (Block & Vogler, 1994; Giangreco & Putnam, 1991). These curricular modifications might include changes to equipment, teaching content, or rules of games.

As was the case with instructional modifications, some modifications will affect only the student with a disability (e.g., lowering a basket or making a target larger), whereas other modifications may affect the entire class (e.g., having all students do a simple locomotor pattern during warm-ups). Changes that affect the entire group should be implemented cautiously; it is important to avoid making changes that will negatively affect the program for students without disabilities. However, as with instructional modifications, some changes that affect the entire class can be positive. For example, providing all students with choices regarding the equipment they use or the locomotor patterns they would like to perform not only accommodates a student with a disability but also helps less-skilled students to be successful and more-skilled students to be challenged. Similarly, offering several activities rather than just one not only accommodates a student with a disability but also allows other students to choose activities that may be more motivating to them. These types of modifications accommodate the range of abilities of typically developing students.

The purpose of this chapter is to introduce a variety of curricular modifications for accommodating students with disabilities during general physical education. These modifications have been organized as follows: 1) a general model for making curricular modifications for all students, 2) curricular modifications for students with specific functional impairments, and 3) modifications for students with specific types of disabilities. The goal of each of these modifications is to allow all students, including students with disabilities, to participate in a general physical education environment that is safe and challenging and affords opportunities for success. As noted in Chapter 6, the techniques you choose to implement will depend on the particular needs of the student with disabilities, the age group with which you are working, the skills on which you are focusing, the make-up of your class, availability of equipment and facilities, availability of support personnel, and your own preferences. Although this chapter provides specific examples of modifications, it is important that you focus on the general process of how to modify your physical education program. If you can understand the general process of creating and implementing appropriate modifications, then you can apply the process to a variety of situations.

Determining Whether a Curricular Accommodation Is Appropriate

As noted in previous chapters, not all modifications are necessarily appropriate at all times for a particular student with a disability. It is important to consider the effect the modification will have on the student with disabilities, his or her peers, and the general physical educator before the modification is implemented. If the modification has a negative effect on any or all of these individuals, then it probably is not the most appropriate modification. In attempting to decide the appropriateness of a particular modification, you should apply the same four criteria that are introduced in Chapter 6 for considering instructional and curricular adaptations. If the modification does not meet the standards set by these criteria, then an alternative modification should be considered.

1. *Does the change allow the student with disabilities to participate successfully yet still be challenged?* For example, a student with mental retardation might not be able to kick a regulation soccer ball back and forth with a partner. A simple mod-

ification might be to allow the student and his partner to kick a large playground ball or volleyball trainer back and forth instead of the regulation soccer ball. Such a modification provides the needed accommodation for the student so that he will be successful, yet it still allows him to be challenged at his level.

2. *Does the modification make the environment unsafe for the student with a disability or for peers?* For example, you want to include a student who uses a wheelchair at a soccer dribbling station, but you are worried that other children will bump into the child. One solution is to mark off an area at this station with cones that the child who uses a wheelchair must stay behind. It may also be helpful to remind peers at the beginning of the class and several times during the class to be careful around the student who uses a wheelchair. Peers quickly will learn to be careful, and the student can safely participate in the activity.

3. *Does the change affect peers without disabilities?* Making all targets larger and asking all students to stand closer to the target is unnecessary and unfair to students without disabilities. Similarly, making all children walk during warm-ups to accommodate a child who uses a walker does not make sense. Rather, the general physical educator should make accommodations that affect only the student with disabilities and not his or her peers. For example, allowing students to choose a target and a distance that challenges them accommodates those students who need such accommodations without affecting students who do not need them. Similarly, a better way to accommodate a student who uses a walker than to force all children to walk is to allow students to choose a locomotor pattern.

4. *Does the change cause an undue burden on the general physical education teacher?* For example, assume that a student who has cerebral palsy and is learning how to walk with a walker is fully included in general physical education. The general physical educator wants to include this student in warm-up activities that include performing locomotor patterns in general space to music. Because this student still needs help to walk with his walker, the general physical educator feels that it is her duty to assist this student during warm-ups. This affects her ability to attend to and instruct the other students. A better modification might be to assist this student for part of warm-ups and then let the student creep on his hands and knees (his most functional way of moving) for part of warm-ups. Or, if walking with the walker is a critical goal for this student, older peer tutors, a teacher assistant, a volunteer, or the physical therapist can come into physical education (at least during warm-ups) to assist this student.

General Categories of Curricular Modifications

Although specific modifications will vary from student to student, generally speaking, three distinct categories of curricular modifications may be necessary: multilevel curricular selection, curricular overlapping, and alternative activities (Block & Vogler, 1994; Giangreco & Putnam, 1991).

Multilevel Curricular Selection

Multilevel curricular selection is designed for students with mild disabilities who can follow the general education curriculum with only slight accommodations. In essence, the general education curriculum is appropriate for the student with a disability, but the level at which the curriculum is presented may be above the student's ability level. For example, a student with mental retardation requiring intermittent support is included in a general physical education throwing and catching unit in fourth grade. Although throwing and catching are appropriate activities for this student, he cannot throw and catch as well as his peers. To accommodate his needs, the teacher allows him to stand closer to targets when throwing; throw at a larger target; stand closer to peers when catching; and use a lighter, larger ball when catching. In fact, this teacher offers all students the opportunity to choose the distance they stand from the target, at which size target to throw, and which balls to use when catching. Thus, this student and other students who have trouble throwing and catching are accommodated. Each student works on the same curricular content but at a level that accommodates his or her individual abilities.

Curricular Overlapping

The general education curriculum may be inappropriate for some students with severe disabilities. In such cases, the student should work on his or her unique physical education IEP objectives. Rather than working on these objectives away from his or her peers, however, these objectives can be embedded or overlapped within the general physical education curriculum. Such a model is known as curricular overlapping because a student's unique curricular needs coincide with the general education curriculum. For example, a second-grade student with severe cerebral palsy is learning how to walk with a walker. Although walking with a walker is not included in the general physical education curriculum, the general physical education class *is* doing a chasing and fleeing unit. While other students work on chasing and fleeing, this student can work on walking with her walker. Therefore, the student gets to participate with her peers in the activities, but she is focused on a unique objective. Figure 7.1 provides other examples of how a student's unique IEP objectives are overlapped within the general physical education curriculum.

Alternative Activities

Some students' unique IEP objectives cannot be safely and/or meaningfully overlapped within the general physical education curriculum. In such cases, the student with disabilities needs to work on his or her unique IEP objectives away from the general physical education activity. For example, a high school student with autism could get hurt during a regulation or even a modified game of speedball or volleyball, and these activities do not match his IEP objectives for physical education. In such a case, the student needs to participate in alternative activities away from the main physical education activity. To make such alternative activities inclusive, peers without disabilities can rotate away from the game to participate in the alternative activity with the student with disabilities. In the above example, five to ten students without disabilities can rotate into the alternative activity (e.g., bowling, tennis, walking, rollerblading) and participate alongside the student with disabilities. This allows the student with disabilities to work on his or her unique objectives while still interacting with peers without disabilities.

Models for Making Curricular Modifications

Rather than implementing specific guidelines for particular students, the following models outline the process that general physical educators and other team members can use to accommodate students with disabilities during general phys-

Student: Emilio   **Grade:** Fourth

Age: 10   **Unit:** Introduction to soccer skills

Emilio's IEP objectives for physical education

Activities in GPE soccer unit	Walk with walker	Throw overhand	Catch	Sidearm strike	Upper-body strength
Move from class to gym	X				
Warm-ups	X				X
Chipping station				X[1]	
Passing/trapping station		X[2]	X[2]		
Shooting station		X[3]			
Dribbling station	X[4]				
Lead-up game	X				
Move from gym to class	X				

1= Emilio uses a bat to hit soccer balls placed on a cone to practice his striking skills.
2= Emilio bends over to pick up balls that are passed to him by a partner; he then throws the ball back to his partner, who traps it.
3= Emilio throws smaller playground balls into the goal rather than trying to kick the ball into the goal.
4= Emilio kicks and then walks after the soccer ball; the focus is on walking with his walker in a cluttered area.

Figure 7.1.   IEP objectives overlapped within general physical education activities.

ical education. Once the process of manipulating the equipment and the task is understood, you can accommodate any student who enters the general physical education program. The following section provides additional general guidelines for changing the curriculum to accommodate students with a wide range of disabilities. Examples of ways to accommodate students who have specific impairments are discussed later in this chapter.

Developmental Task Analysis

A variety of task and environmental factors influence motor performance. Many of these factors can be modified by the teacher to make the activity easier or more challenging for particular students. Herkowitz's (1978) developmental task analysis is designed to systematically identify task and environmental factors that influence movement patterns. The model includes two components: 1) general task analysis (GTA), and 2) specific task analysis (STA). GTA involves outlining all of the task and environmental factors that influence the movements of students in general movement categories (e.g., striking, catching, jumping). These factors are then listed hierarchically in terms of levels of difficulty from simplest to most complex. Figure 7.2 provides an example of a GTA for striking. Note how this grid provides the teacher with information regarding the way in which various task factors influence specific movements and ways that the teacher might modify these factors to make a movement simpler or more complex.

Once the teacher has a general understanding of the ways in which task and environmental factors affect movement, he or she can develop an STA to examine in greater detail the ways in which select factors influence a specific movement. STAs are developed by creating activities that utilize two to four factors from the GTA. Like the GTA, these factors are broken down into levels of difficulty and listed hierarchically from simplest to most complex. The difference between the STA and the GTA is that, on the STA, levels of difficulty refer to specific factors rather than general categories. Figure 7.3 provides an example of an STA for striking. Note how more specific, observable information is provided in this STA than on the GTA in Figure 7.2. The teacher can quickly evaluate the ways that levels of difficulty in various factors influence movement performance in students. The goal is to get the student to perform the task under the most complex circumstances (in this case, using a 36-inch plastic bat to strike a tossed tennis ball). STAs also can be used to help less-skilled students and students with disabilities be more successful at a particular task. In striking, a student who has limited strength could use an 18-inch wooden dowel rather than a 36-inch plastic bat, or a student who has difficulty contacting a tennis ball with his or her bat could hit a 9-inch beach ball instead. Limitations such as strength and visual-motor coordination can mask a student's ability to perform a task using a more skillful pattern. By altering task and environmental demands, these students might be able to demonstrate more skillful patterns. Teachers also can use STAs to evaluate a student's present level of performance (i.e., circumstances under which a student can perform a given task) as well as progress a student is making (i.e., changes in these circumstances over time). (See Herkowitz, 1978, for examples of STA evaluation grids.)

Ecological Task Analysis

Davis and Burton (1991) developed a new type of task analysis that extends Herkowitz's developmental task analysis. They noted that, although it was a great beginning in skill analysis, Herkowitz's model contained two major flaws: 1) It did not consider the goal of the given task, and 2) it did not consider the attributes of the mover.

The goal of the task can have a tremendous influence on a student's movement pattern. For example, a mover might throw using what appears to be a very inefficient movement pattern (e.g., not stepping or stepping with the right leg while throwing with the right arm-side foot, not extending his arm in a backswing, not following through). If the goal of the task is to throw a dart at a dart board 10 feet away, the student's movement pattern might be very appropriate. Similarly, a student might perceive the goal of a task differently from what the teacher actually wants. In such situations, the student might appear to be displaying inefficient movement patterns. For example, a student might demon-

Factors	Size of object to be struck	Weight of object to be struck	Speed of object to be struck	Length of striking implement	Side of body to which object is traveling	Anticipatory locomotor spatial adjustments
Simple	Large	Light	None Slow	None	Favored side	No adjustment
	Medium	Moderate	Moderate	Short	Nonfavored side	Minimal adjustment
Complex	Small	Heavy	Fast	Long	Midline	Maximum adjustment

Modifications →

Figure 7.2.   General task analysis (GTA) for striking. (From Herkowitz, J. [1978]. Developmental task analysis: The design of movement experiences and evaluation of motor development status. In M. Ridenour [Ed.] Motor Development: Issues and applications [p. 141]. Princeton, NJ: Princeton Book Co.; reprinted by permission.)

	Factors	Size of ball	Length of striking implement	Predictability of ball trajectory
	Simple	S1 12" ball	L1 Hand	P1 Rolled along ground
		S2 9" ball	L2 Ping-pong paddle	P2 Bounced along ground
		S3 4" ball	L3 18" dowel rod	P3 Aerial ball
	Complex	S4 Tennis ball	L4 Plastic bat	

Figure 7.3. Specific Task Analysis (STA) for striking. (From Herkowitz, J. [1978]. Developmental task analysis: The design of movement experiences and evaluation of motor development status. In M. Ridenour [Ed.], *Motor development: Issues and applications* [p. 143]. Princeton, NJ: Princeton Book Co.; reprinted by permission.)

strate a chopping movement with very little bat motion in his striking pattern because he wants to hit the pitched ball (i.e., goal is perceived as hitting ball), whereas the teacher wants the student to take a full, horizontal swing at the ball while rotating his body (i.e., goal is perceived as using a certain striking pattern). The intended goal of the task is critical to eventual performance of the movement; however, the goal of the task is not discussed in Herkowitz's model.

The second weakness noted by Davis and Burton is the absence of the person performing the task in the task analysis equation. Herkowitz's developmental task analyses focused on the characteristics of the task rather than the characteristics of the mover. However, movers with different capabilities and physical characteristics will respond quite differently to changes in task factors. For example, Herkowitz listed ball size and balance as factors that can affect throwing performance. However, the size of a mover's hand and his or her own innate balance abilities will affect the degree to which ball size and balance requirements affect performance. For some students with large hands, subtle changes in ball size might not affect throwing performance. However, when a ball that is slightly larger than average is presented to a student with Down syndrome who has smaller hands than those of his peers, his throwing pattern may change from one-handed to two-handed (Block & Provis, 1992). Similarly, balance requirements in the task might not negatively affect a student who has good balance; however, such requirements might have a dramatic effect on a student with ataxic cerebral palsy who has difficulty with even simple balance tasks. Although performer characteristics, such as the goal of the task, are critical determinants of performance, performer characteristics often are absent from previous task analysis models.

In an effort to correct flaws found in Herkowitz's model, Davis and Burton proposed the ecological task analysis (ETA) model. Three of the major tenets of ETA include the following:

1. Actions are the result of the complex relationship between the task goal, the performer, and the environment. ETA includes a description of the task goal and the performer as critical factors in movement outcome.

2. Tasks should be categorized by function and intention rather than movement pattern or mechanism of performance. A specific function often can be

achieved through very different movement patterns. Although a particular pattern might be most efficient for one group of movers who have similar abilities and physical characteristics, other movers who have different abilities and characteristics might find another movement pattern more efficient. This is particularly true for students with disabilities, who often have very unique abilities and characteristics. Rather than describe a movement pattern such as skipping or throwing, ETA utilizes a functional task category that describes the general intent of the movement. Skipping, therefore, becomes one form of the function *locomotion*—to move from one place to another; throwing becomes one form of the function *propulsion*—to propel a stationary or moving object or person. Criteria for performance are specified for each functional task category. For example, under the locomotion category, criteria for performance include moving with efficiency, precision, accuracy, speed, and/or distance. Each mover, however, might use a different pattern to accomplish a given function and criteria.

3. Invariant features of a task and variations within a task may be defined in terms of essential and nonessential variables, respectively. Essential variables, or invariant features, refer to the underlying patterns that organize and define a movement. Relative timing between the two lower limbs during walking or galloping is an example of an essential variable. For practical purposes, broader descriptors of patterns of coordination, such as arm action in throwing, also can be viewed as essential variables. Nonessential variables refer to dimensions or control parameters that, when scaled up or down, may cause the mover to change to a new, qualitatively different pattern of coordination (new essential variable). These control variables can include physical dimensions of the mover such as limb length or weight, body proportions, or postural control; or they can refer to task factors such as ball size, weight of striking implement, or size of target. For example, throwing a ball at a wall from 5 feet away would result in the student displaying a pattern of coordination (essential variable) that is characterized by no stepping, no preparatory backswing, and no trunk rotation. As the student moves away from the wall (nonessential variable is scaled up), his throwing pattern will remain intact up to a critical distance. At that critical distance (and provided that the student has the underlying ability to display a different throwing pattern), the student's pattern will abruptly change to a qualitatively different throwing pattern: stepping with opposition, trunk rotation, and preparatory backswing.

According to Davis and Burton, several of the advantages of using the ETA are that a teacher can more accurately determine 1) under which set of conditions the student is able to achieve the task, 2) the set of conditions that elicit the most efficient and effective pattern (optimal performance), and 3) the dimension values at which the student chooses to use a different skill to perform a specific activity (e.g., changes from galloping to running). ETA appears to be a viable approach to understanding how a mover prefers to move and how changes in task variables affect movement.

Accommodations for Students with Specific Functional Impairments or Particular Disabilities

The previous section provided two models for creating curricular modifications to facilitate the successful inclusion of students with disabilities in general physical education. The models presented outline a process for making curricular modifications so that physical educators can begin to make their own modifications tailored to meet the unique needs of their students. However, some physical educators feel more comfortable if they receive specific suggestions regarding how to accommodate students with specific impairments or disabilities. Therefore, this section presents modifications designed to accommodate students with specific impairments or disabilities and is organized as follows: 1) accommodations for students with specific impairments such as difficulties with endurance or accuracy, and 2) accommodations for students with specific types of disabilities such as cerebral palsy or visual impairments. Although it is difficult to generalize modifications across categories, the specific modifications reviewed in this chapter should give you and other team members ideas for ways in which you can modify activities.

One final note before introducing specific accommodations: Although ideas to accommodate students with specific disabilities (e.g., mental retardation, orthopedic disability) are provided, you should focus on the functional strengths and weaknesses of the particular students rather than on their diagnostic labels. For example, it is difficult to generalize modifications to all students who have cerebral palsy. Functionally, students with cerebral palsy can be quite different. Some may have problems with coordination; others may have problems with strength. Therefore, accommodations should be different for each individual student based on his or her functional needs as opposed to his or her disability. In reading this section, it is useful to first think of the specific disabilities that students have, then return to the introductory section on specific functional impairments to cross-reference the best possible accommodations. You also should ask your fellow team members to provide more specific information regarding functional abilities of particular students.

Accommodations for Students with Specific Functional Impairments

Some students with disabilities have specific difficulties that affect their ability to perform at a level equal to that of their peers. Such impairments can become very frustrating for these students, eventually causing them to dislike physical education and physical activity altogether. Some impairments, such as difficulties with strength or endurance, can often be remediated so that the student can perform the skill at a higher level. However, structural impairments such as extreme short stature (dwarfism), visual impairments, or physical disabilities cannot be remediated. In these situations, modifications to activities may be introduced to allow the student to perform the skill more successfully. Most of these changes do not have to affect other students, although you may want to use some of these techniques to accommodate students without disabilities who are having difficulty with specific tasks. Table 7.1 outlines some general factors that can be manipulated to accommodate students with specific impairments.

Students with Impairments in Strength, Power, and Endurance

1. *Lower targets:* For students who do not have the strength to get an object to a target, the target can be lowered. For example, a student who cannot reach a 10-foot basket in basketball can shoot at a 6-foot or 8-foot basket. Similarly, the net can be lowered for a student who cannot hit a ball or birdie over a regulation volleyball or badminton net. By lowering the target, students will have a greater

Table 7.1. Adaptations for students with functional impairments

---

Adaptations for students with impairments in strength, power, and endurance

    Lower targets.

    Reduce distance/size of playing field.

    Reduce weight and/or size of striking implements, balls, or projectiles.

    Allow student to sit or lie down while playing.

    Use deflated or suspended balls.

    Decrease activity time/increase rest time.

    Reduce speed of game/increase distance for students without disabilities.

Adaptations for students with limited balance

    Lower center of gravity.

    Keep as much of body in contact with the surface as possible.

    Widen base of support.

    Increase width of beams to be walked.

    Extend arms for balance.

    Use carpeted rather than slick surfaces.

    Teach students how to fall.

    Provide a bar to assist student with stability.

    Teach student to use eyes optimally.

    Determine whether balance problems are related to health problems.

Adaptations for students with challenges with coordination and accuracy

    For catching and striking activities, use larger, lighter, softer balls.

    Decrease distance ball is thrown and reduce speed.

    For throwing activities, use smaller balls.

    In striking and kicking, use stationary ball before trying a moving ball.

    Increase the surface of the striking implement.

    Use backstop.

    Increase size of target.

    In bowling-type games, use lighter, less-stable pins.

    Optimize safety.

Adapted from Arbogast & Lavay, 1986; Herkowitz, 1978; and Sherrill, 1998.

opportunity for success, which in turn will encourage them to continue to practice the skill. Targets set at reasonable heights also facilitate the desired movement patterns. For example, students who cannot reach a 10-foot basket with a basketball using a "typical" shooting pattern often resort to different, less-effective shooting patterns (e.g., sidearm hurl, underhand, tossed backward over their heads). However, students often will use a more standard pattern when the basket is lowered.

    2. *Reduce distance/playing field:* Many physical education activities require students to throw, pass, serve, or shoot a ball a certain distance or run a certain distance. For example, when shooting a free throw, the student must be behind the free-throw line; while serving a volleyball, he or she must be behind the back line; and when running to first base, the student must actually run from home to first base. Although these distances are necessary when playing intramural or interscholastic games, they can be altered when teaching skills or playing lead-up or recreational games during physical education. Distances can be reduced so stu-

dents with disabilities can be successful. For example, a student could push his wheelchair to a first base that is half the distance of the general first base to accommodate his limited speed. Similarly, a student who can serve a ball only 10 feet can be allowed to serve from 8 feet away from the net rather than from the back line. Such accommodations do not give either team an advantage; however, they do allow the student with disabilities an opportunity to be successful. For games that require running up and down an entire floor or field (e.g., basketball or soccer), games can be played using the width of the field rather than the length, or half-court games can be played. Another modification that would not affect the entire class would be to allow a particular student to play in just half the field (playing just defense or offense or placing the student in a position that requires less movement [playing defensive back in soccer rather than midfielder; playing lineman in football rather than wide receiver]).

3. *Reduce weight and/or size of striking implements, balls, or projectiles:* Students with limited arm or grip strength or with a smaller than typical hand size may have difficulty holding large or heavy striking implements or balls. For example, a regulation-size tennis racket might be too long and heavy for a student with muscular dystrophy who is very weak in her upper body. Allowing this student to use a racquetball, badminton, or tennis racket with the handle cut off would contribute to her success. Some students with more subtle strength problems might simply need to be encouraged to choke up on the racket. Similarly, a student with small hands might have difficulty gripping a softball with one hand. Because of this, the student might resort to throwing the softball with two hands; however, he could demonstrate a one-handed throwing pattern if he used a tennis ball rather than a softball. Finally, some balls are too heavy for students to handle or may even scare students. Balloons, beach balls, or Nerf balls are good substitutes for volleyballs or basketballs that are too heavy or intimidating for a student.

4. *Allow student to sit or lie down while playing:* Activities played while lying or sitting demand less fitness than games played while standing or moving. Students with limited strength and endurance (e.g., cystic fibrosis, asthma) can be allowed to sit down when the ball is at the other end of the playing field in soccer or to sit while playing in the outfield. These students also can be allowed to sit while practicing some skills during physical education and move while practicing other skills. For example, a student with a heart condition who tires easily can warm up with the class by performing each of the locomotor patterns that the class performs; however, the student can be allowed to sit down when he is not performing a locomotor pattern.

5. *Use deflated balls or suspended balls:* By their nature, balls tend to roll when put in motion. Although most young students enjoy chasing balls, students who fatigue easily may use up all their energy chasing the ball after each turn, thus missing out on important practice trials. Balls that are deflated or paper balls (crumpled up piece of paper wrapped with a few pieces of masking tape) do not roll away as easily as general balls. Also, balls suspended from a basket or ceiling or balls tied to a student's wheelchair are easy to retrieve.

6. *Decrease activity time/increase rest time:* Games and practice sessions can be shortened for students who fatigue easily. Students can be allowed to play for 5 minutes, then rest for 5 minutes; periods can be shortened so that all students play for 3 minutes, then rotate to an activity that requires less endurance; or the number of points needed to win a game can be reduced. For example, a game of

sideline basketball can be played in which three players from each team play for 3 minutes while the other players on each team stand on opposite sidelines prepared to assist their teammates. Such a game would allow a student to be active for 3 minutes then rest for 3 minutes. Another possibility is to allow free substitutions during a game. For example, a student with asthma can come out of a soccer game every 2–3 minutes to make sure he does not have an asthmatic episode (i.e., he would not have to wait until the ball went over the end line or sideline to be substituted).

7. *Reduce speed of game or increase distance for students without disabilities:* Many games can move quite quickly, leaving slower players and players with limited endurance behind. It only takes a few instances of finishing last for a student to begin to dislike his- or herself and physical activity. Modifications can be made so that races and games are more fair for students with limited speed and endurance. For example, in a relay race, slower students might be required only to run one lap, whereas more-skilled students might be required to run two laps. Similarly, a special zone in soccer can be marked off for a student who has limited speed. When the ball goes into the zone, this student is the only one who can kick the ball.

Students with Limited Balance

1. *Lower center of gravity:* Allow student to perform activities while sitting down or while on his or her hands and knees. Also, encourage student to bend his or her knees while moving, stopping, and standing. For example, a student should be encouraged to land with his feet apart when jumping down from a box. When performing locomotor patterns, students should be encouraged to perform animal walks that lower the center of gravity (crawling, creeping, bear walking) or to move with their knees bent when performing locomotor patterns such as running and jumping.

2. *Keep as much of body in contact with the surface as possible:* Allow students with balance problems to walk or run flat-footed rather than on tiptoes, or allow them to perform balance activities on three or four body parts rather than on one or two body parts. For example, when working on locomotor patterns, allow a student with balance problems to jump on two feet while his classmates hop on one foot.

3. *Widen base of support:* Encourage students to stand with feet farther apart to provide more stability. For example, the student with poor balance should be encouraged to stand with his feet apart while preparing to catch a ball. Similarly, students should be allowed to walk or run with feet apart until they develop more postural control.

4. *Increase width of beams to be walked:* Students should be allowed to walk on the floor or on wider beams until they develop postural control. For example, a balance station could have 2-inch x 4-inch, 2-inch x 6-inch, 2-inch x 8-inch, and 2-inch x 10-inch beams so that each student is challenged at his or her own level of ability. In addition, a hierarchy of challenges could be set up; a student could begin by walking with one foot on and one foot off of the beam, then using a shuffle step across the beam, then walking across the beam holding on to the wall or a peer's hand, and, finally, increasing the number of independent steps he or she takes.

5. *Extend arms for balance:* Encourage students to hold their arms out to the side while performing balance activities. For example, have a student hold his or

her arms out to the side while walking on a beam or when learning how to walk, run, jump, or hop.

6. *Use carpeted rather than slick surfaces:* When possible, provide surfaces that increase friction. It is easier to perform various locomotor patterns on a carpeted surface than on a slick surface. For example, learning how to roller skate on a tumbling mat or carpeted surface is easier than learning how to skate on a gym floor. Finally, encourage students to wear rubber-soled footwear rather than shoes with slick bottoms.

7. *Teach students how to fall:* Students who have postural control problems that are not easily remediated (e.g., student with ataxic cerebral palsy) fall often. While teaching these students how to compensate for balance problems, they should also be taught how to fall safely by practicing how to fall on mats. You could even make a game of falling that all students can play. For example, a simple game such as "ring around the rosy" requires all students to fall at the end of the song. During the game, students can practice falling in a forward, backward, and sideward manner.

8. *Provide a bar to assist with stability:* During activities that require balance, allow the student to hold on to a stationary object for extra stability. For example, allow a student with poor balance to hold on to the wall as he or she walks across the beam, or let the student hold on to a chair while practicing the leg action in kicking. Allowing students to use balance aids while learning motor skills such as throwing and kicking may enable them to exhibit more-advanced motor patterns. A student who has difficulty stepping and throwing because of balance problems might be able to demonstrate a step and throw if allowed to hold on to a chair while throwing. The chair then can be gradually faded away as the skill becomes more ingrained.

9. *Teach student to use eyes in an optimal manner:* Vision plays a critical role in postural control. Teach students how to use their vision to facilitate balance. For example, students can be taught to focus their vision on a stationary object on the wall while walking on a beam or while performing standing balance activities.

10. *Determine whether balance problems are related to health problems:* Balance problems may be related to health problems such as inner-ear infections. For example, students with chronic inner-ear infections often walk later than students with no inner-ear problems. Talk to the student's special education teacher, parent, or physician to determine whether any health conditions are present that might negatively affect balance. In addition, find out whether the student is taking any medication that might affect balance. Balance difficulties due to health complications or medication might be acute in nature, in which case the student might need to avoid activities that require balance. If the problem is chronic or will last for several weeks or months, then some of the previously described modifications can be implemented.

Students with Challenges with Coordination and Accuracy

1. *For catching and striking activities, use larger, lighter, softer balls:* Large balls are easier to catch and strike than small balls. However, large balls may promote an immature catching pattern (e.g., scooping into the body rather than using hands). If a student is unsuccessful or frightened of small, hard balls (e.g., softball), then the use of a larger Nerf ball, balloon, or punch ball is appropriate. Gradually introduce a smaller ball to elicit a more skillful pattern. In addition, balls tossed directly

to a student are easier to catch than balls tossed to a student's side, whereas balls tossed to a student's side are easier to strike than balls tossed directly at the student.

2. *Decrease distance ball is thrown and reduce speed:* The distance a ball is tossed should be reduced for students who have difficulty tracking balls. For example, one student might be allowed to hit a ball pitched from 10 feet away in a game of softball, whereas other students are expected to hit a ball pitched from 20 feet away. Similarly, a ball can be tossed slowly for some students, faster for others, and still faster for very skilled students. Ideally, the teacher will vary distance and speed so that each student is challenged at his or her level yet has an opportunity to succeed.

3. *For throwing activities, use smaller balls:* Some students might have trouble gripping a ball (e.g., students with spastic cerebral palsy). Allow these students to use smaller balls or balls that are easily grasped such as yarn balls, koosh balls, paper balls, or bean bags. Again, the teacher should have a variety of balls available from which her students can choose so that each student is challenged yet successful.

4. *In striking and kicking, use a stationary ball before trying a moving ball:* Allow students who have coordination problems to kick a stationary ball or strike a ball on a tee before attempting to kick or hit a moving ball. Suspended balls that move at slower speeds and a known trajectory are also easier to kick or strike than moving balls. Again, allow the student to be successful and demonstrate a skillful pattern with adaptations, then gradually fade away adaptations as the student gains confidence and skill.

5. *Increase the surface of the striking implement:* Allow students to use lighter bats or rackets with a larger striking surface than those used by students without disabilities. Again, offer a variety of striking implements from which students can choose.

6. *Use backstop:* Students who miss the ball often may spend most of their time retrieving the ball rather than practicing the skill. This is not a good use of practice time and can become very frustrating for the student. When working on striking, kicking, or catching activities in which students may miss the ball several times, use a backdrop, backstop, nets, or a rebounder. One end of a piece of string could be attached to a ball and the other end to a student's wheelchair for ease of recovery.

7. *Increase size of target:* Allow students to throw or kick at larger targets, or allow students to shoot at larger baskets. In addition, give points for coming close to targets such as points for hitting the rim or backboard in basketball or points for throwing a ball that hits the side of the target but not the middle. Less-skilled students can be allowed to stand closer to the target in order to promote initial success, then gradually move back.

8. *In bowling-type games, use lighter, less-stable pins:* In games or activities in which the goal is to knock something down, use lighter objects (e.g., milk cartons, aluminum cans) so that any contact with the object will result in success. In addition, use more pins and spread them out farther than normal so that throws or kicks that would normally miss the target still result in success.

9. *Optimize safety:* Students who have problems with coordination are more prone to injury, especially in activities that involve moving balls. Students who are prone to injury should be allowed to wear eyeglass protectors, shin guards,

helmets, and face masks. When necessary, provide the student with a peer tutor who can protect the student from errant balls.

Accommodations for Students with Particular Disabilities

The following provides information regarding adaptations for students who have specific disabilities. The disabilities that are discussed in this section include 1) physical disabilities, 2) mental retardation, 3) hearing impairments, 4) visual impairments, 5) emotional disturbances or autism, and 6) health disorders. For more information regarding the medical and/or motor characteristics of any of these disabilities, refer to an adapted physical education or medical text. As noted previously in this chapter, a diagnostic label does not provide much information about a student's functional abilities. As you think of your particular students, cross-reference the modifications presented in this section with modifications outlined in the previous section on functional impairments.

Students with Physical Disabilities

1. *Confer with the collaborative team to determine the exact nature of the student's disability:* Make sure you obtain medical information from the student's physician and physical therapist, including information regarding contraindicated activities, activities that need modifications, and precautions for safety. Adhere to these restrictions. For example, a student's physical therapist can provide information regarding a student's range of motion in various joints and the best positions for functional movement.

2. *Prepare classmates without disabilities:* Provide classmates with general information about physical disabilities as well as specific information about the particular student who is being included. Talk about wheelchairs (allow students without disabilities to sit in and move a wheelchair to see what it is like). Talk about ways that students without disabilities can informally help a student who uses a wheelchair. For example, students without disabilities can retrieve errant balls or help push a student to a station. They also can be the student's partner during group activities. In general, students without disabilities should be encouraged to welcome the student with disabilities into their class.

3. *Think safety:* Students without disabilities should be aware of other student's wheelchairs or crutches when moving about the environment. Cones could be set up around a student who uses a wheelchair as a buffer to warn students that they are getting close to him or her. Also, peers should be assigned to stand near the student who uses a wheelchair to protect him or her from errant balls or students who get too close to him or her.

4. *Allow students with physical disabilities but typical intelligence to be included in decision-making processes regarding adaptations for certain activities:* The student probably knows better than anyone else what his or her movement capabilities are and how best to accommodate his or her abilities and limitations. For example, if you are working on locomotor patterns, a student who uses a wheelchair can decide how he is going to move his chair to simulate hopping (using one arm) or skipping (moving arms rhythmically) or how best to throw a ball (perhaps backward over his head rather than in the traditional forward manner).

5. *Make accommodations for limited strength, endurance, and flexibility:* Simple modifications that help a student overcome problems with physical fitness (see

previous chapter) can improve a student's success and ability to participate with peers in a variety of group games and sports. Encourage students to find their own modifications to accommodate their limitations.

6. *Make accommodations for limited coordination and reaction speed:* For example, utilize Herkowitz's developmental task analysis model to determine how you can modify task factors such as size of the ball, speed of the ball, trajectory of the ball, and so forth.

7. *Use rebounders or tie balls to a student's wheelchair so that student does not have to spend a lot of time retrieving balls:* For example, a student can practice throwing a ball that is tied to his chair with a 20-foot string. After the throw, the student simply pulls the string to retrieve the ball.

8. *Reduce playing area for student in wheelchair:* Although students without disabilities can be allowed to use the whole field or court, a student who is learning how to push his wheelchair could be allowed to move in a smaller space.

9. *Use "game analysis" techniques to determine the best ways to accommodate students who use wheelchairs in traditional games and sports:* Allow students without disabilities to participate in the decision-making process so that they do not feel that the modifications are being dictated to them. Use cooperative and initiative games, and encourage the group to figure out ways to safely include the student who uses a wheelchair.

10. *Utilize sports rules from specific sports associations* (e.g., National Wheelchair Athletic Association [NWAA], United States Cerebral Palsy Athletic Association [USCPAA], National Amputee Athletic Association [NWAA], or Les Autres Athletic Association [LEAA]): Each of these sports associations have specific rule modifications for various sports. For example, while playing tennis, a person who uses a wheelchair is allowed two bounces before she must hit a ball; in basketball, a person who uses a wheelchair can dribble by pushing his wheelchair while keeping the ball on his lap.

Students with Mental Retardation

1. *Confer with the collaborative team regarding the student's mental abilities and limitations:* Information from the student's special education teacher regarding his or her ability to comprehend verbal cues will be important. The special education teacher and speech-language therapist can give you vital information regarding how best to communicate with the student. Also, find out if the student has any behavior problems and which behavior management techniques are used when the student does misbehave.

2. *Prepare classmates without disabilities:* Provide information in general regarding mental retardation and specifically about the student who will be included in the class. Encourage students without disabilities to help the student with mental retardation in terms of understanding directions, understanding where to go and where to stand in activities and games, and how to practice skills correctly. Also, encourage students without disabilities to invite the student with mental retardation to join their stations or groups. Praise students without disabilities for befriending the student with mental retardation, and sternly reprimand students who tease, ridicule, or take advantage of the student with mental retardation. Students without disabilities should realize that the student with mental retardation wants to do well in physical education and wants to be friends with other students but that he or she may be shy or uncomfortable at first. Students with-

out disabilities can help the student feel more comfortable by simply befriending the student during early physical education sessions.

3. *Do not underestimate the abilities of students with mental retardation:* Given enough instruction, practice, and time, many students with mental retardation can learn skillful movement patterns. For example, most students with mental retardation, particularly those with mental retardation requiring intermittent or limited support, should be expected to demonstrate skillful throwing, striking, and catching patterns that allow them to be successful in a game of softball. Only after exhaustive efforts should less-skillful movement patterns be accepted (e.g., hitting a ball off a tee, throwing without rotating trunk). Most students with mental retardation also can learn to follow the basic rules of individual and group games and sports. There are many examples of Special Olympics athletes playing team sports such as basketball, volleyball, softball, and soccer. These players not only adhere to the rules of the game without any special modifications but also use more complex strategies and team concepts such as zone defenses in basketball and set dead-ball plays in soccer. Again, more instruction, practice, and time may be needed for these students to learn rules and concepts, but every effort should be made to give them an opportunity to learn how to play the game the correct way. Then and only then will these students have an opportunity to participate in community sport programs.

4. *Select activities based on chronological age rather than mental age of skill development:* This is particularly true for older students (middle school and older). Although students with mental retardation may be delayed by 2 years or more in mental and skill development compared with their peers without disabilities, it is important that you teach skills that will allow these students to interact with their peers and develop recreation and fitness skills for postschool life. For example, assume that a high school student with mental retardation requiring extensive support has the mental abilities and motor skills of a 5-year-old. Although it may seem reasonable to work with this student on activities appropriate for a 5-year-old child (e.g., learning basic locomotor and manipulative patterns), such activities will not help this student participate in activities played by his high school peers or help him acquire the skills necessary to independently participate in recreational activities as an adult. Realistically, you may have to work on two or three targeted activities rather than all the activities typically conducted in general physical education. For example, you may want to work only on softball, basketball, weight training, and aerobic dance with a high school student who has mental retardation requiring extensive support because it will take this student a long time to learn the basics of these four activities.

5. *Think safety:* Students with mental retardation often cannot anticipate potentially dangerous situations such as walking in front of a soccer goal when other students are shooting or moving in front of a target toward which students are throwing. Remind students with mental retardation (as well as students without disabilities) of the safety rules, and tell students without disabilities to be extra cautious of students with mental retardation (and to be cautious of other students as well).

6. *Provide direct instruction regarding how to play with toys and physical education equipment* (i.e., actually show students how to play with equipment such as how to throw bean bags, walk on beams, toss and catch balloons): Students with mental retardation may not understand how to play with toys and equipment or how to interact with their peers or teammates. Have students without disabilities act

as role models for appropriate play, and encourage students to invite the student with mental retardation to play with them. For example, if you are playing a co-operative game such as "musical hoops," have other students in the class invite the student with mental retardation to share their hoops.

7. *Keep verbal directions to a minimum and use extra demonstration and physical assistance when providing instruction:* Students with mental retardation do not understand verbal directions as well as their peers without disabilities, and they may miss key points during demonstrations. Help students focus on critical aspects of a movement by providing them with extra, specific verbal cues; demonstrating key movement components; and even physically assisting students to perform the movement correctly. Even if you are using a movement exploration approach, you may need to provide some physical assistance to students with mental retardation to help get the student "in the ball park" of the movement.

8. *Break skills down into smaller components:* For example, if you are working on the task of hopping with a class of kindergartners, most students can learn the skill by breaking it down into three or four critical steps: preparatory position, place arms out to side, bend knee, simultaneously extend knee and hip to lift body up. For students with mental retardation, you may need to extend this task analysis into 10 steps.

9. *Measure progress and reinforce skill development in smaller increments:* Students with mental retardation will learn, but their progress will be much slower than that of their peers without disabilities. Use various ways of detecting and reinforcing progress. For example, progress can include less-intrusive levels of assistance (e.g., going from physical assistance to demonstration, throwing a ball farther or with more accuracy measured in inches rather than feet, noting use of one or two more components in the overall locomotor or manipulative pattern).

10. *Be aware of limited motivation, particularly in activities that require physical fitness:* Plan on providing external reinforcements (e.g., tokens, primary reinforcements, free play) to encourage students with mental retardation to perform activities that are difficult, such as running, sit-ups and push-ups, practicing the correct pattern for throwing, and so forth.

11. *Let students with mental retardation know that they will not be ridiculed for performing a movement or activity incorrectly or more slowly than their peers:* Encourage students without disabilities to be patient with students with mental retardation and to praise them for trying difficult activities.

12. *Plan to help students maintain and generalize skills:* For maintenance, you will need to give the student many extra trials after he or she acquires a skill to help him overlearn the skill. Similarly, students may not generalize skills from one environment to another. That is, if a student is taught how to bowl in the gym, he may not be able to perform this skill at a bowling alley. Therefore, you may need to teach critical lifetime skills in the actual environment in which the activity will take place. This is especially true for high school students who soon will graduate from school and will be using their motor skills in community recreation environments.

13. *Be prepared to provide compensations for processing problems, perceptual problems, and fitness problems:* Students with mental retardation may not be able to process complex verbal instructions as quickly as their peers. Give them extra time to process information, and be prepared to repeat directions at a later time. Ask the student to repeat key parts of the verbal cues to make sure he or she un-

derstands what he or she is supposed to do. Similarly, some students with mental retardation may have problems intaking visual or auditory information, or they may have problems with spatial awareness. To help this student, actually set up activities in which the student can work on improving perception. For example, an activity at one station could include practicing going over, under, and between obstacles without touching them. A peer at the station can change the heights of obstacles to encourage the student to practice making correct decisions (e.g., when should he go over versus under?). In terms of physical fitness, allow the student with mental retardation to do fewer repetitions or run fewer laps at a slower pace than his or her peers. Encourage the student to try to improve his fitness by gradually increasing fitness demands, but be sure to reinforce even small amounts of progress. For example, most of the students do 20 sit-ups as a warm-up activity, but the student with mental retardation requiring limited support works on doing 5 sit-ups. Encourage the student to do additional sit-ups as the year progresses.

Students with Hearing Impairments

1. *Confer with the collaborative team:* Discuss the student's specific hearing impairment and any residual hearing that the student may have. Obtain specific information from the student's audiologist and speech teacher. Ask how the student communicates and how to best communicate with the student. Although learning sign language may be difficult for most teachers, learning a few key signs will help you convey instructional and management cues to the student more effectively. For example, simple signs such as STOP, GO, SIT, STAND UP, RUN, WALK, LINE UP, and COPY ME are relatively easy to learn. Most students do well with a good demonstration.

2. *Prepare classmates without disabilities:* Provide students without disabilities with general information regarding hearing impairments and specific information about the student who will be included. Explain the best way to communicate with the student, and encourage students to learn a little sign language so they can communicate with the student. Also, encourage students without disabilities to interact with the student who is hearing impaired and to invite him or her to join their stations or groups. Encourage students to offer to be a buddy to the student in terms of repeating directions, providing extra demonstrations, and generally watching out for the student if he looks confused.

3. *Position the student in front of the class and as close to you as possible when giving instructions:* If a student has residual hearing, you may want him or her to actually stand next to you. If the student is trying to read your lips, he or she should have a good view from the front of the class. Do not speak any slower or in a more exaggerated way than normal; remember, even good lipreaders understand only about 30% of what the speaker is saying. Be prepared to repeat verbal directions to the student off to the side of the gym after you have given directions to the entire class.

4. *Be prepared to provide extra demonstrations after you have given verbal cues to the class:* After you present information to the class, pull the student with a hearing impairment off to the side of the gym and give him or her a brief demonstration focusing on the exact component of the skill on which you would like the student to focus. For example, you might give a second demonstration in which you focus on the preparatory position for catching. Point to the student and ask him or her to repeat the demonstration to make sure she understands on which skills she should be working.

5. *Use extra visual cues such as written directions or pictures to describe exactly what you want the student to do:* For example, you can have a picture of the correct throwing pattern taped to the wall of a station. Point to the particular aspect of the movement on which you would like the student to focus. Also, provide the student with written information regarding rules and strategies that other students understand through verbal instructions.

6. *Make sure the learning environment has adequate lighting:* When outside, do not have the student face the sun; this will make it difficult for him to read your lips and see your demonstrations. In the gymnasium, make sure the janitor fixes all broken lights and that stations are set up where lighting is best.

7. *For students who use hearing aids, encourage use of residual hearing:* Discuss the student's hearing ability with his or her collaborative team, and determine how much residual hearing the student has. Also, determine whether the student hears better in one ear than the other, and if speaking into that ear would be helpful.

8. *Avoid excessive noise in the environment so that the student with a hearing impairment can focus on key verbal cues and directions:* Physical education classes tend to be noisy, but you can ask for quiet during critical instruction time. Again, if the environment is too noisy when you are relaying information to the class, repeat the directions (using demonstrations and gestures as needed) off to the side in a quieter environment.

9. *Be cautious of the student's hearing aids:* Students should be encouraged to wear their hearing aids during physical education (with the exception of swimming) to assist them in picking up verbal cues and sounds, but they should be aware of these aids during contact activities. Removal of aids in combative activities such as wrestling, karate, and football is probably appropriate, but check with the student's audiologist or physician.

10. *Utilize peer tutors to repeat directions, to give extra demonstrations, and to help the student understand what to do and where to go:* For example, if the teacher gives complex directions regarding which station to go to and how to perform an activity, a peer can repeat the information to the student with a hearing impairment via gestures and demonstrations. Some students without disabilities enjoy learning sign language and may be able to learn enough to communicate more explicit cues to the student.

Students with Visual Impairments

1. *Confer with the collaborative team:* Discuss the student's visual impairment and residual vision, other disabilities he or she may have, and specific safety considerations or contraindications. Obtain information from the student's ophthalmologist and vision specialist. For example, students with a detached retina can lose the little vision they have if they receive a direct blow to the head. Caution should be taken when exposing these students to activities using balls, and most combative activities (e.g., wrestling, karate, football) are contraindicated for these students.

2. *Always think safety:* If a student wears eyeglasses, consider having him or her wear eyeglass protectors during activities in which balls are used. Adhere to recommendations given by the student's collaborative team regarding safety precautions and contraindicated activities. When you are not sure whether a student can protect him- or herself in an activity (e.g., playing outfield in softball or wing fullback in soccer or performing locomotor patterns in a scattered forma-

tion), assign a peer to work with the student. For example, a student with a visual impairment can play deep center field in softball with a peer who plays short center field who can protect the student from line drives and hard-hit balls. When possible, replace hard balls with Nerf balls so that if the student does get hit it will not cause injury. There are new, firmer sponge balls that have the bounce and feel of softballs, basketballs, and soccer balls and that can be used by the class without affecting the game (this would make the game safer for all students, including students without disabilities who have less ability than other students without disabilities).

3. *Do not assume that all students with visual impairments like to play only stereotypical activities that are popular among people who are blind:* For example, although gymnastics, swimming, and bowling are relatively easy activities to learn for students who have visual impairments or are blind, many of these students will want to participate in the same activities as their peers. With modifications and extra assistance from a peer, these students can participate in volleyball, softball, basketball, and soccer—team sports that are not usually played by people who have visual impairments. Although students who are blind might not be able to play these sports independently, they can learn the rules of these sports and gain a better understanding of the various positions and strategies used in the game. This will enhance their enjoyment when listening to high school, college, or professional games, and many students may learn to enjoy working on the skills used in the game such as shooting basketballs or hitting a softball or tennis ball off a tee with verbal cues.

4. *Assist students who are blind or have visual impairments in moving safely and independently in the gym environment:* Have a peer take the student through the locker room to show him where the bathrooms, showers, and lockers are. Also, take the person around the gym to show him the boundaries and where equipment is located. Pay particular attention to stored equipment into which the student might walk. When changing the environment so that new equipment is placed around the gym, take time to show the student where the equipment is, what it is used for, and how it feels. Encourage the student to tactually explore balls, bats, and other pieces of equipment in order to better understand their use.

5. *"Anchor" student to play area:* Anchoring means telling a student who he or she is sitting next to when he or she enters the gym. This can be as easy as having the student sit next to the same students every time he or she enters the gym (e.g., in the same squad). If students sit randomly, have students without disabilities who are next to the student who is blind or has a visual impairment introduce themselves to the student.

6. *Prepare classmates without disabilities:* Students without disabilities should know a little about visual impairments in general and about the specific visual skills of the student who is being included. They should be encouraged to informally assist the student and be his or her friend during physical education. Suggest simple ways in which students without disabilities can provide informal assistance such as retrieving errant balls, helping the student find a station or position on the field, or helping the student perform a particular movement correctly. Also, encourage students without disabilities to talk with the student with a visual impairment, share team strategies, help the student understand where other students are positioned around the playing area, and so on.

7. *Use brightly colored objects and objects that contrast with the surrounding environment to encourage students to use their residual vision:* For example, use yellow balls

when playing outside on grass, or use blue balls when playing inside on an orange gym floor. Use brightly colored cones or tape to mark boundaries.

8. *Use tactile or auditory boundaries:* For example, use cones or change the surface (from grass to gravel) to indicate a boundary. Hang crepe paper from the ceiling for boundaries or mark the floor with tape that the student can feel with his toes or hands. Use beeper cones or music (a tape player works well) to indicate where a target is. For example, place a tape player under the basket during a basketball game to help a student determine the direction in which she should shoot a basketball.

9. *Be prepared to use very specific verbal directions and physical assistance when providing instruction and feedback:* For example, you will have to tell a student (or have a peer tell the student) exactly how he or she missed the target (you missed the target by throwing the ball 1 foot too high and 6 inches too far to the left). You will also have to give explicit feedback regarding a student's movement patterns (e.g., bend your elbow so that it is at a 90° angle when getting into the backswing position of the backhand stroke). In most cases, students with visual impairments will learn best if you provide them with physical assistance. You can physically assist the student through appropriate patterns so that the student "gets a feel" for how he or she should move, or you can have the student hold on to you while you perform the movement. This latter technique (called *reverse manual assistance*) works well as a supplement to more traditional physical assistance and explicit verbal cues. Auxter, Pyfer, and Huettig (1997) noted that you can present a demonstration to the class by using the student with a visual impairment as an assistant. You simply demonstrate the movement and physically assist the student who is blind. This way, you are giving direct tactile feedback to the student who is blind without taking time away from the rest of the class.

10. *Allow the student with visual impairments to use special equipment as needed to ensure success:* For example, bowling guides that are placed parallel to the student allow him or her to know where the side boundary is while taking an approach. This device could be used in similar situations when side boundaries are needed. Another simple modification is to attach one end of a piece of string to a ball and the other end to the student's hand so that balls do not get away easily. When throwing, for example, sighted students can see where their ball goes and easily retrieve it. For students who have visual impairments or are blind, they can throw the ball then retrieve it by pulling the string toward them. Other simple adaptations include having a guide rope when running to first base, running sprints, or swimming; using beep cones to indicate where to run; using foot markers for proper stance when batting; or dangling crepe paper as a reference point throughout the gym to mark certain critical points.

11. *Have the vision specialist translate all handouts and cognitive concepts such as rules of games, strategies, and names of equipment into braille:* For example, have the vision specialist translate a diagram of a baseball diamond with the names of all the positions into braille. Students who are blind also should be allowed to take written tests orally (have someone read him or her the questions; allow him or her to answer verbally).

12. *Utilize rules from the United States Association for Blind Athletes (USABA):* This sports governing body that is specifically for students with visual impairments has a variety of suggestions for modifying traditional sports such as swimming, track and field, and gymnastics. The suggested modifications can help you in-

clude a student who has a visual impairment in general physical education. For example, one of the rules for wrestling is that students must remain in contact at all times. This could be a fair compensation to which students without disabilities should adhere when wrestling a student who is blind. In addition, USABA offers information and rules for unique sports designed specifically for students who are visually impaired such as "Beep Baseball" and "Goal Ball." Although these activities have been designed specifically for students who are blind, they can be fun games to introduce to blindfolded students without disabilities to show them what it is like to have a visual impairment.

Students with Emotional Disorders or Autism

1. *Confer with the collaborative team to determine the student's specific behavior problems and what other team members do to prevent or deal with these behaviors:* Discuss any activities that might "set the student off" or make the student feel uncomfortable, and discuss simple ways that such situations can be modified. Determine which activities, teaching methods, instructional formats, or pieces of equipment (if any) should be avoided for particular students. For example, some students might fear loud sounds such as balloons popping. If you are planning on using balloons with a first-grade class, this student might work at stations away from the balloons or in the hallway with a teacher assistant during this particular activity. Similarly, some students do not do well in large-class formats (too much noise and stimulation). These students might be included slowly (included in part of class during small-group work or stations but removed during group games). Finally, some students are tactually defensive (do not like being touched). These students should be given directions verbally and through demonstrations. Physical assistance can be provided in small doses, and the students should be told ahead of time that someone will be touching them for a few seconds.

2. *Prepare classmates without disabilities:* The classmates of the student with disabilities should know a little about emotional disturbances or autism and how this particular student behaves in certain situations. They should be encouraged to interact with the student, but they also should learn to back off from the student if he or she is having a difficult time. For whatever reason, some students will "set off" students with emotional disturbances or autism. You may need to hand-pick groups so that students who set each other off are separated.

3. *Provide activities that ensure success:* This will help the student feel good about him- or herself and about physical education. As the student feels comfortable with you and the class structure, you can begin to introduce more challenges that may result in occasional failures. For example, initially, you can have the student shoot at a lower basket in basketball so that he will be successful. Later, you can introduce shooting at a higher basket for part of the class while reinforcing the student for good efforts as well as successful baskets. You may even want to set up a scoring system that reinforces good efforts. For example, a student can be reinforced for touching a ball with his or her hands when practicing catching (not just being able to catch the ball).

4. *Teach the student that it is okay to fail and how to accept failure or loss:* Spend some early sessions with the class so that everyone learns appropriate sportsmanship. Set up structured situations in which one team will lose. Warn them ahead of time and explain how to lose properly. Also, play more cooperative and initiative games as well as competitive games that deemphasize winning and losing. For example, play games in which points are scored by passing the ball to

teammates, or play a tag game in which tagged players do five jumping jacks and then can go back into the game.

5. *Provide a release for students who are aggressive:* If a student is prone to hitting other students or throwing things when he or she is angry, set up a special station where he or she can go and throw bean bags at a target. Explain to the student that it is okay to get angry and mad, but throwing bean bags at a target is more appropriate than hitting his or her fellow students. Encourage the student to think of other, more appropriate ways to vent his or her anger and frustration.

6. *Provide extra stimuli to help students focus on relevant information:* Many students with emotional disturbances (especially those with attention-deficit/hyperactivity disorder) or autism have difficulty focusing on the targeted activities. By making the activities fun and reinforcing, the students will be apt to pay attention and stay on task. For example, having a student hit balls off a tee against a wall is not as stimulating as hitting old soda cans off a tee to the wall (soda cans make a lot more noise).

7. *Provide additional external reinforcements for students:* Some students with emotional disturbances or autism (like many students without disabilities) are not intrinsically reinforced by physical education activities. Be prepared to provide extra reinforcements for these students to help motivate them to try new and challenging physical education activities. Although you should not bribe them, use a simple "Premack Principle" (e.g., "If you do a good job with this activity, then you can have a few minutes of free play"). Another technique that works is using a token system in which students receive tokens for displaying good behavior, following directions, or making efforts. Students can then trade in tokens at the end of the day, end of the week, or end of the month for something they want (e.g., playing a special game, using a special piece of equipment, playing with a special partner). Discuss possible behavior programs with the student's special education teacher.

8. *Clearly state consequences for misbehavior and follow through when student misbehaves:* Students need to know exactly what will happen when they perform the desired activities and when they misbehave. Describe in detail to the student both positive and negative consequences *prior to* implementing the program. You may want to practice the consequences one or two times in a nonthreatening way so that students clearly understand them. Once a student knows the program and consequences, make sure you follow through with these consequences when the student misbehaves. Do not give warnings unless they are part of the behavior program. Students will test the program in its early stages, and if you waver in your delivery of consequences, he or she will think he or she can get away with misbehavior. Again, confer with the team regarding specific behavior management techniques.

9. *Allow some flexibility in behavior:* Some students will come to your gym with a "chip on the shoulder" from something that happened at home or in the classroom. The student is often in no mood for physical education, and if you force him or her to participate you will no doubt have to deal with a major behavior problem. Let the student know that you realize he or she is having a hard time today and that he or she can choose to participate with the group or sit out. Point out that this is a special situation and that typically he or she would be expected to participate or face the consequences.

Students with Health Disorders

1. *Confer with the collaborative team to determine specific precautions, modifications, and contraindications to physical activity:* Information from the student's physician is particularly important. Adhere to these guidelines when planning and implementing your program. For example, a student with a congenital heart defect might be able to participate in all physical education activities except for those that raise his heart rate over a long period of time. Examples of activities that would be restricted include long-distance running, basketball, and soccer. However, the student might be allowed to play basketball and soccer if he only plays for 2-minute periods, then rests for 5 minutes or works on skills, then plays for another 2 minutes. Again, any modifications should be approved by the student's physician.

2. *Prepare classmates without disabilities:* Provide students without disabilities with general information regarding health disorders and specific information about the student who is being included (do not give information that will affect the student's right to privacy or cause him undue ridicule). For example, the class should understand why a student who has a seizure disorder must wear a helmet during physical education. They should be told that there is no need to be scared, and they should be encouraged to interact with the student and invite him to participate with them in their stations or on their teams. The right to privacy can create a tricky situation, particularly for students with acquired immunodeficiency syndrome (AIDS), so you will need to confer with the collaborative team regarding how much information you can give to the students without disabilities.

3. *Think about safety:* Although including the student is important, it is of utmost importance that the student participate safely. Modifications can be made so that students with health disorders can participate in general physical education activities. However, care should be taken so that participation will not jeopardize the student's health and safety. For example, a student who has a seizure disorder should not be allowed to participate in climbing activities, but the student should be able to participate in low ropes or low-height gymnastic activities with spotters and mats. Similarly, this student can participate in swimming activities with his peers if he has a one-to-one assistant with him. Again, safe modifications should be a team decision. Students with health disorders should not be immediately dismissed from physical education, nor should they be tossed in without considering their individual conditions. Students with AIDS or hepatitis pose a unique health risk to you and other students in the class. Utilize universal precautions during situations in which injuries such as cuts or scrapes occur. For example, use gloves when treating bloody injuries, and do not allow other students near the student when he or she is bleeding. You will probably want to confer with the school nurse regarding specific procedures for treating an injury sustained by a student with AIDS or hepatitis.

4. *Be aware of the effects of medication:* Some students who have health disorders take medication that has side effects that may affect their physical abilities. For example, some seizure medications can make a person's gums weak and prone to bleeding. Although these students can still participate in physical activity, they may need to be extra careful not to take a blow to the face. Similarly, some medications may affect a student's balance. Students with balance problems should be given a balance aid (can be as simple as a chair) or an assistant (could be a peer) during activities in which balance is needed. Some students

might need to wear helmets during physical education if their seizure disorders are not under control or if their medications cause problems in balance.

5. *Be aware how time of day or seasons affect particular students:* Some students improve once their medication has kicked in (e.g., after a student with attention-deficit/hyperactivity disorder takes Ritalin). Other students (especially some students with heart defects) gradually tire throughout the day and can hardly walk, let alone participate in physical activity, by seventh period. Still other students might be affected by the season (e.g., students with allergy-induced asthma). Whenever possible, accommodations should be made to have the student come to physical education earlier or later in the day depending on his or her condition. Similarly, students with allergy-induced asthma might receive physical education inside during particularly bad pollen days in the fall and spring. Again, confer with the team to determine the best time for the student to participate in physical education and when alternatives to general physical education are warranted.

PERSKE

8

Modifying Group Games and Sports

*Being included in a general PE class has made me feel uncomfortable.
I cannot participate in hardly any of the activities because of my physical limitations. I spend the whole class sitting on the side of the gym,
. . . And when people who don't know me very well come up to me and
ask me why I don't participate, I feel uncomfortable and embarrassed.
. . . But the only other alternative to taking a general PE class would
be in an adaptive PE class, and that seems a bit extreme for my situation. Perhaps another PE class should be offered, one that offers noncompetitive sports and low-impact activities.*

Chaney Hindman, tenth-grade student

Elena is a third grader at Monroe Elementary School. Elena loves to run and move,
and she loves physical education. However, Elena has autism, which makes it difficult for her to follow even the simplest rules of lead-up games that are a part of
general physical education. For example, Elena is easily tagged during tagging
and dodging games, and she gets easily confused regarding what to do and where
to go during relay-type games. The general physical educator is concerned that
Elena is missing out on the game experiences and might get hurt. What should
this physical educator do?

Andre is a sixth grader at Wilson Middle School. Andre has cerebral palsy,
but he gets around quite well with his walker. In fact, he loves to go really fast in
his walker and chase his friends. Andre attends a general physical education class
and does fairly well in warm-ups and skill activities. Problems arise when the
class plays team sports such as basketball and soccer. Although Andre has the
heart and the willingness to play, he cannot keep up with his peers. Andre tried
to play the games early in the semester, but lately he has asked his physical education teacher if he can just sit and watch. Clearly, Andre wants to play these
games with his peers, but he realizes that he cannot keep up. What can Andre's
physical education teacher do to accommodate Andre during team sports?

Mel is an eleventh grader at Hoover High School. She does not like physical
education because she does not move very well compared with her peers. This
may be due to Mel's learning disability and related perceptual problems, or it may
be due to Mel's being a little overweight and her limited fitness. Regardless, because physical education is required in Mel's high school, she must take some
form of physical education. Recently, one of the physical educators at Hoover
High School heard that alternative activities and games might be more appropriate and beneficial for students such as Mel who do not like traditional team
sports. Although this physical educator would like to organize such a program,
he is not familiar with the various types of alternative programs that are available. What are some alternative games for high schoolers like Mel?

Group games and team sports are popular activities in general physical education. When used properly, they can facilitate skill development as well as promote an understanding of rules, strategies, and concepts. Some group games also
can be designed to promote sportsmanship, cooperation, and teamwork. Unfortunately, group games and team sports are often conducted in such a way that
they promote adherence to rules and competition designed for very skilled athletes (Kasser, 1995; Morris & Stiehl, 1999). For example, it is not unusual to see
upper-level elementary school students playing regulation basketball games dur-

ing physical education; students use 10-foot baskets and follow professional rules even though most students at this age cannot reach a 10-foot basket or comprehend the rules of the game. Highly skilled students might enjoy these games, but the majority of students will quickly get frustrated and become passive, unhappy participants. And what of students with disabilities? Many general physical educators assume that group games and team sports are beyond the skill level or cognitive ability of students with disabilities, so these students are relegated to watching from the sidelines, keeping score, or keeping time. When allowed to participate in the game, they rarely enjoy success because they cannot perform the skills as quickly or as accurately as their peers.

Fortunately, many physical educators modify games and team sports so that all students can successfully participate. Some modifications can be relatively simple, such as allowing a student to hit a ball off a tee during softball games or to stand closer to the net when serving during volleyball games. Other modifications might require changes for everyone, such as making all players on the offensive team touch the ball one time before the ball can be shot during a basketball game. Still other modifications might change a game so much that a teacher might want to offer two or three variations of the game (e.g., one volleyball game that is played with regulation rules, another in which students use a volleyball trainer and are allowed to stand closer to the net when serving, a final game with a lower net that has a cooperative rather than a competitive focus).

The purpose of this chapter is to present a variety of modifications to group games and team sports that can be used when including students with disabilities in general physical education. As with Chapters 6 and 7, the first part of this chapter focuses on the general process or model for making modifications to group games or team sports. Once a physical educator understands the general process for modifying group games and the components of games that can be manipulated, he or she can apply this process to a variety of game situations. The second part of this chapter presents a variety of alternatives to group games, including adventure activities, cooperative games, and New Games. Finally, a list of modifications to popular individual and team sports is presented with suggestions for students with physical disabilities, mental retardation, and visual impairments. As mentioned in Chapters 6 and 7, the specific type of game modification you choose to implement will vary based on each individual student's needs, the abilities and competitive nature of the class, the purpose of the game, and the type of game being played. Although examples presented in this chapter might suggest that all students with similar disabilities could benefit from similar modifications, each student and situation should be analyzed separately.

Basic Principles of Adapting Games

Morris and Stiehl outlined three basic premises for modifying games that are ideal guiding principles when trying to include students with disabilities (1999, p. 4):

1. *Games are not sacred; kids are.* If a game is not appropriate for even a single player, it is worth examining and altering to accommodate that player. The design of a game strongly influences each student's experience of it. Children who are always the first to get tagged or are never given the ball are probably not benefiting from the intended purposes of the game.

2. *Games are for everyone, but not always in their traditional configurations.* For example, in its current form, professional baseball might be ideal for some players. Few would argue, however, that professional rules, equipment, and expectations are not appropriate for third graders. Instead, to accommodate this group, substantial alterations are necessary. There are many different ways to play a game such as baseball, and in physical education there does not necessarily have to be a right and wrong way to play the game. If the purpose of your physical education program is to include everyone, regardless of ability level, experience, or motivation, then a single, standard game design with strict rules might not be appropriate.

3. *You can modify any game to include anyone, accommodating a wide spectrum of abilities, interests, needs, and resources.* This will require modifications to various components of games such as the number of players, equipment, and how a player moves (refer to the section on "Games Design Model"). Some modifications might be for only one child (e.g., allowing a child who moves slowly a "safe area" in a tag game), while other modifications might involve several children (e.g., children who miss their first serve in volleyball get to take a step closer and try again). The key is thinking of alternative ways to play the game to accommodate all children.

Determining Whether a Game Accommodation Is Appropriate

As noted in the previous chapters, not all modifications are necessarily appropriate for a particular student with a disability in a particular situation. Again, the following four criteria should be used when considering whether a particular game modification should be used or if an alternative modification should be considered.

1. *Does the game modification allow the student with disabilities to participate successfully yet still be challenged?* For example, in a softball game a student with mental retardation might not be able to hit a pitched softball when it is tossed from the regulation pitching mound. However, this student can hit a pitched ball if the pitcher stands a little closer and tosses it right over the plate. Such a modification provides the needed accommodation for the student so that he or she will be successful, while still challenging the student to hit a pitched ball instead of hitting a ball off a tee (another accommodation that promotes success but may not be as challenging). Game modifications should be designed to meet each individual student's unique needs.

2. *Does the game modification make the setting unsafe for anyone?* For example, you want to include a student who uses a wheelchair in a game of volleyball. You can make a rule that the student must play one of the back positions so that other students are less likely to bump into the student. In addition, you can place cones around the student's chair so that classmates without disabilities who get too close to the student hit the cones first rather than the wheelchair. Finally, you want to remind peers at the beginning of the class and several times during the class to be careful around the student who uses the wheelchair. Peers will quickly learn to be careful, and the student can safely participate in the activity.

3. *Does the game modification negatively affect peers without disabilities?* This point is particularly important when playing group games. For example, an elementary class might be playing a game of tag, and included in the class is a student who

has autistic-like behaviors such that he is not really aware of the rules of the game. To include this student, the teacher makes a rule that, when he is the tagger, all students must sit down and let the student tag them. Obviously, students without disabilities are not thrilled with the idea of sitting down and letting another student, regardless of his ability, tag them. A better modification might be to make the space smaller, eliminate "safe" places, and assist the student to tag his peers. This way, students without disabilities are still challenged to avoid the tagger (perhaps more challenged because of the modifications), yet the student with disabilities can still be included. Similarly, it might be fun for a high school class to play "sit-down" volleyball one day to accommodate a student who uses a wheelchair or "beep softball" to accommodate a student who is blind; however, implementing such changes for an entire unit negatively affects the program for students without disabilities.

4. *Does the game modification cause an undue burden on the general physical education teacher?* For example, a ninth grader with advanced muscular dystrophy (who uses an electric wheelchair) is fully included into general physical education. Yet, the ninth-grade physical education unit is soccer. One solution is to change the game to accommodate this student. However, making major modifications for this student would be difficult for the general physical educator to develop and implement. Another solution is for the general physical educator to work with this student off to the side of the field one-to-one; however, this would not allow the teacher to supervise and instruct the other students. A better solution is to have this student play a "permanent throw-in" position. The student moves his electric wheelchair along the sideline of one side of the field. When the ball goes out of bounds, a player retrieves the ball, gives it to the student in the wheelchair, and then the student in the wheelchair throws it back into play (pushing the ball off his lap). This way the student who uses a wheelchair is a part of the game and gets to work on his goals of moving his electric wheelchair and moving his arms. Furthermore, this simple modification is relatively easy for the general physical educator to implement.

Games Design Model

Morris and Stiehl (1999) developed a systematic approach for analyzing and then changing group games. They built their model around the premises outlined previously: 1) games are not sacred, kids are; 2) games are for everyone, but not necessarily in their traditional configurations; and 3) any game can be modified to include anyone. Their approach uses the following three basic steps.

Step 1: Understanding Any Game's Basic Structure

Various aspects of games can be altered to accommodate the needs of students with different abilities. Table 8.1 outlines the way in which Morris and Stiehl conceptualized six major aspects of games and variations that can change the nature of the game.

Purposes of games can vary from one simple focus (e.g., improving one's motor skills) to the expectation that students will acquire a variety of skills, concepts, and behaviors. Not all students involved in a game necessarily have to work on the same goals. For example, a locomotor game played by students in a kindergarten physical education class could have different goals for various students, including improving walking gait for a student with cerebral palsy; im-

Table 8.1.   Components to be manipulated in the Games Design Model

Purposes	Players	Movements	Objects	Organi-zation	Limits
Develop motor skills	Individuals	Types	Types/uses	Types	Performance
Enhance self-worth	Groups	Location	Quantity	Location	Environment
Improve fitness numbers		Quality	Location	Quantity	
Enjoyment		Relationships			
Satisfaction		Quantity			
Develop cognitive skills		Sequences			

Adapted, by permission, from G.S. Don Morris & Jim Stiehl, 1999, *Changing kids' games,* 2nd Edition, (Champaign, IL: Human Kinetics), 18.

proving hopping skills for students with limited locomotor abilities; and improving body and space awareness while performing various locomotor patterns for skilled students. Similarly, goals for a game of soccer played by all students in tenth-grade physical education could include improving cardiovascular fitness for a student with Down syndrome and range of motion for a student with cerebral palsy, developing basic skills and understanding of the rules of the game for students whose abilities are lower than those of the typical student, and using various strategies for skilled students.

Players involved in the game can vary in two major ways: 1) the way or ways in which the players are grouped and 2) the number of players involved in a game. Players can be grouped homogeneously by gender, size, or skill level; grouped heterogeneously so that each team has an equal representation of skilled and unskilled players; or assigned randomly to groups. Similarly, a game may be played with more, fewer, or the same number of players for which the rules of a particular game call. Group size can be varied so that a particular team has more or fewer players than other teams. The way in which players are selected for a particular group as well as the number of players involved in a game will profoundly affect how successfully a student with disabilities is included. For example, a teacher needs to break down her seventh-grade physical education class into four teams for a modified game of volleyball. The class includes a student named Bill who has muscular dystrophy. He uses an electric wheelchair and has limited strength and mobility in his upper body. The teacher decides to group the teams by skill level, with each team having skilled players, average players, and unskilled players. The student with muscular dystrophy is unskilled, so he is assigned to Team A. Teams B through D also have unskilled players, so the addition of the student with muscular dystrophy is not an unfair disadvantage to Team A. The teacher also could divide the class so that unskilled teams (probably the one that Bill is on) have more players than teams that have more-skilled players.

Movement refers to the types of movements involved in a particular game and the ways in which these movements are used. Types of movements include types of locomotor, nonlocomotor, manipulative, and body awareness skills. Types of movements can be varied so that skilled students work on one skill during the game (e.g., skipping, throwing with a skillful pattern), less-skilled students work on other skills (e.g., galloping, throwing with a basic overhand pattern), and a student with disabilities works on different skills (e.g., pushing his wheelchair forward, grasping and releasing). Other ways in which Morris and Stiehl (1999) suggested that movements could be modified included modifications to locations of movement (e.g., personal space, general space, following certain directions, levels, pathways), quality of movement (e.g., variations in force, flow, speed requirements), quantity of movement (e.g., several repetitions, a few repetitions), variations in relationships (e.g., moving with or without objects or other players), and sequences (e.g., following a particular sequence or having no sequence). Modifications in movement dimensions are one of the best ways to ensure that students with disabilities are appropriately and successfully engaged in general physical education activities.

Susie is a third grader who has mental retardation requiring extensive support and displays autistic-like behaviors. Susie's class is working on the basketball skills of dribbling and passing a playground ball, skills that Susie does not demonstrate independently. The class consists of 25 students who have varying abilities, so the teacher has modified the movement requirements so that all students are challenged yet successful in the activity. Highly skilled students work on dribbling the ball while running between cones and passing by playing a game of keep-away, with one person in the middle trying to steal the pass from two players who pass the ball back and forth using different passing patterns. Students who can dribble and pass but still need practice in dribbling the ball while jogging forward and passing the ball back and forth from various distances, depending on each student's strength. Students who are just learning how to dribble and pass work on dribbling a ball while standing in one place and passing a ball so that it hits a large target on the wall. Finally, with assistance from various peers in her class, Susie works on her dribbling skills by dropping the ball and catching it before it bounces again. Susie also works on passing by handing the ball to a peer upon a verbal request. During relay races at the end of class, each student uses the skills on which he or she has been working. That is, some students have to dribble between cones, some student have to dribble while jogging forward, some students have to dribble the ball 10 times, and Susie has to drop and catch the ball with assistance. The basic movements are similar, but the ways in which these movements are operationalized during practice as well as during the game vary from student to student depending on each student's abilities.

Good example

Objects, equipment used during practice or a game, can vary in terms of how a student moves in relation to the object (e.g., going under, over, or through hoops; catching, kicking, or throwing a ball), how the object moves a student (e.g., scooterboards, skates, tricycles), how an object is used to propel other objects away (e.g., bats, hockey sticks, rackets, feet or hands), or how objects are used to gather other objects in (e.g., gloves, hands, lacrosse sticks, milk cartons). The number and placement of objects in the environment also can vary depending on the needs of each student. For example, some students might use regulation-size bats to propel objects away from their bodies (i.e., batting), other students might use slightly larger bats, and still other students might use very large bats to hit very large balls. Varying the objects will ensure that each student is working at a level that meets his or her unique needs.

Organization refers to decisions regarding the patterns, structure, and location of players. Some games might have very strict patterns to follow, such as relay races in which students are expected to line up behind one another or dodge ball, which is played in a circle. However, the structure also can be undefined, with players being allowed to move anywhere they wish in the environment (with or without set boundaries). Another organizational component is the location of players and objects within the boundaries. Are players in close proximity to each other or are they spread out? For a student with limited mobility or strength, a fair accommodation would be to have other students stand near him when it is his turn to toss a ball to them or tag them. However, if the student was hitting a ball off a tee during a softball game, it would be reasonable to have the defensive team stand far away from him. Similarly, the distance each student has to run during a relay race could vary based on each student's individual abilities.

Limits are the general rules to which players are asked to adhere. Some games might have movements that are deemed acceptable or unacceptable or necessary or unnecessary. For example, it might be necessary for a skilled student to dribble through several cones, though this rule is not necessary for lesser-skilled students. It might be unacceptable for skilled students to spike a volleyball unless it goes into a certain zone (i.e., if the student spikes the ball and it does not go into the zone, the other team gets the ball). *Limits* also refer to the physical aspects of the environment and activity conditions. Physical aspects of the environment can vary (e.g., width of the playing field, special zones for students with disabilities, size and type of equipment, number of players in the game). Activity conditions can vary in terms of how long the game is, how long a particular student gets a turn, scoring, or rules. For example, a skilled student gets one pitch to hit in a softball game, a less-skilled student gets three pitches, and a student with disabilities gets to hit the ball off the tee. In terms of scoring, the skilled student would be safe if he or she ran all the way to second base before the other team could retrieve the ball, the less-skilled student if he or she ran to the regulation first base, and the student with disabilities if he or she made it to first base set up 10 feet away from home plate.

Step 2: Modifying a Game's Basic Structure

This level of game analysis involves applying the components outlined in the first step to specific games. That is, games should be devised and modified based on your answers to questions such as "What is the purpose of the game?" "How many players will be involved?" "What are the movements?" "What objects will be used?" and so forth.

There are two basic ways to modify a game's structure. First, you can manipulate the components in Step 1 to make up a completely new game. For example, if your purpose is to help students develop and improve kicking skills (i.e., purpose/movement components), you can make up a game that works on these skills by manipulating the game components. One game could consist of equal teams with three players each (i.e., players component). Each team is given one large box to kick (i.e., objects component; boxes for washing machines or refrigerators work particularly well), with the object of the game being to kick the box across the gym. The rules are that each player on the team must kick the box at the same time (i.e., count 1, 2, 3, kick) and that players cannot touch or kick another team's box (i.e., organization/limits component). This novel game ensures that teammates work together and that each player gets many turns to practice the skill of forceful kicking.

A second way to manipulate components is to modify traditional games. Traditional games of soccer, basketball, or volleyball often are dominated by one or two skilled players. Game analysis can be used to modify these traditional sports so that everyone gets opportunities to participate, improve skills, and contribute to the game. For example, a basketball game can be modified so that the focus of the game is on improving passing skills and teamwork (i.e., purpose/movement component). Six teams of five players each are selected by the teacher so that each team has an equal representation of skilled and nonskilled players (i.e., players component). Rules are modified to encourage passing and teamwork by changing the ways in which teams can score points. As in regulation basketball, points can be earned by making baskets; but, in the modified game, a team that passes the ball to each player before shooting gets double points for every basket made (i.e., limits component). In addition, every time a different player makes a basket, the team gets five bonus points. This encourages teammates to pass the ball before shooting and to make sure everyone on the team shoots the ball at least once during the game. In addition, some players must shoot at a 10-foot basket, whereas other players can shoot at an 8-foot basket (i.e., objects component). Manipulating game components is an easy way to ensure that the students are focused on specific goals and maximum participation and practice is afforded to each student.

Step 3: Managing a Game's Degree of Difficulty

This level of analysis is perhaps the most important in terms of accommodating students with disabilities. This step involves analyzing each of the game's components and then creating a continuum within each component from easy to difficult. The continuum can then be used to make a game or skill easier or more difficult for particular students. Skilled students can be challenged by making the activity more difficult, and students with lower abilities or specific disabilities can become more successful by making the activity easier. Morris and Stiehl (1999) outlined the following strategy for identifying degree of difficulty:

1. *Action 1: Identify factors that may limit a player's performance.* List the various aspects of the task that can be manipulated. External factors such as ball size, size of targets, and speed of objects should be the focus at this level. According to Morris and Stiehl, a student's personal abilities such as visual perception or strength should not be considered at this level of analysis because these factors cannot be influenced directly by game analysis. However, personal limitations can be accommodated by making simple changes in task complexity. For example, a larger, slower-moving ball can be used for kicking or striking for a student who has a visual perception problem or a visual impairment.

2. *Action 2: Diagram the task complexity spectrum.* Factors identified in Action 1 can now be sequenced along a continuum from less difficult to more difficult. For an example of how the factor "ball speed" in kicking might be listed, see Figure 8.1. All of the factors related to the targeted skills should be sequenced as in Figure 8.1. These sequences will begin to help you understand how to modify activities to accommodate students with varying abilities.

3. *Action 3: Begin to create tasks that vary in difficulty.* The final action is to take all of the factors and the sequences you have developed and compile them into a *task complexity (TC) spectrum* for a particular skill. An example of one of Morris and Stiehl's TC spectrums is presented in Figure 8.2.

Game categories (e.g., limits, players) also can be modified to make a particular game easier or more difficult for a group of students. For example, having four teams shoot at four separate goals during a soccer game would make the

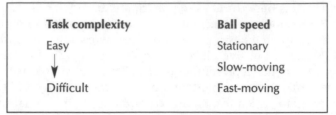

Figure 8.1.   Sequence of factors for kicking.

game more difficult, whereas having two teams of just three players each would make the game easier. Similarly, using a smaller playing field would make soccer easier for players with limited endurance, but using a smaller tennis court would make the game more difficult for a skilled player. The TC spectrum now shows in one schematic the ways in which several factors can be manipulated to accommodate a student with disabilities, make a task slightly less difficult for a student just learning a skill, or make an activity more challenging for a skilled player.

In summary, Morris and Stiehl's Games Design Model involves three basic stages: 1) understanding the basic structure of the game, 2) modifying the structure of a specific game, and 3) managing the game's degree of difficulty. Systematic analysis of games will help the physical education teacher make good decisions regarding how to successfully include students with disabilities into general physical education activities.

Unique Games and Group
Activities that Can Facilitate Inclusion

Project Adventure

Project Adventure (PA) is based on the "philosophy that people are usually more capable (mentally, emotionally, and physically) than they perceive themselves to be. PA games and activities give people opportunities to challenge themselves and to take risks within the supportive atmosphere of the group. Adventure means any new experience that elicits excitement" (Ellmo & Graser, 1995, p. 4; see also Rohnke, 1977). Goals of the adventure program are as follows:

1.   To increase the participant's sense of personal confidence

2.   To increase mutual support within a group

3.   To develop an increased level of agility and physical coordination

4.   To develop an increased joy in one's physical self and in being with others

5.   To develop an increased familiarity and identification with the natural world

These goals are achieved through the use of group initiative activities such as noncompetitive games, group problem solving, initiatives, and rope course activities (e.g., climbing, using rope swings) to create excitement and achieve the goals of facilitating personal learning and growth. Group initiative activities are designed "to increase a student's ability to be an active member of a group which has a problem to solve . . . This problem-oriented approach can be useful in developing each student's awareness of decision-making, leadership, and the obli-

TC	Size of support base	Center of gravity	Speed	Time
Easy	Eight body parts	Directly over and close to base of support	Slow	8 seconds
↓	Four body parts	Slightly off center and above base of support	Fast	18 seconds
Difficult	One body part	Moderately off center and far above base of support	Faster	30 seconds

Figure 8.2.   Task complexity: Balance factors. (From Morris, G.S.D., & Stiehl, J. [1999]. *Changing kids games* [p. 139]. Champaign, IL: Human Kinetics Books; reprinted by permission.)

gation of each member within a group" (Rohnke, 1977, p. 65). In terms of including students with disabilities, group initiative activities can be used to highlight the importance of including all students in the class to achieve a team goal. The rules of the game do not permit exclusion of any participants, which forces the team to figure out how to safely and meaningfully include all participants. In fact, initiative games help team members focus on each person's strengths and how he or she can best contribute to the solution. After they have participated in group initiative activities, students can apply cooperative problem-solving skills learned in initiative games to include students with disabilities in more traditional team sports.

An example of a simple initiative game is Reach for the Sky (Rohnke, 1977) The object of the game is to place a piece of tape as high as possible on a wall. Teams of as few as three and as many as 15–20 players work together to build a human tower to place the tape as high as possible on the wall. Groups quickly realize that heavier students should be on the bottom to support smaller players. A student who uses a wheelchair can be a good support on the bottom of the tower, using his wheelchair as a base and his arms to help hold a person in place. Students with fetal alcohol syndrome (FAS), who tend to be smaller than their peers, can be used near the top of the tower. Therefore, a person's strengths are highlighted rather than his or her weaknesses, and students without disabilities learn to appreciate how each person, regardless of whether he or she has a disability, can contribute to team efforts and successes.

The concept learned in the group initiative game can be transferred to traditional games; students without disabilities can focus on both a student's strengths and weaknesses in a modified game. For example, during a game of basketball, a student who uses a wheelchair can be seen as a tough obstacle to get around as a point guard positioned in a 2-1-2 defense alignment (i.e., typical zone defense alignment in which two players guard the area near the foul line, one player guards the middle, and two players guard the area close to the basket). The student with FAS, who may have attention-deficit/hyperactivity disorder, could be used as a chaser while playing defense, chasing the ball and harassing any player who has the ball. During a game of football, the student who uses a wheelchair can be used as an offensive lineman, protecting the quarterback by moving his wheelchair so that oncoming rushers must run around him. Similarly, the student with FAS can be a rusher who enjoys chasing other players. Obviously, including students who use wheelchairs or other students who use adapted equipment can be dangerous. Make sure that you talk to the group about safety—particularly about being aware of the students who use wheelchairs. In addition, you might want to make special rules for the students who use wheelchairs to limit the area about which they can move so that students without disabilities know where "safe" areas are. Students will learn quickly if they are given proper instruction.

One of the nice aspects of group initiative games is that there are no set solutions or answers to the problems presented by the physical education teacher or group leader. Solutions depend on the unique characteristics of each member and the ways in which these characteristics interact with the characteristics of other group members. This fact should be pointed out to the group at the end of each initiative game or at the end of a class that included several initiative games. Group discussions are a critical part of the adventure process, and participants should be encouraged to share their thoughts regarding how they solved problems during the activity. During group discussion you can focus on the way in which each member of the team contributed to the group goal. Group discussions also can be used to guide students to think about how students with varying abilities can be included in an activity and contribute to the team. For example, the group leader can ask group members how they worked with John (student who uses a wheelchair) to complete their task. The leader could then ask the group members how they would achieve the goals of the task if a student who was blind or a student with cerebral palsy were included in the activity. The group could then learn about and discuss the various disabilities and abilities of individuals who are blind or who have cerebral palsy and how best to modify activities to safely and successfully include those students in the activities. (See Ellmo & Graser, 1995, and Rohnke, 1977, for samples of group initiative games.)

Cooperative Games

Cooperative games are designed to help students play with one another and work together to overcome challenges rather than against one another to overcome other people (Orlick, 1978). The major goal of cooperative games is to create an environment that helps "children play together for common ends rather than against one another for mutually exclusive ends. In the process, [children] learn in a fun way how to become more considerate of one another, more aware of how other people are feeling, and more willing to operate in one another's best interests" (Orlick, 1982, p. 4). Obviously, the atmosphere created by cooperative sports is conducive to including students with disabilities into general physical education.

The major difference between traditional games and cooperative games is their focus and structure. As Orlick explained, traditional games, such as "King of the Mountain" (one student [the "king"] tries to push all others off of the "mountain") requires players to work against each other, and only one player can achieve the goal of the game. Therefore, the game has an inherent competitive focus and structure. In contrast, a cooperative version of the same game, "People of the Mountain," adopts a completely different goal: to get as many people as possible to the top of the mountain. This requires students to work together rather than compete against one another. The focus of the game is inherently cooperative and encourages classmates to help and support each other. In addition, every student is a winner in this game.

Although they focus on skill development, many physical education programs present skill development through competitive activities. Although these competitive activities are fun and motivating for skilled students who can win competitive games, students with less ability, including students with disabilities, rarely have an opportunity to win. In addition, competitive team sports drive skilled players to pressure less-skilled players. Mistakes are more obvious, and more-skilled players often dominate the game and overshadow less-skilled players. Less-skilled players lose confidence and self-esteem and eventually even learn how to avoid fully participating in the game. For example, after miskicking a soccer ball during a soccer game and being ridiculed by his teammates and teased by his opponents, a less-skilled player avoids kicking the ball for the remainder of the game by positioning himself away from the action. Is this what we want for our physical education programs? Is this student going to improve his soccer skills? If this happens to less-skilled students without disabilities, what happens to students with disabilities who are included in such an atmosphere?

An alternative to competition in physical education is cooperation. Cooperative games can be implemented at various levels. One level is to play only cooperative games such as People of the Mountain, in which the focus of all activities is cooperation. This approach is most appropriate for elementary students who are learning how to work together and have not been exposed to traditional sports. A second level is to play within the traditional competitive structure but to focus on cooperation instead of competition. For example, the focus of a game of volleyball can be to see how many different players on a team can hit the ball before it is hit over the net rather than which team scores the most points. Such an approach is appropriate for students just learning game skills who need practice in a game atmosphere without the added pressure of competition. A third level is to include self-paced activities that are not assessed or scored. For example, Clean Out Your Backyard, a fun throwing game for young students in which teams throw yarn balls back and forth toward each other, can be played without highlighting which team has fewer balls on its side. For older students, a basketball game can be made less competitive by simply not keeping score. Finally, the fourth level includes goal-oriented play in some situations and lighthearted play in other situations. For example, some days the class can work on basketball following traditional rules; other days, the focus can be on which team passes the ball the most before shooting or on which team the most players score.

Most traditional physical education activities, including group games and team sports, can easily be made more cooperative by making just a few changes. *The Cooperative Sports and Games Book* (Orlick, 1978) and *The Second Cooperative Sports and Games Book* (Orlick, 1982) present several suggestions for making traditionally competitive games cooperative. For example, Musical Hoops is a cooperative version of Musical Chairs. In traditional Musical Chairs, music is played, chairs are taken away when the music stops, and students fight against each other for a chair in which to sit. The quickest students usually get to sit in the remaining chairs, whereas less-skilled players, including students with disabilities, typically are the first to be eliminated. In Musical Hoops, when the music stops and hoops are taken away, players must share the remaining hoops. Imagine an entire class of kindergartners, including a student who is blind and another with cerebral palsy who is much slower than his peers, working together to fit in one hoop! Another example is Alaskan Rules Baseball. One of the problems in traditional baseball is that players in the field stand around waiting for the ball to be hit to them. Even if a ball is hit to a less-skilled player or a player with a disability, chances are that a more-skilled player will run over and try to field the ball. Consequently, skilled players get more turns and become more skilled, whereas less-skilled players and players with disabilities get fewer practice turns and get bored. In Alaskan Rules Baseball, all players on the field must touch the ball before a player is called out. The first player who gets the ball picks it up, and all other players on the team line up behind that player. The ball is then passed (or tossed) from player to player. When the last player has the ball, he yells "stop," at which time the player's turn is over. The batter gets one point for every base he touches. See Grineski (1996) for more examples of co-operative games and activities.

New Games

New Games are games that allow people of all ages and abilities to play in an atmosphere where fun and creativity are a premium (Fluegelman, 1976). The following points are the principal philosophies of New Games:

1. Individuals choose games and make changes to rules as needed so that every student can be involved.

2. Modifications can occur at any time (even in the middle) during the game.

3. Everyone should enjoy the activities. If not everyone is having fun, then modifications are probably needed.

4. Fair, fun competition is important, but winning is deemphasized.

New Games Book (Fluegelman, 1976) and *More New Games* (Fluegelman, 1980) contain descriptions of hundreds of games that can be played by as few as 2 to as many as 100 players. Games are also categorized in these books by the participants' levels of activity. New Games lend themselves nicely to integrating students with disabilities and can be fun rainy-day activities for students without disabilities. The following are two examples of New Games that easily can accommodate students with varying abilities.

People to People   Students are paired up and stand in a circle facing one player who is the leader. The leader calls the names of two body parts, for example, "back to back," and the partners must touch their backs together. When everyone is touching backs, the leader then calls the names of two more body parts, for example, head to knee, and each partner must touch his or her head to his or her partner's knee. The game continues this way until the leader says, "People to People," at which time everyone (including the leader) tries to find a new partner. Whoever is left without a partner is the new leader.

Amoeba Tag   Players scatter about the playing area, and one player is designated *it*. Players move about the playing area while *it* tries to tag a player (every so often, you can change the way players move, such as requiring them to gallop, skip, jump, hop, travel at different levels [high, medium, low], or follow different pathways [straight, curvy, zigzag]). When a player is tagged, he or she holds *its* hand, and both players become *it*. When another player is tagged, he or she holds hands with the two-person *it* to form a three-person *it*. As new students are tagged, they join the ever increasing *it*. Eventually, all but one player is *it*.

Specific Modifications to Traditional Team and Individual Sports

Many middle and high school physical education programs focus on traditional individual and team sports. It may be easier for physical educators in these types of programs to focus on simple modifications to these traditional sports and activities rather than the game model discussed previously in this chapter. Therefore, the following pages provide information regarding specific ways to modify select individual and team sports to meet the needs of students with disabilities. Information, written in outline form, includes 1) general suggestions for modifying skill work, 2) general suggestions for modifying games, and 3) modifications for students with specific disabilities. This is not supposed to be a comprehensive list but rather provides suggestions for modifying traditional individual and team sports. As you learn more about the functional skills of your students as well as how to utilize these modifications, you will quickly begin to incorporate your own modifications to meet the needs of your particular students.

Again try to focus on the functional requirements of a particular skill and how they relate to the functional abilities of your students. For example, running to first base in a game of softball requires a certain amount of balance and the ability to run (or move) a certain distance. How do these requirements match the particular balance and running abilities of your student or students with disabilities? Similarly, the functional requirements for hitting a tennis ball are strength and coordination. How do these requirements match the particular strength and coordination abilities of your student or students with disabilities? As you review the specific suggestions in the chapter appendixes, look back at Chapter 7 and the section on accommodating students with specific functional impairments as a cross-reference. Also, as noted previously in this chapter, although these suggestions are presented for students who share similar disability labels, your exact modifications should be based on each student's unique abilities and needs as well as the nature of the sport and the focus of your lesson. Do not think that a successful modification for one student who has mental retardation will necessarily work for another student with mental retardation who has very different functional abilities.

Appendix A

Accommodations to Team Sports for Students with Disabilities

Basketball

Dribbling

General

- Use larger or smaller balls.
- Use playground balls, Nerf balls, or punch balls (large balloons).
- Vary distance required to travel.
- Vary speed required.
- Use only dominant hand.

Students who use wheelchairs (typical upper-body strength)

- Hold ball on lap and push wheelchair.
- Push wheelchair a few rotations, bounce ball one time, then push wheelchair again.

Students who use wheelchairs (limited upper-body strength and control)

- Have peer push wheelchair while student holds ball in lap or in hands.
- Have peer physically assist student in bouncing ball.
- While being pushed, have student repeatedly hit ball as it sits on lap tray.

Students with visual impairments

- Allow student to dribble in place.
- Allow student to use two hands to dribble.
- Allow student to dribble in place a few times, then walk forward toward sound of peer.
- Allow student to walk forward while dropping and catching ball for dribbling.
- Attach string to ball and to student's wrist so that ball is easy to retrieve.
- Have student stand in corner of gym while dribbling so that ball is less likely to bounce away.
- Put bell or beeper in ball so that student can retrieve it when it bounces away.

- Have peers assist student by giving verbal cues for direction and by retrieving balls that get away from student.

Students with mental retardation or learning disabilities

- Allow student to walk while dribbling.
- Allow student to stand, bounce, and catch ball.
- Allow student to walk while holding ball.
- Allow student to use two hands to dribble.
- Allow student to walk forward while dropping and catching ball for dribbling.
- Encourage proper technique.

Passing and catching

General

- Use suspended balls.
- Use larger or smaller balls.
- Use textured balls.
- Use playground balls, Nerf balls, or punch balls (large balloons).
- Vary distance required to pass (have peers stand closer).
- Toss ball slower than required.
- Toss ball at known trajectory.

Students who use wheelchairs (typical upper-body strength)

- Encourage student to find the best way to pass (e.g., overhead versus chest versus sidearm).
- Use soft balls (Nerf balls) for safety as needed.

Students who use wheelchairs (limited upper-body strength and control)

- Use soft balls (Nerf balls) for safety.
- Push ball down ramp.
- Push ball off lap.
- Swing arm and hit ball held by peer.
- Kick ball if legs have more control than arms.
- Hit ball off tee (or held by peer) with head.

Students with visual impairments

- Use soft balls (Nerf balls) for safety.
- Use verbal cues (tell student when ball is released for catching; tell student where to pass).
- Use bounce pass (ball makes sound).

- Put bells or beeper in ball.
- Use physical assistance to instruct student.

Students with mental retardation or learning disabilities

- Use soft balls (Nerf balls) for safety.
- Start with a balloon and gradually work toward faster-moving balls.
- Use suspended balls.
- Use physical assistance when teaching the skill.
- Encourage proper technique.

Shooting

General

- Use larger-or smaller-than-regulation-size balls.
- Use playground balls, Nerf balls, or punch balls (large balloons).
- Vary distance required to shoot.
- Vary height of basket.
- Vary size of basket (use large box for basket or hang hula hoop on wall).

Students who use wheelchairs (typical upper-body strength)

- Encourage student to find best way to shoot (overhead versus chest versus sidearm).
- Use soft balls (Nerf balls) for safety as needed.

Students who use wheelchairs (limited upper-body strength and control)

- Use soft balls (Nerf balls) for safety.
- Push ball down ramp into box.
- Push ball off lap into box.
- Swing arm and hit ball held by peer into box.
- Kick ball into box if legs have more control than arms.
- Hit ball off tee (or held by peer) with head into box.

Students with visual impairments

- Use soft balls (Nerf balls) for safety.
- Use verbal cues to tell student where to shoot.
- Give student specific verbal feedback to tell him or her how close his or her shot was to the basket.
- Use physical assistance to instruct student.
- Tie string to ball and to student's wrist so that ball is easy to retrieve.
- Place radio under basket to cue student.
- Put bells or beeper in ball.

Students with mental retardation or learning disabilities

- Use soft ball (Nerf ball) for safety.
- Use physical assistance when teaching skill.
- Place handprints on ball to show proper technique.
- Encourage proper technique.

Basketball game

General

- Encourage students without disabilities to develop modified rules that will be fair for everyone, including students with disabilities.
- Allow student to shoot at a lower basket.
- Allow student to use a different ball when it is his or her turn to dribble or shoot.
- Make a rule that no student can steal ball when the student is dribbling.
- Make a rule that no student can block or interfere with the student's pass.
- Have student play a zone position away from the basket.
- Match student with disability with a less-skilled student without disabilities.
- Give student a peer to assist him or her during game.
- Allow free substitution for student if he or she tires easily.
- Give student's team extra player (six versus five players).
- Allow student to play only offense or defense if he or she has limited mobility.
- Split the class and allow skilled students to play competitive, full-court games while allowing less-skilled players (including student with disabilities) to play slower, less-competitive games (e.g., half-court, three versus three, run set plays).
- Play lead-up basketball games such as half-court basketball, horse, or relays.

Students who use wheelchairs (typical upper-body strength)

- Caution peers about wheelchair.
- Have student play away from basket on defense and offense for safety.

Students who use wheelchairs (limited upper-body strength and control)

- Provide student with peer to assist him or her.
- Allow student to use adapted equipment practiced during skills work (e.g., ramps).
- Bring basket (can be box or trash can) to student.

Students with visual impairments

- Have peer guide student around court.
- Have a guide rope across the gym so student can move up and down the court.
- Place a carpet square on floor to mark where student should stand for defense and offense.

- Have teammates give extra verbal cues to student to describe where he or she is, where teammates are, and where opponents are.
- Use ball with bell.
- Place radio under basket.
- Have teammates wear brightly colored pinnies or jerseys.
- Use brightly colored ball.
- Put brightly colored ribbons or streamers on basket.

Students with mental retardation or learning disabilities

- Provide student with peer to assist him or her during game.
- Give student extra time to pass and shoot without being defended.
- Give student free shot at basket.

Soccer

Dribbling

General

- Use larger or smaller balls.
- Use playground balls, Nerf balls, or punch balls (large balloons).
- Vary distance required to travel.
- Vary speed required (allow student to walk).
- Use only dominant foot.

Students who use wheelchairs (typical upper-body strength)

- Hold ball on lap and push wheelchair.

Students who use wheelchairs (limited upper-body strength and control)

- Have peer push wheelchair while student holds ball in lap or in hands.
- Have peer physically assist student in moving foot to kick ball.
- Have student repeatedly hit ball when it sits on lap tray while being pushed.

Students with visual impairments

- Tie string to ball and to foot so that ball can be retrieved.
- Provide student with peer to guide student with visual impairments in correct direction.
- Put bells or beeper in ball.
- Dribble toward sound of peers.
- Use deflated ball.
- Place student along wall or fence so that he or she can place hand against wall for balance and for reference.

Students with mental retardation or learning disabilities

- Allow student to walk while dribbling.
- Allow student to use deflated ball.
- Tie ball to student's foot so that it is easy for student to retrieve.
- Practice on grass (ball moves slower).
- Have peer assist student (extra verbal and physical cues).
- Encourage proper technique.

Passing and trapping

General

- Use suspended balls.
- Use larger or smaller balls.
- Use playground balls, Nerf balls, or punch balls (large balloons).
- Vary distance required to pass (have peers stand closer).
- Pass balls slower as required.
- Try to pass ball directly to student.

Students who use wheelchairs (typical upper-body strength)

- Allow student to pass ball by throwing or rolling it instead of kicking it.
- Encourage student to find best way to pass if using arms instead of legs (over-head versus chest versus sidearm).
- Use soft ball (Nerf ball) for safety as needed.

Students who use wheelchairs (limited upper-body strength and control)

- Use soft balls (Nerf balls) for safety.
- Kick (push with foot) ball down ramp.
- Kick ball held by peer.
- Push ball off lap.
- Hit ball off tee (or held by peer) with head.

Students with visual impairments

- Use soft balls (Nerf balls) for safety.
- Use verbal cues (tell student when ball is released for trapping; tell student where to pass).
- Put bells or beeper in ball.
- Use physical assistance to instruct student.

Students with mental retardation or learning disabilities

- Use soft balls (Nerf balls) for safety.
- Start with a balloon and gradually work toward faster-moving balls.

- Use suspended balls.
- Use physical assistance when teaching skill.
- Encourage proper technique.

Shooting

General

- Use larger or smaller balls.
- Use playground balls, Nerf balls, or punch balls (large balloons).
- Use balls with varying texture.
- Vary distance required to shoot (allow student to stand closer).
- Vary size of goal (larger goal for less-skilled students).

Students who use wheelchairs (typical upper-body strength)

- Allow student to substitute throwing for shooting.
- Encourage student to find best way to shoot (overhead versus chest versus sidearm).
- Use soft balls (Nerf balls) for safety as needed.

Students who use wheelchairs (limited upper-body strength and control)

- Use soft balls (Nerf balls) for safety.
- Kick ball or push ball down ramp toward goal.
- Push ball off lap toward goal.
- Kick or swing arm and hit ball held by peer toward goal.
- Hit ball off tee (or held by peer) with head toward goal.
- Allow student to kick or strike ball into box next to chair as goal.

Students with visual impairments

- Use soft balls (Nerf balls) for safety.
- Use verbal cues (goalie) to tell student where to shoot.
- Give student specific verbal feedback to tell him or her how close his or her shot was to goal.
- Use physical assistance to instruct student.
- Place radio in middle of goal to cue student.
- Put bells or beeper in ball.
- Use target that makes noise when it's hit.

Students with mental retardation or learning disabilities

- Use soft balls (Nerf balls) for safety.
- Use overinflated playground balls (travel farther with less strength).
- Use physical assistance when teaching skill.
- Encourage proper technique.

Soccer game

General

- Encourage students without disabilities to develop modified rules that will be fair for everyone, including students with disabilities.
- Set up special zone for student inside of which only he or she can touch the ball.
- Allow student to shoot at wider goal.
- Allow student to use different ball when it is his or her turn to dribble or shoot.
- Make rule that no student can steal ball when student with disabilities is dribbling.
- Make rule that no student can block or interfere with student's pass.
- Have student play a wing position away from fastest action.
- Match student with disability with a less-skilled student without disabilities.
- Give student a peer to assist him or her during the game.
- Allow free substitution for student if he or she tires easily.
- Give student's team an extra player (12 versus 11 players).
- Allow student to play only offense or defense if he or she has limited mobility.
- Split the class and allow skilled students to play competitive, full-field games while allowing less-skilled players (including student with disabilities) to play slower, less-competitive games (half-field, six versus six, keep-away games, cooperative games).
- Play lead-up soccer games.

Students who use wheelchairs (typical upper-body strength)

- Caution peers about wheelchair.
- Have student play goalie (requires less mobility) and make rule that skilled students cannot shoot from closer than 20 yards away.

Students who use wheelchairs (limited upper-body strength and control)

- Provide student with peer to assist him or her.
- Allow student to use adapted equipment on which he or she practiced during skills work (e.g., ramps).
- Allow student free shot at goal from close distance.

Students with visual impairments

- Ask peer to guide student around field.
- Designate special zone for student marked with rope or cones where only he or she can play ball (make rule that ball should be played into zone every 2–3 minutes).
- Have teammates give extra verbal cues to student to describe where he or she is, where teammates are, and where opponents are.
- Use ball with bell.
- Use brightly colored ball.

- Place radio inside of goal.
- Have teammates wear brightly colored pinnies or jerseys.
- Allow student free shot from penalty line at least once during game.

Students with mental retardation or learning disabilities

- Provide student with peer to assist him or her.
- Give student extra time to pass and shoot without being defended.
- Give student occasional free shot at goal.

Softball

Throwing, catching, and fielding

General

- Use suspended balls.
- Use Velcro balls and Velcro mitts.
- Use larger or smaller balls.
- Use playground balls, Nerf balls, or punch balls (large balloons).
- Vary distance required to throw (have peers stand closer).
- Throw balls slowly, as required.

Students who use wheelchairs (typical upper-body strength)

- Encourage student to find best way to throw (overhead versus sidearm).
- Use soft balls (Nerf balls) for safety as needed.

Students who use wheelchairs (limited upper-body strength and control)

- Use soft balls (Nerf balls) for safety.
- Push ball down ramp, then have peer throw it rest of way.
- Push ball held by peer, then have peer throw it rest of way.
- Push ball off lap, then have peer throw it rest of way.
- Hit ball off tee (or held by peer) with head, then have peer throw it rest of way.
- Use legs and kick ball if student has more control over legs.

Students with visual impairments

- Use soft balls (Nerf balls) for safety.
- Use suspended ball.
- Use verbal cues to help student stand facing correct direction.
- Use verbal cues (tell student when ball is released for catching; tell student where to throw).
- Put bells or beeper in ball.
- Use physical assistance to instruct student.

Students with mental retardation or learning disabilities

- Use soft balls (Nerf balls) for safety.
- Start with a balloon and gradually work toward faster-moving balls.
- Use suspended balls.
- Use physical assistance when teaching skill.
- Encourage proper technique.

Batting

General

- Use larger or smaller balls.
- Use playground balls, Nerf balls, or punch balls (large balloons).
- Use larger or smaller striking implements.
- Use lighter striking implements.
- Hit ball off tee.
- Vary distance ball is pitched.

Students who use wheelchairs (typical upper-body strength)

- Encourage student to find best way to position chair for batting.

Students who use wheelchairs (limited upper-body strength and control)

- Use soft balls (Nerf balls) for safety.
- Hit ball off tee with hand.
- Strap small striking implement to hand for striking.
- Push ball down ramp.
- Push ball off lap.
- Swing arm or use head to hit ball held by peer.
- Kick ball if legs have more control than arms.

Students with visual impairments

- Use verbal cues to tell student when ball is pitched.
- Give student specific verbal feedback to tell student how close he or she was to hitting the ball.
- Use physical assistance to instruct and help student.
- Put bells or beeper in ball.
- Hit ball rolled across table.

Students with mental retardation or learning disabilities

- Use physical assistance when teaching skill.
- Encourage proper technique.
- Hit ball rolled across table.

Base running

General

- Vary distance to first base.
- Vary width of base path.

Students who use wheelchairs (typical upper-body strength)

- Allow student to push wheelchair.

Students who use wheelchairs (limited upper-body strength and control)

- Have peer push chair while student tries to keep arms up.
- Have peer push chair while student tries to keep head up and look at first base.

Students with visual impairments

- Use verbal cues to tell student where to run (first baseman).
- Use physical assistance to instruct and help student.
- Put bells or beeper at first base.
- Put radio by first base.
- Have rope between home and first to guide student's path.

Students with mental retardation or learning disabilities

- Use physical assistance as needed.
- Encourage proper running technique.

Softball game

General

- Encourage students without disabilities to develop modified rules that will be fair for everyone, including students with disabilities.
- Establish special rule such as ground rule double (batter only allowed to advance to second base) when ball is hit to student with disabilities.
- Give student extra strikes.
- Allow student to hit ball off tee.
- Allow pitcher to stand close to player and pitch ball slowly.
- Allow student to use larger ball when it is his or her turn to bat.
- Allow student to use lighter, larger bat (or even a racket) when batting.
- Have student play outfield with peer assistant.
- Have student play catcher (requires less mobility).
- Place first base closer to home for student.
- Give student a peer to assist him or her during game.
- Allow student to only play offense or play every other inning if he or she tires easily.

- Give student's team extra player (11 versus 10 players).
- Split the class and allow skilled students to play competitive, regulation game while allowing less-skilled players (including student with disabilities) to play slower, less-competitive game or modified game (e.g., cooperative game).
- Play lead-up softball games.

Students who use wheelchairs (typical upper-body strength)

- Caution peers about wheelchair.
- Have student play catcher or first base (requires less mobility).

Students who use wheelchairs (limited upper-body strength and control)

- Provide student with peer to assist him or her.
- Allow student to use adapted equipment used during skills work (e.g., ramps).
- Force players without disabilities to play "regular depth" on defense to give student fair chance to make it to first base.
- Make different rules for scoring (if student hits ball a certain distance, he or she gets a single, double, triple, or home run).

Students with visual impairments

- Have peer assist student in field.
- Have teammates give extra verbal cues to student to describe where he or she is and where teammates are.
- Use ball with bell or beeper and first base with beeper.
- Place radio at first base.
- Use brightly colored ball.
- Make first base brightly colored.
- Make different rules for scoring (if student hits ball a certain distance, he or she gets a single, double, triple, or home run).

Students with mental retardation or learning disabilities

- Provide student with peer to assist him or her.
- Have student play catcher or outfield (less mobility and skill needed).

Volleyball

Setting and passing

General

- Use larger-or smaller-than-regulation-size balls.
- Use lighter and softer balls (Nerf balls, balloons, beach balls, volley trainers).
- Vary distance requirements (stand closer to net).
- Vary speed required (slow down the ball).
- Lower the net.

Students who use wheelchairs (typical upper-body strength)

- Vary distance requirements (position closer to net).
- Use lighter, softer balls (Nerf balls, balloons, beach balls, volley trainers).

Students who use wheelchairs (limited upper-body strength and control)

- Hit suspended ball.
- Push ball held by peer, then have peer pick up ball and pass it to other team-mates.
- Push ball off lap tray, then have peer pick up ball and pass it to other team-mates.
- Push ball down ramp or across table, then have peer pick up ball and pass it to other teammates.
- Use legs or head if student has better control with these body parts, then have peer pick up ball and pass it to other teammates.
- Provide physical assistance as needed.
- Allow student to touch ball, then have peer pick it up and pass it to other teammates.

Students with visual impairments

- Use brightly colored balls.
- Have peers tell student which direction to face and where to pass.
- Put bells or beeper in ball.
- Hold ball for student and let him or her hit it out of your hands.
- Allow student to self-toss, then set ball.

Students with mental retardation or learning disabilities

- Allow students with limited coordination to toss ball rather than hit it.
- Have peer assist student (extra verbal and physical cues).
- Encourage proper technique.

Bumping

General

- Use larger or smaller balls.
- Use lighter and softer balls (Nerf balls, balloons, beach balls, volley trainers).
- Vary distance requirements (stand closer to net).
- Vary speed required (slow down the ball).
- Lower the net.

Students who use wheelchairs (typical upper-body strength)

- Encourage student to lean forward to bump or to bump to side of chair.
- Allow overhead passing to be used as substitute for bumping.

Students who use wheelchairs (limited upper-body strength and control)

- Hit suspended ball.
- Push ball held by peer, then have peer pick up ball and bump it to other team-mates.
- Push ball off lap tray, then have peer pick up ball and bump it to other team-mates.
- Push ball down ramp or across table, then have peer pick up ball and bump it to other teammates.
- Use legs or head if student has better control with these body parts, then have peer pick up ball and bump it to other teammates.
- Provide physical assistance as needed.
- Allow student to touch ball, then have peer pick it up and bump it to other teammates.

Students with visual impairments

- Use brightly colored balls.
- Have peers tell student which direction to face and where to bump ball.
- Provide physical assistance as needed.
- Put bells or beeper in ball.
- Hold ball for student and let him bump it out of your hands.
- Allow student to self-toss, then bump ball.

Students with mental retardation or learning disabilities

- Allow students with limited coordination to toss ball rather than bump ball.
- Have peer assist student (extra verbal and physical cues).
- Encourage proper technique.

Serving

General

- Use larger or smaller balls.
- Use lighter and softer balls (Nerf balls, balloons, beach balls, volley trainers).
- Vary distance requirements (stand closer to net).
- Lower the net.

Students who use wheelchairs (typical upper-body strength)

- Encourage student to find best way to serve (overhand versus sidearm).

Students who use wheelchairs (limited upper-body strength and control)

- Hit suspended ball.
- Push ball held by peer, then have peer pick up ball and serve it over net.
- Push ball off lap tray, then have peer pick up ball and serve it over net.

- Push ball down ramp or across table, then have peer pick up ball and serve it over net.
- Use legs or head if student has better control with these body parts, then have peer pick up ball and serve it over net.
- Provide physical assistance as needed.
- Allow student to touch ball, then have peer pick it up and serve it over net.

Students with visual impairments

- Use brightly colored balls.
- Have peers tell student in which direction to stand and where to serve.
- Provide physical assistance as needed.
- Put bells or beeper in ball.
- Put radio under net to help student locate net.

Students with mental retardation or learning disabilities

- Allow students with limited coordination to throw ball rather than serve it.
- Have peer assist student (extra verbal and physical cues).
- Encourage proper technique.

Volleyball game

General

- Encourage students without disabilities to develop modified rules that will be fair for everyone, including students with disabilities.
- Set up special zone for student where only he or she can play ball.
- Have student play back and side positions for safety.
- Allow student to throw ball rather than hit it.
- Allow student to use different ball when it is his or her turn to serve.
- Make rule that student's team gets an extra hit.
- Make rule that no student can block or interfere with student's pass.
- Match student with disability against lower-ability student without disabilities.
- Give student a peer to assist him or her during game.
- Allow free substitution for student if he or she tires easily.
- Give student's team extra player (seven versus six players).
- Split the class and allow skilled students to play competitive, regulation games while allowing less-skilled players (including student with disabilities) to play slower, less-competitive game (e.g., cooperative games).
- Play lead-up games.

Students who use wheelchairs (typical upper-body strength)

- Caution peers about wheelchair.
- Have student play back and side positions only.

Students who use wheelchairs (limited upper-body strength and control)

- Provide student with peer to assist him or her.
- Allow student to use adapted equipment used during skills work (e.g., ramps).

Students with visual impairments

- Have peer guide or assist student during game.
- Mark floor with carpet squares to help student find position.
- Have teammates give extra verbal cues to student to describe where he or she is, where teammates are, and where opponents are.
- Use brightly colored ball.
- Put brightly colored ribbons or streamers on net.
- Use ball with bell.
- Place radio under net.
- Have teammates wear brightly colored pinnies or jerseys.
- Allow student to hit ball held by peer.

Students with mental retardation or learning disabilities

- Provide student with peer to assist him or her.
- Allow student to hit ball held by peer.

Appendix B

Accommodations to Individual Sports for Students with Disabilities

Tennis
Forehand

General

- Use larger or smaller balls.
- Use lighter and softer balls (Nerf balls, balloons, beach balls, volley trainers).
- Use shorter, lighter rackets (racquetball racket, pantyhose racket).
- Use rackets with larger heads.
- Vary distance requirements (stand closer to net).
- Vary speed required (slow down the ball).
- Lower the net or do not use net.

Students who use wheelchairs (typical upper-body strength)

- Encourage student to find best position to hit forehand.
- Hit ball off tee.
- Encourage student to work on maneuvering wheelchair and then hitting ball.

Students who use wheelchairs (limited upper-body strength and control)

- Strap or Velcro racket or striking implement to student's hand.
- Hit suspended ball.
- Hit or push ball held by peer, then have peer pick up ball and hit it over net.
- Hit or push ball off lap tray, then have peer pick up ball and hit it over net.
- Hit or push ball down ramp or across table, then have peer pick up ball and hit it over net.
- Use legs or head if student has better control with these body parts, then have peer pick up ball and hit it over net.
- Provide physical assistance as needed.
- Allow student to touch ball, then have peer pick it up and hit it to other player.

Students with visual impairments

- Use brightly colored balls.
- Have peers tell student which direction to face and where to hit ball.
- Provide physical assistance as needed.
- Put bells or beeper in ball.
- Put radio by net for direction.
- Hold ball for student and let him hit it out of your hands.
- Allow student to self-toss, then hit ball.
- Attach string to student and to ball so that student can quickly retrieve ball.

Students with mental retardation or learning disabilities

- Allow students with limited coordination to hit suspended ball.
- Allow students with limited coordination to hit ball off tee.
- Have peer assist student (extra verbal and physical cues).
- Encourage proper technique.

Backhand

General

- Use larger or smaller balls.
- Use lighter and softer balls (Nerf balls, balloons, beach balls, volley trainers).
- Use shorter, lighter rackets (racquetball racket, pantyhose racket).
- Use rackets with larger heads.
- Vary distance requirements (stand closer to net).
- Vary speed required (slow down the ball).
- Lower the net or do not use net.

Students who use wheelchairs (typical upper-body strength)

- Encourage student to find best position to hit backhand.
- Hit ball off tee.
- Encourage student to work on maneuvering wheelchair and then hitting ball.

Students who use wheelchairs (limited upper-body strength and control)

- Hit suspended ball.
- Hit or push ball held by peer, then have peer pick up ball and hit it over net.
- Hit or push ball off lap tray, then have peer pick up ball and hit it over net.
- Hit or push ball down ramp or across table, then have peer pick up ball and hit it over net.
- Use legs or head if student has better control with these body parts, then have peer pick up ball and hit it over net.
- Provide physical assistance as needed.

- Allow student to touch ball, then have peer pick it up and hit it to other player.

Students with visual impairments

- Use brightly colored balls.
- Have peers tell student which direction to face and where to hit ball.
- Provide physical assistance as needed.
- Put bells or beeper in ball.
- Put radio by net for direction.
- Hold ball for student and let him or her hit it out of your hands.
- Allow student to toss and then hit the ball.
- Attach string to student and to ball so that student can quickly retrieve ball.

Students with mental retardation or learning disabilities

- Allow students with limited coordination to hit suspended ball.
- Allow students with limited coordination to hit ball off tee.
- Have peer assist student (extra verbal and physical cues).
- Encourage proper technique.

Serving

General

- Use larger or smaller balls.
- Use lighter and softer balls (Nerf balls, balloons, beach balls, volley trainers).
- Use shorter, lighter rackets (racquetball racket, pantyhose racket).
- Use rackets with larger heads.
- Vary distance requirements (stand closer to net).
- Lower the net or do not use net.

Students who use wheelchairs (typical upper-body strength)

- Encourage student to find best way to serve (overhand versus sidearm).
- Serve ball off tee or have ball tossed to person to serve.

Students who use wheelchairs (limited upper-body strength and control)

- Hit or push ball held by peer, then have peer pick up ball and hit it over net.
- Hit or push ball off lap tray, then have peer pick up ball and hit it over net.
- Hit or push ball down ramp or across table, then have peer pick up ball and hit it over net.
- Use legs or head if student has better control with these body parts, then have peer pick up ball and hit it over net.
- Provide physical assistance as needed.

- Allow student to touch ball, then have peer pick it up and serve it to other player.

Students with visual impairments

- Use brightly colored balls.
- Have peers tell student which direction to face and where to hit ball.
- Provide physical assistance as needed.
- Put bells or beeper in ball.
- Put radio by net for direction.
- Allow student to hit ball off of tee.
- Allow student to bounce ball then hit it.

Students with mental retardation or learning disabilities

- Allow students with limited coordination to hit ball off tee.
- Toss the ball to student if this is easier for him or her.
- Have peer assist student (provide extra verbal and physical cues).
- Encourage proper technique.

Tennis game

General

- Allow student to hit ball after two to three bounces.
- Allow student to hit to doubles line while opponent hits to singles line.
- Match student with student without disabilities who has limited abilities.
- Play lead-up games rather than regulation games.
- Play games without net.
- Play doubles and allow team with student to have extra player (3 versus 2).
- Play modified or lead-up games.

Students who use wheelchairs (typical upper-body strength)

- Allow student to serve ball off tee or have ball tossed to him or her to serve.

Students who use wheelchairs (limited upper-body strength and control)

- Give student peer assistant.
- Make special rules that if ball is hit a certain distance, it counts as over the net. Then, peer assistant can hit ball over net to opponent.
- Allow student to use adapted equipment.

Students with visual impairments

- Use brightly colored balls.
- Have textured markers on court or guide wires so that student knows where he or she is on court.

- Have peers tell student which direction to face and where to hit ball.
- Provide physical assistance as needed.
- Put bells or beeper in ball.
- Put radio by net for direction.
- Allow student to hit ball off tee for serving.
- Allow student to bounce ball then hit it.

Students with mental retardation or learning disabilities

- Allow students with limited coordination to hit ball off tee for serving.
- Toss the ball to student if this is easier for him or her when serving.
- Have peer assist student.

Golf

Hitting ball

General

- Use larger balls.
- Use lighter balls.
- Use shorter, lighter clubs (junior clubs or students' plastic clubs).
- Make club with a large head.
- Vary distance requirements (allow student to hit it shorter distance than peers).
- Always put ball on tee.

Students who use wheelchairs (typical upper-body strength)

- Encourage student to find best way to hit ball.

Students who use wheelchairs (limited upper-body strength and control)

- Hit or push ball held by peer.
- Hit or push ball off lap tray.
- Hit or push ball down ramp or across table.
- Use legs or head if student has better control with these body parts.
- Provide physical assistance as needed.
- Use switch that activates machine that hits ball off tee.

Students with visual impairments

- Use brightly colored balls.
- Have peers tell student which direction to face and which direction to hit ball.
- Provide physical assistance as needed.

- Put bells or beepers in ball.
- Put radio out in field for target.

Students with mental retardation or learning disabilities

- Have peer assist student (provide extra verbal and physical cues).
- Encourage proper technique.

Archery[1]
Shooting

General

- Use shorter arrows.
- Use lighter bows.
- Use shorter, smaller, lighter bows.
- Vary distance requirements (move target closer).
- Make target larger.

Students who use wheelchairs (typical upper-body strength)

- Encourage student to find best way to shoot with bow.
- Allow use of adapted release cuffs.
- Use adapted archery bow

Students who use wheelchairs (limited upper-body strength and control)

- Use crossbow with adapted trigger device.
- Use adapted archery bow.
- Shoot with physical assistance.

Students with visual impairments

- Use brightly colored arrows and targets.
- Have peers tell student which direction to face and which direction to shoot.
- Provide physical assistance as needed.
- Put bells or beeper in target.
- Put radio in front of target.
- Rig target so it makes sounds if it is hit.
- Use special auditory device for lining up shot.

---

[1]For more information on the crossbow with adapted trigger, adapted archery bow, adapted release cuff, or other unique adaptations of archery to meet the needs of individuals with specific disabilities, see Adams, R., & McCubbin, J. (1991). *Games, sports, and exercises for the physically disabled* (4th ed.). Philadelphia: Lea & Febiger.

Students with mental retardation or learning disabilities

- Use crossbow with adapted trigger device if strength is a problem.
- Use adapted archery bow if coordination is a problem.
- Shoot with physical assistance.
- Encourage proper technique.

Badminton[2]
Forehand

General

- Use larger badminton rackets or birdies.
- Use lighter and softer birdies (Nerf balls, balloons).
- Use shorter, lighter rackets (pantyhose racket).
- Use rackets with larger heads.
- Vary distance requirements (stand closer to net).
- Vary speed required (slow down the birdie).
- Lower the net or do not use net.
- Practice with suspended birdie.

Students who use wheelchairs (typical upper-body strength)

- Encourage student to find best position to hit forehand.
- Hit birdie off tee.
- Encourage student to work on maneuvering wheelchair and then hitting birdie.

Students who use wheelchairs (limited upper-body strength and control)

- Strap racket to player's hand.
- Hit or push birdie held by peer, then have peer pick up birdie and hit it over net.
- Hit or push birdie off lap tray, then have peer pick up birdie and hit it over net.
- Hit or push ball down ramp or across table, then have peer pick up birdie and hit it over net.
- Use legs or head if student has better control with these body parts, then have peer pick up birdie and hit it over net.
- Provide physical assistance as needed.
- Allow student to touch birdie, then have peer pick it up and hit it to other player.

---

[2]For more information on unique adaptations of badminton to meet the needs of individuals with specific disabilities, see Adams, R., & McCubbin, J. (1991). *Games, sports, and exercises for the physically disabled* (4th ed.). Philadelphia: Lea & Febiger.

Students with visual impairments

- Use brightly colored birdies or balls.
- Have peers tell student which direction to face and where to hit birdie.
- Provide physical assistance as needed.
- Put bells or beeper in birdie.
- Put radio by net for direction.
- Suspend birdie from string with Velcro so that birdie releases when hit.
- Place birdie on tee.
- Allow student to self-toss, then hit birdie.
- Attach string to student and to birdie so that student can quickly retrieve birdie.

Students with mental retardation or learning disabilities

- Allow students with limited coordination to hit suspended birdie.
- Allow students with limited coordination to hit birdie off tee.
- Have peer assist student (extra verbal and physical cues).
- Encourage proper technique.

Serving

General

- Use larger birdies.
- Use lighter and softer birdies (Nerf balls, balloons).
- Use shorter, lighter rackets (pantyhose racket).
- Use rackets with larger heads.
- Vary distance requirements (stand closer to net).
- Lower the net or do not use net.

Students who use wheelchairs (typical upper-body strength)

- Encourage student to find best way to serve (overhand versus sidearm).
- Serve birdie off tee, or have birdie tossed to person to serve.

Students who use wheelchairs (limited upper-body strength and control)

- Strap racket to player's hand.
- Hit or push birdie held by peer, then have peer pick up birdie and hit it over net.
- Hit or push birdie off lap tray, then have peer pick up birdie and hit it over net.
- Hit or push birdie down ramp or across table, then have peer pick up birdie and hit it over net.
- Use legs or head if student has better control with these body parts, then have peer pick up birdie and hit it over net.

- Provide physical assistance as needed .
- Allow student to touch birdie, then have peer pick it up and hit it to other player.

Students with visual impairments

- Use brightly colored birdie or ball.
- Have peers tell student which direction to face and where to hit birdie.
- Provide physical assistance as needed.
- Put bells or beeper in birdie.
- Put radio by net for direction.
- Allow student to hit birdie off tee.

Students with mental retardation or learning disabilities

- Allow students with limited coordination to hit birdie off tee.
- Toss the birdie to the student if this is easier for him or her.
- Have peer assist student (provide extra verbal and physical cues).
- Encourage proper technique.

Badminton game

General

- Allow student to hit to wider court while opponent hits to narrower court.
- Match student with student without disabilities who has limited abilities.
- Play lead-up games rather than regulation games.
- Lower net or play game without net.
- Play doubles and allow team with student to have extra player (three versus two players).
- Play modified or lead-up games.

Students who use wheelchairs (typical upper-body strength)

- Allow student to serve birdie off tee or have birdie tossed to him or her to serve.

Students who use wheelchairs (limited upper-body strength and control)

- Provide student with peer assistant.
- Make special rules that if birdie is hit a certain distance, it counts as over the net. Then, peer assistant can hit birdie over net to opponent.
- Allow student to use adapted equipment.

Students with visual impairments

- Use brightly colored balls.
- Use textured markers on court or guide wires so that student knows where he or she is on court.

- Have peers tell student which direction to face and where to hit birdie.
- Provide physical assistance as needed.
- Put bells or beeper in birdie.
- Put radio by net for direction.
- Allow student to hit birdie off tee for serving.
- Allow student to bounce birdie, then hit it.

Students with mental retardation or learning disabilities

- Allow students with limited coordination to serve birdie off tee.
- Toss the birdie to student if this is easier for him or her when serving.
- Have peer assist student.

Dancing

General

- Use colored markers or cones on floor for direction.
- Use colored markers on hands and feet for left and right.
- Practice small portions of dance and gradually add more steps.
- Slow down music.

Students who use wheelchairs (typical upper-body strength)

- Substitute arm movements for leg movements.
- Allow partner to push student's wheelchair as needed.

Students who use wheelchairs (limited upper-body strength and control)

- Substitute any controllable movement the student has for more traditional movements.
- Allow peers to assist students in movements.
- Allow students to push wheelchair.
- Encourage student to maintain proper posture and to focus eyes on partner.

Students with visual impairments

- Use brightly colored markers on floor.
- Have partner wear brightly colored pinny or shirt.
- Have partner wear bells on wrist.
- Have partner tell student which direction to face and where to move.
- Have partner provide physical assistance as needed.

Students with mental retardation or learning disabilities

- Have peers assist student (extra verbal and physical cues).
- Encourage proper technique.

9

Facilitating Social
Acceptance and Inclusion

I think about the issue of inclusion on a daily basis. I never spend time wondering if it's the right answer for a child in the physical education setting, I know that it is. Most importantly kids know that it is. My students are motivated to work with other kids, they learn from each other, and they succeed with a smile on their face! They demonstrate that inclusion helps every child to accept the strengths and weaknesses in themselves and others and take pride in their accomplishments. Children grow socially, physically and cognitively in the inclusive setting. . . .

Kris Grant, general physical educator

Devin is a very bright, very energetic third grader at Redland Elementary School. Devin has autism, and although he really enjoys physical education—particularly running, climbing, and tumbling—he has a very difficult time following the routines and rules. In addition, Devin does not respond very expressively to his peers and has a tendency to make strange sounds and hand movements. Devin's physical education teacher is able to keep Devin with the rest of the group fairly easily with a few extra verbal cues and gestures in addition to some pictures. In fact, Devin's physical education teacher really enjoys having Devin in his class; however, he is concerned that Devin is not getting the full benefits of general physical education. The problem is that none of Devin's classmates really talk to or interact with Devin. They certainly look at him, especially when he makes the strange sounds, but they just are not sure what to make of Devin. Some seem interested in befriending Devin, whereas others seem scared of him. What can this physical educator do to facilitate more social interactions between Devin and his classmates?

Brianna is a seventh grader at Yellowfield Middle School. Like Devin, Brianna enjoys physical education. She particularly enjoys kicking and dribbling balls and hitting balls off a tee. She does not particularly like running laps or doing calisthenics, but what seventh grader does? Brianna has mental retardation requiring extensive support, which affects the degree to which she is able to comprehend the activities and teacher's directions in physical education class. In fact, her individualized education program (IEP) team believed that Brianna's cognitive and motor limitations were so significant that she needed her teacher assistant, Mrs. Jung, to accompany her to physical education. Mrs. Jung is a wonderful woman who cares very deeply for Brianna and truly wants to help her in general physical education. Unfortunately, Mrs. Jung is constantly around Brianna, helping her do everything. For example, when the physical education teacher asks students to pair up to do sit-ups, Mrs. Jung is Brianna's partner. Similarly, when Brianna is assigned to a group or station with other students, Mrs. Jung goes with her and hovers around her constantly. Brianna's peers seem very willing to befriend Brianna, but they cannot seem to get close to her because of Mrs. Jung. What can the general physical education teacher do to help Mrs. Jung facilitate more social opportunities for Brianna?

Ryan is an eleventh grader at Greenwood High School. Several years ago, Ryan was a rising star on Greenwood's junior varsity soccer and baseball teams

---

This chapter is based in part on the following two articles:

Block, M.E. (1998). Don't forget the social aspects of inclusion. *Strategies, 12*(2), 30–34.

Block, M.E., & Brady, W. (1999). Welcoming children with disabilities into regular physical education. *Teaching Elementary Physical Education, 10*(1), 30–32.

and was well liked by his classmates and teachers. Unfortunately, Ryan was in a car accident when he was in ninth grade and sustained a traumatic brain injury. After intense rehabilitation, Ryan is now back at Greenwood High. Ryan uses a manual wheelchair to move around, although quite slowly; can move his upper body slowly through the normal range of motion; has slurred but generally understandable speech; and can follow simple directions. Ryan needs help in many physical education activities, but Ryan's IEP team has decided that the help should come from classmates rather than a teacher assistant. Ryan's parents were thrilled with the idea of Ryan's peers helping him during physical education and hoped that Ryan might make some new friends. However, when Ryan's parents came to observe Ryan during physical education, they were disappointed. Ryan's classmates *were* in fact helping Ryan through the various activities presented in general physical education, but they were treating Ryan like a tutee rather than a peer. They talked down to him, and they helped him do things that he actually could do himself; there were few real friendship-like interactions. Ryan's parents voiced their concerns to the general physical education teacher regarding how Ryan's peers were treating him. What can this general physical educator do to promote more natural interactions between Ryan and his classmates?

Although students with disabilities never should be placed in general physical education solely for social development (Block & Garcia, 1995), clearly one of the greatest benefits of inclusion is the opportunity for social acceptance and interactions between students with and without disabilities. Inclusion, if done correctly, can promote social factors such as how to interact with peers, play cooperatively, take turns, deal with anger, follow directions, listen quietly, stay on task, and behave appropriately. For many students (e.g., some students with behavior problems), social development during physical education can be as important as motor and cognitive development. In such cases, social goals should be addressed in the student's IEP. In addition, peers without disabilities can learn that classmates who seem different from them on the outside may actually share similar interests, pleasures, problems, and concerns. Finally, when social inclusion is done very well through appropriate interactions and contact, the opportunity for true acceptance, appreciation, and friendships between peers with and without disabilities becomes possible (Falvey & Rosenberg, 1995; Forest, Pearpoint, & O'Brien, 1996).

Simply placing a student with a disability into general physical education, however, does not ensure appropriate and meaningful social interactions and acceptance. Meaningful interactions and subsequent acceptance have to be carefully planned and facilitated. Physical educators often unwittingly create barriers to social interactions and acceptance. For example, not telling students without disabilities that a student with Tourette syndrome might make strange sounds or that a student with mental retardation and a heart condition does not have to run the mile like everyone else in class because of his condition could create barriers to social interactions. In fact, placing students with disabilities into general physical education without preparing students without disabilities often can lead to feelings such as, "Why is *he* in my class?" "Why is *she* making all those weird noises?" Why does *he* get to run around and not follow directions?" Why does *she* have to be on my team?" or, "*he* will ruin the game for everyone."

This chapter discusses ways that general physical educators can remove barriers to social acceptance and interactions and at the same time foster more interactions between students with and without disabilities. The chapter focuses on the two major players who can facilitate the social acceptance and inclusion of students with disabilities: 1) the general physical educator, who can promote social inclusion during class, and 2) the student's classmates, who can be prepared to accept and interact with peers with disabilities. Discussion of the two major players will be followed by examples of three common problems in general physical education classes that can hinder social inclusion and some possible solutions to these problems.

Teacher Behaviors that Can Facilitate Social Inclusion

The general physical educator is perhaps the most important determinant in successful inclusion. General physical educators can either welcome students with disabilities or show disinterest; they can either view students with disabilities as part of the class and their responsibility or they can view the student as a visitor and someone else's burden. The attitude and commitment a general physical educator displays affect how classmates without disabilities accept the students with disabilities. Although general physical educators might not feel prepared to work with and help students who have disabilities, there are things they can do from the very beginning to help the student with disabilities feel welcome and part of the group. The following section provides some suggestions for methods general physical educators can use to facilitate the social acceptance and inclusion of students with disabilities (see Table 9.1).

Have a Positive Attitude

It is very reasonable for general physical educators to feel nervous and even incompetent when working with students who have disabilities. In fact, such feelings are quite common among general physical educators (Janney, Snell, Beers, & Raynes, 1995; LaMaster, Gall, Kinchin, & Siedentop, 1998). These feelings, however, should not be used as an excuse to not include students or to ignore them when they do participate in general physical education. General educators have noted that these fears tend to be based on misconceptions, misunderstandings, and general inaccurate preconceptions about their ability to teach students with disabilities. For example, Janney and her colleagues (1995) interviewed both general and special education teachers who had undergone the change from segregated to inclusive programming. A high school general physical education teacher who was interviewed in the study suggested the following to other general physical educators dealing with inclusion for the first time:

> Well, I just, I would go in with an open mind, don't be closed-minded. . . . I think what's on every teacher's mind is the fact that, oh no, this is double the workload and double the problems that you might have. And I think the best thing they can do is wait, and talk it over and see the situation, and at least try. There are always modifications you can make if something is not working out. (p. 435)

Table 9.1. Ways for a teacher to facilitate social inclusion

Have a positive attitude.
Be the teacher for all students in your general education classes.
Model appropriate behavior.
Include the student in as many activities as possible.
Individualize the curriculum and instruction.
Reinforce positive interactions.
Be knowledgeable about the student.

Although feelings of apprehension and incompetence may be common, these feelings should not be used as an excuse to disclude students or to ignore them when they do come into general physical education. General physical educators should make an honest attempt to learn about and include students with disabilities, and they should be willing to experiment with different ways to include the students in the general physical education program. There are plenty of resources, particularly special education teachers, therapists, adapted physical education specialists, and other general physical educators, in or around most school districts who can help general physical educators with the mechanics of how to safely and successfully include students with disabilities. The first step, however, is to simply be willing to try. General physical educators will be surprised at how quickly they can become experts on working with, motivating, and helping particular students with disabilities in their general physical education programs. In fact, many physical educators may find working with students who have disabilities to be more rewarding than working with students without disabilities. As another physical educator noted in Janney et al., "These kids seem to appreciate you a lot more . . . and that's a little pat on the back for the teacher" (1995, p. 435).

Bricker (1995) and Janney et al. (1995) noted it might not be enough to assume that staff will embrace inclusion and have a positive attitude toward students with disabilities; in fact, specific strategies may need to be employed to help these professionals develop positive attitudes. One particularly interesting recommendation was careful selection of staff. There are always going to be general educators who simply do not want to deal with students with disabilities. Because of this, it makes sense for general educators who are more positive toward including students with disabilities to be the first teachers to receive these students. Because often there is more than one physical educator in a building, students with disabilities should be included with the physical educator who seems to be the most receptive toward inclusion. This physical educator should then be given ongoing training and support to make sure he or she and the student with disabilities have successful, positive experiences. This physical educator can then serve as a role model for other physical educators who are more apprehensive about inclusion. Janney et al. (1995) noted that when teachers see trusted colleagues having success with inclusion, they are more likely to be open to change.

One final note regarding attitude: Lipsky and Gartner (1998) noted that the way inclusion is introduced as well as the extent to which all staff members participate in the change process had a profound impact on teachers' attitudes. Slower, incremental changes with involvement from all staff members promote favorable attitudes more than quick, comprehensive changes dictated by one or two administrators or teachers (Janney et al., 1995; Kelly, 1994). Again, placing one or two students with disabilities with selected physical educators promotes successful inclusion experiences that can gradually be expanded to other students and physical educators. Including general physical educators throughout the planning process also promotes positive attitudes and a feeling of ownership of the plan (Janney et al., 1995; Lipsky & Gartner, 1998). Trying to include too many students with disabilities too quickly can lead to negative attitudes toward inclusion and children with disabilities.

Be the Teacher for All Students in Your General Education Classes

It is common for general physical educators to feel that students with disabilities who have been placed in their general physical education classes are not really their students or part of their caseload. For example, it is not uncommon for a general physical educator to say something such as, "I have 50 students in my third-period physical education class plus Cassandra (the student with disabilities). But it really hasn't been too bad—Mrs. Jones (Cassandra's teacher assistant) works with Cassandra." General physical educators with this type of attitude often feel they are "hosting" a special visitor in their general physical education class and, therefore, are not responsible for the student's education. When the general physical educator perceives his or her role to be that of host, it becomes someone else's responsibility (e.g., paraprofessional, adapted physical education specialist) to teach and work with this student (Giangreco, 1997). The general physical educator ends up having minimal contact with the student with disabilities and has little say in the student's program.

Unfortunately, when the general physical educator chooses to act like a host instead of a primary physical education teacher to the student with disabilities, major curricular and instructional decisions are left up to others; these others, including underqualified teachers, paraprofessionals, specialists, and peer tutors, may not even know the rules of various games and sports played in general physical education or how to make modifications to these activities.

One of the most important things general physical educators can do, in addition to being willing to give inclusion a try, is to truly perceive themselves as the primary educators for all students who enter their gymnasium, including students with disabilities. Although support personnel might accompany a student with disabilities to general physical education, the general physical educator should take the lead in making key decisions regarding what the student with disabilities is doing and how and with whom he or she is doing it. This requires the physical educator to personally spend time with each student in the class, including the student with disabilities. Do not become an "outsider" in your own gymnasium when it comes to students with disabilities. Finally, keep this important concept in mind: "If you are successful teaching students without disabilities, then you have the skills to be successful teaching students with disabilities" (Giangreco, 1997, p. 11).

Model Appropriate Behavior

Many students learn how to act around students with disabilities by modeling behavior of respected adults, such as their physical education teacher. One of the simplest things you as the physical education teacher can do to show that you welcome students with disabilities is to model welcoming, friendly behavior through your actions and words (Giangreco, 1997). Do not be afraid to greet and talk to the student with disabilities just like you would greet and talk to students without disabilities, even if the student does not fully understand what you are saying. Giving pats on the back, slapping high-five, choosing the student first, and simply calling out the student's name during activities (e.g., "Good job pushing your wheelchair, Billy!") are ways to show that the student is part of the group and that it is okay to talk to and interact with him or her.

Include the Student in as Many Activities as Possible

Whenever possible, avoid excluding the student from activities. Too often, students with disabilities are "placed" in general physical education but are not really "included"; they may even spend a large portion of their time in general physical education away from their peers doing different activities. Time spent away from peers in general physical education inhibits learning with and from peers and can lead to social isolation (Giangreco, 1997). For inclusion to be successful, it is critical that the student with disabilities be included in as many general physical education activities as possible (although the goals for the student with disabilities might be different from those of his or her peers). The student should be included, with modifications as necessary to ensure safety and fairness, in warm-ups, skill and drill work, and games. For example, a student with mental retardation who cannot keep up with the fast warm-up routine of a fifth-grade class can still warm up with the group. However, the student can be encouraged to focus on three or four key warm-up activities (e.g., sit-ups, push-ups, jumping jacks, hurdler stretches) rather than on all of the movements. Also, you may want to position the student closer to you so you can give him extra feedback. Similarly, in a lead-up game of soccer, a student in a wheelchair can participate by using her hands instead of her feet and by being positioned in a special zone near the perimeter of the field so that other students do not run into her wheelchair (see Block, 1994c; Kasser, 1995; and Morris & Stiehl, 1999, for other examples of modifications to activities and games). Remember, "Where students spend their time, what they do, when, and with whom play a major role in defining affiliations and status within the classroom (and gymnasium)" (Giangreco, 1997, p. 13).

Individualize the Curriculum and Instruction

Related to attitudes is a commitment by general educators to change their curricula and the way in which they present information to account for individual differences created by inclusion (CIRA/CAHPER, 1994; Sherrill, 1998). Interestingly, many authors of general education texts talk about individualization for general physical education classes (e.g., Graham, Holt/Hale, & Parker, 1998; Mosston & Ashworth, 1994; Pangrazi, 1998). However, dealing with diversity and individualizing instruction require a fundamental shift in philosophy and teaching style for many general physical educators.

Chapters 6 through 8 discuss various ways to modify the curriculum to account for individual differences, including multilevel curricular selection, curricular overlapping, and multiple activities. Modifications to help students who learn differently from their peers include the use of 1) peer tutoring, 2) cooperative learning, 3) different cues, 4) different start and stop signals, 5) different equipment, and 6) different levels of motivation. For inclusion to be successful, general physical educators must be trained in and then embrace these and similar types of modifications that accommodate individual abilities and learning styles. An effective training tool is to either observe a peer teacher who is implementing these types of accommodations or co-teach with an adapted physical educator who is familiar with these types of accommodations (Lipsky & Gartner, 1998; Sherrill, 1998).

The inclusion of students with disabilities and the realization that students (even students without disabilities) have individual needs can make general physical educators better teachers for all of their students. As noted by Ginny Popiolek, an adapted physical educator in Maryland who specializes in helping general physical educators with inclusion,

> The best thing that has happened with inclusion is that we have all become better physical education teachers. With inclusion, our regular physical education staff was forced to use a larger array of teaching strategies and materials to accommodate students with disabilities. These teachers quickly found that individualizing instruction and creating a variety of accommodations helped all the students in the physical edu-

cation classes. These teachers have become aware of the fact that all students learn differently and that adaptations create a positive atmosphere and facilitate the development of all their students. (as quoted in Block, 1994b, p. 49)

Another important aspect of accommodating individual differences is realizing that some students with disabilities will benefit and learn differently from peers without disabilities. Again, this realization can be difficult for general physical educators who are used to more homogeneous groups. For example, students with severe attention-deficit/hyperactivity disorder may be so distracted and off task that they get only half the number of turns as peers in general physical education. However, given the student's level of attending, they may be benefiting from physical education to the best of their abilities. Similarly, a child with autism might benefit from physical education if she interacts with peers, demonstrates appropriate behavior, does not wander away from the group, and follows directions given in a large group setting. Expectations should continue to be high, but they also need to be individualized to meet the unique learning as well as physical and motor needs of students with disabilities.

Reinforce Positive Interactions

Encourage peers to befriend students with disabilities by being their partners, including them on their teams, and generally interacting with them during activities. The simple act of asking a student with disabilities to be part of a group or team can do wonders for the student's self-esteem. When necessary, also encourage peers to help the student with disabilities determine where to go and what to do during physical education. This is particularly true for students with mental retardation or autism who might not understand exactly what is going on during physical education class. Be careful not to assign one peer to a student with a disability for an entire period because that peer will miss out on his or her physical education practice time. Encourage peers to provide as little assistance as possible rather than "parent" students with disabilities. Also, just as you reinforce positive interactions, do not tolerate teasing or negative interactions. If you hear teasing or if you see students excluding the student with disabilities, it may be necessary to talk to those peers or to the class about the student and his or her needs (see p. 269 for a section on preparing peers).

Be Knowledgeable About the Student

Although it is impossible to know everything about the student with disabilities, there is some basic information you will need to know. This information includes 1) medical and health information (e.g., Does the student take medications? Are their any activities in which the student should not participate because of health concerns?), 2) how to communicate with the student (Does the student understand verbal directions, or does he or she need additional demonstrations and physical assistance?), 3) how to deal with behavior problems (Is the student aggressive, withdrawn, impulsive, hyperactive, or a wanderer? What is the behavior plan to cope with these behaviors?), and 4) any activity that the student really enjoys (What reinforcements can be used to motivate the student to participate and demonstrate appropriate behaviors?). Information about the student can be obtained from the student's parents, special education teacher, therapists, and, in some cases, even the student him- or herself (see Chapter 5 for forms to collect this type of information). Arming yourself with knowledge about the student will help you create individualized accommodations and explain to peers why you are doing certain things. For example, some students with Down syndrome refuse to do activities that they do not want to do. It will be important to find out how the student's parents and special education teacher cope with this type of behavior so you can deal with it during physical education class. You also should explain this behavior plan to peers so they know what is going on. The key is to know as much as possible about the student so you can accommodate his or her unique needs and help peers understand why you are making certain modifications.

Preparing Classmates without Disabilities for Social Acceptance and Inclusion

Peer acceptance can be the critical difference between successful and unsuccessful inclusion. Research suggests that many students without disabilities have positive attitudes toward including classmates with disabilities in physical education and sports activities (Block, 1995a; Block & Malloy, 1998). For example, Block and Malloy found that girls without disabilities ages 11–13 overwhelmingly accepted a student with a disability into their competitive, fast-pitch softball league. Furthermore, they were willing to allow modifications to ensure this peer's success.

Unfortunately, because they have no experience with peers who have disabilities, the initial response of many peers without disabilities may be negative. Some students without disabilities will be scared of students with disabilities, particularly students with physical disabilities. Others will immediately reject students with disabilities because they feel that these students will ruin their physical education program. Still others may be sympathetic toward students with disabilities and try to parent these students. None of these responses will facilitate successful inclusion; however, these responses are understandable given that most students without disabilities know very little about students with disabilities. Therefore, an important part of the process of including students with disabilities is to prepare the students' peers.

Several professionals have suggested ways in which teachers can help peers without disabilities develop a positive attitude toward students with disabilities (e.g., Auxter, Pyfer, & Huettig, 1997; Block & Brady, 1999; Clark, French, & Henderson, 1985; Getskow & Konczal, 1996; Stainback & Stainback, 1985). The key is helping classmates 1) become more knowledgeable about disabilities in general to avoid myths and stereotypes, 2) learn how to view peers with disabilities in a positive manner, and 3) learn how to interact with peers with disabilities during general physical education. There are several different ways this can be accomplished. The following sections address some of these methods (see Table 9.2).

Table 9.2. Suggestions for preparing classmates without disabilities for social acceptance and inclusion of students with disabilities

Conduct Circle of Friends exercise.
Invite guest speakers with disabilities to speak to the class.
Role-play.
Discuss the concept of rules and handicapping.
Lead a discussion about disabilities.
Talk about famous people who have disabilities.
Discuss the specific student who will be included.
Explain how to interact with specific students with disabilities.
Provide ongoing information, encouragement, and support for acceptance.

Circle of Friends

A circle of friends is a systematic way of identifying and outlining all the friends, acquaintances, and other key people with whom we come into contact on a regular basis (Falvey, Forest, Pearpoint, & Rosenberg, 1997). Most students without disabilities have an extensive network of friends with whom they play and interact on a regular basis. However, some students with disabilities do not have any friends at all. The circle of friends process can help students without disabilities realize how important friends are in their life and understand how students who do not have friends (e.g., some students with disabilities) must feel. Through this exercise, students without disabilities often gain a greater appreciation of the importance of accepting and befriending peers with disabilities.

The circle of friends process begins with a "social scan," which results in a picture of the key people in a person's life. The "social scan" also helps students without disabilities see very clearly what type of people (e.g., friends, paid adults) might be involved in certain activities and what circles need to be filled. For the "social scan," each student in the class draws four concentric circles (see Figure 9.1). The students are told that they are in the center of their circles. They are then prompted

You

Circle of Intimacy

Circle of Friendship

Circle of Participation

Circle of Exchange

Figure 9.1.   Circle of friends. (From Falvey, M. A., Forest, M., Pearpoint, J., & Rosenberg, R. L. (1997). All my life's a circle: Using the tools: Circles, MAPS & PATH. Toronto: Inclusion Press.

to fill in the people who are in each of the four circles around them. The first circle, the *circle of intimacy*, lists the people most intimately connected to the student's life—those people the student could not imagine living without (e.g., parents, siblings, grandparents). The second circle, the *circle of friendship*, lists each student's good friends, those people who almost made the first circle. The third circle, the *circle of participation*, lists people, organizations, and networks with whom or which the student might be involved (e.g., sports teams, clubs, scouts)—people with whom the student participates. Finally, the fourth circle, the *circle of exchange*, lists people who are paid to provide services to the student (e.g., teachers, specialists, medical professionals) (Falvey et al., 1997).

Once all of the students have finished their social scans, the teacher leads a discussion about the results. In terms of inclusion, the focus should be on the students with disabilities and how their social scans look. Students will quickly see that students with disabilities generally have fewer names in their *circle of friends*, fewer names in their *circle of participation*, and more names in their *circle of exchange* compared with other students in the class. Students are led to discover, through questioning and comparison, that students with disabilities have fewer friends, participate in fewer activities, and often interact only with family members or people who are paid to provide services. Students without disabilities could be asked how they would feel if that were their circle. The process concludes with a discussion of ways that members of the class can help this student fill in the various circles, have more friends, and participate in more activities (Forest et al., 1996).

To apply this process to general physical education, ask students to draw and fill in three circles: 1) students with whom they play and interact during physical education on a daily basis, 2) students with whom they play and interact occasionally, and 3) students with whom they never play or interact. Through this process, students can learn that they interact only with some of their peers and not others and that some students never really interact with anyone during physical education. Through discussion and prompting, the teacher can then help students realize that some of their peers might be very lonely and isolated during physical education but that this situation can change if classmates make an effort to interact with and befriend more of their fellow students, including students with disabilities.

Guest Speakers

One method to help change students' attitudes about people with disabilities is to bring in guest speakers who have disabilities who participate in sports such as wheelchair racing or basketball, sit-skiing or skiing for the blind, or the Special Olympics. These speakers can dispel the stereotypes that people with disabilities cannot play sports. Local sports organizations that are affiliated with national sports associations are excellent resources for recruiting speakers (see appendix at the end of the book for list of sports organizations that serve individuals with disabilities).

Role Playing

Role playing, an activity during which students without disabilities are "given" a disability, is another effective method for changing the attitudes of students without disabilities. This technique has been used for years in Red Cross adapted aquatics classes as well as in physical education programs in which students with disabilities are to be included (Mizen & Linton, 1983). Some examples of role plays that can be conducted during physical education include blindfolding a student and asking him or her to move through an obstacle course; making students sit in chairs while playing volleyball or basketball; or tying up a student's arm, then having him or her try to hit a softball. The teacher should facilitate a discussion regarding how a peer with a disability might feel when he or she is trying to participate in similar activities. Discussions should also include reasons that, in some situations, a person with a disability is actually at an advantage. For example, a person who is blind can move around an unlit house much better than a sighted person. Auxter et al. (1997) provided a nice list of role-playing activities (see Table 9.3).

Discuss the Concept of Rules and Handicapping

A third method for changing attitudes of students without disabilities is to discuss the purpose of rules in sports and how these rules can be modified to successfully include all students. Discussion should include the concept of *handicapping* (e.g., in sports such as golfing and horse racing) in order to equalize competition. Encourage students to discuss ways of handicapping (i.e., making rule modifications) to equalize competition during physical education. For example, a student who is blind might experience difficulty hitting a pitched ball and running to first base. A fair modification for this student might include allowing him to hit the ball off a tee when he is batting. When the student must run to first base, a peer can guide him toward the base. Because it takes longer for the student to run to first base, the base can be moved closer to home plate. Moving the base closer to home plate would also make it more challenging for the students without dis-

Table 9.3.   Role-playing ideas to teach children without disabilities about disabilities

General role-playing ideas

Spend a day in a wheelchair.

Wear mittens when attempting to perform fine motor tasks.

Endeavor to trace an object reflected in a mirror.

Spend a day not speaking a word.

Spend a day with cotton wads covered with Vaseline in or a headset on your ears.

Wear eye patches.

Use crutches for a day.

Spend a day with a yardstick splint on your dominant arm.

Listen to teacher instructions given in a different language.

Role-playing specific to physical education

Navigate an obstacle course in a wheelchair.

Wear mittens when trying to play catch with a friend.

Play in the gymnasium and on the playground using only gestures to communicate.

Wearing a headset to block hearing, attempt to play a game.

Wearing eye patches, allow a classmate to walk you around the playground and help you use each piece of equipment.

Kick a ball while supporting yourself on crutches.

With a yardstick splint on your dominant arm, try to catch, throw, and dribble with your nondominant hand and arm.

Participate in a class in which the teacher uses only sign language to communicate.

From Auxter, D., Pyfer, J., & Huettig, C. (1997). *Principles and methods of adapted physical education and recreation* (8th ed., pp. 115–116). Madison, WI: Brown & Benchmark; reprinted by permission.

abilities to get this student out. Ideally, several distances to first base should be developed so that highly skilled students run farther than students with typical skills who run farther than low-skilled students. If students are involved in the process of developing modifications to accommodate students with varying abilities, then they are more likely to "buy in" to these modifications and be more accepting when they are implemented.

Lead a Discussion on Disabilities

A fourth way to prepare peers is to have them answer a questionnaire about students with disabilities and then discuss the answers as a group. For example, you could ask the following question: "Would you pick a student who uses a wheelchair to be on your basketball team in physical education?" Make sure the students understand that there are no right or wrong answers to these questions. Rather, explain to the students that their answers reveal how they feel about their classmates with disabilities. Then, through group discussion, you can explore stereotypes, fears, and the reasons why some students have more favorable attitudes toward students with disabilities than other students. Two tools that lend themselves to these types of discussions are located in Figures 9.2 and 9.3. The Children's Attitudes Towards Integrated Physical Education–Revised (CAIPE–R) Inventory in Figure 9.3 was designed for children in fifth through twelfth grades. After reading a short vignette describing a student with a disability, students respond to a series of statements regarding how they feel about 1) having this student in their class, and 2) specific modifications to a sport to facilitate inclusion. Figure 9.3 provides a sample vignette and questions.

Talk About Famous People Who Have Disabilities

A fifth way to change students' attitudes about disabilities is to discuss famous people who have disabilities (Zygmunt, Larson, & Tilson, 1994). Choose several names from the appendix at the end of this chapter and ask students to write down the first thing they think of when they hear each name. Then, when all the names have been read, ask the students to imagine what these people have in common. Finally, explain to the students that each of these famous people had or have a disability but that we recognize each for his or her individual talents and abilities. Finally, discuss with the class what they have learned about people with disabilities and how this will affect the way that they treat their classmates with disabilities (Zygmunt et al., 1994).

Discuss the Specific Student Who Will Be Included

In addition to the previously listed general methods designed to change students' attitudes, a final and critical method is to discuss with students the specific disabilities (and abilities) of the student who will be included in general physical education class (Block & Brady, 1999; CIRA/CAHPER, 1994). Focus on ways that the student with disabilities is similar to them. For example, stress that this student is the same age they are, likes to wear similar clothes, enjoys playing and watching sports, hates the food in the cafeteria, and argues with his mom about bedtime. Discuss positive ways in which students without disabilities can assist the student during physical education; for example, they can retrieve balls or help the student locate stations or move from one part of the gym to another. Also, students should be allowed to visit this student in his or her special class or in other integrated classes—such as art, history, industrial arts, and music—during the day. Similarly, the student with disabilities should be encouraged to visit

Statements About Disabilities

Directions: For each statement below, place a check on the line that best describes how you feel. (**Important:** There are no right or wrong answers! Just think about how you feel, then answer honestly.)

	Yes	No	Maybe
1. I feel okay around people who have disabilities.	___	___	___
2. I think people who have disabilities should live and work with everybody else.	___	___	___
3. I have seen people with disabilities working at a local business.	___	___	___
4. People with disabilities are able to ride bicycles, drive cars, and participate in sports.	___	___	___
5. A person who has a disability can marry a person who does not have a disability.	___	___	___
6. People who have disabilities can be good parents.	___	___	___
7. Kids who have disabilities should go to the same schools as everyone else.	___	___	___
8. Kids who have disabilities can be just as smart as those who do not have disabilities.	___	___	___
9. Kids who have disabilities can have many friends.	___	___	___
10. I would like to make friends with someone who has a disability.	___	___	___
11. During recess on the school playground, I would play with kids who have disabilities.	___	___	___
12. I would invite someone who has a disability over to my house to play.	___	___	___
13. Kids who have disabilities are the same in many ways as those who do not have disabilities.	___	___	___
14. Kids who have disabilities can be as happy as those who do not have disabilities.	___	___	___
15. Kids who have disabilities can live on their own when they grow up.	___	___	___

- Bring in newspaper or magazine articles that support your point of view about disabilities.
- Share the articles with the class.

A Teacher's Guide to Including Students with Disabilities in General Physical Education, 2nd ed.
by Martin E. Block, copyright ©2000 Paul H. Brookes Publishing Co.

Figure 9.2. General questions that facilitate discussion about disabilities. (From Getskow, V., & Konczal, D. [1996]. *Kids with special needs* (p. 34). Santa Barbara, CA: The Learning Works, Inc.; reprinted by permission.)

Questions from the Children's Attitudes towards
Integrated Physical Education–Revised (CAIPE–R) Inventory

Directions: Read the following vignette, then answer each statement with yes, probably yes, probably no, or no.

Michael is the same age you are. However, he has mental retardation, so he doesn't learn as quickly as you do. Because of his mental retardation, he also does not talk very well, so sometimes it is hard to understand what he is saying. Michael likes playing the same games you do but does not do very well in the games. Even though he can run, he is slower than you and he tires easily. He can throw and catch and hit a softball, but not very well. He likes soccer, but he cannot kick a ball very far. He also likes basketball, but he is not very good at shooting or dribbling, and he doesn't really know the rules of the game. When you read each sentence, think about Michael. Remember, there are no right or wrong answers. The answers you put will depend on you, and your answers will probably be different than those of other kids in your class.

	Yes	Probably Yes	Probably No	No
1. It would be OK having Michael come to my PE class.	____	____	____	____
2. Because Michael cannot play sports very well, he would slow down the game for everyone else.	____	____	____	____
3. If we were playing a team sport such as basketball, it would be OK having Michael on my team.	____	____	____	____
4. PE would be fun if Michael was in my class.	____	____	____	____
5. If Michael was in my PE class, I would talk to him and be his friend.	____	____	____	____
6. If Michael was in my PE class, I would like to help him practice and play the games.	____	____	____	____

Specific questions related to modifications to a sport (e.g., softball)

	Yes	Probably Yes	Probably No	No
7. Michael could hit a ball placed on a batting tee.	____	____	____	____
8. Someone could tell Michael where to run when he hits the ball.	____	____	____	____
9. The distance between home and first base could be shorter for Michael.	____	____	____	____
10. Someone could help Michael when he plays in the field.	____	____	____	____
11. If the ball was hit to Michael, the batter could only run as far as second base.	____	____	____	____

A Teacher's Guide to Including Students with Disabilities in General Physical Education, 2nd ed. by Martin E. Block, copyright ©2000 Paul H. Brookes Publishing Co.

Figure 9.3. Questions from the Children's Attitudes towards Integrated Physical Education–Revised (CAIPE–R) Inventory. Reprinted by permission from Martin E. Block, 1995, Development and Validation of the Children's Attitudes Toward Integrated Physical Education–Revised [CAIPE–R] Inventory. *Adapted Physical Education Quarterly, 12*(1), 60–77.

general physical education classes (if the student has not yet been included), and the peers without disabilities should be encouraged to introduce themselves and chat with the student. By preparing classmates ahead of time, many of the fears, misconceptions, and stereotypes surrounding students with disabilities can be shattered before they begin.

Explain How to Interact with Specific Students

Many students may want to interact with a student who has a disability, but they are not quite sure how to approach the student or if it is even okay to approach the student. For example, some students with more severe disabilities come to physical education with a teacher assistant. Often, peers see the teacher assistant helping the student with disabilities and think that they are not supposed to interact with or include the student. Explain to peers that it is acceptable and even desirable to talk to and play with the student with disabilities, and explain how important it is for this student to have many opportunities to interact with peers and really feel like part of the class. Then, demonstrate how to talk to the student (i.e., if the student has unique communication techniques), include the student in activities (i.e., which simple modifications might work), and befriend the student (e.g., making the student feel like a part of the group by patting him or her on the back, giving high fives, encouraging him or her to be part of the team). For example, many elementary-age students would love to learn some basic signs so they can communicate with a deaf student or a student with autism who uses sign language.

Similarly, it can be fun and challenging for peers to determine the best way to modify various physical education activities to include peers who use wheelchairs or peers who are blind. Simply explaining that it is okay to interact with classmates with disabilities and then providing some suggestions on ways to interact with classmates who have disabilities will help peers be more understanding and welcoming to these students. Note that these discussions may need to take place several times during the school year. For example, students may be very friendly and helpful to a student with mental retardation in the beginning of the school year when inclusion is still novel. However, after several months, students may begin to ignore the student or forget that the student needs some modifications to activities in order to participate successfully. In such cases you may need to sit down with the group again to remind them of the student's needs and how to help him or her feel like a part of the class.

Provide Ongoing Information, Encouragement, and Support for Acceptance

Preparing peers is an important part of successful inclusion, but preparation should not stop once the student with disabilities is included. Too often, students with disabilities are ignored in physical education because their classmates do not know how to interact with or assist them (Block & Brady, 1999). In these cases, the teacher should provide ongoing encouragement to peers (both through modeling and direct suggestion) to talk to the student with disabilities, to provide feedback and positive reinforcement, to gently correct or redirect the student when he or she misbehaves, and to ask the student if he or she needs assistance. Rather than assigning one peer to the student, the entire class should take responsibility for the student with disabilities. For example, if a student who has mental retardation does not know which station to go to, one of his peers can assist him. Similarly, if a student who is blind has lost the ball she was dribbling, one of her peers can retrieve it for her. Students should be continuously prompted and reinforced for interacting with the student with disabilities. As the year progresses and classmates begin to feel more comfortable with the student who has a disability, interactions will become more spontaneous.

Common Problems and Possible Solutions to Social Aspects of Inclusion

Unfortunately, the social aspects of inclusion are rarely addressed in general physical education. Simply placing a student with disabilities in general physical education will not ensure socialization. Furthermore, many physical educators unknowingly create situations that prevent the social development of students with disabilities. The purpose of this section is to focus on three problems that prevent socialization in inclusive physical education and ways that these problems can be overcome. Problems include 1) teacher assistants who are overly helpful, 2) general education activities that are inappropriate, and 3) peers who serve only as tutors and not as friends.

Problem #1: Teacher Assistants Trying Too Hard

As noted previously, students with severe disabilities who attend general physical education often are accompanied by a teacher assistant. These teacher assistants often know a lot about the student with disabilities, but very little about physical education; however, despite their lack of training in physical education, they feel compelled to assist the students to whom they are assigned as much as possible. After all, that is their job! Unfortunately, a teacher assistant who hovers around a student with a disability unwittingly prevents that student from interacting with his or her peers without disabilities. The hovering teacher assistant is comparable to a bubble placed around the student with disabilities. For example, when partnering up to do sit-ups in the beginning of class, the teacher assistant is almost always partnered with the student with disabilities.

Similarly, peers often feel uncomfortable approaching the student with disabilities when there is a teacher assistant working with the student. For example, a teacher assistant is instructing a student with a disability on the overhand throw at a throwing station. She also retrieves bean bags that the student has thrown. Peers watching this interaction may not want to interfere with the instruction that is taking place. At the same time, the student becomes very dependent on the teacher assistant in this activity.

Solution: Awareness Training for Teacher Assistants

Teacher assistants want to do what is best for the students with disabilities to whom they are assigned, and they also want to be useful. Simply explaining to the teacher assistant that you want to encourage more interactions between the student with disabilities and his or her peers is a big start to solving the problem. Explain that hovering around a student with disabilities prevents important social interactions with peers. Instead, the teacher assistant could help a student with a disability get started at a station, then move away and help other students at the station while still keeping an eye on the student with disabilities. In fact, a teacher assistant can be assigned to a group of students that includes the student with disabilities rather than to *just* the student with disabilities.

Teacher assistants also can be given specific ideas regarding ways to promote more interactions between peers with and without disabilities. For example, when students are looking for partners, the teacher assistant can encourage peers to choose the student with disabilities as a partner. When a student needs assistance retrieving balls or going to another station, the teacher assistant can encourage peers to help the student. When the class is playing a group game, the teacher assistant can encourage peers to help the student know where to stand and what to do. The teacher assistant should be in the general vicinity for safety reasons, but he or she does not need to hover around the student with disabilities the entire period. By "backing off" a little, the student is given a greater opportunity for interaction with peers and a chance to become more independent.

Problem #2: Student Cannot Participate in the General Activity

In some cases, students with disabilities cannot participate in a particular activity because of health and safety issues. Although it may seem appropriate to have the student engage in a more suitable activity off to the side of the gym, such separation from peers encourages isolation and prevents social interactions. For example, it may be unsafe for a tenth grader with cerebral palsy who uses an electric wheelchair to play soccer with his peers or for a third grader with Down syndrome to do forward rolls during a tumbling unit; however, asking the student to sit off to the side and watch or play by himself is not an appropriate solution to the problem.

Solution: Utilize Peers without Disabilities

One relatively simple solution to this problem is to have peers rotate over to the student with a disability and participate with him or her in an alternative activity. Using the soccer example above, each player in the soccer game could be given a number from 1 to 6. Because there are 30 students in the class, five players will have the number 1, five will have the number 2, and so on. At the start of the soccer game, players with the number 1 could be off to the side of the soccer field working with the student with cerebral palsy in an alternative activity. In keeping with the theme of soccer, students could practice dribbling as quickly as they can through cones or could pass a ball back and forth with a partner. The student with cerebral palsy could practice maneuvering his wheelchair through the cones or pushing his ball off his lap tray to a partner. After about 3 minutes, the "1's" rotate "in" and the "2's" rotate "out". Peer participation at the alternative activity creates opportunities for social interactions.

Another way to promote additonal interactions with peers when an activity is inappropriate for a student with disabilities is to add more activities. For example, a student with Down syndrome cannot do forward rolls due to the potential for sustaining a neck injury; however, you were planning on doing forward rolls with your class as part of your tumbling unit. A solution is to set up another area of the gym with mats for other tumbling-type activities, such as log rolls, or strength activities (e.g., seal walks, crab walks). All the students in the class could then rotate between the forward roll station, the log roll station, and the strength station. However, the student with Down syndrome would rotate only through the last two stations. This setup allows the student with Down syndrome to participate in activities that are important for him (i.e., body awareness, strength) yet still be part of the general activity. While the student with Down syndrome is working on motor and fitness skills, he also has an opportunity to interact with his peers, wait his turn, and observe appropriate behavior.

The activity off to the side of the gym can be anything that is appropriate for the student with a disability. Although, ideally, it should match what the other students in class are doing, this is not always possible. Regardless of whether the activities match, it is critical to the social well-being of the student with a disability for him or her to interact with his or her peers without disabilities. For example, a third-grade class is learning softball skills, but a student with autism needs to work on learning how to ride a bicycle. On Tuesdays and Thursdays, she works on this skill with an adapted physical educator outside on the black top. Because the student's peers already know how to ride bicycles, bicycle riding is not a skill on which they need to work; however, it is important for this student to be around her peers, see peers doing the same activity she is doing, and generally learn how to behave appropriately around peers. Using bicycles donated by the PTA, three students go outside and ride alongside the student with autism. These peers are encouraged to talk to and interact with the student with autism as much as possible. Similarly, the student with autism is encouraged to watch her peers ride their bicycles. After 10 minutes, these three students come back into class and three more students go outside to ride. By utilizing the classmates of the students with disabilities, the students in the examples above have opportunities to interact with and observe the behaviors of their peers without disabilities.

Problem #3: Peers Are Tutors, not Friends

Using peers as tutors to facilitate inclusion has been promoted for the past several years (e.g., Block, 1996; Houston-Wilson, Lieberman, Horton, & Kasser, 1997). Peers are a free, readily available source of support for students with disabilities who need extra attention or extra help. However, if peers only serve as tutors to the students with disabilities, then the relationship is unbalanced. This imbalance promotes the idea that students with disabilities always need help and are somehow "less than" students without disabilities. In addition, such unbalanced relationships can lead to lower self-esteem for students with disabilities (Sherrill, 1998).

Solution: Utilize Peers as Friends as well as Tutors

Although you still can use peers as tutors to help students with disabilities, you should also create situations in which students with disabilities can serve as tutors. Known as the reciprocal style of teaching (Mosston & Ashworth, 1994), or classwide peer tutoring (Block, Oberweiser, et al., 1995; Houston-Wilson, Lieberman, et al., 1997; Sherrill, 1998), the student with disabilities and a peer take turns serving as tutor and tutee. This works particularly well for students with mild disabilities such as learning disabilities or behavior problems. As the tutee, the student with disabilities learns how to listen to and accept feedback. As the tutor, the student with a disability learns how to carefully observe others and to provide feedback in a "nice" way. Furthermore, taking turns as tutor and tutee leads to increased interactions and discussions between the two students. For example, a fourth grader with a behavior problem (does not follow directions, is hyperactive, can be belligerent) is paired with a peer during a classwide peer tutoring throwing activity. Students are given a score sheet with the components of the overhand throw, and each student takes a turn being the tutor (watching and giving feedback about the throw) and the tutee (performing the throw and listening to feedback). The student with the behavior problem starts as the tutor.

The tutee encourages her to watch her throw, paying particular attention to the way she steps with the opposite foot. The tutor watches the throw and gives immediate feedback following a script written out by the teacher: "Good throw, you stepped with the opposite foot." During this activity, the student with the behavior problem is learning how to give feedback in a nice way, and she also is learning, through observation, how to respond to feedback. After five throws, the students switch roles. The student with a behavior problem now gets to throw and receive feedback; because she just served as the tutor, the tutee with whom she worked already has provided a model of how to stay on task, listen to feedback, and accept feedback properly.

Another solution to the imbalance of peer tutoring is to set up situations in which peers are simply friends and not tutors. For example, a ninth grader with fetal alcohol syndrome has motor delays (he is about 3 years delayed compared with peers) as well as behavior problems (short attention span, impulsive, hyperactive, lies a lot). The general physical education class is doing a basketball unit; in the past, this student has been assigned a peer to help him stay on task, follow directions, and stay with the group. However, the physical education teacher decides to do something new in this unit: He asks the entire class to be this student's "friend" by taking responsibility in helping him stay on task and generally behave more appropriately during physical education. The class discusses this new model to help John, the student with fetal alchol syndrome, be more successful in general physical education and their new roles as John's friends. For example, when students line up in squads for role call and warm-ups, peers in John's squad call him over to say hi and then remind him to line up. During warm-ups, peers in his squad remind John when it is time to change to a new warm-up activity, and several peers try to be his partner when it is time for sit-ups. When the teacher gives instructions, John's peers provide gentle reminders to sit and listen quietly. During the basketball game, teammates guide John; they tell him where to stand, to whom to pass, and not to play too rough on defense. The other team, aware that John is not as skilled as his peers without disabilities, allows John a little more room to pass and to shoot, and they do not call "traveling" unless it is blatant. This subtle approach to helping John provides more dignity and promotes a natural delivery of support. Furthermore, the student with disabilities has a chance to interact with all of his classmates rather than just one peer tutor.

Appendix

Famous People with Disabilities

Athletes

Jim Abbott (baseball)	Physical disability (one hand)
Mohammed Ali (boxing)	Brain injury
Larry Brown (football)	Hearing impairment
Harold Connelly (track and field)	Physical disability (withered left arm)
Tom Dempsey (football)	Physical disability (congenital foot deformity [half a right foot])
Jim Eisenreich (baseball)	Tourette syndrome
Sean Elliot (basketball)	Kidney disease (has one kidney)
Pete Gray (baseball)	Physical disability (one arm)
Nancy Hogshead (swimmer)	Asthma
Catfish Hunter (baseball)	Diabetes, Amyotrophic Lateral Sclerosis (ALS)
Bruce Jenner (track and field)	Learning disability
Magic Johnson (basketball)	HIV
Jackie Joyner-Kersee (track and field)	Asthma
Tony Lazzeri	Epilepsy
Greg Louganis (diver)	Asthma (Louganis' mother enrolled him in a children's gymnastics class to help him strengthen his lungs); AIDS
Walter Payton (football)	Kidney disease
Wilma Rudolph	Physical disability (birth defects and polio)
Ron Santo	Epilepsy
O.J. Simpson (football)	Learning disability
Kenny Walker (football)	Deafness

Politicians

Winston Churchill	Learning disability
Robert Dole	Physical disability (cannot use right arm as a result of war injuries)

John F. Kennedy	Physical disability (Kennedy's back was injured in WW II; he used crutches to get around the White House when he was not in the public eye.)
Abraham Lincoln	Depression and Marfan syndrome
George Patton	Learning disability
Ronald Reagan	Alzheimer's disease
Franklin D. Roosevelt	Physical disability (Polio at age 39 greatly reduced ability to use his legs.)
Woodrow Wilson	Learning disability

Actors and Actresses

Chris Burke	Mental retardation (Down syndrome)
Cher	Learning disability (dyslexia) (Cher uses a reading coach to learn TV, movie, and commercial scripts.)
Tom Cruise	Learning disability (dyslexia) (Cruise went to the LAB school in Washington, D.C., and he uses a reading coach to learn scripts)
Sammy Davis, Jr.	Visual impairment
Walt Disney	Learning disability (Disney did not learn how to read until he was 9. He drew pictures to help himself remember what he was learning.)
James Earl Jones	Communication disability (stutter) (Jones did not speak in school because he was so embarrassed. He learned to speak without stuttering by reading poetry. [Because poetry and musical lyrics have a rhythm, people who stutter often can read poetry or sing.])
Annette Funicello	Multiple sclerosis
Danny Glover	Learning disability (Glover was placed in a class for students with mental retardation until he was in high school, and he did not learn how to read or write until after he graduated from school.)
Whoopi Goldberg	Learning disability (dyslexia) (Goldberg uses a reading coach to help her learn scripts.)
Katherine Hepburn	Parkinson's disease
Marlee Maitlin	Deaf
Richard Pryor	Multiple sclerosis
Christopher Reeves	Quadriplegia

Musicians

Beethoven	Deaf
Ray Charles	Blind

John Lennon	Learning disability
Itzhak Perlman	Physical disability (paraplegic)
Stevie Wonder	Blind

Other Famous People

Hans Christian Anderson (author)	Learning disability
Agatha Christie (author)	Learning disability
Thomas Edison (inventor)	Learning disability
Albert Einstein (scientist)	Learning disability
Stephen Hawking (scientist and author)	Amyotrophic lateral sclerosis (ALS)
Helen Keller (author)	Deaf and blind

10

Making Inclusive
Physical Education Safe

Lifetime wellness is of concern for all individuals, but the impact for individuals with disabilities is significantly more profound. . . . I have had the opportunity to observe children with disabilities who are included in general physical education at the elementary, middle, and high school level. . . . Lifetime activities, which are provided within the general physical education setting, are provided and instruction is given in order for students to choose appropriate leisure activities. Physical education is an integral part of improving the quality of life for children with disabilities. It provides health benefits, social opportunities, independence, job enhancement, and appropriate use of leisure time.

Ginny Popiolek, adapted physical education specialist

Mrs. Richards does not mind having students with disabilities in her general physical education class. Over the years she has had students with Down syndrome, learning disabilities, and attention disorders; she once even had a student who was deaf. However, this year, Mrs. Richards has Malcolm, a student with autism, and Chandra, a student who uses a wheelchair, in one of her ninth-grade classes. Malcolm comes to general physical education with a teacher assistant, but Mrs. Richards has heard that he runs away from the group for no apparent reason and with no warning. Mrs. Richards is particularly concerned for Malcolm's safety when she takes the class outside to the upper field for physical education. If Malcolm runs away while they are there, he could easily go through a small wooded area and end up on a busy road. What would happen if this student were hit by a car? In addition, Mrs. Richards heard that Malcolm sometimes hits other kids when he gets upset or confused. What if Malcolm were to hit another student during physical education?

Mrs. Richards also worries about Chandra. Chandra has a condition that Mrs. Richards has never heard of—Werdnig-Hoffman disease, a form of spinal muscular atrophy. Chandra has typical intelligence, but she is very weak. Most of her muscles appear very atrophied (withered), and she has severe scoliosis (curvature of her spine) that affects her breathing. She can move about in her electric wheelchair, but she moves her wheelchair relatively slowly (at the pace of someone walking). Consequently, Mrs. Richards worries that she will not be able to move out of the way of balls or other students. Moreover, Chandra cannot move her hands quickly enough to catch a ball tossed to her, let alone to protect herself from a volleyball, basketball, or soccer ball during a game. She could easily get hurt. Finally, Chandra's chair is so big that Mrs. Richards is afraid that other students might bump into it when they are focusing on an activity. Mrs. Richards wants to do what is best for Malcolm and Chandra, but including them in general ninth-grade physical education just does not seem "doable." What are Mrs. Richard's options?

Gallahue noted that "the very nature of physical education classes, which take place in the gymnasium, swimming pool, or playground, exposes the teacher to greater liability for accidents and injuries than any other area of the school curriculum" (1996, p. 244). Safety issues in physical education are only com-

---

This chapter is based on Block, M.E., & Horton, M.H. (1996). Include safety: Do not exclude children with disabilities from regular physical education. *Physical Educator, 53,* 58–72.

pounded when students with disabilities are included in general physical education programs. There are three major safety concerns for included students with disabilities: First, safety is a problem for students with disabilities who do not have the same level of speed, strength, stamina, balance, or coordination as their peers without disabilities. In addition, many students with disabilities have cognitive and perceptual ability problems that can add to their confusion and inability to react to situations as quickly as their peers. Such differences easily can lead to injuries. For example, in a dodging or fleeing activity, a student with cerebral palsy who is very unstable in standing could easily be knocked down by all of the movement. Similarly, a student who has mental retardation may not know that he or she is standing too close to the batter during a softball game. The student could be in danger of getting hit by the ball or the bat.

Second, safety is an issue for students who have medical conditions that can lead to emergency complications. For example, many students have such severe asthma that their attacks require emergency medical attention (Butterfield, 1993). Similarly, changes in diet and exercise patterns can have severe consequences for students who have diabetes (Petray, Freesemann, & Lavay, 1997). Of even greater concern are students with disabilities who are medically fragile, such as students who have tracheostomies to correct airway problems, gastric tubes for feeding problems, shunts for hydrocephalus, and colostomies and ileostomies for bowel problems. Students with such severe medical conditions used to receive education in hospitals and special schools; however, in recent years, a greater number of these students are being placed in general school environments and attending general classes, including general physical education (Graff, Ault, Guess, Taylor, & Thompson, 1990; Troher, 1992). In fact, in 1999, the Supreme Court of the United States ruled that public schools must now provide a wide array of medical care for students with disabilities, including in general education and general physical education classrooms (Biskupic, 1999).

Third, including students with disabilities in general physical education poses dangers to students without disabilities. For example, a student who uses a wheelchair may be involved in a game of tag. During the excitement of the game, one of the student's peers could easily run into the student's wheelchair. Similarly, a student with crutches could accidentally hit or trip another student during a soccer game, and a student with an artificial arm could accidentally bump into and injure a peer during movement exploration activities.

Safety certainly should be a priority in physical education for students with and without disabilities, and there are, in fact, some cases in which students with disabilities cannot safely be included in general physical education. However, safety concerns should not be used as a blanket excuse to simply place *all* students with disabilities in separate physical education programs. As noted in Chapters 1 and 2, placements need to be made on an individual basis. In addition, supplementary aids and services should be used as needed to ensure that students with disabilities receive a safe, appropriate, individualized physical education program within the general environment. Only when the environment is deemed unsafe or inappropriate following attempts to make it safe and appropriate through supplementary aids and supports can the student be placed in a separate environment (Block, 1996; Individuals with Disabilities Education Act [IDEA] Amendments of 1997, [PL 105-17], §1412[5][B]; *Oberti v. Board of Education*, 1993).

The purpose of this chapter is to share strategies that can be used to make general physical education environments and activities safe for all students, including those with disabilities. First, the issues of liability and negligence, as they pertain to physical education and students with disabilities, are discussed. This is followed by a discussion of six key aspects of making inclusive environments safe: 1) the student with disabilities, 2) the general environment, 3) the equipment, 4) class organization, 5) content, and 6) emergency procedures. It is understood that some students in some activities and environments may not be able to participate safely and, therefore, should receive physical education in alternative environments. Nevertheless, by considering each of these six factors, you will be able to make more objective decisions regarding which students might need alternative programs or placements. However, you will find that most students with disabilities, including those with more severe disabilities, can be accommodated safely within general physical education.

A Primer on Legal Liability

Liability

From a legal standpoint, *legal* or *tort liability* refers to 1) someone being at fault, 2) this "fault" leading to or causing an injury or death, and 3) that "someone" being legally responsible for the injury or death (Appenzeller & Appenzeller, 1980; Black, 1990; Gallahue, 1996). With regard to physical education, tort liability means that a student basically is holding a physical education teacher liable for injuries sustained during physical education class. For example, a student with a visual impairment is knocked down during a dodging and fleeing game. Her parents sue the physical education teacher for their child's injuries. Although the parents have the right to hold the physical education teacher liable for their daughter's injuries, it is up to the court to show that the cause of the student's injuries was due to the physical education teacher's negligence.

Negligence

Fault that results in personal injury is also known as *negligence* (Appenzeller, 1983; Dougherty, 1987). Negligence is defined as failure on the part of the physical education teacher to act in a manner that is judged to be reasonable, careful, and prudent for someone with his or her level of training or status (Dougherty, 1987; Gallahue, 1996; Gray, 1995). This is also known as the *prudent or reasonable person principle* (Appenzeller & Appenzeller, 1980; Dougherty, 1987). That is, would another reasonably prudent physical education teacher placed in the same situation have done the same thing to ensure the safety of the student who was injured? A physical educator who places students in unnecessarily risky situations or who does not provide proper supervision of activities may be considered negligent. Appenzeller (1983), Dougherty (1987), Gallahue (1996), and Pangrazi (1998) noted that negligence must be proved in a court of law and that the following three factors must be shown if negligence is to be established.

Duty It must be determined that the defendant (i.e., the physical education teacher) had a responsibility to provide for the safety and welfare of the plaintiff (i.e., the student). If the injured party is a student in the defendant's physical education class, then established duty is a foregone conclusion. It is important to note that the licensed physical education teacher is responsible for providing for the safety and welfare of all students who enter his or her physical education program, including students with disabilities. This is the case even if the student with a disability is accompanied by a teacher assistant, volunteer, or peer tutor. In fact, the licensed physical education teacher is also responsible for the safety of the teacher assistants, volunteers, and peer tutors who enter his or her physical education environment.

Breach of Duty   It must be shown that the defendant failed to provide the standard of service that reasonably could be expected of a professional under similar circumstances. A duty can be breached by 1) *nonfeasance* or *act of omission*—failure to do something that a prudent physical educator would have done, such as not providing alternative instruction to students who are deaf or who have learning disabilities and might not fully understand typical instruction given to other students; 2) *malfeasance* or *act of commission*—doing something that a prudent physical educator would not have been doing, such as allowing a student with Down syndrome who tested positive for atlantoaxial instability (problem in the neck that can lead to paralysis if pressure is placed on the neck) to do forward and backward rolls with the other students; or 3) *misfeasance*—following proper procedures but not to the required standard of conduct expected by a prudent physical education teacher, such as supervising students in a game of tag but having too small a space and too many students moving at once, causing a student with low vision to collide with another student.

If a breach of duty is established, then the plaintiff must prove that there was a reasonable relationship between the defendant's breach of duty and the student's injury. In other words, was it the physical education teacher's specific breach of duty that led to the damage incurred by the student? If, for example, a student with mental retardation who was properly supervised and instructed got hurt due to "an act of God" (e.g., the student tripped over his own feet and broke an ankle while working at a basketball station), then the physical education teacher is not necessarily liable. As noted by Appenzeller,

> The fact that an accident occurs does not necessarily mean the teacher or coach is negligent or liable for damages. It must be proved that the injury is reasonably connected with negligence. . . . No court has held a defendant liable where there was substantial evidence that the defendant acted with prudence and caution in the performance of his duties. (1983, p. 183)

Related to the concept of breach of duty is *foreseeability.* It must be shown that the physical education teacher could have predicted the likelihood of an accident or injury occurring due to the specific circumstance or situation. For example, could the physical education teacher have foreseen that a third-grade peer tutor did not have the strength or control to safely push a student in a wheelchair down a steep hill? Could the physical education teacher have foreseen that a student with asthma might have an attack when running a mile on a hot June day?

Damage   *Damage* basically refers to actual injury or loss. The plaintiff has to prove damage to receive some sort of compensation from the defendant. Real damages can comprise, for example, medical expenses, rehabilitation expenses, psychological stress, and time away from school. Compensation for damages, then, could be in the form of payment of medical expenses, compensation for medical discomfort, psychological counseling, home tutoring, or even a legal restraint on the physical education teacher (e.g., taking away his or her teaching license).

When Is an Injury to a Student Not Negligence?

Under the following circumstances, a physical education teacher could be found *not negligent* in relation to an injury incurred by a student during physical education class: contributory negligence, proximate cause, and act of God (Appenzeller, 1983; Dougherty, 1987; Gallahue, 1996; Pangrazi, 1998). The following sections describe each of these conditions.

Contributory Negligence   *Contributory negligence* refers to the plaintiff (i.e., the student) being held partially or wholly responsible for the injury he or she received. Note that a court will take into consideration a student's age, physical capabilities (both mental and physical), and training before it rules with regard to fault. In other words, the defense tries to prove that the activity and equipment were familiar to the student, that the student received training in the activity or with the equipment, and that the injured student did not follow proper safety procedures that would be expected of other students of his age and with his capabilities. For example, a 16-year-old student who uses a wheelchair, has no intellectual impairments, and has been in the same school in the same gymnasium for 3 years wheels his chair into the wall while playing basketball, causing a broken leg and concussion. Because the wall has been in the same place for all 3 years that this student has been at the school, the court could reasonably rule that the student was old enough and capable enough to move his wheelchair safely within the confines of the gymnasium and that running into the wall was at least partially the student's own fault. In some states, the concept of *comparative negligence* is used, which means that fault for a given situation is apportioned based on the information presented to the court (e.g., physical education teacher is 30% at fault; student is 70% at fault). In such cases, the student can still receive compensation for damages, but on a prorated basis.

Proximate Cause   *Proximate cause* suggests that the injury was not caused by negligence on the part of the physical education teacher. There must be a close relationship between the breach of duty by the teacher and the resulting injury to the student. For example, a teacher sets up five stations at which students work on various physical fitness skills. The teacher would normally move around the room supervising the stations but not directly assisting any of the students (all students could do each of the fitness activities independently). However, at one point during class, a therapist comes into the gym to ask the physical education teacher a "quick question." While the physical education teacher is talking to this therapist, a student with a physical disability (uses crutches but has excellent upper-body strength) who is working at a pull-up station strains to do one more pull-up. With her last effort, she slips off the bar, falling so that the back of her head hits the mat on the floor, causing her to have a concussion and a bruised spinal cord. Even if the physical education teacher was watching this student as he normally would have been, the student still could have fallen and hurt herself. Therefore, although it could be argued that the physical education teacher was not providing proper supervision, this lack of supervision was not the proximate cause of the student's injury.

Act of God   *Act of God* suggests that the injury occurred due to an event that was completely unexpected and could not have been foreseen. In other words, something happened that caused an accident that was beyond the reasonable control of the teacher. For example, while playing outside, a sudden gust of wind knocks down a student who has muscular dystrophy, causing him to break several bones. To prove an act of God, the defense must show that the accident still would have occurred even though reasonable action had been taken.

In summary, teachers who act responsibly, with common sense, and with an attitude that they are going to create the safest environment possible while still allowing students to be involved actively in movement and fitness activities should not be scared of liability and negligence. Ask yourself what another prudent physical educator would do in a particular situation. Also, think of worst-case scenarios in an attempt to foresee potential safety concerns. The key is to learn as much as you can about each student so you can anticipate any possible problems, provide proper supervision and instruction, make sure equipment is in working order, and provide activities and progressions that are appropriate for each student's abilities. Figure 10.1 provides a checklist to help you ensure the safe inclusion of students with disabilities. The following section reviews key components of creating a safe, inclusive physical education environment.

Legal Issues Specific to Students with Disabilities

Many students with disabilities present an immediate concern to the physical educator (e.g., students who use wheelchairs, students who are blind). Others have hidden disabilities that may not be immediately recognized by simply observing the student (e.g., seizure disorders, asthma, diabetes, HIV/AIDS). This is particularly dangerous because special educators and parents often forget to inform physical education staff members about medical conditions that can result in injury or illness. Being unaware of a student's health or medical problems can lead to participation in unsafe activities and possible lawsuits. Ultimately, you, as the physical educator, are responsible for the safety of all the students you serve (Cotton, 1994; Dougherty, 1987). Thus, it is imperative that you learn as much as possible about each student with disabilities before determining how to cope with safety concerns.

The first step is simply to identify students with health problems and/or specific disabilities. This can be done by carefully reviewing the medical records of all of the students you teach (Pangrazi, 1998). An easier way is to review the emergency cards on file in the main office. These cards usually highlight students' health problems such as asthma, diabetes, or allergies and list medications that the students take. In addition, you can go to the school nurse or to each classroom teacher and ask him or her to identify students with special health concerns or disabilities.

Once you have identified these students, you should examine detailed medical records and cumulative folders for the particular student; these items also should be available in the main office. If, for some reason, detailed records are outdated or are not available, contact each student's parents to obtain additional information. A relatively simple way to obtain information about students with special health problems or disabilities is to send home a form that the parents and/or physician can fill out (see Figure 10.2 for an example). Some school districts actually require such forms to be sent home and filled out before a student with a disability can participate in physical education (Fairfax County Public Schools, 1994). Information about each student with special health problems or disabilities can then be placed in a database on your computer or in a file in the physical education office and updated annually. For example, a database can be sorted to print out the names of all students who have asthma. Proper precautions (e.g., having an inhaler or other medicine available, not doing strenuous exercise in the fall during heavy pollen season) could then be taken for these students.

Although this may seem like an enormous task, it is critical that you know as much as possible about each student with special health problems or disabilities in order to ensure safe participation in general physical education. For example, some students with cerebral palsy are prone to hip dislocations if lifted or positioned improperly (Orelove & Sobsey, 1996). Physical activity can lower blood sugar in a student with diabetes, which can cause a hypoglycemic reaction (Petray et al., 1997). Many students with spina bifida have shunts in their heads that drain

Checklist to Ensure the Safe Inclusion of Students with Disabilities

1. **Have you taken the time to get to know the student with disabilities?**
   —Have you identified specific health/medical problems?
   —Have you learned about each child's specific disability and learning character-
     istics as they relate to safety in physical education?
   —Have you talked with each child's parents?

2. **Have you gotten involved in the IEP process?**
   —Have you attended IEP meetings?
   —Have you shared your concerns for physical education with team members?
   —Have you provided specific information about your program to team members?
   —Have you helped write the IEP for physical education?
   —Have you talked with specialists who work with the student with disabilities?

3. **Have you determined each student's abilities through formal and informal assess-
   ment?**
   —Have you observed the student in general physical education?
   —Have you noted the student's behavior as it relates to potential safety concerns?
   —Have you determined the student's fitness as it relates to potential safety con-
     cerns?
   —Have you determined motor abilities as they relate to potential safety concerns?

4. **Have you examined the teaching environment for safety concerns?**
   —Have you examined the environment for adequate movement space for all chil-
     dren?
   —Have you established clear boundaries that all children can recognize?
   —Have you set up equipment in a safe manner for all children?
   —Have you examined accessibility of your environment, including lockers and
     playing fields?

5. **Have you examined all of your equipment for safety concerns?**
   —Have you recently checked equipment for adequate repair?
   —Do you have necessary adapted equipment for children with disabilities?
   —Do all children know the proper use of equipment?

6. **Have you utilized safe teaching techniques?**
   —Have you established safety rules, and have you made sure all children under-
     stand these rules?
   —Can you adequately supervise all areas, especially areas where children with
     disabilities are moving?
   —Have you modified instruction so that all children understand directions?
   —Have you provided adequate time for all children to participate in a sufficient
     warm-up?
   —Have you planned activities that are progressive so that all children are not par-
     ticipating in activities beyond their abilities?

7. **Have you considered modifications to content to ensure safety?**
   —Have you examined the need for multilevel curricular selection to ensure
     safety?
   —Have you examined the need for curricular overlapping to ensure safety?
   —Have you examined the need for an alternative curriculum to ensure safety?

A Teacher's Guide to Including Students with Disabilities in General Physical Education
by Martin E. Block, copyright ©2000 Paul H. Brookes Publishing Co.

Figure 10.1. Checklist to ensure safe inclusion of students with disabilities.

Physical Education Information Form

I. General information (to be filled out by parent/guardian)

Name: _____ Date of birth: _____

Parent/guardian: _____ Telephone: _____

Person filling out this form/relationship to child: _____

Signature:_____ Date: _____

II. Medical information (to be filled out by parent/guardian and/or doctor)

Part A: Nature of disability (if your child does not have a disability, skip to B)

1. What type of disability(ies) does the child have? _____ _____
    _____

2. Please describe in more detail the characteristics of the child's disability(ies).
    _____
    _____

3. Is there anything I should be aware of in physical education? _____
    _____

Part B: Specific health problems (if your child does not have any health problems, skip to C)

Does your child have . . .

Asthma? _____ yes _____ no
1. If you answered yes, is there an inhaler at school? _____ yes _____ no
2. If you answered yes, where is it located at school (e.g., office, classroom)?
    _____

Allergies to bee stings? _____ yes _____ no
1. If you answered yes, is there a bee sting kit at school? _____ yes _____ no
2. If you answered yes, where is it located at school (e.g., office, classroom)?
    _____

Diabetes? _____ yes _____ no
1. If you answered yes, does your child take insulin? _____ yes _____ no
2. If you answered yes, where is it located at school (e.g., office, classroom)?
    _____

Heart problems? _____ yes _____ no
1. If you answered yes, please explain in more detail. _____
    _____

A Teacher's Guide to Including Students with Disabilities in General Physical Education, 2nd ed.
by Martin E. Block, copyright ©2000 Paul H. Brookes Publishing Co.

Figure 10.2.   Physical education information form. (*Sources:* Fairfax County Public Schools, 1994; Kelly & Wessel, 1986; Markos & Jenkins, 1994.)

Figure 10.2. (*continued*)

Other health problems? _____ yes _____ no

1. If you answered yes, please explain in more detail. _____

_____

_____

Part C: Medications

Does your child take any medications? _____ yes _____ no

1. If you answered yes, what is the name of the medication and what is it used for?

_____

_____

2. When is it administered? _____

_____

_____

3. Does the medication have any effects on physical/motor performance (if yes, please explain)? _____

_____

_____

4. Are there any specific concerns regarding health or medications of which I should be aware during physical education, including any activities in which your child should not participate (see lists in part III for more detail)?

_____

_____

III. PE activities that may be inappropriate (to be filled out by parent, PT, or doctor)

Some activities can be dangerous for children with particular disabilities. Please circle any activity about which you have concerns for this student. Please comment on any activities that you have circled (e.g., note the types of supervision/modifications that would allow this student to participate safely in the activity).

Elementary (K–5)

Locomotor skills	Manipulative skills	Body management	Fitness
Running	Throwing	Twisting	Continuous running
Jumping	Catching	Turning	Sprinting
Galloping	Striking	Stretching	Stretching
Hopping	Kicking		Push-ups/pull-ups
Skipping	Dribbling (feet)		Sit-ups
Bouncing			Rope climbing
			Aerobic dance
			Weightlifting
			Stationary bike

Figure 10.2. *(continued)*

Elementary (K–5) (continued)

Tumbling	**Games**	**Activities**
Balance beam	Chasing/fleeing	Getting wet
Log roll	Dodging	Standing in water
Forward roll	Tag	Floating
Backward roll	Racing	Basic strokes
Headstand/handstand	Team sports	Lap swimming
Vaulting	Skating	Diving
Pyramids	Jumping rope	
Rope climbing		

Middle/high school

Team sports	**Individual sports**	**Gymnastics**	**Dance**
Basketball	Golf	Rings	Aerobic
Softball	Tennis	High bar	Square
Volleyball	Archery	Parallel bars	Folk
Soccer	Bowling	Vault	Modern
Flag football	Badminton	Floor exercise	
Floor hockey	Wrestling		
Lacrosse			

Comments on activities that you circled: _____

_____

_____

_____

_____

_____

_____

_____

_____

_____

_____

_____

_____

_____

fluid from their brains, and most physicians recommend some restrictions in physical education activities (French, Keele, & Silliman-French, 1997). Students with exercise-induced asthma are particularly sensitive to continuous exercise (Butterfield, 1993). A physical educator who is not aware of these and other medical conditions could put his or her students into dangerous situations.

Another way to obtain this and other information is to participate in the individualized education program (IEP) team meeting. All critical team members, including parents, attend this meeting and share information about the student with disabilities. This meeting also is a great place to educate IEP team members about your program and what you know about the student. You can share information such as the student's fitness level, gross motor skills, perceptual motor abilities, skills in specific activities, and general motivation and behavior during physical education. Once team members begin to understand your program, the unique aspect of the physical education environment, and the gross motor/fitness skills of the student, they can provide more specific suggestions to make your program safe. In addition, by attending team meetings, team members might become more sympathetic to your request for extra support, such as the use of peer tutors and teacher assistants, consultation with specialists, and adapted equipment.

Although medical and health information is extremely important, there is other information that will help you determine how to make safety adjustments for students with disabilities. Most important, you will want to know about each student's physical fitness level, body and space awareness level, balance, eye–hand coordination, and other motor abilities and how they might affect safe participation in general physical education. For example, if a student has difficulty with eye–hand coordination, you could plan accommodations during dodging, catching, rebounding, and striking activities. A relatively simple modification is to allow the student to use a foam ball when striking or catching so that if he or she does miss the ball, there is a reduced risk of injury. Similarly, you could allow students who have trouble with balance, including students who use walkers or canes, to move in a special zone so that they will not get bumped or knocked down during chasing-and-fleeing activities. Figure 10.3 provides a list of questions that should be asked regarding a student's fitness level and gross motor abilities.

Finally, you will want to find out about the student's communication skills and behavior problems. Again, you can obtain much of this information at the IEP meeting by listening and talking to parents, general and special education teachers, therapists, and teacher assistants. These key people can provide you with specific information to help you make the program safer for the student with disabilities. For example, the general and special educators can note behaviors that could create safety problems (e.g., aggressive behaviors or running away), and the speech-language therapist can note how much verbal information the student understands. The checklist in Figure 10.4 provides a list of questions that can guide you when meeting with these professionals. As with the forms displayed in Figures 10.2 and 10.3, this completed form can be placed on file in your office for future reference.

Safe Teaching Environment

Making the general physical education environment safe for students with disabilities is very similar to best practices for making physical education safe for all students. The following sections address safety considerations within the teaching environment: space, boundaries, unique environmental considerations, adapted equipment, and teaching students how to use the equipment properly.

Questions Regarding the Safety of the Student with Disabilities
(for the general physical educator or the physical therapist)

Does the student have specific problems with space awareness? ___ yes ___ no

Activities that might be affected: _____

Possible solutions/modifications: _____

Does the student have specific problems with body awareness? ___ yes ___ no

Activities that might be affected: _____

Possible solutions/modifications: _____

Does the student have specific problems with upper-body strength? ___ yes ___ no

Activities that might be affected: _____

Possible solutions/modifications: _____

Does the student have specific problems with lower-body strength? ___ yes ___ no

Activities that might be affected: _____

Possible solutions/modifications: _____

Does the student have specific problems with endurance? ___ yes ___ no

Activities that might be affected: _____

Possible solutions/modifications: _____

Does the student have specific problems with flexibility? ___ yes ___ no

Activities that might be affected: _____

Possible solutions/modifications: _____

Does the student have specific problems with speed? ___ yes ___ no

Activities that might be affected: _____

Possible solutions/modifications: _____

Does the student have specific problems with eye–hand coordination? ___ yes ___ no

Activities that might be affected: _____

Possible solutions/modifications: _____

Does the student have specific problems with balance? ___ yes ___ no

Activities that might be affected: _____

Possible solutions/modifications: _____

Figure 10.3.   Questions regarding the safety of the student with disabilities for the general physical educator or the physical therapist.

Important Information About the Student
(to be filled out by parent, teacher, and/or therapist)

Communication skills

1. Does the child understand simple verbal directions? _____ yes _____ no

2. If you answered no, do you have suggestions regarding how to facilitate communication? _____

_____

_____

3. Can the child convey his or her wishes and/or needs? _____ yes _____ no

_____

_____

4. If you answered no, do you have any suggestions regarding how I might know what the student wants or needs? _____

_____

_____

Behaviors

5. Does the child understand simple rules of games? _____ yes _____ no

6. If you answered no, do you have suggestions for helping the child play safely?

_____

_____

7. How does the child handle disappointments such as being on the losing team?

_____

_____

8. Is the child ever aggressive? If so, what do you do when this happens?

_____

_____

9. Does the child have a hard time paying attention and staying on task? If so, what do you do when this happens? _____

_____

_____

Reinforcements

10. What activities, objects, and/or people does the child like? _____

_____

11. What activities, objects, and/or people does the child dislike? _____

_____

Figure 10.4. Important information about the student form.

Space

First and foremost, the general physical educator should consider the amount of teaching space available. The area in which students will be working should allow for movements that are free from restrictions (Graham, Holt/Hale, & Parker, 1998). This is particularly true for students with mental retardation or learning disabilities who may not be as aware of personal space. For example, if a student with mental retardation is working on striking with a bat, there should be enough space to swing the bat freely without being hazardous to peers. If a student who uses a wheelchair is involved in an activity such as a chasing-and-fleeing game, extra space may be required to ensure his or her safety. The teacher also should remind students without disabilities to be extra careful when moving near students who use wheelchairs or students with visual impairments. Maintaining self-space is important for everyone at all times, regardless of abilities or disabilities.

Boundaries and Equipment Set-Up

The teaching environment also should have set boundaries that separate activity and hazardous areas. You may need to highlight boundaries for students with low vision, perceptual motor concerns, or attention-deficit/hyperactivity disorder (ADHD). Students with visual impairments might benefit from brightly colored cones or tape markings used to designate activity areas from storage space as well as to mark off boundaries on playing fields. Peers can provide extra physical assistance and verbal cues to students with autism or ADHD who may not be aware of safe boundaries.

Working space should be organized to ensure safe participation. One of the easiest yet most effective safety measures is to keep extraneous equipment away from the activity area. Large equipment such as volleyball standards and parallel bars should be placed off to the side of the activity area and padded. Smaller equipment that you plan to use that day should be kept compact and out of the way until it is needed. This is particularly important when you have students with visual impairments or ADHD or students who use wheelchairs or walkers. For example, during a warm-up activity in which students are moving in general space to music, a student with ADHD who is impulsive and hyperactive might fall over balls that have been scattered around the play area for the next activity. A safer set-up would be to bag the balls and place them off to the side until warm-ups are completed. Although this may be a little inconvenient, it will make the environment much safer for all students.

Unique Environmental Considerations

Some students present unique concerns in terms of creating a safe environment. For example, it will be necessary to familiarize students who have visual impairments with their surroundings. This includes telling the student where equipment is set up, where boundaries are, and where extraneous equipment, such as chairs, tables, steps, ramps, and the water fountain, is placed. Similarly, it will be necessary for students who use walkers or wheelchairs to have an uncluttered environment through which to move (Auxter, Pyfer, & Huettig, 1997). As noted previously, extraneous equipment should be off to the side until needed. In addition, peers without disabilities need to be sensitized to the fact that students who use walkers or wheelchairs might move at different speeds. Finally, for students with asthma or other respiratory disorders, the teaching environment should be well ventilated and the temperature should be set at a comfortable level. In addition, the gym should be as dust-free as possible. This can be difficult, but you can request to have duct work and support beams cleaned annually and the floors dusted. Finally, you may need to allow students who are sensitive to pollen to participate inside with other physical education classes during days when the pollen count is high. If you are not sure how the student is supposed to use special equipment, whether special equipment is fitted properly, or if special equipment is in good repair, consult with the student's physical and occupational therapists or special education teacher or parent (CIRA/CAHPER, 1994).

Adapted Equipment

Equipment should accommodate the unique movement needs of each student. This can be accomplished by varying the size, weight, and texture of catching and throwing objects, striking implements, and other manipulative equipment. For example, a catching station should have balls ranging in size from small to large, in weight from light to heavy, and in material from foam to rubber. At a striking station, balloons may be more appropriate for students with limited object control skills, whereas beep balls can assist students who are blind. Such equipment accommodations ensure that students with disabilities will be able to perform the skills of catching and striking without feeling threatened by a hard object traveling rapidly toward them. In addition, peers need to be sensitive to the motor skills of classmates with disabilities by varying components such as speed, distance, and force when participating in activities with these students. For example, when tossing a ball to a partner with mental retardation and limited catching skills, students should use light force and stand closer to the catcher.

When adapting equipment, it also is important to consider the developmental level of the student with disabilities. Just as it would be unsafe for kindergartners to practice the skill of striking using regulation-size tennis rackets, it is unsafe for a student with Down syndrome who has small hands to use a regulation-size softball bat when striking. Instead, he or she should strike with his or her hand and then progress to small, light foam paddles that can easily be controlled. Grips of such implements may also need to be altered for students with limited grasping skills. As mentioned previously, some situations require special equipment, such as beep balls for students who have visual impairments or bowling balls with quick-release handles for students with cerebral palsy who may have limited strength and gripping ability.

Teaching Students How to Use Equipment Properly

Perhaps the greatest concern for students with disabilities, particularly students with mental retardation and emotional disturbances, is teaching them safe and appropriate use of equipment. Some students with mental retardation may not be aware of safe ways to use physical education equipment; for example, they may not look around before swinging a golf club or a racket. Students with behavior problems may exhibit inappropriate behavior with equipment, such as using improper force when throwing balls to peers. Students with ADHD may be so impulsive with equipment that they do not take the time to think of the consequences of their actions. In all of these cases, it is important to teach these students how to use equipment safely.

Safe Teaching Techniques

Quality physical education presumes that general techniques regarding safety are common practice among physical educators. Teachers have a responsibility for providing appropriate instruction and proper supervision and for conducting activities in a safe manner (Nichols, 1994; Pangrazi, 1998). The following safe teaching techniques should be considered when including students with disabilities: establishment of safety rules, supervision, delivery of instructional cues, warm-ups, activities, and attitude.

Establishment of Safety Rules

The first safe teaching technique is to establish and review safety rules with the class. Although you do not need to have hundreds of safety rules and regulations, it is important to establish a few critical rules such as stop/start signals, maintaining personal space, adhering to set boundaries, avoiding equipment that is off-limits, and so forth. These rules should be posted in a visible area and should be reviewed frequently with all students in the class. Focus special attention on students with mental retardation, ADHD, or emotional disturbances who may tend to forget or ignore these rules. In addition, it is important to constantly remind students without disabilities to move cautiously around students who use wheelchairs or walkers or who are blind.

Supervision

As noted, physical educators are legally responsible for everything that goes on in the physical education environment. Therefore, it is imperative that physical education teachers are able to observe all that is going on in the class, particularly when students with disabilities are included. Observing the entire class involves establishing a position such as the "back-to-the-wall" technique and scanning, which allows you to see all students at all times (Graham et al., 1998). Always be aware of students who have impulsive tendencies, students who can be aggressive, and students who wander away from the group; they need extra supervision. When possible, place students with such characteristics close by you. If this is not possible, utilizing peers is always an option. For example, a peer can be assigned to make sure a student with autism stays with the group. For more extreme situations (e.g., a child who often runs away), utilize teacher assistants. Note that when opting to utilize peers or aides, you should provide them with information about the student, including specific precautions, and regarding their responsibilities in assisting the student.

Delivery of Instructional Cues

The delivery of instructional cues should be provided in such a manner that everyone understands directions and safety cues. Do not assume that all students in your class will understand verbal cues. For example, students who have hearing impairments may need visual aids such as demonstrations, written materials, or pictures to understand complex directions. Students with mental retardation or autism or students who are blind may need physical assistance to understand how to move. Even students with relatively mild disabilities, such as specific learning disabilities, may benefit from extra demonstrations. If students do not understand directions and safety cues, such as having only one person on the mat at a time during tumbling activities, a greater chance of injury exists.

Another factor in the delivery of instructional cues involves positioning students. Students with visual impairments who have some residual vision might benefit from demonstrations if they are positioned at the front of the class. Similarly, students with hearing impairments should be positioned so that they can read lips and have a better vantage point for picking up visual cues. Finally, students with ADHD, emotional disturbances, or autism should be positioned away from distractions including antagonizing peers, extraneous equipment, and markings on the floor. Students who are apt to physically attack their peers (e.g., biting, hitting, scratching) should be positioned close to you.

Warm-Ups

One of the most important safe teaching techniques is preparing students for activity through participation in some type of warm-up activity prior to actual skill instruction. For students with disabilities, this is particularly important. For example, a student with cerebral palsy needs to stretch his or her hamstrings and groin muscles prior to walking with a walker during a movement exploration activity. Similarly, students with autism often need to experience repetition in warm-ups before they can be expected to participate in new activities.

Although most students with disabilities can participate in the same warm-up activities as their peers, some students might need special warm-up activities. In the previous example, the student with cerebral palsy might need to work on special leg stretches designed by the physical therapist and carried out by a teacher assistant while his peers work on different stretches. Similarly, students with limited strength can be allowed to do modified sit-ups and push-ups, and students with asthma can be allowed to alternate between walking and running laps. Such individualization can be implemented with minimal disruption to your general program.

Activities

Not only is warming up a safe practice, but it is important to plan activities that are progressive in nature. When activities are progressive, injuries that occur when prerequisite skills have not been taught or when activities are beyond the readiness of the student can be avoided (CIRA/CAHPER, 1994; Pangrazi, 1998). To illustrate, consider a student with low muscle tone who is working at a station that focuses on the handstand. This student could receive a serious injury because she is not ready to support her total body weight on her hands. Instead, there should be various levels of weight transfer at this station that eventually lead to a handstand. This student may simply need to work on transferring weight from her feet to her hands before focusing on an actual handstand.

Many unsafe practices can be avoided with careful planning that allows for the foreseeability of accidents (Gray, 1995; Grosse, 1990; Pangrazi, 1998). When planning activities that carry a high risk for accidents, such as gymnastics, aquatics, or the rope climb, extra precautions should be taken from the start. Although this is important for all students, it is especially essential for students with disabilities who may lack the requisite motor ability or cognitive awareness or who may have other physical limitations. For example, during an aquatics session, the teacher can arrange for peers to assist students who use walkers and need extra help walking around the pool area. At the same time, a student with a seizure disorder may need to take part in a "buddy system" in case he or she has a seizure while in the water. During a tumbling or gymnastics unit, students with ADHD, autism, or mental retardation may not be aware of the inherent risks of using the equipment without supervision. A student might try to swing on the uneven bars or climb the rope unsupervised, which could lead to injury. When you have students who exhibit impulsive behaviors in your class, you should constantly review safety rules with them, assign peers to assist in preventing them from using the equipment inappropriately, and, in extreme cases, assign a teacher assistant to the student. In all cases, each student's unique characteristics must be considered (CIRA/CAHPER, 1994).

Attitude

Finally, safe teaching techniques include having a positive attitude toward teaching students with disabilities. This involves serving as a role model for students without disabilities on how to interact with, assist, and befriend students with disabilities (Block, 1994a, 1999a). Peers can be a tremendous resource in terms of making the environment safe, but they will not know what to do unless you show them by example. Demonstrating safe practices for students with disabilities begins with the teacher. However, although safety should be of utmost concern, care should be taken to not be overly protective. All students should be allowed certain experiences without the hindrance of exorbitant safety concerns (CIRA/CAHPER, 1994). For example, students who use wheelchairs often are excluded from team sports such as basketball and soccer. Although participation in such activities can pose a risk to the student in the wheelchair as well as to his or her peers, with proper modifications and a careful review of safety rules, many of these students can participate safely in team sports. An excellent way to illustrate how modifications to team sports might work is to invite an athlete from the community who participates in wheelchair sports such as wheelchair basketball to speak to the class.

Content

One of the biggest misconceptions about inclusion is that students with disabilities have to follow the same content at the same level as their peers without disabilities. Actually, all students should be presented with physical activities that are individualized to meet their unique needs. In some cases, these needs can be met by following the general curriculum with simple modifications; in other cases, an alternative curriculum will need to be followed. In either case, forcing a student with or without a disability to participate in an activity that he or she is not physically, mentally, and/or emotionally ready for can lead to injury. Therefore, it is important to 1) determine if the content that you are presenting is appropriate for the student's abilities; and 2) if it is not appropriate, determine what adjustments (or alternatives) will be needed to ensure safe participation in physical education.

Multilevel Curricular Selection

In most cases, students with disabilities can follow the same content as their peers without disabilities. However, the difficulty level of the skill as well as the way that you present information may need to be adjusted. Presenting the same content but at different levels for students with disabilities is known as *multilevel curricular selection* (Block & Vogler, 1994; Giangreco & Putnam, 1991). In multilevel curricular selection, all students work on the same content but at different levels matched to their physical, mental, and emotional abilities. This can best be facilitated by organizing the content in a generally progressive sequence of difficulty (Block, Provis, & Nelson, 1994; CIRA/CAHPER, 1994). For example, a student with a learning disability and related motor delays might hit a ball off a tee using a plastic bat; other students may hit a ball off a tee using a wooden bat; and still other students may hit pitched balls using a wooden bat. Similarly, a student with mental retardation who requires extensive support might work on shooting a Nerf basketball into a 6-foot basket during a game of HORSE while peers shoot at an 8- or 10-foot basket from 5, 7, 9, or 11 feet away using a Nerf basketball, rubber playground ball, or junior-size basketball. In both of these cases, all students work on the same content (softball and basketball, respectively). Only the level of content and the equipment used are modified to accommodate the student's unique needs and to ensure safety. Other simple adjustments that promote safety within the same content area include allowing students with muscular dystrophy or asthma to take frequent breaks during an activity; manipulating speed, distance, and movement requirements in relay races; changing movement requirements in tag games; and making rule changes to accommodate individual students (see Chapters 6–8 for more specific examples).

Curricular Overlapping

Although many students with disabilities can follow the same content as their peers without disabilities, students with more severe disabilities may need to work on completely different curricular goals. Presenting alternative curricular goals within the same activity is known as curricular overlapping (Block & Vogler, 1994; Giangreco & Putnam, 1991). For example, in a third-grade basketball activity, partners take turns dribbling across the gym. A student with cerebral palsy who uses a walker is working on improving her walking skills, and it would be inappropriate and unsafe to have her try to walk while dribbling a basketball. Instead, when it is her turn, she walks with her walker back and forth across the gym (a shorter distance). Therefore, she is still part of the activity and interacts with and cheers on her partner (who also cheers her on), but she works on different skills. Similarly, a high school student with Down syndrome has a goal of improving cardiovascular endurance. During a soccer unit, this student, who plays a wing position, is encouraged by peers to run up and down the field continually. While this student works on cardiovascular endurance within the context of a soccer game, his peers work on soccer skills and strategies.

Alternative Curriculum

In extreme cases, a student with a disability might need to work on goals that cannot be incorporated into general physical education activities. In such cases, the student with a disability should be allowed to work on activities that are more appropriate and safe. For example, a tenth grader with severe cerebral palsy and mental retardation is in general physical education during the week of a basketball unit. The class is now playing full-court basketball games, and it would be extremely inappropriate and unsafe to attempt to alter the game to accommodate this student. This student needs opportunities to work on his individual goals, which include bowling and boccie (using a ramp) and swimming at the local YMCA. The student goes swimming at the YMCA during general physical education two times per week with two peers. During the other 3 days of physical education, this student works on bowling or boccie in the corner of the gym with peers who rotate out of the basketball game to play alongside the student. Therefore, this student gets to work on his bowling and boccie goals and interact with his classmates, and his classmates get to enjoy taking a break from the hectic pace of basketball to test their skills in bowling or boccie.

Emergency Procedures

Make sure you have proper training in emergency procedures in the unlikely event that a student does sustain an injury (see Table 10.1). First and foremost,

Table 10.1.   Emergency procedures—action plan

Preparation

1. Identify kinds of injuries, emergencies, and health accidents that might occur.
2. Learn emergency care for each of these incidents.
3. Create an incident surveillance system to track all incidents for a particular student, for the facility, or for the program.
4. Examine medical information and talk to parents and other professionals for clues to possible medical situations for particular students with disabilities.

Plan

1. Create a written emergency action plan.
2. The plan should include, but not be limited to, the identification of the injured person, recognition of injury or medical need, initiation of first aid, and the obtaining of professional help.
3. Detailed protocols for seeking assistance and talking with medical personnel should be posted in appropriate places.

Learn and rehearse

1. Each employee and classmates knows his/her role in the emergency plan.
2. First-aid, rescue, and emergency equipment are adequate, routinely checked, and ready for use.
3. Staff members know how to use all equipment.
4. The system has been created with input from community emergency medical crews.
5. The plan is rehearsed with the staff and with the community emergency medical crews. Approximate times required to reach a facility is determined by each of these agencies.
6. Rehearsals are conducted periodically and whenever new staff are employed.
7. Records of all practices and those involved are prepared and retained.

Follow-up

1. Follow-up procedures for seriously injured persons exist and are unused.
2. Parents are notified in a uniform fashion.
3. A means of working with the media exists and is used.
4. The entire system is known by all, rehearsed often, and periodically monitored for flaws.
5. Legal counsel and insurance representatives are invited to review the entire system.

Adapted from Clements, 2000.

the physical education teacher should know cardiopulmonary resuscitation (CPR) and first aid (Pangrazi, 1998). In addition, familiarize yourself with universal precautions for handling blood (see Brown & Richter, 1994, for an example). Rubber gloves, gauze, and other essentials should be readily available in the event of an accident. Also, have an ice cooler with ice and bags in the gym. Ice usually can be obtained from the school cafeteria each morning. If you know you have students with specific health concerns, talk to the school nurse and the students' parents about special emergency procedures. For example, there may be a special way to handle a student who has a particular type of seizure disorder. If your school does not have a school nurse, implement a plan in case of emergencies such as contacting a rescue squad or a doctor's office that is close to the school.

The next step involves having emergency cards for all students. In addition, notations should be made in your roll book to identify students who have medical problems such as asthma, diabetes, seizures, and allergies. By noting this information in your roll book, you will constantly remind yourself of potential emergencies. For example, a student who is stung by a bee might be allergic to bee stings. By noting this allergy on an emergency card or in your roll book, you will know right away to immediately contact the nurse for assistance. Similarly, you may be more sensitive to a student who you know has asthma and is wheezing after a tag activity.

You will need to establish special emergency plans for some students with health problems or disabilities, such as a plan for removing students who are in wheelchairs from the gymnasium in the event of a fire or other emergency. Students with health problems may need to bring emergency materials to physical education in the event of an emergency. For example, students who are prone to asthma attacks should bring an inhaler with them to physical education, and orange juice and insulin should be available for students with diabetes. Although you may not feel comfortable with medical procedures such as giving insulin, you should have these materials available when qualified personnel arrive. Finally, notify the main office in the event of a medical emergency or injury, and complete a student accident report immediately (see Pangrazi, 1998, for an example).

11

Accommodating Students with Behavior Problems

with Ron French and Lisa Silliman-French

I like both. Adapted physical education is easier because you move slower. I like general physical education with everybody. I like being involved. I like the much faster pace, and I like being with my friends. I like that I am included and doing this together.

Robin Shuler, middle-school student

Ms. Zippay is a junior high school physical educator. She is a very structured teacher who has a set routine and very specific rules of conduct for her students. Peter, a student with autistic tendencies, has just been placed in her third-period class. A paraeducator accompanies Peter to class. Even with the paraeducator's assistance, Peter continually does not follow the traditional routines and demonstrates inappropriate behaviors. Ms. Zippay has heard about these behaviors but never has had to deal with them in her classroom. For example, when Ms. Zippay is leading warm-ups, Peter often makes loud sounds and strange movements with his hands. When the students are supposed to be sitting and listening to directions, Peter often gets up and runs around the gym. Ms. Zippay is beside herself. The structure and harmony that she has worked so hard to establish are quickly deteriorating. What can Ms. Zippay do?

A clear need exists for behavior management techniques in the school environment to assist students in learning and demonstrating (within their innate capabilities) the appropriate behaviors, attitudes, knowledge, and skills that they will need to become responsible and productive members of society. This need has increased during the 1980s and 1990s as a result of a variety of societal changes: 1) the deterioration of the family unit, 2) increased poverty, 3) increased number of working mothers, 4) increased drug abuse by children, and 5) the inclusion of students with disabilities in general education environments. Specifically related to inclusion, more and more students who exhibit maladaptive behaviors are being placed in general physical education environments. These students often are identified as having *attention-deficit/hyperactivity disorder, autism, emotional disturbances, mental retardation,* or *traumatic brain injuries.* Although not all of these students will necessarily demonstrate behavior problems, many of these students tend to display behaviors that can make teaching physical education difficult (see Table 11.1).

The purpose of this chapter is to provide physical educators with basic information regarding teaching students with behavior problems. The use of a behavioral approach to prevent behavior problems and cope with students who display behavior problems in physical education is emphasized. This chapter begins with a detailed outline of how to analyze behaviors and develop a behavior plan using the behavioral approach in physical education. Lists and explanations of specific techniques that can be used within the behavioral approach to increase or decrease behaviors follow this outline. The chapter concludes with some basic educational assumptions that need to be in place in order to make behavior management effective.

A Behavioral Approach to Behavior Management

Although there are a variety of approaches for dealing with students who display behavior problems, the behavioral approach seems to be the most popular, ap-

Table 11.1. Common disabilities and related behaviors that can affect learning

Disability	Related behaviors
Attention-deficit/ hyperactivity disorder (ADHD)	A combination of inattention and hyperactivity. ADHD is marked by impulsive symptoms, which are present in at least two environments and must interfere with academic, social, and occupational functioning. Common characteristics include poor attention, hyperactivity, impulsivity, and noncompliance.
Autism	A disability noted by problems with social interactions, language used during social interactions, play skills, repetition, and/or stereotyped patterns of behavior. Common characteristics of students with autism include making inappropriate sounds and gestures, having inappropriate affect (e.g., laughing when no one else is laughing), being withdrawn, being anxious in new and different situations, and running away.
Emotional disturbance	A condition involving one or more of the following behaviors over a long period of time, which must adversely affect educational performance: 1) inability to learn, which cannot be explained by intellectual, sensory, or health factors; 2) inability to build or maintain satisfactory interpersonal relationships; 3) demonstratation of inappropriate behavior or feeling; 4) general pervasive mood of unhappiness or depression; or 5) a tendency to develop physical symptoms or fears. Common characteristics for these children vary widely based on the specific type of emotional disability ranging from juvenile delinquency, depression, obsessive-compulsive disorder, eating disorders, and manic-depresive disorders.
Mental retardation	Substantial limitations in personal capabilities manifested as significantly subaverage intellectual functioning occurring with significant impairments in adaptive behavior (e.g., self-help skills, communication, working, academics). Common characteristics of children with mental retardation vary based on the specific cause and level of functioning. For example, many children with fetal alcohol syndrome are impulsive and hyperactive, whereas children with Down syndrome tend to have trouble understanding and following complex directions.
Traumatic brain injury	Permanent damage to the brain caused by concussion, contusion, or hemorrhage. In many cases, this condition may cause severe impairments in perception, emotion, cognition, and motor function. Again, common characteristics will vary widely based on the extent and location of the brain injury.

propriate, and effective for physical education environments (Auxter, Pyfer, & Huettig, 1997; Henderson & French, 1993; Jansma & French, 1994; Seidentop & Rushall, 1972). The key to the behavioral approach is to determine which antecedents within the specific school environment are causing the behavior problem and which consequences could effectively be used to reduce or eliminate the behavior.

The approach is based on an A–B–C paradigm, in which a stimulus or antecedent, *A*, precedes the behavior, *B*, that is followed by a consequence, *C* (Hen-

Table 11.2.   Creating a behavior plan

Identify the behavior in objective, measurable terms.
- Describe what the student is doing.
- Describe how the student is acting.
- Record the behavior.

Examine antecedents for possible causes.
- When does behavior usually occur?
- Where does behavior usually occur?
- What is usually happening when behavior occurs?

Examine possible functions of behavior.
- Does the student want attention?
- Does the student want to be involved?
- Is the student angry?
- Is the student frustrated?
- Is the student in pain or discomfort?
- Does the student need help with something?
- Determine other possible reasons.

Explore the consequences.
- What happened when the behavior occurred?
- When did the consequences take place (immediate or delayed)?
- How did the student react to the consequences?

Consider simple alternatives that might prevent or reduce the behavior.
- Move the student.
- Rearrange the environment.
- Change the activity.
- Give the student a partner.
- Regroup the class.

Create the behavior plan.
- Clearly state targeted behavior in measurable terms.
- Outline procedures for increasing appropriate behaviors.
- Outline procedures for preventing or reducing the behavior.
- Outline consequences for dealing with the behavior if it occurs.

derson & French, 1993; Jansma & French, 1994). The focus is on carefully analyzing the antecedents and consequences that surround the behavior as well as examining the behavior itself to determine what might be responsible for producing it. Physical educators who use this approach manipulate A and/or C to increase or decrease B. That is, changing things in the environment (antecedents) prevents inappropriate behaviors, and adding reinforcement (positive consequences) increases appropriate behaviors. When prevention does not work, other techniques (e.g., negative consequences such as time-out) can be used in order to eliminate or reduce the behavior.

The following outlines a model for 1) identifying a behavior, 2) analyzing antecedents and consequences to determine why a student might be displaying the behavior, and 3) developing an individualized behavior management plan to increase appropriate and decrease inappropriate behaviors (see Table 11.2). It is important that each step in the process be followed in order to create the most appropriate and most effective plan possible. The following section details each step in the process.

Identify the Behavior in Objective, Measurable Terms

Identifying the behavior(s) seems to be a simple task. However, all too often, physical educators have trouble specifying exactly what the student is doing that is bothering the educators and the student's peers. Saying things such as "he is always in my face," "he is constantly in motion," "she is destroying my gym," or "this student is here to torture me" certainly conveys the teacher's emotions but does not identify what the student is doing wrong. The physical educator, along with other professionals, needs to carefully examine the student's behaviors and write them down in measurable, objective terms. For example, "he is always in my face" might mean that the student approaches the physical educator in the middle of an activity to ask him or her questions 10–15 times in a 30-minute class. Similarly, "he is constantly in motion" might mean that the student does not sit to listen to instructions or stay at a station independently for more than 1 minute.

Note how these last two descriptions are measurable: Someone can come into the gymnasium and actually measure how often or how long the student displays the particular behavior. Being able to measure the behavior is important; measurements allow the physical educator to chart progress. There are three common ways to measure behaviors in physical education. In *event recording*, the physical educator records the number of times a student exhibits a particular behavior in a given time period. For example, a teacher might record the number of times (e.g., 1 time, 10 times, 20 times) a student inappropriately touches other students during a 30-minute class. In *duration recording*, a physical educator records how long a student exhibits a behavior during a given period of time. For example, a teacher might record the length of time (e.g., 1 minute, 5 minutes, 10 minutes) that a student makes inappropriate sounds during physical education. In *interval recording*, a physical educator divides the class period into intervals (e.g., 1-minute intervals) and records if the behavior occurs at any time during that interval. For example, at the end of each 1-minute interval during a 30-minute period, a physical educator monitors and records if a student is on- or off-task. If the student is off-task when the teacher observes the student at the end of a 1-minute interval, then he or she notes it on a piece of paper. At the end of the class, the teacher can tally the number of intervals (e.g., 1/30, 10/30, 20/30) during which the student was off-task (see Figure 11.1 for examples).

The type of recording mechanism used should be based on the nature of the behavior. Behaviors that occur frequently but for short durations (e.g., touching peers) should be recorded using event recording. Behaviors that do not occur frequently but last a long time (e.g., crying) should be measured using duration recording. Behaviors that occur so frequently that it is too difficult to count specific instances (e.g., tics) should be measured using interval recording. Regardless of the recording method, these types of baseline information provide the teacher with a clear idea of the extent to which the behavior occurs. Later, the physical educator can chart whether the behavioral intervention is effective (i.e., there is a reduction in targeted behavior).

Examine Antecedents for Possible Causes

Once the behavior has been identified, defined, and measured, the next step in the process is to examine what environmental factors might be causing the behavior. Often, something in the environment triggers the behavior. For example, having to sit and wait while the teacher takes roll might cause a student with ADHD to get "antsy" and eventually misbehave. Similarly, a student with autism

Event recording (e.g., How many times in 30 minutes does the child talk back to the general physical educator?)

Day	Tally count per day	Total
Monday	1 1 1 1 1 1 1 1 1 1 1 1 1 1 1 1 1 1 1 1	20
Tuesday	1 1 1 1 1 1 1 1 1 1 1 1 1 1 1 1	16
Thursday	1 1 1 1 1 1 1 1 1 1 1 1 1 1 1 1 1	17
Friday	1 1 1 1 1 1 1 1 1 1 1 1 1 1 1 1 1 1	18

Average: 17.75 occurrences

Duration recording (e.g., How long does the child choose to pout in the corner of the gym?)

Day	Duration of each episode (in minutes)			Total time
Monday	2	4	1	7 minutes
Tuesday	3	3.5		6.5 minutes
Thursday	2			2 minutes
Friday	5	1.5		6.5 minutes

*Average: 5.5 minutes
per 30-minute class*

Interval recording (e.g., During how many intervals is the child touching other children?)

Day	Intervals (2 minutes each)	# of intervals in 30-minute period
Monday	y n y y y n y n y n n y n y y	9/15
Tuesday	n n y y y y n y y y n n n y y	9/15
Thursday	y y n n n y y n n n n n n y y	6/15
Friday	n n n n y n y y y y y n y n y y	8/15

Average: 8/15 intervals

Figure 11.1.   Examples of ways to measure behavior in general physical education.

who does not like loud noises might yell and try to scratch and bite his teacher assistant just before the music used for warm-ups is played. In both cases, it appears that something in the environment agitates the student and precipitates his or her behavior. Through careful analysis of the antecedents to the behavior, the physical educator might be able to determine those causes. Factors to examine can be divided into three categories:

1. When does the behavior usually occur (e.g., when student is changing into his or her uniform, during role call, during warm-ups, during skill work, during a game, when the student is paired with a particular peer or group of peers)?

2. Where does the behavior usually occur (e.g., in the locker room, in the gym, outside, in the pool area)?

3. What is usually happening when the behavior occurs (e.g., sitting and waiting, doing exercises, doing skill work, picking teams, playing the game)?

Although the causes of all behaviors cannot be determined by analyzing the antecedents in the environment, such an analysis often reveals why the student is displaying certain behaviors.

Examine Possible Functions of Behavior

Once the environment has been analyzed for possible causes of the behavior, the next step is to examine why the student might be displaying the behavior. That is, what does the student want or hope to accomplish by displaying the inappropriate behavior? Rarely does a student display inappropriate behavior without a goal in mind, even if he or she does not really understand the goal. For example, a student with autism might suddenly strike out at his teacher assistant or peer for no apparent reason. A close examination of antecedents in addition to some guesswork by the general and adapted physical educators reveals that the student is avoiding playing with balloons. Perhaps the student is scared of the sound of balloons when they pop or of the way they feel. For whatever reason, the student clearly gets agitated when balloons are mentioned or introduced. The student communicates his fear of balloons by scratching others and screaming. With this information, part of the behavior plan for the student with autism might include having him do a different activity at the other end of the gym while his peers are playing with balloons. Other possible functional causes of behavior include 1) an attempt to gain attention; 2) a desire to be involved; 3) anger against a student, teacher, or situation; 4) frustration; 5) pain or discomfort; 6) a need for help with something; 7) a need to go to the bathroom; and/or 8) a dislike for the peers to whom he or she has been assigned. As was the case with antecedents, it may not be possible to fully understand why a student displays particular behaviors. However, in many cases, a functional analysis will help the physical educator begin to see why some students behave the way they do. Figure 11.2 provides a sample behavioral observation data sheet to help you collect data regarding antecedents, behaviors, and consequences.

Explore the Consequences

What occurs following the display of a particular behavior is known as a consequence; determining the effects of consequences can be as important as analyzing antecedents and functions. Consequences may be the reason a student displays a behavior in the first place. For example, a student with a learning disability who does not like physical education displays noncompliant behavior and talks back to the teacher, resulting in time-out during physical education. In this case, time-out is exactly what the student wanted all along! Consequences can make a behavior stronger or weaker, depending on how the student reacts to the consequences. In examining consequences of a student's behavior, one should ask the following three questions.

1. What happened immediately after the behavior occurred? For example, a student who reputedly is mean pulls another student's hair, causing the student to cry. This makes the reputedly mean student laugh. Even a verbal reprimand from the teacher and being sent to time-out are not sufficient deterrents compared with the reinforcement of hearing the girl cry.

Behavioral Observation Data Sheet

Student's name: _____ Class period: _____

Evaluator: _____ Date: _____

Behavior: *How is the student acting?*

Describe what the student is doing in measurable terms.

_____

_____

_____

Examine antecedents: *What in the environment might be causing inappropriate behaviors?*

When does the behavior typically occur?

_____

_____

_____

Where does the behavior typically occur?

_____

_____

_____

What typically is happening when the behavior occurs?

_____

_____

_____

Examine function: *What might the student be trying to communicate?*

_____ Does the student want attention?

_____ Does the student want to tell you something?

_____ Does the student want a particular piece of equipment?

_____ Does the student want to be with a particular friend?

_____ Does the student want to avoid the activity?

_____ Does the student need to go to the bathroom?

_____ Does the student want to escape the situation?

_____ Is the student angry?

_____ Is the student frustrated?

A Teacher's Guide to Including Students with Disabilities in General Physical Education, 2nd ed.
by Martin E. Block, copyright ©2000 Paul H. Brookes Publishing Co.

Figure 11.2.   Behavioral observation data sheet.

Figure 11.2. (*continued*)

_____ Is the student in pain or discomfort? _____

_____ Does the student need help with something? _____

_____ Are there other possible reasons? If yes, what are they? _____

_____

Examine consequences: *What were the consequences? How did the student react?*

_____ Received angry look   Student's reaction:_____

_____ Physical educator moved   Student's reaction:_____

     closer to the student

_____ Received verbal warning   Student's reaction:_____

_____ Received verbal reprimand   Student's reaction:_____

_____ Had to apologize to peer   Student's reaction:_____

_____ Had to clean up mess   Student's reaction:_____

_____ Lost use of equipment   Student's reaction:_____

_____ Changed partner or group   Student's reaction:_____

_____ Sent to time-out   Student's reaction:_____

_____ Received physical assistance   Student's reaction:_____

_____ Physically restrained   Student's reaction:_____

_____ Sent to principal   Student's reaction:_____

_____ Other:_____ Student's reaction:_____

Suggestions for plan: _____

_____

_____

_____

_____

_____

_____

_____

_____

2. When did the consequences take place: were they immediate or delayed? If consequences are delayed for too long, the student might forget why he is receiving the consequences in the first place.

3. How did the student react to the consequences? Did the student happily gallop off to time-out, or did he curse and yell at the physical educator? Did the student apologize to the peer he pushed, or did he fold his arms and choose to go to time-out? Again, the way in which the student reacts to the consequences that result from the behavior may provide insight into why the student displayed the behavior in the first place and which consequences will and will not work in the future (Figure 11.2 includes a checklist of possible consequences).

Consider Simple Alternatives that Might Prevent or Reduce the Behavior

Once information about the behavior, antecedents, possible functional causes, and results of consequences has been gathered, the physical educator and other team members are ready to develop a behavior plan. However, it is important to look carefully at the previous analysis—which might reveal that some very simple, one-time changes might stop the behavior immediately and forever—before a full-blown plan is developed. Although many behavior problems are not solved so simply, some might be. For example, the behaviors of a student with autism who has trouble making the transition from his classroom to the gymnasium have grown worse (he often hits peers or his teacher when walking down the hall to the gym) ever since the physical educator started to do a different activity for warm-ups every day. The special educator suggested that the physical educator should have the students do the same thing every time the student's class enters the gym (e.g., run one lap, gallop one lap, and then skip one lap). This simple change in routine to make each physical education class consistent has helped this student feel more confident when he comes to the gym. Although he still displays inappropriate behaviors at times during physical education, the transition from the classroom to the gym is no longer a problem. Other simple changes that might work immediately with some students include 1) moving the student closer to you or away from particular peers, 2) rearranging the environment (e.g., not putting out equipment until you are ready to use it), 3) changing the activity from competition to cooperation (at least making this a choice for some students), 4) having a special-colored ball or special spot on the floor especially for the student, or 5) giving the student a partner (see Table 11.3 for a more detailed list).

Create the Behavior Plan

If simple solutions do not work, the team may need to develop a behavior plan. The behavior plan should include 1) a clear statement of the targeted behavior written in measurable terms, 2) specific procedures for increasing appropriate behaviors, 3) a description of specific procedures for preventing and/or reducing the behavior, and 4) specific procedures for presenting consequences if the behavior does occur. Figure 11.3 presents an example of a behavior plan. Although the plan is designed for physical education, it may be appropriate for a variety of team members to participate in its development. For example, the student's special education teacher and parents may know what things are reinforcing to the student. They also will know which behaviors occur in other environments such as the classroom, recess, and at home.

Table 11.3.   Techniques for preventing behavior problems

- *Determine cause of behavior.* Try to determine what might be causing the misbehavior, then try to rearrange the environment or the situation to prevent the behavior from reoccurring.
- *Tune in to your class.* Be aware of what is going on; pay particular attention to students who have a history of problem behavior.
- *Set the right pace.* Teach your lesson so that there is a smooth flow from activity to activity; set a comfortable pace—one that is not too fast or too slow.
- *Manage time efficiently.* Reduce nonteaching time to prevent misbehavior that occurs when children are bored or waiting.
- *Encourage clarification of instructions.* Make sure students understand instructions by repeating instructions, asking students to repeat instructions back to you, or giving some students extra cues or help from peers.
- *Set realistic goals.* Set goals or help students set goals that are both achievable and challenging—students get bored if activities are too easy and frustrated if they are too hard.
- *Make sure students are appropriately placed.* Some students cannot handle large classes or classes that are very competitive. Either try to place the child in a smaller or less competitive class or break the class into smaller groups, with some participating in competitive activities and others participating in cooperative activities.
- *Involve the entire group.* Organize the class to encourage maximum active participation—avoid waiting in line, elimination games, and sharing equipment.
- *Hold students accountable for what you teach them.* Make sure students know what they are supposed to be working on and what is expected of them, then hold them accountable for their performance.
- *Keep the class attentive.* Use creative techniques such as unique equipment, novel games, and having high school or college athletes come in and help teach an activity to keep the students' attention.
- *Keep the students motivated.* Be aware of the motivational level of the class and of individual students—note that it is better to stop an activity when kids are still enjoying it rather than wait until they become bored.
- *Be assertive but gentle.* Face problems immediately and do not ignore them; be direct, yet calm, when dealing with children who display behavior problems.
- *Use humor.* Use humor to reduce tension and defuse stressful situations.
- *Appeal to your students' values.* Appeal to students' sense of fairness, commitment to the group's code of behavior, and to the positive relationship you have and want to continue to have with them.
- *Generate enthusiasm.* Show your students genuine enthusiasm about physical activity and about how you care about their success by cheering, clapping hands, and generally having a good time.
- *Know your stuff.* Students respect and want to learn from teachers who are competent in the skills and activities being taught. Make sure you are prepared for your lessons, and get experts in the community to help you with units with which you do not feel comfortable.
- *Take responsibility for managing behavior.* Try to deal with students' behavior problems in the gymnasium rather than always sending students to the principal.
- *Establish a consistent behavior management plan.* Develop your plan for physical education with plans used in other parts of the building by other professionals.
- *Use proximity control.* Students will be less likely to misbehave if you stand closer to them.
- *Take an interest in your students.* Students are more willing to cooperate with a teacher who shows interest in them by discussing their interests, asking about their weekend, noting their achievements, and so forth.

(continued)

From Henderson, H.L., & French, R.W. (1993). *Creative approaches to managing student behavior* (2nd ed., pp. 14–16). Park City, UT: Family Development Resources; reprinted by permission.

Table 11.3.   *(continued)*

- *Be a good role model.* Because many students imitate their teacher, model appropriate dress, talk, and conduct, including showing self-control when you get angry or when a child gets angry at you.
- *Redirect disruptive behavior.* Try to redirect disruptive or dangerous situations into more productive tasks.
- *Provide vigorous activities.* Help students release their anger and frustration through vigorous activities such as sprints, volleyball spiking, hitting a softball, or aerobics.
- *Befriend a disliked student.* A teacher who befriends a disliked student often helps other students accept the student.
- *Use nonverbal cues.* Teach and then use simple gestures such as finger to the lips, the time-out sign, or direct eye contact to deal with minor disruptions.
- *Establish class rules early.* Establish and review class rules and consequences from the first day of class; post the rules in a conspicuous place, and review the rules often.
- *Grade fairly.* Establish clear, fair criteria for grades, explain the grading system on the first day of class, and keep careful records of progress for calculating grades.
- *Avoid nagging.* Continual nagging can make students anxious or may cause them to "tune out" the teacher—give one warning or reminder, then give consequences.
- *Create an appropriate physical environment.* Create an environment that promotes enthusiasm, learning, and participation; make sure the environment is as comfortable as possible; ensure that students have enough space for a given activity; try to limit auditory and visual distractions in the environment.

Procedures to Maintain or Strengthen a Behavior

Once the behavior has been targeted and the plan is ready to be implemented, the final step is to decide which specific techniques will be used to increase appropriate behaviors and decrease inappropriate behaviors. Techniques within the behavioral approach are based on the principles of operant conditioning. In operant conditioning, a systematic application of consequences is presented following a specific behavior in order to strengthen, maintain, or weaken the behavior (Eichstaedt & Lavay, 1992). When something is presented or taken away that increases the likelihood that the behavior will be repeated, it is known as *reinforcement*. When something is presented or taken away that decreases the likelihood that the behavior will be repeated, it is known as *punishment*.

Reinforcement

Reinforcement, which can be positive or negative, refers to consequences of behavior that increase the future rate of that behavior. *Negative reinforcement* refers to taking something away that has the effect of maintaining or increasing a behavior. Negative reinforcement is a less commonly used method of increasing behaviors (Henderson & French, 1989). There are two major procedures involved in negative reinforcement. The first is the avoidance procedure. For example, the physical educator may state that all students who run a mile in less than 10 minutes will not be required to run the mile the next day. Because most students do not want to run the mile a second day, they will attempt to run the mile in less than 10 minutes. The second is the escape procedure. For example, a group of students in a gymnastics class are preparing for a school demonstration. The presentation is the next day and the physical educator tells the students that everyone must know their routines perfectly. He states that during this class the students must repeat their routines until they do them without error before he will allow them to take a break.

Name: _Edward Smith_   Class: _Mrs. Control's sixth grade_

Age: _13_   School: _Wildwood Elementary_

Date: _August 21, 2000_

Targeted behavior

Edward does not sit or stand still and listen when the teacher is giving instructions.

Measure

Edward has to be reminded to sit an average of 10 times during a 30-minute period.

Possible antecedents

The class is supposed to get into their squads.

The teacher is giving instructions.

Kids are supposed to be listening to the teacher's instructions when practicing a skill.

Possible functions

Boredom   Does not like to sit and listen to instructions

Enjoys running around   Does not understand instructions

Targeted objectives

Edward will sit and listen to the first minute of instruction without getting up.

Edward will sit in his squad and wait for the teacher to take roll without getting up.

Edward will stop what he is doing and listen to instructional feedback from the teacher when in the midst of practicing a skill.

Plan to prevent the behavior

When Edward is sitting in his squad, allow him and peers near him to talk softly to one another. Encourage peers near Edward to engage him in conversation while roll is taken.

Encourage Edward to sit in front near the teacher when teacher gives instructions.

Have teacher try to use Edward as an assistant to demonstrate instructions.

If Edward is particularly antsy, allow him to go to a station and start an activity with a peer. Make sure other classmates understand why Edward is allowed to do this.

Have teacher try to limit how long he or she has the students sit and listen.

Have teacher stand near Edward when he stops the group to give instructional feedback to the group.

Plan to reinforce behavior

Give Edward verbal praise when he sits quietly.

Give Edward free time in the beginning of class to look at all the equipment.

Have peers give Edward verbal praise when he sits quietly.

If appropriate, give Edward free time at the end of class if he sits and listens.

Consequences if behavior occurs

Verbal reminders of what he is supposed to do

Verbal reprimand (e.g., "Edward, I don't like it when you get up when I am talking; you need to sit down right now!")

Get Edward to communicate what he wants; when he sits and calms down, then you can allow him to get up and move around the gym.

Response cost—Edward loses some free time at the end of the class.

Figure 11.3. Sample behavior plan.

Some caution is advised when using negative reinforcement. Some students have encountered considerable negative reinforcement situations in their lives and have developed resistance to it by adopting a belligerent, "make me" attitude that sometimes leads to an escalation of punishments as a consequence for non-compliance. Therefore, negative reinforcement can set a negative tone for the student and the physical educator (Rizzo & Zabel, 1988). However, negative reinforcement can be used in a positive way, too. For example, imagine that a student with mental retardation who is overweight does not want to get dressed for physical education when the class is doing the mile run. Because of low cardiovascular fitness, he knows he will not be able to run the entire mile. The physical education teacher realizes that the student will not participate if she makes him run the entire mile. She decides to tell the student that he only needs to run as far as he can, and then he can walk the rest of the way (she takes away the threat of making him run a mile). The student feels less threatened, gets dressed for physical education, and runs farther and faster than ever before (he actually runs a mile for the first time).

Positive reinforcement involves the presentation of something following a particular response that has the effect of maintaining or increasing that response. For example, allowing students to ride scooter boards (positive reinforcement) after completing their warm-ups without complaining (targeted response) may increase the likelihood that the students will do their warm-ups next time without complaining. Because positive reinforcement is easier, more appropriate, and more effective than negative reinforcement, the following discussion focuses on the many different forms of positive reinforcement. The key is to begin at the most natural level of reinforcement and move down the continuum until the type of reinforcement selected actually has reinforcing power (see Table 11.4 for guidelines for using reinforcement). Also, note that a "one size fits all" approach when selecting a reinforcer generally is ineffective. There are individual differences among students as to what is reinforcing. Even a single student's response to reinforcements will be better when he or she has a variety of reinforcements from which to choose. Student observations, reinforcement preference surveys (Figure 11.4), and talking to other teachers and the student's parents can be used to determine which reinforcement will be most effective.

Table 11.4.   Guidelines for using reinforcement

- Make sure the student is performing the target behavior before you provide reinforcement.
- Reinforce the behavior immediately after it occurs.
- Be specific in your praise. For example, tell the student "good swinging your leg when you hop" rather than "good job."
- When students are first learning to perform a skill or display a behavior appropriately, make sure you reinforce that skill or behavior every time it is done correctly.
- After a skill or behavior has been learned, you need reinforce that skill or behavior only periodically.
- If social praise is effective in maintaining or increasing a behavior, do not use other rewards. Use more tangible rewards only when social praise is not effective.
- If you have to introduce tangible rewards, pair them with social praise so that you can eventually fade away the use of tangible reinforcers.
- Make sure that what you are using as a reward for the student is reinforcing to that student. Each student might find different things rewarding.

From Henderson, H.L., & French, R.W. (1993). *Creative approaches to managing student behavior* (2nd ed. p. 18). Park City, UT: Family Development Resources; reprinted by permission.

Reinforcement Survey

Directions: Please place an *x* in the column that most accurately explains your feelings about each item or activity.

Questions	Like very much	Like	Dislike
Do you like juice?	_____	_____	_____
Do you like fruit?	_____	_____	_____
Do you like candy?	_____	_____	_____
Do you like sports equipment?	_____	_____	_____
Do you like to rollerblade?	_____	_____	_____
Do you like soccer?	_____	_____	_____
Do you like basketball?	_____	_____	_____
Do you like football?	_____	_____	_____
Do you like softball?	_____	_____	_____
Do you like recess?	_____	_____	_____
Do you like to be a squad leader?	_____	_____	_____
Do you like to demonstrate a skill?	_____	_____	_____
Do you like to play in groups?	_____	_____	_____
Do you like activities that you can do alone?	_____	_____	_____
Do you like your teacher to ask you for help?	_____	_____	_____
Do you like to win at relays and games?	_____	_____	_____
Do you like certificates and awards?	_____		_____
Do you like to help other students?	_____	_____	_____
Do you like to play music during class?	_____	_____	_____
Would you like to talk to a sports star?	_____	_____	_____

Please respond to the following questions

What is your favorite activity at home? _____

_____

What is your favorite activity at school? _____

_____

What is your favorite activity in physical education? _____

_____

What is your least favorite activity in physical education? _____

_____

A Teacher's Guide to Including Students with Disabilities in General Physical Education, 2nd ed. by Martin E. Block, copyright ©2000 Paul H. Brookes Publishing Co.

Figure 11.4.   Reinforcement survey. (*Source:* Walker & Shea, 1984.)

Types of Positive Reinforcement

The following sections describe major types of positive reinforcement beginning with the most natural type (intrinsic) and concluding with more artificial types (e.g., tokens, tangibles). As noted previously, the specific type or types of reinforcements used will vary from student to student.

Intrinsic   The activity itself is reinforcing to the student. It is our goal to have all students function at this level. Students who are intrinsically motivated have sufficient interest in the physical education class activities to perform and learn at their capacity. For example, a student does not need external motivation or reinforcement to happily join her peers when the parachute is taken out. Playing with the parachute is reinforcing in and of itself.

Social Praise   Social praise involves communicating to the student that you are pleased with some aspect of his or her performance or behavior. Social praise is the most common and easiest form of reinforcement used in physical education, and it can be quite effective for many students. Although social praise can be overused, it generally is not used enough with students who are learning to behave or master a new task. Some types of social praise include gestures (e.g., look of pleasure, a grin), statements (e.g., "better," "excellent," "great," "terrific"), or a pat on the shoulder or back. Another type of social recognition is public posting. This technique involves posting in public view (e.g., physical education bulletin board) the names of students who have demonstrated a specific level of citizenship or who have mastered an individual challenge.

Physical Activity   Use a favorite physical activity as a reward for demonstrating appropriate behavior. Physical activity is an excellent type of reward that is highly appropriate in physical education (Jansma, 1978). Using physical activity as a positive reinforcement can lead to numerous student and program benefits compared with many other types of positive reinforcements (Armstrong, Rosengard, Condon, Sallis, & Bernal, 1993). For many students, physical activity itself may be a behavioral intervention. After an in-depth review of the literature by Sallis and Owen (1999), it was concluded that there is a positive relationship between exercise and emotional health, particularly in reducing depression and anxiety. Some other benefits include 1) it does not add extra cost to the physical education budget, 2) there are many different types of equipment available and games from which to choose that increase the possibility that the physical educator will find an activity suited to each individual student, and 3) the use of physical activity as a positive reinforcement not only serves as a reward to most students but also has the potential to improve the student's level of physical fitness and motor skills (Eichstaedt & Lavay, 1992).

Sensory Reinforcements   Auditory, visual, or kinesthetic sensations can be used as reinforcements for appropriate behaviors. This technique is particularly effective with students who have autism. For example, allowing a student to swing (vestibular stimulation) after he or she completes a set of warm-up exercises can be very reinforcing to a student with autism. Another type of reinforcement that has had positive results in improving the physical fitness levels of students with and without disabilities is music. Music can be played while a student rides a stationary bike or walks on a treadmill. If the student stays within his or her target heart range, the music continues to play; if he or she does not stay within his or her target heart range, the music is stopped. This type of reinforcement dispensation is very functional and community-linked for older students because wearing a headset and walking or jogging is performed daily by millions of people in the United States.

Tangibles   This type of reinforcement involves giving something to a student that reinforces a behavior. There are a variety of tangibles that are appropriate to use in physical education environments. The two major categories of tangibles are objects and edibles. Objects used in physical education include stickers, stamps, certificates, award ribbons, patches, trophies, plaques, and even money. For example, one item on a physical fitness test administered to a student with an emotional disturbance was how far the student could throw a softball. In three attempts, the farthest distance the student threw the ball was 23 feet. The physical educator felt that, despite being given social praise, the student was not giving his best effort. Therefore, the student was told that he could earn 50 cents if he could throw the softball more than 50 feet. The student took one of the softballs and threw it 73 feet! A completely inappropriate individualized education program (IEP) goal could have been written from the results of the first testing!

Edibles are the least desirable type of reinforcement and should be used only if the student is not motivated by other methods. However, the use of edibles should not be ignored as a viable method. Edibles can be used to teach students who have the ability to perform an activity, but who are basically passive and noncompliant. For example, based on the results of his physical fitness test, a student with a learning disability could perform only three sit-ups. Because the physical educator knew that the student could do more than three sit-ups, he offered the student a dish of nacho chips if the student would try to perform the test again and do as many sit-ups as possible. The boy performed 53 sit-ups. Again, how reliable would his IEP goals and objectives have been based on the initial test results?

Group Contingencies   This technique refers to the presentation of a reinforcement to a group of students as a unit based on whether they follow an appropriate set of rules. This technique may be more effective with older students who seek and desire peer approval more than the approval of the physical educator. For example, if all the students sit quietly in their squad while the teacher takes role, then the squad gets to choose one warm-up activity. Each squad member uses peer pressure to control the behavior of the other squad members. This technique has proven to be very successful in the physical education environment, and, in certain instances, it is superior to the individual reinforcement technique for managing behavior.

Group contingencies can be categorized into three basic types (Kauffman, Mostert, Trent, & Hallahan, 1998). First, there is the dependent group contingency, in which a target student must earn the desired reinforcement for the entire squad. To ensure that undue peer pressure is not placed on the student, the teacher must be certain that the target student is capable of earning the reinforcement. For example, if the group can get Billy (a student with Down syndrome who often refuses to walk or run on the track) to run one lap, then the group gets to play a game of soccer. The second type is independent group contingency, in which a squad goal is stated, and students work individually to earn the desired reinforcement. This eliminates the competitive nature of other group contingencies. For example, each person in the squad has to complete his or her own prescribed number of push-ups and sit-ups. Once everyone in the squad completes his or her sit-ups, the squad gets to shoot baskets for a few minutes. The third type of group contingency is interdependent contingency, in which the desired reinforcement is dependent on the behavior of the entire squad or class. This is the most commonly used and the most effective group contingency method. Note that if one student consistently ruins the chances of the entire group to earn the desired reinforcement, an individual behavior management technique may need to be implemented within the group contingency procedure.

The Good Behavior Game (Vogler & French, 1983) is an example of an interdependent group contingency. The physical educator places the students in various squads and explains that they will earn 10 minutes of free time if the squad members follow the class rules. Each squad begins with 10 points. Free time is then awarded at the end of the class or week if a squad has retained 8 or more points. Those squads that have lost more than 2 points have to continue with the class activity. It is possible that all squads can win because they are not competing against each other. It must be made clear to the students that *free play* means that the students can select an activity from a menu of activities derived from daily or weekly instructional goals and objectives chosen by the teacher.

Token Economies   Token economies are effective methods for modifying the behavior of individuals as well as groups. Tokens are symbolic rewards used as temporary substitutes for more substantial reinforcements for which the tokens will eventually be traded. Tokens may take the form of checkmarks, points, poker chips, colored strips of paper, or play money that are assigned a predetermined value and earned for performing specific behaviors. An advantage of a token system is that the symbolic rewards can be presented immediately following the demonstration of the appropriate behavior or task with minimal interference in the ongoing activity. In addition, token awards can easily be added to contracts. Paraeducators as well as the student's peers could assist in providing the tokens.

Other Methods to Increase Appropriate Behaviors

Methods other than reinforcement that can increase appropriate behaviors include contracts, prompts, shaping, and chaining. These methods work best when paired with the reinforcement methods discussed previously.

Contracts   A contract is a written agreement between the physical educator and the student regarding improvement in a behavior or task performance (see Figure 11.5). Many authorities consider contracts to be the most sophisticated behavior management technique. In addition, they are very adaptable to a variety of behaviors and situations. There are three basic types of contracts. First, there is the physical educator–controlled contract, in which the educator determines the target behavior and the reinforcements (see Figure 11.6). This type of contract is commonly referred to as a *proclamation*. Second, there is the student-controlled contract, in which the student determines the task and the reinforcement (see Figure 11.7). Third, there is the mutual contract, in which both the physical educator and the student determine the terms of the contract together (see Figure 11.8). Perhaps the most appealing feature of the latter two types of contracts is the removal of the onus of responsibility from the educator's shoulders (see Table 11.5 for guidelines for designing and implementing contracts).

Prompts   Prompts are cues that help a student identify target behaviors. There are three major types of prompts. First, there are visual prompts such as markings on the gymnasium floor or picture posters on the wall. Second, there are auditory prompts such as a whistle or verbal directions. Third, there is physical guidance in which the physical educator may hold the student's hand or put his or her hand on the student's shoulder when walking from one activity to another (see Chapter 6 for more detail on prompts). Prompts are especially effective with students who are hesitant or reluctant to perform a skill. Prompts also aid in the student's success. For example, assisting a student with mental retardation to

This is an agreement between Shawn Jackino and his physical education teacher. This contract begins on September 1, 2000, and will be reviewed daily by the physical education teacher.

I, Shawn Jackino, agree to discuss my behavior with the physical education teacher each day immediately after class. At that time, we will determine whether I earned a point in each of four categories: 1) class attendance, 2) class participation, 3) appropriate interaction with peers, and 4) use of appropriate language. A maximum of four points per day can be earned. A weekly behavior chart will be used to keep track of my points. Once I have earned enough points, I can choose from the reinforcement menu I developed with my physical education teacher (shown below).

_____   _____
Shawn Jackino, Student   Date

_____   _____
George McCall, General Physical Educator   Date

_____   _____
Jennifer E. Austin, Licensed School Psychologist   Date

Reinforcement menu

Reinforcement	Points needed
Free time with peer (e.g., shooting baskets)	10
Opportunity to be teacher's aide	10
Opportunity to lead daily stretching activities	5
Opportunity to choose class activity	10
Sports drink	5

A Teacher's Guide to Including Students with Disabilities in General Physical Education, 2nd ed.
by Martin E. Block, copyright ©2000 Paul H. Brookes Publishing Co.

Figure 11.5. Token economy contract.

hold a bat and hit a ball off a tee may make the student more willing to try the activity because he knows he will be successful with the physical prompts.

Shaping   *Shaping* refers to the development of a new behavior by reinforcing a series of behaviors that are gradually and progressively similar to the desired new behaviors. This is also referred to as *reinforcing successive approximations*. For example, the targeted goal for a student is to come into the gym and go

Billy will pay attention in physical education this week. He will earn the right to choose the class activity from four choices on Monday.

_____   _____
Billy Smith, Student   Date

_____   _____
George Matthews, General Physical Educator   Date

A Teacher's Guide to Including Students with Disabilities in General Physical Education, 2nd ed.
by Martin E. Block, copyright ©2000 Paul H. Brookes Publishing Co.

Figure 11.6. Teacher-controlled contract.

My physical education contract for success:

I, Jeramias Williams, promise to

- Follow teacher directions
- Participate in all physical education activities without arguing 4 out of 5 days a week
- Get dressed for physical education and do all activities Monday through Thursday
- Not fight with other students
- Not curse in class

If I do all of the above, I will be rewarded by

- Not having to get dressed for physical education on Fridays
- Passing physical education

_____   _____

Jeramias Williams, Student   Date

_____   _____

Clarence Thompson, General Physical Educator   Date

_____   _____

Sallie H. Swisher, Licensed School Psychologist   Date

A Teacher's Guide to Including Students with Disabilities in General Physical Education, 2nd ed.
by Martin E. Block, copyright ©2000 Paul H. Brookes Publishing Co.

Figure 11.7. Student-controlled contract.

directly to his squad. However, this student tends to run directly to the equipment and start playing until the physical educator literally pulls him away from the equipment and takes him to his squad. Rather than waiting for the student to display the complete targeted behavior, the physical educator may want to reinforce this student when he comes in, runs over to the equipment but does not touch it, then goes and sits down in his squad. Reinforcing successive approxi-

Michelle will dress for class for the next 15 class periods. After Michelle reaches the 15th class period, Coach Morales will award Michelle with a shirt with the logo of her favorite soccer team.

_____   _____

Michelle Roberson, Student   Date

_____   _____

Anthony Morales, Coach   Date

A Teacher's Guide to Including Students with Disabilities in General Physical Education, 2nd ed.
by Martin E. Block, copyright ©2000 Paul H. Brookes Publishing Co.

Figure 11.8. Mutual contract.

Table 11.5.   General guidelines for designing and implementing contracts

- Read and explain the conditions of the contract aloud with the student.
- Make sure the contract is fair for all persons.
- Design the contract in a positive manner.
- Design the contract in small approximations that lead to the target behavior or skill.
- Allow for frequent reinforcement that is given immediately following successful achievement.
- Be consistent and systematic in using a contract.
- Whenever possible, all people concerned should sign and receive a copy of the contract.
- Renegotiate contract if it is not effective.
- Start the contract as soon as possible after signing.

From Jansma, P., & French, R. (1994). *Special physical education* (p. 385). Englewood Cliffs, NJ: Prentice-Hall; reprinted by permission.

mations rather than waiting to reinforce the student until he or she has mastered the skill is more likely to result in the student's success.

Chaining   Chaining is a procedure of identifying a series of steps needed to perform a specific target behavior and then taking the student through those steps. In this procedure, each step is taught separately, then the separate steps are linked together. There are two types of chaining: backward and forward. Backward chaining involves teaching the steps to perform a target behavior in the reverse order of that in which they would normally occur. For example, in backward chaining, a student first would work on the follow-through in the overhand throw, then, working backward, would work on releasing the ball, then trunk rotation, then extending his arm backward, and finally side orientation. Typically, in backward chaining, the physical educator assists the student through each step of the movement except for the last step (e.g., in the previous example, the last step would be follow-through). Once the student has mastered the last step, the teacher then assists with all components except the last two, and so forth. This type of backward chaining provides more errorless learning. In contrast, forward chaining involves teaching the steps to perform a target behavior in the order that they normally occur.

Procedures to Reduce or Eliminate Behaviors

When reinforcement alone is ineffective in developing, maintaining, or increasing the demonstration of an appropriate behavior or task, it may be necessary for the physical educator to use techniques that decrease the problem behavior that is interfering with the learning process. There are two main techniques that a physical educator can use to reduce or eliminate behaviors: differential reinforcement and punishment.

Differential Reinforcement

There are three general differential reinforcement strategies: 1) differential reinforcement of low rates of behavior (DRL), 2) differential reinforcement of other behaviors (DRO), and 3) differential reinforcement of incompatible behaviors (DRI) (Alberto & Troutman, 1990).

Differential Reinforcement of Low Rates of Behavior   In this procedure, a specific schedule of reinforcement is applied to decrease the rate of a problem behavior that may be tolerable or even desirable at low rates but is inappropriate when it occurs too often or too rapidly. For example, one student may talk to his friends during the entire class; another student performing warm-up activities may not perform them at a level of exertion required to receive the full benefit.

There are two types of DRL reinforcement delivery schedules, each of which is based on the frequency, intensity, and duration of the problem behavior. The first type is the full-class DRL in which the total number of inappropriate responses in the entire class is compared with a preset criterion. A reinforcement is given if the occurrences of the problem behavior are at or below a predetermined criterion. The second type is interval DRL, which involves dividing the class period into an activity or time interval in which the behavior occurs during numerous intervals. This approach can be used if 1) the problem occurs during various times in the class period, and 2) it is believed that reinforcement will be effective only if it is awarded at various times during the class rather than at the end of the class. For example, there could be time periods after each activity within a lesson (e.g., getting dressed for class, role taking, instruction, warm-up, activity, cooldown, closure). At the completion of each activity, the student can be given a reward if the number of inappropriate responses during a specified period was less than or equal to a predetermined limit. As the problem behavior improves, the number of activities in which this behavior is awarded increases until the student is on a full-class DRL delivery schedule. The procedure is then gradually removed until the student is just receiving traditional reinforcement like the other students in the class.

Differential Reinforcement of Other Behaviors   This DRO strategy involves a reinforcement of other behaviors that are unrelated to the targeted behavior. The idea is to show the student that he or she will be reinforced for displaying appropriate behavior. For example, Hayden frequently talks to a peer while the physical educator tries to give him instructions. Rather than reprimand Hayden, the physical educator reinforces other positive behaviors that Hayden is displaying, such as not touching peers or not playing with equipment inappropriately. The hope is that Hayden will respond positively to being reinforced for these other behaviors. Later, when Hayden is not talking while the physical educator is giving instructions, the physical educator can reinforce Hayden's behavior.

Differential Reinforcement of Incompatible Behaviors   In this strategy, a behavior that is incompatible with the inappropriate behavior is reinforced. For example, a student receives reinforcement for standing on his spot or for being quiet in line, which is incompatible with standing in an inappropriate spot or being disruptive in line. Similarly, students are reinforced for clapping their hands to the music, which is incompatible with waving their hands in an inappropriate manner. This procedure has been reported to be quite effective in reducing aggressive behavior and other inappropriate behaviors (Goldstein, 1995).

Punishment

Punishment is defined as the presentation of an aversive event or consequence immediately following a behavior that leads to a decrease in the occurrence of that behavior. If punishment is used appropriately, it can improve a student's behavior. For instance, at the beginning of class, Frank runs over to the playground equipment instead of lining up with his class. As a consequence for this behavior, Frank's teacher has Frank walk to and from the locker room to his class squad 10 consecutive times (overcorrection). The next class, Frank walks directly to his squad. The teacher then rewards him for the appropriate behavior by patting him on the back and verbally praising him.

Physical educators must take care when using punishment. Punishment can be abusive, leading to withdrawal, anger, frustration, and even further misbehavior. Therefore, punishment should be used only when positive techniques have not been effective. Even when punishment is used, it is important to remember that it is easy to focus on decreasing or eliminating an inappropriate behavior and forget the importance of teaching positive, alternative behaviors. The educator must target both the behavior that the student should increase as well as the behavior the student should decrease. For example, in the previous case, Frank's teacher reinforced him (e.g., gave him a high-five, patted him on the back) for walking directly to his squad the day after Frank's negative behavior was corrected.

If it is determined that punishments must be used, it is important that certain guidelines be followed (see Table 11.6). Also, it is important to obtain approval from the student's parents and special education teacher before implementing a punishment program. There are numerous techniques, ranging from mild to intrusive, that can be used. There are six basic types of punishments that are appropriate in physical education: angry looks, verbal reprimands, extinction, time-out, overcorrection, and response cost. Each of these punishments is discussed briefly in the following sections.

Angry Looks   Sometimes, an angry look by the physical educator when a student exhibits an inappropriate behavior is sufficient punishment to stop the recurrence of the behavior. For example, a physical education teacher stops speaking and glares at a student who is talking while the teacher is trying to give directions. The student then realizes he is disturbing the teacher and stops talking.

Verbal Reprimands   This form of punishment is used widely and, in many cases, effectively in physical education. The key, however, is always to address the student's behavior problem and not the student him- or herself. The following illustrates appropriate ways to use verbal reprimands: "Do not bounce the ball while I am talking!" "You are not standing in the circle that I requested you to stand in!" "You were asked to run around all four cones, not just three!" Henderson and French (1990) listed numerous verbal reprimands in which the student, not the behavior, is attacked. Examples of inappropriate verbal reprimands include "You can't do anything right!" "You should be ashamed of yourself!" "Can't you control yourself and act your age?" "That is the worst thing I have ever seen!" and "You have lost my respect!"

Extinction   A student who mutters, "You can't make me" or whines about having to run an obstacle course is setting a bad example for other students. Such behavior can easily anger and frustrate the physical educator. Usually, the reinforcing consequence is some response from the physical educator or other students in the class. There are students whose main goal is to upset, frustrate, or anger their teachers and peers. These students receive reinforcement in two ways. First, they receive attention from the teacher or other students. Second, they get revenge. One way to reduce or eliminate this type of behavior is to use an extinction procedure (Ninness & Glenn, 1988). During this procedure, the physical educator eliminates or extinguishes maladaptive behaviors by simply ig-

Table 11.6. Guidelines for the use of punishment

- Always talk to the student privately first to determine the cause of the misbehavior.
- Establish classroom rules so students know beforehand what the punishable behaviors are and what their consequences will be.
- Post the rules in the gym and go over them with the students.
- Send a list of the rules and unacceptable behaviors and consequences home to parents so they know what is expected of their child.
- Provide models of acceptable behavior so students are aware of appropriate ways to behave.
- Do not allow a student to exhibit an inappropriate behavior for too long a period of time so that it increases in intensity before you attempt to intervene. Punishment must occur immediately after the behavior is first observed. Afterward, it is important that you provide opportunities for the student to behave appropriately and to receive positive reinforcement for this appropriate behavior.
- Distinguish between intentional and unintentional disruptions. Do not treat students who make accidental mistakes the same way as those who misbehave on purpose. For instance, a student who accidentally throws a ball that hits another person should be treated differently from a student who throws a ball with the intention of hitting someone. Make the punishment suit the behavior.
- Do not lose control of your own emotions. The problem will only become worse if both the student and the teacher have lost control.
- Avoid confrontations with the student, especially in front of peers. Secondary-level students, in particular, tend to function as members of a group and are quite protective of each other. By confronting one student, you may lose the respect of other students as well.
- Avoid the use of sarcasm. Some teachers use sarcasm to chastise or demean a student in an attempt to control behavior. Using words as weapons of control can alienate all students in the class. Many times, the teacher unconsciously slips into using this technique or considers it a form of joking to get the point across. Sarcasm is generally not considered funny by the students and could negatively affect their self-image and status with their peers. It is not a recommended way to manage behaviors.
- Be consistent in your use of punishment. What is wrong today must be wrong tomorrow, and the consequences must be the same.
- Be fair. Behavior that is wrong for Tommy to exhibit must also be wrong for Mary to exhibit.
- When a student does misbehave, make sure that in your reprimand you specify that it is the behavior, *not* the student, of which you disapprove. For example, do not say, "You are a bad person, and I will not tolerate you in my class," but rather, "That behavior is inappropriate, and I will not tolerate that behavior in this class."
- Avoid touching a student when you are angry. Physical restraint may be appropriate with aggressive, self-destructive, or dangerous behaviors when the teacher is unable to successfully use a more gradual, positive approach due to the possibility that the student may cause harm to him- or herself or to others. When using physical restraint, hold the student firmly but not roughly to give the student a sense of protection—not punishment. The preferred technique is for the teacher to stand behind the student and hold the student's wrists with the arms crossed over the chest.
- Never hit a student. Hitting is totally inappropriate for a teacher. There are too many negative side effects of hitting a student for it ever to be an approved management technique. In addition to all of the negative repercussions of hitting a student, there is an issue of legal liability.

From Henderson, H.L., & French, R.W. (1993). *Creative approaches to managing student behavior* (2nd ed. pp. 31–32). Park City, UT: Family Development Resources; reprinted by permission.

Table 11.7. Guidelines for using an extinction procedure

- Generally, combine with other methods such as strategies related to differential reinforcement.
- Be consistent, and do not occasionally reinforce the problem behavior.
- Practice not responding to the misbehavior.
- Be aware of "extinction bursts." After the extinction procedure is initiated, the inappropriate behavior may occur more often, more vigorously, or for longer periods of time by the student in an effort to gain attention. Eventually, the extinction burst will fade, and the problem behavior will gradually diminish.
- Do not make eye contact, verbal cues provide verbal contact, or make physical contact.
- Some form of punishment may be the procedure of choice if the problem behavior intensifies over a long period of time.

From Alberto, P.A., & Troutman, A.C. (1990). *Applied behavior analysis for teachers.* Columbus, OH: Merrill; adapted by permission.

noring them. Extinction is the most effective known way to permanently remove an inappropriate response and, like other punishments, is most effective when combined with positive reinforcement. Extinction, however, can be difficult to implement; it takes a great deal of self-control on the parts of the physical educator and the student's peers (see Table 11.7 for extinction guidelines).

Time-Out   This technique involves the removal of the student from positive reinforcement for a fixed period of time. There are different thoughts regarding the recommended length of the time-out period. Some authorities suggest that this time period should be no longer than 2–3 minutes. Others have stated that the student should stay in time-out for the equivalent of 1 minute for each year of his or her age. There are three general forms of time-out. The first form is *observational time-out,* in which the student is removed from the activity but is allowed to view the activity without participating. The second form is *seclusionary time-out,* in which the student is required to sit or stand in a corner within the physical education environment but is not allowed to see students participating in the activity from which he or she was removed. The third form is *exclusionary time-out,* in which the student must leave the environment to go to an environment that is supervised and not more reinforcing than the environment that he or she has left.

Advantages of time-out are that it is simple to implement in a short amount of time and has been shown to be effective in decreasing many undesirable behaviors in students. The major disadvantage of time-out is that the student is not allowed to participate in the activities. Also, students who wish to avoid participating in physical education will find time-out reinforcing.

Overcorrection   Overcorrection was designed to reduce the inappropriate side effects of intense punishment. There are two basic types of overcorrection. First, in *restitutional overcorrection,* the student is required to restore the environment. For example, if a student put his chewing gum on top of his locker, he would be required to clean the gum off of his locker plus all of the gum that others have put on their lockers. Second, in *positive practice overcorrection,* a student is required to repeatedly practice a positive behavior in the correct manner. For example, suppose the physical educator sees a student running in the locker room. In positive overcorrection, the student may be required to walk correctly at the required speed 10 consecutive times.

Advantages reported when using overcorrection are that it reduces the undesired behavior faster, more completely, and for a longer time than other punishment techniques such as time-out. Although it is also an effective technique for reducing extreme behavior problems, the physical educator must be aware of a number of disadvantages associated with using overcorrection: It is a difficult and time-consuming procedure to implement, and an additional staff member usually is required to ensure that the corrective procedure is implemented accurately. Finally, as with the use of most techniques used to eliminate or reduce severe behavior, informed consent from the student's parents needs to be obtained.

Response Cost   This procedure refers to the removal of a specific quantity of previously earned reinforcement from a student, such as minutes of time to perform an activity, loss of equipment, or points taken away from a grade. This system of punishment is used in most traditional sports. For instance, if a player inappropriately hits another player in football, the penalty will cost the team valuable yardage or, as in basketball, even possession of the ball. In using this type of punishment, the physical educator must consider the following: 1) magnitude of the cost in relation to the problem behavior exhibited, 2) provision of opportunities to regain the lost privilege or points when the appropriate behavior has replaced the inappropriate behavior, and 3) assurance that the student understands the rules for the removal of the reinforcing event (Jansma & French, 1994).

Some Final Thoughts on Managing Behavior Problems

The previous sections present a great deal of information regarding how to understand and help students who display behavior problems in general physical education. The following sections provide some final details that should be considered when working with these students.

Plan on Teaching Appropriate Behaviors

The management of behavior problems should be treated in the same way as the management of instructional problems. For example, if a student makes an error while performing a motor task, a correction procedure is implemented and the student is provided with more practice and review. If the problem is not corrected, the physical educator rediagnoses the problem and then rearranges the practice session. However, there may be different reactions on the part of the physical educator with the occurrence of an inappropriate behavior. Typically, when an inappropriate behavior occurs, the student may be given a reminder of the disregarded rule or expected behavior, told what not to do, and penalized or punished for exhibiting the inappropriate behavior. Just like physical fitness or motor skills, behavior also must be taught in the physical education curriculum.

Communicate with Students

Communication is vital to developing positive interactions with students that lead to trust and acceptance. In physical education programs that promote a great deal of communication, students are more likely to do what teachers ask of them. Even intermittently talking or listening to students will help. Some researchers have suggested that physical educators should interact, either through verbal or nonverbal communication, with each student in the class during each class period. In large classes, this may take two class periods. One technique that can be used to increase student–teacher interactions is to meet students at the door

Table 11.8.   Techniques to consider when communicating with students

- Focus on behaviors, not the student. Do not say "behavior problem student"; rather, say "student with a behavior problem."

- Listen to the student as long as the student is not using the opportunity to control you. For example, during an elementary physical education class, a primary-grade student kept approaching the teacher and holding her hand. The physical educator, in an attempt to manage and instruct the class of 28 students, kept asking the student to go back to the spot or station. This behavior continued throughout the class period. After school, the physical educator went to the classroom teacher to see if this behavior also occurred in the classroom. The classroom teacher informed the physical educator that the young child had upset his father the night before, and the father had forced the child to sleep alone outside the home. It would have been great if the physical educator had been informed of this information earlier.

- Understand your feelings toward the student. With diversity in the levels of behavior and learning of students, teachers must modify traditional teaching styles. If a student has a cognitive impairment, techniques must be implemented to ensure that the student understands the instructions. If this does not occur, the teacher may be constantly frustrated because a particular student is continually in the wrong place and talking to other students to figure out what he is supposed to do in class.

- Accentuate students' strengths. With large classes, it seems that it is a constant chore just to "put out fires." Focusing on a student's appropriate behavior and learning his or her strengths and not just his or her weaknesses may decrease many of the problems that he or she exhibits in the class. Students who are never reinforced will be more likely to display inappropriate behavior.

- Respect students' legitimate opinions. When a student provides his or her opinion, reinforce that you support the opinion, especially when it is honest and not negative. Many times these opinions can improve instruction. Sometimes, the student states that it is too cold out, he or she is bored with a particular activity, or that he or she never gets to play a certain position during a game. This particular student may not be the only one to feel this way. Make sure that you listen and make the appropriate modifications and do not simply ignore a student's opinion.

From Pangrazi, R.P., *Dynamic physical education for elementary school children* (12th ed., pp. 67–68). Copyright © 1998 by Allyn & Bacon. Reprinted by permission.

when they are entering or leaving the gym. Another technique is to stand near students during the daily activity and provide feedback. For instance, if students are jogging, position yourself in one corner of the gym so you can provide a friendly look, a high-five, or words of encouragement as the students pass by. Table 11.8 presents some techniques to consider when communicating with students.

Communicate with Parents

Parents should be kept abreast of their child's progress or lack of progress in all school environments, including physical education. This is particularly true for students who have a history of displaying inappropriate behaviors. Communication with parents can be by telephone, e-mail, or notes sent home with the student. Items that should be communicated to the parents include the student's appropriate behaviors during class as well as the student's behavior in physical education. Also, you should contact parents (and other team members) if you notice changes in the student's behavior. Sometimes parents and teachers forget to tell you if the student's medication is being changed or there are changes in the home situation. For example, a new medication that a student is taking to combat a seizure disorder may be affecting his or her coordination and stamina in physical education. Similarly, a student who seems very depressed and does not want to get dressed for physical education might be having trouble coping with her parents' divorce. The key is to view parents as your allies in helping you develop the most appropriate behavior management program possible.

Establish Class Rules

Establishing rules, consequences, and a clear class structure for your general physical education class will prevent many students (including students with disabilities) from displaying inappropriate behaviors. Class rules for all students should be established and clearly defined early in the school year. Most physical educators review the rules with their classes at the beginning of the school year and then periodically throughout the school year. Some educators will ask their students to repeat the rules either verbally or in a written quiz in order to determine their understanding. Others actually send the rules home in a written format for parents to review, sign, and send back. Generally, it is recommended not to have more than eight rules. Some of the traditional rules and consequences used in physical education can be found in Table 11.9.

Be Consistent in Enforcing Rules

In addition to establishing class rules and consequences, it is critical that these rules and consequences be consistently enforced. If students perceive that some students can get away with misbehavior whereas others cannot, then students will become confused and angry. You can, however, establish some alternative rules and consequences for students with disabilities. Just make it clear to all of the students why such an alternative is necessary. For example, a student with mental retardation often tries to talk to peers while the teacher is giving instructions. Rather than send the student to time-out, instruct peers to gently and quietly tell the student not to talk while the teacher is talking. Later, have peers talk to the student on the way to a station or at other appropriate times.

Table 11.9.   Common rules and consequences used in physical education

Rules for physical education

• Raise your hand.	• Listen to instructions.
• Be quiet when others talk.	• Enter and exit the room quietly.
• Remain in your spot.	• Show respect to your classmates/teachers.
• Practice the assigned task.	• Take care of equipment.
• Follow directions.	• Throw chewing gum away before class.

Consequences used in physical education

For following the rules	*For not following the rules*
• Free play at end of period or week	• First warning
• Choice of activity (e.g., parachute)	• Second warning
• Game at end of class	• 3-minute time-out
• Choice of music during the activity	• Letter home to parents (negative)
• Stickers or stamps	• Send back to classroom teacher
• Letter home to parents (positive)	• Send to principal

Utilize a Team Approach

Collaboration among faculty, staff, parents, and the community may be required to modify problem behaviors. As many team members as possible should be included in the diagnosis of the problem and development of a plan. This should include a consensus on how the plan will be implemented and who will be responsible for each part of the plan. For example, although a teacher assistant might not be needed to accompany a student with an emotional disability to physical education every day, she may be asked to be available in emergencies. Similarly, in large high schools that have several vice principals, the team should decide which principal is in charge of behavior problems for particular students.

A growing concept is a schoolwide behavior management program that can be a proactive means of reducing discipline problems in the school. This type of plan broadens the shared knowledge about the student's behavioral and learning needs that influence performance and learning and the various appropriate interventions. In some communities, there are even communitywide programs. In this instance, the student would truly be viewed as part of the ecosystem. Specific behaviors, such as honesty, helping others, and using manners, become the focus of the school and the community. Changing these behaviors then becomes the responsibility of the community, not just the school.

Ensure Generalization

Generalization refers to the likelihood that a behavior or activity learned in the physical education environment will also occur in different environments such as the home or the community. Only behaviors and activities that can be generalized should be selected for instruction. In addition, activities in which the student has received instruction should be checked periodically to make sure they are maintained. For instance, it is not an effective use of time to teach a skill such as bowling if you do not ensure that the skill is maintained over time and in different environments. Waiting until the following year when the unit is taught again only leads to regression of skill performance and time lost having to reteach the skill.

Know the Laws

Physical educators must know federal, state, and local policies and laws related to discipline. For instance, based on Section 504 of the Rehabilitation Act (PL 93-112) and the Individuals with Disabilities Education Act (IDEA) Amendments of 1997 (PL 105-17), different procedures related to discipline are used for students with and without disabilities. For example, under most circumstances, a student with a disability cannot be expelled from school unless a trained and knowledgeable group of people first determine whether the student's misconduct is related to his or her disability. This is commonly termed *manifestation determination*. Disciplinary action and behavior intervention plans are two additional concepts that physical educators need to know and understand.

1. *Disciplinary action:* No more than 10 days following the date to take disciplinary action against a student with a disability, the school district must conduct a review of the relationship between the student's disability and the behavior that is the subject of the disciplinary action. The IEP committee may determine that the student's behavior was or was not a manifestation of the student's disability based on the evaluation and diagnostic results, observations of the stu-

dent, and review of the appropriateness of the student's IEP and placement. If it is determined that the student's disability did not impair his or her ability to understand the impact and consequences of the behavior subject to the disciplinary action, the student can be disciplined in the same manner as a student without disabilities. However, if the student is suspended or expelled, the district must continue to provide the student with a free appropriate public education to decrease the possibility of educational regression. These laws do not require this provision for students without disabilities who were suspended or expelled for the same inappropriate behavior. If the behavior is determined to be a manifestation of the student's disability, the student cannot be disciplined for the behavior. Instead, the district must attempt to remediate the impairment in the student's IEP and/or its implementation. This could mean a revision in the IEP and the development and revision of the student's behavior intervention plan. There are some exceptions. A student with a disability may be placed in an alternative education environment, determined by the IEP committee, for the same amount of time that a student without a disability would be subjected to discipline but for no more that 45 days if the student carries a weapon to school or school function or knowingly possesses or uses illegal drugs or sells or solicits the sale of a controlled substance while in school or at a school function.

2. *Behavior intervention plan (BIP):* A BIP contains strategies to address specific behaviors exhibited by a student that interfere with his or her performance or the learning of others. This plan must include strategies, consequences (rewards and punishments), and educational supports to increase the student's performance and learning. This plan is designed by a student's IEP committee, which includes a student's general education teacher. The BIP must be developed for any student who has committed a drug or weapon offense, and the IEP committee must meet no later than 10 days after the offense to 1) develop a functional behavior assessment plan or 2) review and modify an existing BIP for the student.

12

Including Students in General Aquatics Programs

with Phillip Conatser

Inclusion, like peace, is a justice issue, and no one should ignore the roles they play. Despite all the variables, examples, or excuses implying now is not the time. . . . The visions of inclusion and peace demand our immediate attention!!

Aleita Hass-Holcombe, adapted physical education specialist

Andrea, a sixth-grade student, is especially popular with several girls in her class who love to sit and talk to Andrea during lunch. Despite the fact that Andrea has severe diplegic cerebral palsy (involvement in all four limbs but affects legs more than arms) and mental retardation requiring extensive support and needs assistance with virtually every activity of daily living, all of Andrea's classmates really like her, and Andrea enjoys their attention. Andrea's parents, special education teacher, general education teacher, teacher assistant, and specialists all have worked together to create a global individualized education program (IEP) for Andrea. Each of these professionals has done a wonderful job of determining ways to embed Andrea's unique objectives into general education classes throughout the school day; and Andrea, her parents, her teachers, and her classmates all seem pleased with Andrea's progress and socialization.

The one class in which the team has had great difficulty determining how to include Andrea has been general physical education. Sixth-grade general physical education at Andrea's school involves many team sports, and the general physical education teacher and other team members are concerned about Andrea's safety. Andrea often works on alternative activities off to the side of the gym with several of her classmates and her teacher assistant, which seems to have worked fairly well. However, the next unit for Andrea's sixth grade is aquatics. Although everyone on Andrea's team agrees that aquatics would probably be an ideal activity for Andrea, the thought of Andrea in the water with just the help of her teacher assistant really scares her parents and her aquatics instructor. How will the instructor be able to supervise and instruct a class of 25 sixth graders while he provides the necessary individual attention that Andrea and her teacher assistant will need?

Aquatics has long been recognized as a means of developing physical and motor fitness, social skills, and self-esteem in individuals with disabilities (Christies, 1985; Daniels, 1954; Grosse, 1996; Sherrill, 1998; Skinner & Thompson, 1983). Aquatics activities not only are a common form of recreation in mainstream society but also provide exercise that is both relaxing and socially acceptable (Broach & Dattilo, 1996; Koury, 1996; Lepore, Gayle, & Stevens, 1998; Morris, 1999). Swimming can be a fun way to improve cardiorespiratory endurance, muscle strength, motor coordination, flexibility, postural stability, and overall fitness without putting undue pressure on joints (*Exceptional Parent* Staff, 1993; Grosse, 1995; Horvat & Forbus, 1989; Hutzler, Chacham, Bergman, & Szeinberg, 1997; Reid, 1979). Finally, aquatics activities often increase normal muscle tone through proprioception and sensory stimulation while decreasing pain and stereotypic behaviors (Geis, 1975; Horvat, Forbus, & Van Kirk, 1987; Koury, 1996; Langendorfer, 1986).

Traditionally, swimming programs for individuals with disabilities have been provided in segregated programs (i.e., special swimming programs just for individuals with disabilities [Conatser, Block, & Lepore, 2000]). Also, in the past, many aquatics organizations mistakenly believed that federal laws mandating equality and inclusion did not apply to them (Osinski, 1993). In fact, there are many aquatics programs around the United States that continue to offer separate swimming programs for individuals with disabilities (Conatser et al., 2000). Currently, however, there is a trend to include individuals with disabilities in general community recreation and school-based swimming programs (Berry, 1990; Conatser et al., 2000). Over time, the impact of federal laws such as the Individuals with Disabilities Education Act (IDEA) of 1990 and the Americans with Disabilities Act (ADA) heightened the awareness of parents and advocacy groups, leading to more inclusive aquatics opportunities for individuals with disabilities (Christies, 1985; Grosse, 1995, 1996; Langendorfer, 1990). Consequently, many individuals with disabilities and their parents are now opting for participation in general aquatics programs (American Red Cross, 1992a, 1992b; Bryant & Graham, 1993). The emphasis on being with peers without disabilities in general aquatics classes has forced aquatics instructors to rethink their instructional strategies, teaching methods, and use of equipment (Conatser et al., 2000; Osinski, 1993).

This chapter presents information regarding ways to safely and meaningfully include students with disabilities in general swim programs in public schools or in the community. The chapter focuses on the following three areas: 1) planning for a general aquatics program that includes students with disabilities, 2) specific instructional and equipment modifications that can be used to facilitate the inclusion of students with disabilities into general aquatics programs, and 3) safety considerations unique to inclusive aquatics programs. Assessment, which is a critical part of the process, is addressed within each of these key areas (i.e., how is assessment used to facilitate planning, develop appropriate modifications, and ensure safety?).

Planning for an Inclusive Aquatics Program

As noted in Chapter 4, planning is a multistep approach that helps physical educators determine what to teach students with disabilities, how well the students' unique goals and objectives will fit into the general physical education environment, methods for teaching these goals and objectives, and who should teach these goals and objectives. The following section applies the model for planning for inclusion that was outlined in Chapter 4 to a student with a disability who will be included in a general aquatics class.

Determining What to Teach

The first step in the planning process is to determine what aquatics skills to teach the students. Aquatics goals for students with disabilities can range from simply tolerating the water to mastering complex strokes. In addition, social and behavioral goals such as interacting with peers, exhibiting appropriate social behaviors, displaying improved awareness of peers and surroundings, and improving self-confidence can be embedded within the aquatics venue. Carter, Dolan, and LeConey (1994) grouped goals for students with disabilities who participate in aquatics programs under the following headings: 1) therapeutic goals, 2) adapted/specialized goals, and 3) mainstream/integrative goals (see Table 12.1). For most students, a combination of goals from each of the three areas will be most appropriate. For example, Andrea's goals might be to improve ambula-

Table 12.1. Aquatics goals for students with disabilities

Therapeutic goals	Adapted/specialized goals	Mainstream/integrative goals
• Improve range of motion. • Improve strength of trunk and/or extremities. • Improve sitting or standing balance. • Reduce muscle contractions. • Improve ambulation. • Improve cardiovascular endurance. • Improve respiratory function. • Improve cognitive functioning, such as problem solving. • Improve posture. • Improve body awareness. • Improve perceptual and spatial awareness.	• Develop and improve swimming skills. • Develop and improve water and personal safety skills. • Improve self-care skills related to swimming, such as dressing. • Improve independence, such as water entry/exit and ambulation. • Increase social interaction skills. • Improve self-concept.	• Develop age-appropriate social interaction skills. • Develop fitness and physical well-being. • Develop community resource awareness and access. • Create awareness by the community at large of swimming abilities of person with disabilities. • Develop friendships among swimmers with and without disabilities.

From Carter, M.J., Dolan, M.A., & LeConey, S.P. (1994). *Designing instructional swim programs for individuals with disabilities* (p. 7). Reston, VA: AALR/AAHPERD; reprinted by permission.

tion and standing balance (therapeutic), to learn how to float on her back and develop a modified backstroke (adapted), and to improve her awareness of and trust in peers (integrative). These broad goals can then be written into long-term goals and short-term instructional objectives for the IEP that are based on assessment and information regarding the student's present level of performance (see Figure 12.1 for an example). Assessment information that can help guide this process includes 1) the student's physical, cognitive, and social/emotional strengths and weaknesses, 2) the student's capabilities with regard to the amount of time he or she realistically has to learn to swim, 3) parent and student interests, and 4) other goals that are already in place in the IEP (e.g., motor, speech-language, and social goals) that can be embedded within the aquatics environment.

Analyzing the General Aquatics Curriculum

Once the team has determined the student's long-term goals, evaluated the student on these goals, and developed short-term instructional objectives based on the evaluation, the next step is to carefully analyze the general aquatics program to determine whether the student's individual goals and objectives match the goals and objectives of the general program. This should include an analysis of both the activities that will be presented during the unit and the general format of each class.

For example, in Andrea's school, the sixth-grade aquatics unit lasts 6 weeks and includes the following components: introductory and safety activities (1 week), learning basic strokes (3 weeks), and refining and mastering select

Long-term goal 1: *Andrea will improve her ability to stand and walk in the water.*

Present level of performance: *Andrea can stand in 4 feet of water without support for about 10 seconds. She tends to lean back too far, and she does not use any righting or balance responses to keep herself from falling. She can take about three steps in 4 feet of water before she loses her balance. Again, she does not use righting or balance responses to keep herself from falling.*

Short-term instructional objectives:
1. *Andrea will stand in 4 feet of water for 1 minute without any support in three out of four trials.*
2. *Andrea will walk in the 4-feet-deep water for a distance of 10 feet without any support in three out of four trials.*

Long-term goal 2: *Andrea will develop the ability to float and swim on her back.*

Present level of performance: *Andrea will lie on her back in the water wearing a neck flotation device for about 15 seconds before she panics and tries to turn over. She needs to work on extending her arms out to the side and relaxing more. When attempting to propel herself, Andrea will move her arms, but she does not do a good job of coordinating the left and right sides of her body. This causes her to angle off to the side. She also panics after three to four arm strokes and tries to turn over. It is important for Andrea to stay on her back for several reasons; on her front, she drinks the pool's water and cannot breathe, and her body position on her back allows her to propel herself better through the water.*

Short-term instructional objectives:
1. *Andrea will float on her back independently wearing a neck support flotation device so that she floats for 3 minutes without turning over in three out of four trials.*
2. *Andrea will swim on her back wearing a neck support flotation device in 4-feet-deep water using her arms simultaneously to propel herself so that she travels a distance of 10 feet in three out of four trials.*

Long-term goal 3: *Andrea will improve her awareness of and trust in her peers (this is a carry-over goal from other parts of her IEP, so refer to those objectives).*

Present level of performance: *See other parts of IEP.*

Figure 12.1. Sample long-term goals and short-term instructional objectives for Andrea, a sixth grader with cerebral palsy.

strokes (2 weeks). The general format of the class is as follows: Change into swimsuit in the locker room (10 minutes), warm up in the shallow water (10 minutes), introduce/practice select strokes (20 minutes), cool down in water while learning safety skills (5 minutes), and change back to street clothes (10 minutes). Andrea could work on her standing balance in the water while the other students warm up in the water (e.g., bobbing, treading water). Because Andrea also is working on basic strokes, she could participate with her peers during stroke work. Then, while Andrea's peers work on some of the more complex strokes, Andrea could work on floating, walking, and a modified backstroke (with support from a teacher assistant or flotation device). During cool-down time, Andrea could work on the standing balance and floating or participate in

---

Locker room: *Change into physical education uniform (approximately 10 minutes).*
  Modifications for Andrea: *Andrea's teacher assistant or other support personnel will help her change into her swimsuit. This is a good time to help Andrea work on her self-help skills. Perhaps allow her to enter the locker room a few minutes earlier to work on these skills.*

Squads/attendance: *Students stand in squads in water while attendance is taken (2 minutes).*
  Modifications for Andrea: *Aquatics instructor will need to help the teacher assistant get Andrea into the pool. This is a good place to work on Andrea's objective of standing independently. Also, it is a good place for Andrea to show regard for and awareness of peers (encourage peers in front of and behind Andrea to talk to her).*

Warm-ups: *Students led by instructor in several warm-up activities in the water (10 minutes).*
  Modifications for Andrea: *This is a good time to work on standing and walking balance with Andrea's teacher assistant. Also, encourage peers around Andrea to say hi to her, and encourage Andrea to regard her peers.*

Skill focus: *Work on specific swimming strokes as prescribed each day by instructor (20 minutes).*
  Modifications for Andrea: *Andrea should work on walking in the water, floating on her back, and doing a modified backstroke. She will need her neck flotation device for floating and for the backstroke. Andrea should be in close proximity to peers without disabilities as much as it is safely possible. Encourage peers around Andrea to say hi to her, and encourage Andrea to regard her peers.*

Cool-down: *Work on relaxing and safety skills (5 minutes).*
  Modifications for Andrea: *This is a good place to work on slow movements for all of Andrea's extremities to help her relax. Also, this a good place to work on standing balance. If the class is going to work on rescue techniques—for example, throwing a rescue line—then Andrea could hold onto the rope and help secure the line. The aquatics instructor will need to help the teacher assistant get Andrea out of the pool.*

Locker room: *Shower, groom, and put on street clothes (10 minutes).*
  Modifications for Andrea: *Good place for Andrea to work on dressing and grooming skills. Have her stay an extra 10 minutes with the teacher assistant to work on these skills.*

Travel: *Take the bus, van, or walk (approximately 15 minutes).*
  Modifications for Andrea: *Good time to work on friendships and fun interactive activities. Andrea can play all types of sitting games such as cards or Tic-Tac-Toe with assistance. Although Andrea takes longer to dress, there will be other students who are equally slow. Therefore, have faster dressers do an activity while they are waiting, or have more than one bus or van available for shuttling.*

Figure 12.2.   General daily lesson plan for sixth-grade aquatics unit with comments regarding Andrea.

aquatics safety techniques (e.g., she could be the student who is being rescued or hold the hands of fellow students in a human rescue chain). Finally, Andrea's social goals can be worked on throughout the class, during dressing and grooming, or during the bus drive from the aquatics facility to the school (see Figure 12.2). Andrea probably will require additional support (e.g., teacher assistant, other aquatics personnel, peers) to be included safely and successfully in this unit. Also, Andrea likely will need special or adapted instruction and equipment. However, with the aforementioned modifications, Andrea can be included in the general aquatics program alongside her peers without disabilities while working on her unique aquatics objectives.

Table 12.2.   Quick modification reference list for lesson plan

Skills	Match, partial match, or no match	Modifications for Andrea
Water entry: Dive from side of pool	Partial match	Sits and rolls into water
Water adjustment: Rotary breathing	Match	Rotary breathing
Buoyancy and breath control: Supine float for 10 minutes	Partial match	Supine floats for 3 minutes, unassisted
Locomotion/strokes: Front crawl, etc.	Partial match	Moves through water with personal flotation device (PFD)
Personal safety: Treads water for 5 minutes	No match	Walks/moves in shoulder-deep water
Game: Water tag	Partial match	Uses PFD (designated "un-freezer")

To accommodate the student with disabilities, instructors should organize a quick and easy-to-read reference that lists 1) the student's skills or objectives, 2) whether these skills match the activities and instructional arrangements in general physical education, and 3) modifications to instructor's activities and instructional arrangements for the student with disabilities (refer to Table 12.2 for an example of a quick reference list).

Determining How to Teach Students with Disabilities in General Aquatics Programs

The next step in the planning process is to determine how to teach targeted goals and objectives within the inclusive environment. This will require curricular and instructional modifications and the use of adapted aquatics equipment.

Curricular Modifications   Three possible curricular modifications can be employed to help the student with disabilities work on his or her objectives within the general aquatics environment. If the student's objectives are similar to those found in the general aquatics curriculum but are performed at a different level of difficulty, then *multilevel curricular selection* is appropriate. Recall from Chapter 7 that multilevel curricular selection involves all students (including the student with disabilities) working on the same objectives, but at different levels of ability. For example, all students in the class might be learning how to float on their backs; however, the student with disabilities either requires the help of a flotation device or a teacher assistant or is expected to float for a shorter period of time. Another way to individualize the same objectives for all students is with the use of extended skill stations. Students all go to the same station to work on the same skill, but each student works on the skill at his or her own level of ability.

For example, all students go to a station to work on the back crawl kick; however, once they are at the station, each student works on the same component of the skill at his or her own level, including

1. Holding onto kickboard and trying to kick while wearing personal flotation device

2. Holding onto kickboard and kicking using good form while wearing personal flotation device

3. Holding onto kickboard and kicking using good form without the use of a personal flotation device—5 yards

4. Holding onto kickboard and kicking using good form—25 yards

5. Without kickboard, kicking using good form—5 yards

6. Kicking using good form—25 yards

7. Incorporating arms and legs when kicking

Another multilevel curricular selection technique that can be used in the water is cooperative learning. Recall that cooperative learning involves a group of students with varying abilities working together to accomplish a team goal (Johnson & Johnson, 1989). For example, the aquatics instructor sets a team goal of treading water continuously for 10 minutes. Because each person in this beginning-level team of five members can tread water only for 1–3 minutes, each person will have to take a turn to achieve the team goal. Jonathan goes first and treads water for 1 minute and 30 seconds. When he says he needs to stop, Jamisha takes over; she treads water for 2 minutes and 30 seconds. When Jamisha gets tired, Jo, a girl with cerebral palsy, takes her turn and, with the aid of "floaties" around her arms, treads water for 1 minute and 30 seconds. Next, Felipe treads water for 2 minutes; and, finally, Kara, the strongest swimmer in the group, treads water for 3 minutes. Thus, the team works together to accomplish a goal that no group member could do independently.

Another way to use multilevel curricular selection is to "teach by invitation" (Mosston & Ashworth, 1994). In this technique, the teacher invites, but does not demand, the students to perform gradually more difficult movements. By giving the students choices, students with disabilities can still participate successfully with the group. For example, an aquatics teacher asks her students to swim across the pool using an elementary backstroke. The next lap, the teacher invites students to either continue the elementary backstroke or attempt a regular back crawl stroke. This allows the student who does not feel comfortable with or who cannot perform the regular back crawl to still be successful.

Although many students with severe disabilities have unique IEP objectives that are different from objectives in the general aquatics curriculum, they can still be included in the general aquatics program using *curricular overlapping* (see Chapter 7 for more detail). In this model, students with disabilities will work on their unique aquatics objectives while other students work on their general aquatics objectives. For example, suppose a seventh-grade general aquatics class is working on increasing their endurance in selected strokes (swimming 50 yards or more using any stroke). Included in this class is William, a student with Duchenne muscular dystrophy. William participates in aquatics primarily to relax his muscles, practice standing (which he is no longer able to do outside the pool), and to enjoy the water with his peers. William works on standing and stretching with the aid of his physical therapist at one end of the pool. When a peer swims by William, William needs to move (walk) so that he does not interfere with this student. In addition, because William is able to see the large clock at the end of the pool, he calls out lap times to two students who are using the same lanes he is using. William works on standing and stretching while his peers work on their endurance; however, William still is part of the group and has an opportunity to interact with and assist his peers.

Another way to overlap two different curricular areas is to use cooperative learning. However, unlike the previously explained cooperative learning method, in which students work on basically the same objectives, in this form of cooperative learning, the student with disabilities helps the team by working on his or her own objectives. For example, students are placed in groups of five students each, and each group member works on an individualized objective. The group goal is to earn 50 points, and each member of the team can earn 10 points by meeting his or her unique objective:

- Student 1: elementary backstroke for 160 yards (10 points)
- Student 2: scull on back for 30 yards (10 points)
- Student 3: back crawl for 50 yards (10 points)
- Student 4: dive off diving board (10 points)
- Student 5 (student with muscular dystrophy): walk 5 yards in the pool (with assistance for balance from PT)

Therefore, the objective of walking for the student with disabilities is just as important to achieving the team goal as the objective of diving off the diving board for a student without disabilities.

Another way to overlap curricular areas is give the student with a disability a special role within the activity that matches his or her objectives. For example, William can be the permanent "unfreezer" in a game of freeze tag that takes place in the water. When a student gets tagged and is "frozen," William has to walk over to the student and unfreeze him or her by tapping the student on the back. Thus, students work on swimming while William works on walking in a fun, interactive way.

In very unique cases, a student with a disability might not be allowed to swim (e.g., a student with a skin condition, a student who cannot tolerate the cold water). This student still can be part of the group through *alternative activities*. For example, assume that an eleventh grader is just returning to school after a year of rehabilitation following a car accident. Because of some decubitus ulcers (sores resulting from lying or sitting down for long periods of time), the student's doctor has recommended that he not swim. However, because the student's goals include continuing to improve upper-body range of motion as well as grasping and releasing skills, the student throws sponges into the pool (with the help of his teacher assistant) that the other students must retrieve and then take across the pool using whichever stroke they want. Thus, the student gets to interact with peers and work on his unique goals.

Students with disabilities can work on alternative activities in the water, too. To make this alternative activity inclusive, the teacher can rotate peers without disabilities into the activity. For example, the aquatics instructor might set up two stations—one for lap swimming and the other for treading water. At the treading station, the student with disabilities works on stretching on his back with the help of his adapted physical education instructor. Because the students with and without disabilities are practicing their individual skills in the same area, there are increased opportunities for interactions. Similarly, a student who is not allowed to swim could work on bowling using a ramp on the pool deck. Peers who have finished their laps and are resting can go to the student's activity and help set up pins and take turns bowling. Even better, the student with disabilities could roll sponge balls into the pool using the bowling ramp, and peers could retrieve the balls for the student.

Instructional Modifications   Chapter 6 reviews several instructional modifications that should be considered when including students with disabilities

Table 12.3. Accommodations in how information is presented

Instructional factor	General considerations	Modifications for Andrea
Teaching style	Command, problem-solve, discover	Use command
Teaching methodology	Verbal, demos, physical assistance	Verbal, pictures, physical assistance
Student's communication	Verbal, sign, pictures, interpreter	Verbal, pictures
Starting/stopping signals	Whistle, hand signals, physical assistance	Verbal
Time of day	Morning, before lunch, afternoon	Morning—she often sleeps in the afternoon
Duration	Student on task	Short, many tasks
Order of learning	What is the best order of learning?	Likes routine, start with familiar activity first
Size/nature of group	Small/large group	Small group if possible
Group instruction	Station/whole class/peer tutoring	Peer tutoring utilizing TA
Instructional setting	Indoor or outdoor pool	Indoor with warm water
Eliminating distractions	Equipment, lighting, people	Andrea likes to play with flotation devices
Providing structure	Organization of instruction	N/A
Level of difficulty	Complexity of instruction	Simple, skill needs to be broken down; have a peer or TA assist
Level of motivation	Use of reinforcements if necessary	Needs extra verbal reinforcement; loves hugs in the water

in general physical education. These modifications, with slight adaptations, are also relevant to including students with disabilities in general aquatics programs. For example, the class format you choose (e.g., whole group, small groups, stations, peer buddies) could have a profound impact on the degree to which the students with disabilities follow directions and behave in the pool. Similarly, the level of methodology you choose (e.g., verbal cues versus demonstrations versus physical prompts) will affect how well a student with cognitive or sensory disabilities will understand your instructions in the pool. Table 12.3 highlights key instructional factors, considerations, and modifications as they relate to aquatics for a student with disabilities.

Equipment and Task Modifications Equipment and task modifications can make a big difference in the success or failure of a student with disabilities in a general aquatics program. The addition of personal flotation devices (PFDs), kickboards, mats, and other equipment allows a student with disabilities to participate in the same activities as his or her peers. For example, allowing a student to use "floaties" for safety and confidence may help a student with mental retardation requiring extensive support feel comfortable swimming the length of the pool independently. In addition, pool toys can be used to motivate students who are not intrinsically motivated by the pool or by the aquatics instructor's plan. For example, a student with autism who initially is fearful of the pool can be encouraged to stand in the shallow end of the pool for 1–2 minutes while he hits a balloon in the air using his hand (something this student really enjoys).

Table 12.4. Sample task/equipment modifications

Limited strength	• Use Velcro (e.g., for limited grip strength, attach one part of the Velcro on a glove and put the other part on the desired piece of equipment), which should help students to grip. • Use equipment in different sizes, weights, lengths, shapes, and textures. • Use flotation devices if student does not have enough strength to keep him- or herself afloat. • Use switches (e.g., pump-up water guns, switch-activated floating toys).
Limited speed or endurance	• Create special zones in tag games or make area smaller (e.g., tag game in pool is played in a very small space when student who is walking is "it"). • Shorten distances for swimming (e.g., number of laps). • Allow more rest periods for some students. • In relay or tag games, put constraints on students without disabilities (e.g., have to swim using only one side of the body). • In relay races or tag games, have students without disabilities perform more difficult skills (butterfly stroke) or slower strokes (breaststroke).
Limited balance or coordination	• Provide student with a disability with physical assistance if necessary. • Use different types of flotation devices that are more or less buoyant. • Use several flotation devices at once. • Use different water levels (waist deep, chest deep, shoulder deep). • Allow student to hold on to line dividers or edge of pool when doing activities.

There are many types of equipment modifications that can be used for students of varying abilities in different situations. The key is to first determine what the student's strengths and weaknesses are before deciding what equipment might be necessary. For example, a student with visual impairments who has good endurance and strength might require equipment that cues him as to where he is in the pool and when he is getting close to the end of the pool. Similarly, a student who is working on walking balance in the pool can use the side rail of the pool for balance. Table 12.4 presents various types of functional impairments along with suggested equipment and task modifications that can help students overcome these impairments. In addition, Table 12.5 presents other considerations regarding equipment and the pool environment. For more information on adapted aquatics equipment, refer to Lepore et al. (1998) and Priest (1990).

Preparing the General Aquatics Instructor

Most experts support the notion that a key factor for a successful inclusive swimming program is the aquatics instructor (Conatser et al., 2000; Reid, 1979; Weiss & Karper, 1980). Unfortunately, many aquatics instructors have had limited training and experience teaching students with disabilities (Conatser et al., 2000). Despite these limitations, aquatics instructors are still expected to provide

Table 12.5.   Necessary equipment and the pool environment

- Send checklists home with students the day before swimming to remind parents to send a towel, swimsuit, and, if needed, plastic pants, earplugs, goggles, and so forth. Remember that some students with disabilities will need to wear plastic pants because of bladder incontinence or eye protection because of hypersensitive eyes.
- When water temperature is in the 80s, the instructor should be in the water for only 5 hours at a time; when it is in the 90s, the instructor should be in the water for no more than 3 hours at a time.
- Provide towels in case the students forget theirs.
- Personal flotation devices (PFDs) (Type I, II, or III) should fit the student properly (i.e., straps should not leave an impression on the skin for more than a few minutes after release) and should not impede the student's swimming mechanics.
- Swimming/lap pool water temperature should be 76°–78°, 85°–87° for water aerobics, and 90°–94° for therapy pools. Most students with disabilities prefer warmer water due to circulation problems, lack of intense exertion, and/or respiratory problems. However, students with multiple sclerosis usually prefer cooler water.
- The air temperature in the pool area and changing room should be 3° above that of the water temperature.
- If the water temperature is unpleasant and uncontrollable, keep the swimming session short.
- Visible signs need to be posted indicating where the changing room is and where to enter and exit the pool.
- Slip-resistant surfaces should be used in heavy-traffic areas.
- Develop and implement regular inspection and maintenance schedules for all equipment (e.g., ramps, switches, railings and pool lifts, facilities).

appropriate swimming instruction to students with disabilities (American Red Cross, 1992b). Insufficient training and a lack of experience and specific instruction in conducting inclusive aquatics programs are major reasons why aquatics instructors and, consequently, aquatics programs fail (Conatser et al., 2000; Lepore et al., 1998; Priest, 1979). In addition, lack of training and experience leads to unfavorable attitudes toward working with individuals with disabilities in general swimming programs (Conatser et al., 2000). A major part of making an inclusive physical education, recreation, or aquatics program successful is the training, experience, and attitudes of the aquatics instructor (Conatser et al., 2000; Lepore et al., 1998).

The most important thing that can be done to help general aquatics instructors feel more comfortable having a student with disabilities in their general aquatics program is to give them information. Aquatics instructors need information regarding the student with disabilities, activities and objectives on which the student should be working, availability of support (if necessary), the student's behavior, ways to communicate with the student, and adapted equipment needs.

For example, Jamal, a student with autism, is going to be included in a general aquatics class. The aquatics instructor is apprehensive about communicating with this student and about the student's safety in the locker room and in the pool. The team invites the aquatics instructor to three short (15-minute) introductory training sessions during the week of in-services before the school year starts. The art teacher, physical educator, and music teacher are part of this training as well. Team members first explain to the aquatics instructor that Mr. Higgins, Jamal's teacher assistant, will be assisting Jamal when he goes to aquatics on Monday and Friday; and Mrs. Carter, his physical therapist, will be assisting him on Wednesday. The team members also explain to the aquatics instructor that, despite the fact that these people will help Jamal, the instructor is responsible for Jamal as well; the aquatics instructor will help decide what to teach Jamal, reinforce Jamal, decide what equipment Jamal might need to be successful, take responsibility for Jamal's safety in an emergency, and encourage interactions between Jamal and his classmates. Team members then show the aquatics instructor a short videotape in which team members demonstrate how they present information to Jamal using a picture schedule. The team notes that they will create a picture schedule for the aquatics instructor and show him how to use it. Finally, they talk about Jamal's behaviors and how to cope with them. Again, team members ensure the aquatics instructor that Jamal's teacher assistant, Mr. Higgins, knows how to deal with Jamal's behaviors as does the physical therapist, but there are things that the aquatics instructor can do to prevent behavior outbursts (they provide him with a list of these things).

The more information an aquatics instructor has, the more competent he or she will feel working with students with disabilities. However, overwhelming the aquatics instructor with reams of paper and charts will not work. As illustrated previously, brief face-to-face meetings over the course of several days with a variety of team members is the best way to present information. In addition, demonstrating and then physically assisting the aquatics instructor in how to work, communicate, lift, and transfer a student with disabilities will help this instructor feel more confident. Finally, providing ongoing support is critical for the success of the student and the comfort level of the aquatics instructor. Team members should be prepared to assist the aquatics instructor and the student with disabilities several times during the first part of the unit to make sure the aquatics instructor is doing things correctly and feels comfortable with the student (see Chapter 4 for more information on training general physical educators for inclusion).

Preparing Students without Disabilities

Without a doubt, students without disabilities will notice differences in the appearance and/or behavior of students with disabilities who are included in the general aquatics program. As Chapter 9 notes, helping students without disabilities accept, interact, and befriend peers with disabilities can greatly improve the aquatics experience for the student with disabilities. Students without disabilities can benefit from knowing 1) why the student with a disability looks and behaves the way he or she does, 2) why he or she is in the general aquatics class, and 3) what they can do to help this student and make his or her experience as positive as possible. This information can be provided through a relatively informal, 10-minute chat with students in the beginning of the aquatics program. Figure 12.3 presents an outline of this type of presentation for a student with autism who was included in a seventh-grade aquatics class.

Other activities that can help classmates accept peers with disabilities include 1) talking about students with disabilities in general and how swimming can be an important fitness and leisure activity for them; 2) role-playing various types of disabilities in the water, such as trying to swim with your eyes closed or with your legs tied together; 3) inviting guest speakers with disabilities to your class who have benefited from swimming in some way (e.g., a person with mental retardation who has won gold medals in swimming at the Special Olympics); 4) showing videotapes of elite swimmers with disabilities, such as highlights from

---

Who is the student with disabilities?
Jerry is 12 years old, and he has just transferred here from a special school for students with autism. His new homeroom is with Mr. Johnson, so some of you may see him in the morning. Has anyone seen or met Jerry yet?

Why does Jerry look and act the way he does?
Jerry has autism. Has anyone heard of that term before, or do you know anyone who has autism? Autism basically affects the way Jerry learns and deals with his environment. For example, Jerry does not like loud noises. He gets really upset at the fire alarm or when the bell rings between classes. Jerry also does not like change. He will have the most difficult time in the beginning of the aquatics unit because he was used to going to the gym and playing basketball. It will take him a few days to adjust to the new setting and new routine. Jerry also does not talk very well or understand a lot of what you say. However, you can still talk to him; just talk slower and use shorter sentences. He really does best when you show him what you want. Finally, Jerry gets confused easily and doesn't always know what to do. His way of coping with this is to withdraw into his own little world, not look at anyone, and sometimes make strange sounds or do strange things with his arms and hands. But Jerry will not harm you, and he really likes being around kids his own age. Does anyone have any questions?

Why is he in our class?
Jerry is the same age and in the same grade that you are in, and his parents and teachers felt that Jerry would enjoy swimming and would benefit from being around other students his age. His parents, in particular, were hoping that some of you would help Jerry and even try to be his friend. Do some of you think you can help Jerry and try to be his friend?

What can we do to help?
Even though Jerry comes to aquatics with Mrs. Brady, his teacher assistant, we need all of you to help us watch out for Jerry. Mrs. Brady and I are here to help Jerry, but it would be great if you all would help him, too. We want Jerry to learn how to respond and interact with kids his own age rather than just with adults. What are some things you think you can do to help Jerry? Here are some other things you can do. Sometimes he does not know where he is supposed to go, so you can tell him or show him where to go. If he seems confused about what he is supposed to do, you can repeat my directions but in a simpler way. If he begins to get anxious and makes strange sounds and movements, simply go up to him and tell him to stop. This usually works. And the big thing is to just go up to him whenever you can and talk to him, be his friend, include him in activities and conversations, and just try to make him feel comfortable and part of the group. If you ever have any questions, just ask me or Mrs. Brady.

Figure 12.3.   Sample discussion to prepare peers without disabilities for inclusion of a student with autism.

the Paralympics; 5) providing specific information about the student who will be coming to the class (focus on abilities rather than just disabilities); and 6) demonstrating ways that students without disabilities can support the student in the pool and in the locker room. The key is doing everything possible to help peers without disabilities feel comfortable with the student with disabilities and to increase their willingness to help and befriend the student.

Preparing Support Personnel

Many students with severe disabilities come to an aquatics class with a teacher assistant or other support person (e.g., peer tutor, community volunteer). These support personnel are committed to helping the students with disabilities, yet they often have no formal training or experience in working with students with disabilities in aquatics. Therefore, these support personnel typically are unsure of exactly what they should be doing with the students with disabilities in aquatics. Obviously, such a situation prevents the student with disabilities from learning targeted objectives and even can be dangerous, depending on what activities the support person chooses to attempt. For example, a student with cerebral palsy may require help getting into the pool and may do best with a particular flotation device and certain types of physical assistance. The teacher assistant, however, may not be aware of this information. Therefore, he or she may attempt to carry the student into the pool in a manner that is unsafe for both the assistant and the student, use flotation devices incorrectly, and ineffectively assist the student with skill development. Consequently, the student probably will not learn the targeted objectives and may, in fact, be in danger of injury. Clearly, careful training of support personnel is a critical part of the inclusion process.

Training of support personnel for assisting a student with disabilities in aquatics should be the ongoing responsibility of all team members. Training should focus on 1) general information about the support person's role, 2) specific information about the student with whom the support person will be working, and 3) how the support person will facilitate the inclusion of the student into the general aquatics program. Table 12.6 suggests specific information that team members should provide to support personnel who will work in an aquatics environment. Note how much information the aquatics instructor can (and should) contribute to the training of the support personnel.

Other Considerations for Inclusion in Aquatics Programs

Lifting, Transferring, and Positioning

It is beyond the scope of this chapter to detail each of the various ways to lift, transfer, and position students with disabilities in the pool environment. Carter et al. (1994) and Lepore et al. (1998) provide detailed information on lifting and transferring in aquatics. Still, there are some general considerations that need to be taken into account when lifting, transferring, and positioning students with physical disabilities in the pool area. Pool lifts, portable or stationary ramps, railing systems, or two- to four-man lifts are all appropriate ways for students with physical limitations to enter and exit the water. The exact type of lift will depend on the student's abilities and disabilities. Consult the student's physical or occupational therapist and ask him or her to show you the most appropriate way to lift a student and transfer him or her into the pool; then, practice lifting and transferring the student while the specialist is present to provide additional instruction if necessary. Note that regardless of the technique, the utmost safety for all involved needs to be ensured. Inappropriate techniques can frighten or injure the student or the instructor. Table 12.7 provides general guidelines for lifting and transferring in the pool.

Safety Considerations

The aquatics environment contains many potentially serious hazards (e.g., falling on a wet floor; being submerged in the water, which could cause brain damage); therefore, aquatics instructors need to be on guard for possible problems con-

Table 12.6.   Preparing support personnel for aquatics

Information	Team member who can provide information
Provide general information (perhaps in the form of a brochure or handout) regarding the support person's role as a support person and what is expected of him or her.	Aquatics instructor, APE specialist
Provide information regarding the philosophy of the aquatics program and the general goals that the student might work on during aquatics (e.g., opportunities to interact with peers without disabilities, improve social behavior, improve communication skills, improve independence in a variety of functional skills).	Aquatics instructor, APE specialist, special education teacher
Provide information regarding resources and key personnel to whom they can go with questions or if they need help (e.g., go to the aquatics instructor or adapted physical educator if they have questions regarding modifying specific aquatics activities; go to the physical therapist if they have specific questions about positioning or contraindicated activities).	APE specialist, special education teacher
Provide detailed description of student, including IEP objectives related to aquatics, medical/health concerns, unique behaviors, likes and dislikes, special friends, and so forth.	APE specialist, special education teacher, parents
Describe specific information regarding safety/emergency procedures for the pool area (e.g., what to do if a student has a seizure or an asthma attack, how to make sure particular students warm up properly)	Aquatics instructor, APE specialist, nurse, parents
Provide general suggestions for modifying activities and instructions for the use of adapted equipment.	Aquatics instructor, APE specialist, PT
Provide alternative activities when general aquatics activities are deemed inappropriate (e.g., when kids are working on diving, student can work on entering and exiting the pool with assistance).	Aquatics instructor, APE specialist
Provide several suggestions for facilitating interactions with peers without disabilities.	APE specialist, special education teacher, parents

APE = adapted physical education; PT = physical therapist.

stantly. "Pool hazards exist in any aquatics programs, but are a greater risk for some individuals with disabilities. The person's vision, balance, sense of direction, concept of space, perception of space and distance, and muscular control should all be considered" (Red Cross, 1992a, p. 217a). For example, a teacher assistant was helping Josh, a student with autism, dress in the locker room. The teacher assistant turned his back on Josh for what seemed like a second, and Josh, now fully dressed, ran out of the locker room and jumped into the pool!

Most aquatics instructors are already very aware of safety issues for their general education students. However, they have to be even more aware of po-

Table 12.7.   General guidelines instructors should consider before lifting students

- How heavy is the student (heavier students may need two people or a mechanical lift)?
- Does the student have a seizure disorder? What triggers the seizure?
- Does the student have primitive reflexes, and are these reflexes stimulated by vestibular movement or tactile pressure (could cause student to thrust into extension)?
- Does the student have joint deformities or limited range of motion requiring unusual grip placement?
- Is the student's motor control and strength limited, making arm and leg movements difficult at best?
- Are you using your legs when picking up the student (i.e., and not bending at the waist, never lifting and twisting simultaneously)?
- Are you lifting the student completely out of his or her chair before turning? Do you turn by walking using your feet rather than twisting using your back?
- Do you ensure that the wheelchair brakes are locked and/or electric wheelchair is turned off prior to moving the student?
- Do you make sure student's straps are off and out of the way before lifting begins?

tential risks, safety precautions, and emergency techniques when students with disabilities are included in their general aquatics classes. Chapter 10 provides information regarding sending home medical information forms for the student's parents to fill out, which can provide a great deal of information about medications, seizure disorders, diabetes, and other health/medical problems that could affect the student's safety in the pool. Readers are encouraged to read this chapter carefully. In addition, Table 12.8 provides safety guidelines with specific reference to aquatics.

In some cases, it may be contraindicated for students with disabilities to participate in swimming programs. Some situations in which a student with or without a disability should not be allowed in the pool include 1) contact precautions (e.g., bacterial infections), 2) open or oozing wounds, 3) conjunctivitis (pink eye), 4) ring worm, 5) lice, and 6) menses without protection. Although other students with disabilities may be allowed in the pool, they may have medical equipment that requires special precautions. Talk with the student's physician, physical therapist, parent, or other knowledgeable person about any necessary precautions. Examples of medical equipment or conditions requiring precautions include 1) staples or stitches, 2) any indwelling tube, such as nasogastric or peg tubes, 3) bowel and bladder incontinence, 4) tracheostomies, 5) fluctuating blood pressure, 6) healing wounds (that need covering), 7) limited respiratory function, 8) cardiac insufficiencies, and 9) seizures.

Some students have disabilities (e.g., spinal injury, traumatic brain injury, multiple sclerosis, spina bifida) that may inhibit their ability to feel pressure and/or pain or to adjust and compensate for extreme hot or cold water. Extra attention needs to be given to cuts, bruises, scrapes, and overexertion in hot water or prolonged periods in cold water. Furthermore, "taking precautions" in the aquatics environment does not mean that students should not participate. Instructors and aquatics personnel merely need to devise safety guidelines and/or adapt instruction to consider the student's condition.

Table 12.8.   Safety guidelines and considerations for aquatics

- Ensure that parents'/guardians' permission report has been signed. The report should include a place for students' personal and medical characteristics (see form in Chapter 10).
- Have a signed eligibility report by a licensed physician. The report should include type of impairment, precautions, restrictions, and recommendations.
- Before the student comes to the pool, make sure all necessary paperwork is properly processed.
- Keep effective incident report documents.
- Lifeguards, instructors, and aquatics administrators need sufficient supervisory skills with current credentials and certifications appropriate to their area of responsibility.
    Lifeguards: (1) Lifeguard Training, (2) CPR, (3) Standard First Aid, and (4) on-site inservice
    Aquatics Instructors: (1) Water Safety Instructor Certification, (2) Lifeguard Training, (3) CPR, (4) Standard First Aid, (5) on-site in-service
    Aquatics Administrators: (1) Water Safety Instructor certification or Lifeguard Training Instructor, (2) CPR, (3) Standard First Aid, (4) pool operator training or additional experience/training, (5) good personal attributes and management skills
- Conduct regular on-site in-services for aquatics staff, and include information about specific students with disabilities who will be using the facility and specific problems that might be associated with those particular students.
- Never, under any circumstances, leave individuals with disabilities unattended in or around a pool.
- The instructor to student ratio for testing should be one to three for students with severe disabilities and one to six for students with mild disabilities. Factors that may influence this ratio include the student's age and his or her physical, cognitive, and social skills. In addition, the instructor or teacher assistant's competence, confidence, and attitude toward inclusion will contribute to the size and ratio of the class.
- Be aware of the location of the pool's emergency plan, first aid equipment, rescue equipment, and phone.
- Before entering the pool area, all rules should be explained clearly to the student. Rules need to be explained at the student's level (e.g., pictures, demonstrations, sign language). Rules often include no diving, running, horseplay, climbing on benches or railing, and so forth. All rules should be posted in a clearly defined space.
- Try to keep the floors of all decks, ramps, and changing areas dry and free of objects.
- Store unused equipment that could become a hazard around the pool.
- Glass or breakable items should be prohibited in the pool area.
- Scum gutters collect the pool's unwanted bacteria and items, so encourage swimmers to avoid them.
- Keep environmental noise to a minimum around the pool.
- Wheelchairs should be locked or turned off (if electric) and stored out of the way when not in use.
- Clearly mark varying water depths steps, slides, diving areas, ramps, and lifts in the pool.
- Clearly mark rules and safety procedures for pool equipment and paraphernalia.
- During cold weather, allow students ample time to dry completely before exiting the facility.
- Make provisions if the pool is outside (e.g., sunscreen, shade, clothing).
- Know your local weather conditions and have alternate plans if needed.
- Develop, use, and maintain a comprehensive reevaluation plan of every aspect of your facility (i.e., equipment, personnel, instruction, safety).
- Always shower after being in the pool and use plenty of lotion on your skin; advise your students to do the same.

References

Adams, R., & McCubbin, J. (1991). *Games, sports and exercises for the physically disabled* (4th ed.). Philadelphia: Lea & Febiger.

Alberto, P.A., & Troutman, A.C. (1990). *Applied behavior analysis for teachers*. Columbus, OH: Merrill.

American Red Cross. (1992a). *American Red Cross swimming and diving*. St. Louis: Mosby–Year Book.

American Red Cross. (1992b). *Water safety instructor's manual*. St. Louis: Mosby–Year Book.

Americans with Disabilities Act (ADA) of 1990, PL 101-336, 42 U.S.C. §§ 12101 *et seq.*

Appenzeller, H. (1983). *The right to participate*. Charlottesville, VA: Michie.

Appenzeller, H., & Appenzeller, T. (1980). *Sports and the courts*. Charlottesville, VA: Michie.

Aquatic sports. (1993, July-August). *Exceptional Parent*, 30–31.

Arbogast, G., & Lavay, B. (1986). Combining students with different ability levels in games and sports. *Physical Educator*, 44, 255–259.

Armstrong, C.A., Rosengard, P.F., Condon, S.A., Sallis, J.F., & Bernal, R.F. (1993). *Self management program: Level 2*. San Diego: San Diego University Foundation.

Arnold, J.B., & Dodge, H.W. (1994). Room for all. *The American School Board Journal*, 22–26.

Aufsesser, P.M. (1991). Mainstreaming and the least restrictive environment: How do they differ? *Palaestra*, 7(2), 31–34.

Auxter, D., Pyfer, J., & Huettig, C. (1997). *Principles and methods of adapted physical education and recreation* (8th ed.). Madison, WI: Brown & Benchmark.

Bateman, B.D. (1996). *Better IEPs*. Longmont, CO: Sopris West.

Bateman, B.D., & Chad, D.J. (1995). Legal demands and constraints on placement decisions. In J.M. Kauffman, J.W. Lloyd, D.P. Hallahan, & T.A. Astuto (Eds.), *Issues in educational placement*. Mahwah, NJ: Lawrence Erlbaum Associates.

Bayley, N. (1969). *Manual for the Bayley Scales of Infant Development*. New York: The Psychological Corporation.

Beirne-Smith, M., Patton, J.R., & Ittenbach, R. (1994). *Mental retardation* (4th ed.). Upper Saddle River, NJ: Prentice Hall.

Berry, W.D. (1990). Contemporary trends in aquatics. *Journal of Physical Education, Recreation and Dance*, 60(5), 35.

Biskupic, J. (1999, March 4). Disabled pupils win right to medical aid. *The Washington Post*, p. A1.

Black, H.C. (1990). *Black's law dictionary* (6th ed.). St. Paul, MN: West.

Blinde, E. M., & McCallister, S. G. (1998). Listening to the voices of students with disabilities. *Journal of Physical Education, Recreation and Dance*, 69(6), 64–68.

Block, M.E. (1991). The motor development of children with Down syndrome: A review of the literature. *Adapted Physical Activity Quarterly*, 8, 179–209.

Block, M.E. (1992). What is appropriate physical education for students with the most profound disabilities? *Adapted Physical Activity Quarterly*, 9, 197–213.

Block, M.E. (1994a). All kids can have physical education the regular way. In M.S. Moon (Ed.), *Just for the fun of it: Community physical education and leisure programs* (pp. 137–162) Baltimore: Paul H. Brookes Publishing Co.

Block, M.E. (1994b). *A Teacher's Guide to Including Students with Disabilities in Regular Physical Education*. Baltimore: Paul H. Brookes Publishing Co.

Block, M.E. (1994c). Why all students with disabilities should be included in regular physical education. *Palaestra*, 10(3), 17–24.

Block, M.E. (1995a). Development and validation of Children's Attitudes towards Integrated Physical Education–Revised (CAIPE-R) Inventory. *Adapted Physical Activity Quarterly*, 12, 60–77.

Block, M.E. (1995b). Using task sheets to facilitate peer tutoring of students with disabilities. *Strategies*, 8(7), 9–11.

Block, M.E. (1996). Implications of U.S. federal law and court cases for physical education placement of students with disabilities. *Adapted Physical Activity Quarterly*, 13, 127–152.

Block, M.E. (1998). Don't forget the social aspects of inclusion. *Strategies, 12*(2), 30–34.

Block, M.E. (1999a). Part 1: Did we jump on the wrong bandwagon? Problems with inclusion in physical education. *Palaestra, 15*(3), 30–38.

Block, M.E. (1999b). Part 2: Did we jump on the wrong bandwagon? Making general physical education work. *Palaestra, 15*(4), 34–42.

Block, M.E., & Block, V.E. (1999). Functional versus developmental motor assessment for children with severe disabilities. In P. Jansma (Ed.), *The psychomotor domain and the seriously handicapped* (5th ed.). Lanham, MD: University Press of America.

Block, M.E., & Brady, W. (1999). Welcoming children with disabilities into regular physical education. *Teaching Elementary Physical Education, 10*(1), 30–32.

Block, M.E., & Burke, K. (1999). Are your children receiving appropriate physical education? *Teaching Exceptional Children, 31*(3), 18–23.

Block, M.E., & Conatser, P. (1999). Consultation in adapted physical education. *Adapted Physical Activity Quarterly, 16,* 9–26.

Block, M.E., & Garcia, C. (Eds.). (1995). *A position statement on inclusion in physical education.* Reston, VA: National Association of Sport and Physical Education (NASPE).

Block, M.E., & Horton, M.H. (1996). Include safety: Do not exclude children with disabilities from regular physical education. *The Physical Educator, 53,* 58–72.

Block, M.E., & Krebs, P.L. (1992). An alternative to least restrictive environments: A continuum of support to regular physical education. *Adapted Physical Activity Quarterly, 9,* 97–113.

Block, M.E., & Malloy, M. (1998). Attitudes of girls towards including a child with severe disabilities in a regular fast-pitch softball league. *Mental Retardation, 36,* 137–144.

Block, M.E., Oberweiser, B., & Bain, M. (1995). Utilizing classwide peer tutoring to facilitate inclusion of students with disabilities in regular physical education. *Physical Educator, 52*(1), 47–56.

Block, M.E., & Provis, S. (1992, October). *Effects of ball size on throwing patterns in children with Down Syndrome.* Paper presented at the North American Federation of Adapted Physical Activity Symposium. Montreal, Canada.

Block, M.E., Provis, S., & Nelson, E. (1994). Accommodating students with severe disabilities in regular physical education: Extending traditional skill stations. *Palaestra, 10*(1), 32–38.

Block, M.E., & Rizzo, T.L. (1995). Attitudes and attributes of physical education teachers towards including students with severe and profound disabilities into regular physical education. *Journal of The Association for Persons with Severe Handicaps, 20,* 80–87.

Block, M.E., & Vogler, E.W. (1994). Including children with disabilities in regular physical education: The research base. *Journal of Physical Education, Recreation, and Dance, 65*(1), 40–44.

Block, M.E., & Zeman, R. (1996). Including students with disabilities into regular physical education: Effects on nondisabled children. *Adapted Physical Activity Quarterly, 13,* 38–49.

Brasher, B., & Holbrook, M.C. (1996). Early intervention and special education. In M.C. Holbrook (Ed.), *Children with visual impairments: A parent's guide* (pp. 175–204). Bethesda, MD: Woodbine House.

Bricker, D. (1995). The challenge of inclusion. *Journal of Early Intervention, 19,* 179–194.

Bricker, D., & Cripe, J.J.W. (1992). *An activity-based approach to early intervention.* Baltimore: Paul H. Brookes Publishing Co.

Broach, E., & Dattilo, J. (1996). Aquatic therapy: Making waves in therapeutic recreation. *Parks & Recreation, 31*(7), 38–43.

Brown v. Board of Educ., 347 U.S. 483 (1954).

Brown, J.D., & Richter, J. (1994). How to handle blood and body fluid spills. *Strategies, 7*(7), 23–25.

Brown, L. (1994, December). *Including students with significant intellectual disabilities in regular education.* Paper present at the Annual Conference of The Association for Persons with Severe Handicaps, Atlanta, GA.

Brown, L., Branston, M.B., Hamre-Nietupski, S., Pumpian, I., Certo, N., & Gruenewald, L. (1979). A strategy for developing chronological-age-appropriate and functional curricular content for severely handicapped adolescents and young adults. *The Journal of Special Education, 13,* 81–90.

Brown, L., Long, E., Udvari-Solner, A., Schwarz, P., VanDeventer, P., Ahlgren, C., Johnson, F., Gruenewald, L., & Jorgensen, J. (1989). Should students with severe intellectual disabilities be based in regular or in special education classrooms in home schools? *Journal of The Association for Persons with Severe Handicaps, 14,* 8–12.

Brown, L., Schwarz, P., Udvari-Solner, A., Kampschroer-Frattura, E., Johnson, F., Jorgensen, J., & Gruenewald, L. (1991). How much time should students with severe intellectual disabilities spend in regular education classrooms or elsewhere? *Journal of The Association for Persons with Severe Handicaps, 16,* 39–47.

Bruininks, R.H. (1978). *Bruininks-Oseretsky Test of Motor Proficiency: Examiner's Manual.* Circle Pines, MN: American Guidance Service.

Bryant, M.D., & Graham, A.M. (1993). *Implementing early intervention from research to effective practice.* New York: Guilford Press.

Butterfield, S.A. (1993). Exercise-induced asthma: A manageable problem. *Journal of Physical Education, Recreation, and Dance, 64,* 15–18.

Carnine, D. (1991). Direct instruction applied to mathematics for the general education classroom. In J.W. Lloyd, N.N. Singh, & A.C. Repp (Eds.), *The regular education initiative: Alternative perspectives on concepts, issues, and models* (pp. 163–176). Sycamore, IL: Sycamore Press.

Carter, M.J., Dolan, M.A., & LeConey, S.P. (1994). *Designing instructional swim programs for individuals with disabilities.* Reston, VA: American Association for Leisure and Recreation (AALR)/American Alliance for Health, Physical Education, Recreation, and Dance (AAHPERD).

Chadsey-Rusch, J. (1990). Social interactions of secondary-aged students with severe handicaps: Implications for facilitating the transition from school to work. *Journal of The Association for Persons with Severe Handicaps, 15,* 69–78.

Chandler, J.P., & Greene, J.L. (1995). A statewide survey of adapted physical education service delivery and teacher in-service training. *Adapted Physical Activity Quarterly, 12,* 262–274.

Chaves, I.M. (1977). Historical overview of special education in the United States. In P. Bates, T.L. West, & R.B. Schmerl (Eds.), *Mainstreaming: Problems, potentials, and perspectives* (pp. 25–41). Minneapolis: National Support Systems Project.

Christies, I. (1985). Aquatics for the handicapped: A review of literature. *Physical Educator, 42*(1), 24–33.

CIRA/Canadian Association of Health, Physical Education, and Recreation (CAHPER). (1994). *Moving to inclusion.* Gloucester, Ontario, Canada: Author.

Clark, G., French, R., & Henderson, H. (1985). Teaching techniques that develop positive attitudes. *Palaestra, 5*(3), 14–17.

Conatser, P., Block, M.E., & Lepore, M. (2000). Aquatic instructor's attitude toward teaching students with disabilities. *Adapted Physical Activity Quarterly, 14,* 38–49.

Condon, M.E., York, R., & Heal, L.W. (1986). Acceptance of severely handicapped students by nonhandicapped peers. *Journal of The Association for Persons with Severe Handicaps, 11,* 216–219.

Cooper Institute for Aerobics Research. (1992). *The Prudential Fitnessgram test administration manual.* Dallas: Author.

Cotton, D. (1994). Students acting as teachers: Who is liable? *Strategies, 8,* 23–25.

Council for Exceptional Children. (1975). What is mainstreaming? *Exceptional Children, 42,* 174.

Council for Exceptional Children. (1999). *IEP team guide.* Reston, VA: Author.

Council on Physical Education for Children. (1992). *Developmental appropriate physical education practices for children.* Reston, VA: Author.

Covey, S.R. (1989). *The 7 habits of highly effective people.* New York: Fireside/Simon & Shuster.

Cowden, J.E., & Eason, R.L. (1991). Legislative terminology affecting adapted physical education. *Journal of Physical Education, Recreation, and Dance, 62*(8), 34.

Craig, S.E., Haggart, A.G., & Hull, K.M. (1999). Integrating therapies into the educational setting: Strategies for supporting children with severe disabilities. *Education and Related Services, 17,* 91–110.

Daniels, S.A. (1954). *Adapted physical education.* New York: Harper & Brothers.

Dattilo, J. (1991). Recreation and leisure: A review of the literature and recommendations for future directions. In L.H. Meyer, C.A. Peck, & L. Brown (Eds.), *Critical issues in the lives of people with severe disabilities* (pp. 171–194). Baltimore: Paul H. Brookes Publishing Co.

Davis, W.E. (1984). Motor ability assessment of populations with handicapping conditions: Challenging basic assumptions. *Adapted Physical Activity Quarterly, 1,* 125–140.

Davis, W.E., & Burton, A.W. (1991). Ecological task analysis: Translating movement behavior theory into practice. *Adapted Physical Activity Quarterly, 8,* 154–177.

Depaepe, J.L. (1984). Mainstreaming malpractice. *Physical Educator, 41,* 51–56.

Dougherty, A.M. (1995). *Case studies in human services consultation.* Pacific Grove, CA: Brooks/Cole.

Dougherty, N.J. (1987). Legal responsibility for safety in physical education and sport. In N.J. Dougherty (Ed.), *Principles of safety in physical education and sport* (pp. 15–22). Reston, VA: American Alliance of Health, Physical Education, Recreation, and Dance (AAHPERD).

Downing, J.E. (1996). *Including students with severe and multiple disabilities in typical classrooms.* Baltimore: Paul H. Brookes Publishing Co.

Doyle, M.B. (1997). *The paraprofessional's guide to the inclusive classroom.* Baltimore: Paul H. Brookes Publishing Co.

DuBow, S. (1989). Into the turbulent mainstream: A legal perspective on the weight given to the least restrictive environment in placement decisions for deaf children. *Journal of Law and Education, 18,* 215–228.

Dunn, J. (1997). *Special physical education* (7th ed.). Madison, WI: Brown & Benchmark.

Dunn, L.M. (1968). Special education for the mildly retarded: Is much of it justifiable? *Exceptional Children, 35,* 5–22.

Education for All Handicapped Children Act (EHA) of 1975, PL 94-142, 20 U.S.C. §§1400 *et seq.*

Education of Handicapped Children: Implementation of part B of the Education of the Handicapped Act. (1977, August 23). 42(163) Fed. Reg. 42, 474–42, 518.

Eichstaedt, C.B., & Lavay, B.W. (1992). *Physical activity for individuals with mental retardation.* Champaign, IL: Human Kinetics.

Ellmo, W., & Graser, J. (1995). *Adapted adventure activities.* Dubuque, IA: Kendall/Hunt.

Exceptional Parent Staff (1993, July-August, 1993). Aquatic sports. *Exceptional Parent,* 30–31.

Fairfax County Public Schools. (1994). *Fairfax County Public Schools: Physician Referral Form—Physical Education.* Fairfax, VA: Author.

Falvey, M.A., & Rosenberg, R.L. (1995). Developing and fostering friendships. In M.A. Falvey (Ed.), *Inclusive and heterogeneous schooling: Assessment, curriculum, and instruction* (pp. 267–284). Baltimore: Paul H. Brookes Publishing Co.

Falvey, M. A., Forest, M., Pearpoint, J. & Rosenberg, R. L. (1997). All my life's a circle: USing the tools: Circles, MAPS, & PATH. Toronto: Inclusion Press.

Ferguson, D.L. (1995). The real challenge of inclusion: Confessions of a "rabid inclusionist." *Phi Delta Kappan, 77*(4), 281–306.

Fluegelman, A. (1976). *New games book.* New York: Doubleday & Company.

Fluegelman, A. (1980). *More new games.* New York: Doubleday & Company.

Folio, M. & DuBose, R.F. (1974). *Peabody Development Motor Scales.* Nashville, TN: George Peabody College for Teachers.

Forest, M., & Lusthaus, E. (1989). Promoting educational equality for all students: Circles and maps. In S. Stainback, W. Stainback, & M. Forest (Eds.), *Educating all students in the mainstream of regular education* (pp. 43–58). Baltimore: Paul H. Brookes Publishing Co.

Forest, M., Pearpoint, J., & O'Brien, J. (1996). MAPs, Circle of Friends, and PATH: Powerful tools to help build caring communities. In S.W. Stainback & W. Stainback (Eds.), *Inclusion: A guide for educators* (pp. 67–86). Baltimore: Paul H. Brookes Publishing Co.

French, R., Keele, M., & Silliman-French, L. (1997). Students with shunts: Program considerations. *Journal of Physical Education, Recreation, and Dance, 68*(l), 54–56.

Gabbard, C. (2000). *Lifelong motor development* (3rd ed.). Needham Heights, MA: Allyn & Bacon.

Gallahue, D.L. (1996). *Developmental physical education for today's children* (3rd ed.). Madison, WI: Brown & Benchmark.

Gallahue, D.L., & Ozmun, J.C. (1998). *Understanding motor development* (4th ed.). Boston: WC Brown/ McGraw-Hill.

Geis, G.C. (1975). Therapeutic aquatics program for quadriplegia. *American Corrective Therapy Journal, 29*(5), 155–157.

Getskow, V., & Konczal, D. (1996). *Kids with special needs.* Santa Barbara, CA: The Learning Works, Inc.

Giangreco, M.F. (1997). *Quick-guides to inclusion.* Baltimore: Paul H. Brookes Publishing Co.

Giangreco, M.F., & Putnam, J.W. (1991). Supporting the education of students with severe disabilities in regular education environments. In L.H. Meyer, C.A. Peck, & L. Brown (Eds.), *Critical issues in the lives of people with severe disabilities* (pp. 245–270). Baltimore: Paul H. Brookes Publishing Co.

Givner, C.C., & Haager, D. (1995). Strategies for effective collaboration. In M.A. Falvey (Ed.), *Inclusive and heterogeneous schooling: Assessment, curriculum, and instruction* (pp. 41–57). Baltimore: Paul H. Brookes Publishing Co.

Goldstein, S. (1995). *Understanding and managing children's classroom behavior.* New York: John Wiley & Sons.

Graff, J.C., Ault, M.M., Guess, D., Taylor, M., & Thompson, B. (1990). *Health care for students with disabilities.* Baltimore: Paul H. Brookes Publishing Co.

Graham, G., Holt/Hale, S., & Parker, M. (1998). *Children moving: A reflective approach to teaching physical education* (4th ed.). Mountain View, CA: Mayfield.

Gray, G.R. (1995). Safety tips from the expert witness. *Journal of Physical Education, Recreation, and Dance, 66*(l), 18–21.

Grineski, S. (1996). *Cooperative learning in physical education.* Champaign, IL: Human Kinetics.

Grosse, S. (1991). Is the mainstream always a better place to be? *Palaestra, 7*(2), 40–49.

Grosse, S. (1995). Try a water aerobics course. *Strategies, 9*(3), 18–21.

Grosse, S. (1996). Aquatics for individuals with disabilities: Challenges for the 21st century. *International Council for Health, Physical Education, Recreation, Sport, and Dance, 33*(1), 27–29.

Grosse, S.J. (1990). How safe are your mainstreamed students? *Strategies, 4*(2), 11–13.

Gutkin, T.B., & Curtis, M.J. (1982). School-based consultation: Theory and techniques. In C.R. Reynolds & T.B. Gutkin (Eds.), *The handbook of school psychology* (pp. 796–828). New York: John Wiley & Sons.

Hanft, B.E., & Place, P.A. (1996). *The consulting therapist.* San Antonio, TX: Therapy Skill Builders.

Hastad, D.N., & Lacy, A.C. (1989). *Measurement and evaluation in contemporary physical education.* Scottesdale, AZ: Gorsuch, Scarisbrick.

Helmstetter, E. (1989). Curriculum for school-age students: The ecological model. In F. Brown & D.H. Lehr (Eds.), *Persons with profound disabilities: Issues and practices* (pp. 239–264). Baltimore: Paul H. Brookes Publishing Co.

Henderson, H., & French, R. (1989). Negative reinforcement or punishment? *Journal of Physical Education, Recreation and Dance, 60*(5), 4.

Henderson, H., & French, R. (1990, Winter). How to use verbal reprimands in a positive manner. *Physical Educator,* 193–196.

Henderson, H., & French, R. (1993). *Creative approaches to managing student behavior* (2nd ed.). Park City, UT: Family Development Resources.

Herkowitz, J. (1978). Developmental task analysis: The design of movement experiences and evaluation of motor development status. In M. Ridenour (Ed.), *Motor development: Issues and applications* (pp. 139–164). Princeton, NJ: Princeton Book Co.

Heron, T.E., & Harris, K.C. (1993). *The educational consultant: Helping professionals, parents, and mainstreamed students* (3rd ed.). Austin, TX: PRO-ED.

Hollis, J., & Gallegos, E. (1993). Inclusion: What is the extent of a school district's duty to accommodate students with disabilities in the regular classroom? *Legal Digest 9*(9), 1–8, 17.

Horvat, M.A., & Forbus, W.R. (1989). *Using the aquatic environment for teaching handicapped children* (2nd ed.). Kearney, NE: Educational Systems Associates.

Horvat, M.A., Forbus, W.R., & Van Kirk, L. (1987). *Teacher and parent guide for the physical development of mentally handicapped in the aquatic environment.* Athens: The University of Georgia, Department of Physical Education.

Houston-Wilson, C., Dunn, J.M., van der Mars, H., & McCubbin, J. (1997). The effects of peer tutors on the motor performance in integrated physical education classes. *Adapted Physical Activity Quarterly, 14,* 298–313.

Houston-Wilson, C., Lieberman, L. Horton, M., & Kasser, S. (1997). Peer tutoring: A plan for instructing students of all abilities. *Journal of Physical Education, Recreation, and Dance, 68*(6), 39–44.

Hutzler, Y., Chacham, A., Bergman, U., & Szeinberg, A. (1997). Effects of exercise on respiration in children with cerebral palsy. *Palaestra, 13*(4), 20–24.

Individuals with Disabilities Education Act (IDEA) Amendments of 1997, PL 105-17, 20 U.S.C. §§ 1400 *et seq.*

Individuals with Disabilities Education Act (IDEA) of 1990, PL 101-476, 20 U.S.C., §§ 1400 *et seq.*

Janney, R.F., Snell, M.E., Beers, M.K., & Raynes, M. (1995). Integrating students with moderate and severe disabilities into general education classes. *Exceptional Children, 61,* 425–439.

Jansma, P. (1978). Operant conditioning principles applied to disturbed male adolescents by a physical educator. *American Corrective Therapy Journal, 32*(3), 71–78.

Jansma, P., & Decker, J. (1990). *Project LRE/PE: Least restrictive environment usage in physical education.* Washington, DC: U.S. Department of Education, Office of Special Education.

Jansma, P., & French, R. (1994). *Special physical education.* Englewood Cliffs, NJ: Prentice Hall.

Johnson, D.W., & Johnson, R.T. (1989). Cooperative learning and mainstreaming. In R. Gaylord-Ross (Ed.), *Integration strategies for students with handicaps* (pp. 233–248). Baltimore: Paul H. Brookes Publishing Co.

Johnston, T., & Wayda, V.K. (1994). Are you an effective communicator? *Strategies, 7*(5), 9–13.

Karagiannis, A., Stainback, W., & Stainback, S. (1996). Rationale for inclusive schooling. In S. Stainback & W. Stainback (Eds.), *Inclusion: A guide for educators* (pp. 3–16). Baltimore: Paul H. Brookes Publishing Co.

Kasser, S.L. (1995). *Inclusive games.* Champaign, IL: Human Kinetics.

Kauffman, J.M. (1993). How we might achieve the radical reform of special education. *Exceptional Children, 60,* 294–309.

Kauffman, J.M., Mostert, M.P., Trent, S.C., & Hallahan, D.P. (1998). *Managing classroom behavior* (2nd ed.). Needham Heights, MA: Allyn & Bacon.

Kelly, L. (1994). Preplanning for successful inclusive schooling. *Journal of Physical Education, Recreation and Dance, 65*(1), 37–38.

Kelly, L.E. (1991). National standards for adapted physical education. *Advocate, 20*(1), 2–3.

Kelly, L.E. (1995). *Adapted physical education national standards.* Champaign, IL: Human Kinetics.

Kelly, L.E. (1998). National certification in adapted physical education. *Virginia Journal of Physical Education, Recreation and Dance, 20*(1), 21–22.

Kelly, L.E., et al. (1991). *Achievement-based curriculum: Teaching manual.* Charlottesville: University of Virginia.

Kelly, L.E., & Gansneder, B.M. (1998). Preparation and job demographics of adapted physical educators in the United States. *Adapted Physical Activity Quarterly, 15,* 141–154.

Kelly, L.E., & Wessel, J.A. (1996). *Achievement-based curriculum development in physical education.* Philadelphia: Lea & Febiger.

Kimble, K.B., Ball, B., & Jansma, P. (1999). Role of the physical therapist and occupational therapist: Addressing serious disabilities. In P. Jansma (Ed.), *The psychomotor domain and the seriously handicapped* (4th ed., pp. 67–74). Lanham, MD: University Press of America.

Kirchner, G. (1992). *Physical education for elementary school children* (8th ed.). Madison, WI: WC Brown & Benchmark.

Kirchner, G., & Fishburne, G.J. (1998). *Physical education for elementary school children* (10th ed.). Boston: WC Brown/McGraw Hill.

Koury, J.M. (1996). *Aquatic therapy programming: Guidelines for orthopedic rehabilitation.* Champaign, IL: Human Kinetics.

Kraus, R.G., & Curtis, J.E. (1986). *Creative management in recreation, parks, and leisure services* (4th ed.). St. Louis: Times Mirror/Mosby College Publishing.

Krebs, P.L. (1990). Rhythms and dance. In J.P. Winnick (Ed.), *Adapted physical education and sport* (pp. 379–390). Champaign, IL: Human Kinetics.

Krebs, P.L., & Block, M.E. (1992). Transition of students with disabilities into community recreation: The role of the adapted physical educator. *Adapted Physical Activity Quarterly, 9,* 305–315.

Kurpius, D.J., & Rozecki, T.G. (1993). Strategies for improving interpersonal communication. In J.E. Zins, T.R. Kratochwill, & S.N. Elliott (Eds.), *Handbook of consultation services for children* (pp. 137–158). San Francisco: Jossey-Bass Publishers.

LaMaster, K., Gall, K., Kinchin, G., & Seidentop, D. (1998). Inclusion practices of effective elementary specialists. *Adapted Physical Activity Quarterly, 15,* 64–81.

Langendorfer, S.J. (1986). Aquatics for the young child: Facts and myths. *Journal of Physical Education, Recreation and Dance, 57*(6), 61–66.

Langendorfer, S.J. (1990). Contemporary trends in infant/preschool aquatics: Into the 1990s and beyond. *Journal of Physical Education, Recreation and Dance, 60*(5), 36–39.

Lavay, B., & Depaepe, J. (1987). The harbinger helper: Why mainstreaming in physical education doesn't always work. *Journal of Health, Physical Education, Recreation, and Dance, 58*(7), 98–103.

Lepore, M., Gayle, G.W., & Stevens, S.F. (1998). *A professional guide to conducting adapted aquatic programs.* Champaign, IL: Human Kinetics.

Lewis, R.B., & Doorlag, D.H. (1991). *Teaching special students in the mainstream* (3rd ed.). New York: Macmillan.

Lieberman, L.J. (1996). The effects of trained hearing peer tutors on the physical activity levels of deaf students in inclusive elementary physical education classes. *Dissertation Abstracts International, 57–03A,* 1074.

Lipsky, D.K., & Gartner, A. (1987). *Beyond separate education: Quality education for all.* Baltimore: Paul H. Brookes Publishing Co.

Lipsky, D.K., & Gartner, A. (1998). *Inclusion and school reform: Transforming America's classrooms.* Baltimore: Paul H. Brookes Publishing Co.

Lipton, D. (1994, April). *The full inclusion court cases: 1989–1994.* Paper presented at the Wingspread Conference, Racine, WI.

Luckasson, R., Coulter, D.L., Polloway, E.A., Reiss, S., Schalock, R.L., Snell, M.E., Spitalnik, D.M., & Stark, J.A. (1992). *Mental retardation: Definition, classification, and systems of supports* (9th ed.). Washington, DC: American Association on Mental Retardation.

Maloney, M. (1994). Courts are redefining LRE requirements under the IDEA. *Inclusive Education Programs, 1*(1), 1–2.

Margolis, H., & Fiorelli, J. (1987, Winter). Getting past anger in consulting relationships. *Organization Development Journal,* 44–48.

Margolis, H., & McCabe, P.P. (1988). Overcoming resistance to a new remedial program. *The Clearing House, 62*(3), 131–134.

Marks, N. & Jenkins, D. (1996). Medical information form-Broadus Wood Elementary School. Earlysville, VA: Author.

McCubbin, J., Jansma, P., & Houston-Wilson, C. (1993). The role of the adapted (special) physical educator: Implications for educating persons with serious disabilities. In P. Jansma (Ed.), *Psychomotor domain training and serious disabilities* (4th ed., pp. 29–40). Lanham, MD: University Press of America.

Mills v. Board of Education of District of Columbia, 348 F. Supp. 866 (D.D.C. 1972).

Minner, S.H., & Knutson, R. (1982). Mainstreaming handicapped students into physical education: Initial considerations and needs. *Physical Educator, 39,* 13–15.

Mizen, D.W., & Linton, N. (1983). Guess who's coming to P.E.: Six steps to more effective mainstreaming. *Journal of Health, Physical Education, Recreation, and Dance, 54*(8), 63–65.

Moon, M.S., & Bunker, L. (1987). Recreation and motor skills programming. In M.E. Snell (Ed.), *Systematic instruction of persons with severe handicaps* (pp. 214–244). Columbus, OH: Charles E. Merrill.

Morreau, L.E., & Eichstaedt, C.B. (1983). Least restrictive programming and placement in physical education. *American Corrective Therapy Journal, 37*(1), 7–17.

Morris, B. (1999). I just want to be a normal kid at summer camp. *Palaestra, 15*(2), 26–28.

Morris, G.S.D., & Stiehl, J. (1999). *Changing kids games* (2nd ed.). Champaign, IL: Human Kinetics.

Mosston, M. (1981). *Teaching physical education.* Columbus, OH: Charles E. Merrill.

Mosston, M., & Ashworth, S. (1994). *Teaching physical education* (4th ed.). New York: Macmillan.

Murata, N.M. (1995). *The effects of physical educators, teacher assistants, and peer tutors on the academic learning time of students with and without disabilities in regular physical education.* Unpublished doctoral dissertation, The Ohio State University, Columbus.

NASDE. (1991). Physical education and sports: The unfulfilled promise for students with disabilities. *Liaison Bulletin, 17*(6), 1–10.

National Association for Sport and Physical Education. (1992). *The physically educated person.* Reston, VA: Author.

National Association for Sport and Physical Education Outcomes Committee. (1992). Definition and outcomes of the physically educated person. *In Outcomes of quality physical education programs* (p. 7). Reston, VA: NASPE.

National Therapeutic Recreation Society. (1995). *About therapeutic recreation.* Arlington, VA: Author.

National Consortium on Physical Education and Recreation for Individuals with Disabilities (NCPERID). (1995). *Adapted physical education national standards.* Champaign, IL: Human Kinetics.

Nichols, B. (1994). *Moving and learning: The elementary school physical education experience* (3rd ed.). Boston: McGraw-Hill.

Ninness, H.A.C., & Glenn, S.S. (1988). *Applied behavior analysis and school psychology.* New York: Greenwood.

Nirje, B. (1969). The normalization principle and its human management implications. In R.B. Kugel & W. Wolfensberger (Eds.), *Changing patterns in residential services for the mentally retarded* (pp. 179–195). Washington, DC: U.S. Government Printing Office.

Oberti v. Board of Education of the Borough of Clementon School District, 995 F.2d 1204, 1009 (3rd Cir. 1993).

O'Brien, J., Forest, M., Snow, J., & Hasburg, D. (1989). *Action for inclusion*. Toronto, Ontario, Canada: Frontier College Press.

Orelove, F.P., & Sobsey, D. (1996). *Educating children with multiple disabilities* (3rd ed.). Baltimore: Paul H. Brookes Publishing Co.

Orlick, T. (1978). *The cooperative sports and games book*. New York: Pantheon Press.

Orlick, T. (1982). *The second cooperative sports and games book*. New York: Pantheon Press.

Osborne, A.G. (1996). *Legal issues in special education*. Needham Heights, MA: Allyn & Bacon.

Osinski, A. (1993). Modifying public swimming pools to comply with provisionals of the Americans with Disabilities Act. *Palaestra, 9*(1), 13–18.

Pangrazi, R.P. (1998). *Dynamic physical education for elementary school children* (12th ed.). Needham Heights, MA: Allyn & Bacon.

Pangrazi, R. P., & Dauer, V. P. (1992). Dynamic physical education for elementrary school children (10th ed.). New York: MacMillan.

PARC (Pennsylvania Association for Retarded Citizens) v. Commonwealth of Pennsylvania, No. 71-42 (E.D. Pa. 1971).

Peck, C.A., Donaldson, J., & Pezzoli, M. (1990). Some benefits nonhandicapped adolescents perceive for themselves from their social relationships with peers who have severe handicaps. *Journal of The Association for Persons with Severe Handicaps, 15,* 211–230.

Pedron, N.A., & Evans, S.B. (1990). Modifying classroom teachers' acceptance of the consulting teacher model. *Journal of Educational and Psychological Consultation, 1,* 189–200.

Petray, C., Freesemann, K., & Lavay, B. (1997). Understanding students with diabetes: Implications for the physical education professional *Journal of Physical Education, Recreation, and Dance, 68*(l), 57–64.

President's Council on Physical Fitness and Sports. (1991). *Get fit! A handbook for youth ages 6–17*. Washington, DC: Author.

Priest, E.L. (1990). Aquatics. In J.P. Winnick (Ed.), *Adapted physical education and sport* (pp. 391–408). Champaign, IL: Human Kinetics.

Priest, L. (1979). Integrating the disabled into aquatics programs. *Journal of Physical Education and Recreation, 50*(2), 57–59.

Pyfer, J., French, R., Babcock, G., Berends, K., Buswell, D., Meyer, S., Piletic, C., Rocco, S., Shephard, D., Stearns, D., Trocki, P., & Woosley, L. (1997). *The survival series: Including students with disabilities in regular physical education*. Unpublished manual, Texas Woman's University, Denton.

Rainforth, B., York, J., & Macdonald, C. (1992). *Collaborative teams for students with severe disabilities: Integrating therapy and educational services*. Baltimore: Paul H. Brookes Publishing Co.

Rainforth, B., & York-Barr, J. (1997). *Collaborative teams for students with severe disabilities* (2nd ed.). Baltimore: Paul H. Brookes Publishing Co.

Rehabiliation Act of 1973, PL 93-112, 29 U.S.C. §§ 701 *et seq.*

Reid, G. (1979). Mainstreaming in physical education. *McGill Journal of Education, 14,* 367–377.

Rizzo, J.V., & Zabel, R.H. (1988). *Educating children and adolescents with behavior disorders: An integrative approach*. Needham Heights, MA: Allyn & Bacon.

Rohnke, K. (1977). *Cowtails and cobras: A guide to ropes courses, initiative games, and other adventure activities*. Hamilton, MA: Project Adventure.

Safrit, M.J. (1990). *Introduction to measurement in physical education and exercise science* (2nd ed.). St. Louis: Times Mirror/Mosby College Publishing.

Sailor, W., Gee, K., & Karasoff, P. (1993). Full inclusion and school restructuring. In M.E. Snell (Ed.), *Instruction of students with severe disabilities* (4th ed., pp. 1–30). New York: Merrill.

Sallis, J.F., & Owen, N. (1999). *Physical activity and behavioral medicine*. Thousand Oaks, CA: Sage.

Santomier, J. (1985). Physical educators, attitudes and the mainstream: Suggestions for teacher trainers. *Adapted Physical Activity Quarterly, 2,* 328–337.

Schleien, S.J., Ray, M.T., & Green, F.P. (1997). *Community recreation and people with disabilities* (2nd ed.). Baltimore: Paul H. Brookes Publishing Co.

Seaman, J.A., & DePauw, K.P. (1989). *The new adapted physical education: A developmental approach*. Mountain View, CA: Mayfield.

Seidentop, D., & Rushall, B.S. (1972). *The development and control of behavior in sport and physical education*. Philadelphia: Lea & Febiger.

Semmel, M.I., Gottlieb, J., & Robinson, N.M. (1979). Mainstreaming: Perspectives on educating handicapped children in the public school. *Review of Research in Education, 7,* 223–279.

Sherrill, C. (1993). *Adapted physical activity, recreation, and sport: Crossdisciplinary and lifespan* (4th ed.). Madison, WI: WC Brown & Benchmark.

Sherrill, C. (1998). *Adapted physical activity, recreation, and sport: Crossdisciplinary and lifespan* (5th ed.). Madison, WI: WCB McGraw Hill.

Sigmon, S. (1983). The history and future of educational segregation. *Journal for Special Educators, 19,* 1–13.

Skinner, A.T., & Thompson, A.M. (Eds.). (1983). *Duffield's exercises in water* (3rd ed.). London: Bailliere Tindall.

Snell, M.E. (1988). Gartner and Lipsky's "Beyond special education: Toward a quality system for all students": Messages for TASH. *Journal of The Association for Persons with Severe Handicaps, 13,* 137–140.

Snell, M.E. (1991). Schools are for all kids: The importance of integration for students with severe disabilities and their peers. In J.W. Lloyd, N.N. Singh, & A.C. Repp (Eds.), *The regular education initiative: Alternative perspectives on concepts, issues, and models* (pp. 133–148). Sycamore, IL: Sycamore Press.

Snell, M.E., & Drake, G.P. (1994). Replacing cascades with supported education. *The Journal of Special Education, 27,* 393–409.

Snell, M.E., & Eichner, S.J. (1989). Integration for students with profound disabilities. In F. Brown & D.H. Lehr (Eds.), *Persons with profound disabilities: Issues and practices* (pp. 109–138). Baltimore: Paul H. Brookes Publishing Co.

Snell, M.E., & Zirpoli, T.J. (1987). Intervention strategies. In M.E. Snell (Ed.), *Systematic instruction of persons with severe handicaps* (pp. 110–150). Columbus, OH: Charles E. Merrill.

Special Olympics International. (1986). *Athletics sports skills guide*. Washington, DC: Author.

Stainback, S., & Stainback, W. (1985). *Integration of students with severe handicaps into regular schools*. Reston, VA: Council for Exceptional Children.

Stainback, S., & Stainback, W. (1987). Educating all students in regular education. *TASH Newsletter, 13*(4), 1, 7.

Stainback, S., & Stainback, W. (1990). Inclusive schooling. In W. Stainback & S. Stainback (Eds.), *Support networks for inclusive schooling* (pp. 3–24). Baltimore: Paul H. Brookes Publishing Co.

Stainback, W., & Stainback, S. (1991). A rationale for integration and restructuring: A synopsis. In J.W. Lloyd, N.N. Singh, & A.C. Repp (Eds.), *The regular education initiative: Alternative perspectives on concepts, issues, and models* (pp. 225–239). Sycamore, IL: Sycamore Press.

Stainback, W., Stainback, S., & Bunch, G. (1989a). Introduction and historical background. In W. Stainback, S. Stainback, & M. Forest (Eds.), *Educating all students in the mainstream of regular education* (pp. 1–14). Baltimore: Paul H. Brookes Publishing Co.

Stainback, W., Stainback, S., & Bunch, G. (1989b). A rationale for the merger of regular and special education. In W. Stainback, S. Stainback, & M. Forest (Eds.), *Educating all students in the mainstream of regular education* (pp. 15–28). Baltimore: Paul H. Brookes Publishing Co.

St. Clair, S.A. (1995). Differences in gross motor performance among multihandicapped deaf children using inclusion versus special day class models in adapted physical education (Masters Thesis, California State University—Fullerton). *Masters Abstracts International, 33–06,* 1662.

Sutherland, S. (1999). Special Olympics' United Sports, Partner's Club, and Sports Partnership Models. In P. Jansma (Ed.), *The psychomotor domain and the seriously disabled* (4th ed., pp. 333–340). Lanham, MD: University Press of America.

Taylor, S.J. (1988). Caught in the continuum: A critical analysis of the principle of the least restrictive environment. *Journal of The Association for Persons with Severe Handicaps, 13,* 41–53.

Troher, K. (March 1, 1992). Handle with care: Fragile kids fit into normal classes. *Chicago Tribune,* Section 18, p. 3.

Turnbull, H.R. (1990). *Free appropriate public education: The law and children with disabilities* (3rd ed.). Denver: Love.

Ulrich, D.A. (1985, August). *Current assessment practices in adapted physical education: Implications for future training and research activities.* Paper presented at the annual meeting of the National Consortium on Physical Education and Recreation for the handicapped, New Carollton, MD.

Ulrich, D.A. (1995). The Test of Gross Motor Development. Austin, TX: PRO-ED.

U.S. Department of Health and Human Services (USDHHS). (1996). *Physical activity and health: A report of the Surgeon General.* Washington, D.C.: Author.

Vandercook, T., & York, J. (1990). A team approach to program development and support. In W. Stainback & S. Stainback (Eds.), *Support networks for inclusive schooling: Interdependent integrated education* (pp. 95–122). Baltimore: Paul H. Brookes Publishing Co.

Vandercook, T., York, J., & Forest, M. (1989). The McGill Action Planning System (MAPS): A strategy for building the vision. *Journal of The Association for Persons with Severe Handicaps, 14,* 205–215.

Voeltz, L.M. (1980). Children's attitudes toward handicapped peers. *American Journal of Mental Deficiency, 84*(5), 455–464

Voeltz, L.M. (1982). Effects of structured interactions with severely handicapped peers on children's attitudes. *American Journal of Mental Deficiency, 86,* 380–390.

Voeltz, L.M., Wuerch, B.B., & Bockhaut, C.H. (1992). Social validation of leisure activities training with severely handicapped youth. *Journal of The Association for the Severely Handicapped, 7*(4), 3–13.

Vogler, E.W., & French, R. (1983). The effects of a group contingency strategy on behaviorally disordered students in physical education. *Research Quarterly for Exercise and Sport, 54,* 273–277.

Vogler, E.W., van der Mars, H., Cusimano, B., & Darst, P. (1990). Relationship of presage, context, and process variables to ALT-PE of elementary-level mainstreamed students. *Adapted Physical Activity Quarterly, 7,* 298–313.

Walker, J., & Shea, T. (1984). *Behavior management* (4th ed.). Upper Saddle River, NJ: Merrill.

Wang, M.C., & Baker, E.T. (1986). Mainstreamed programs: Design features and effects. *The Journal of Special Education, 19,* 503–521.

Wang, M.C., Peverly, S.T., & Randolph, R. (1984). An investigation of implementation and effects of a full-time mainstreamed program. *Remedial and Special Education, 5,* 21–32.

Wang, M.C., Reynolds, M.C., & Walberg, H.J. (1987). Rethinking special education. *Journal of Learning Disabilities, 20,* 290–293.

Webster, G.E. (1987). Influence of peer tutors upon academic learning time: Physical education of mentally handicapped students. *Journal of Teaching in Physical Education, 6,* 393–403.

Weiss, R., & Karper, W.B. (1980). Teaching the handicapped child in the regular physical education class. *Journal of Physical Education and Recreation, 51,* 22–35,77.

Wessel, J.A., & Curtis-Pierce, E. (1990). *Ballhandling activities: Meeting special needs of children.* Belmont, CA: Fearon Teacher Aids.

Wessel, J.A., & Kelly, L. (1986). *Achievement-based curriculum development in physical education.* Philadelphia: Lea & Febiger.

West, J.F., Idol, L., & Cannon, G.S. (1989). *Collaboration in the schools: An inservice and preservice curriculum for teachers, support staff, and administrators.* Austin, TX: PRO-ED.

Will, M.C. (1986). Educating children with learning problems: A shared responsibility. *Exceptional Children, 52,* 411–416.

Winnick, J.P. (1991). Program organization and management. In J.P. Winnick (Ed.), *Adapted physical education and sport* (pp. 19–36). Champaign, IL: Human Kinetics.

Winnick, J.P. (1995). An introduction to adapted physical education. In J.P. Winnick (Ed.), *Adapted physical education and sport* (2nd ed., pp. 3–16). Champaign, IL: Human Kinetics.

Wolfensberger, W. (1972). *The principle of normalization in human services.* Toronto, Ontario, Canada: National Institute on Mental Retardation.

Woodruff, G., & McGonigel, M.J. (1988). Early intervention team approaches: The transdisciplinary model. In J.B. Jordan, J.J. Gallagher, P.L. Hutinger, & M.B. Karnes (Eds.), *Early childhood special education: Birth to three* (pp. 163–182). Reston, VA: Council for Exceptional Children.

York, J., Giangreco, M.F., Vandercook, T., & Macdonald, C. (1992). Integrating support personnel in the inclusive classroom. In S. Stainback & W. Stainback (Eds.), *Curriculum considerations in inclusive classrooms: Facilitating learning for all students* (pp. 101–116). Baltimore: Paul H. Brookes Publishing Co.

York, J., & Rainforth, B. (1991). Developing individualized adaptations. In F.P. Orelove & D.J. Sobsey (Eds.), *Educating children with multiple disabilities: A transdisciplinary approach* (2nd ed., pp. 259–295). Baltimore: Paul H. Brookes Publishing Co.

York, J., Vandercook, T., Macdonald, C., Heisse-Neff, C., & Caughey, E. (1992). Feedback about integrating middle-school education students with severe disabilities in general education classes. *Exceptional Children, 58*(3), 244–258.

Zygmunt, L., Larson, M.S., & Tilson, G.P. (1994). Disability awareness training and social networking. In M.S. Moon (Ed.), *Making school and community recreation fun for everyone* (pp. 209–226). Baltimore: Paul H. Brookes Publishing Co.

Resources

Adaptive Equipment for Sports and Recreation

Adapted Physical Education/ Sports Equipment

Flaghouse
601 Flaghouse Drive
Hasbrouck Heights, NJ 07604
Phone: 800-793-7900
Fax: 800-793-7922
http://www.flaghouse.com

Gym Closet
6515 Cotter Avenue
Sterling Heights, MI 48314
Phone: 800-445-8873
Fax: 810-997-4866
http://www.gymcloset.com
E-mail: email@gymcloset.com

Play with a Purpose
220 24th Avenue NW
Post Office Box 998
Owatonna, MN 55060-0998
Phone: 800-533-0446
Fax: 800-451-4855
http://www.gophersport.com
E-mail: email@gophersport.com

S & S
Post Office Box 513
Colchester, CT 06415-0513
Phone: 800-266-8856
Fax: 800-566-6678
http://www.snswwide.com
E-mail: service@snswwide.com

Sporttime
One Sporttime Way
Atlanta, GA 30340
Phone: 800-283-5700

Fax: 800-845-1535
E-mail: catalog.request@sporttime. com

U.S. Games
Post Office Box 117028
Carrollton, TX 75011-7028
Phone: 800-327-0484
Fax: 800 899 0149
http://www.us-games.com
E-mail: feedusg@ sportsupplygroup.com

Bibs

Event Promotion Supply
11420 East 51st Avenue
Denver, CO 80239
Phone: 800-227-0337
Fax: 303-371-9149
http://www.eventpromo.com
E-mail: webmaster@eventpromo. com

Reliable Racing Supply
643 Upper Glen Street
Queensbury, NY 12804-2014
Phone: 800-274-6815
Fax: 800-585-4443
http://www.reliableracing.com
E-mail: customerservice@ reliableracing. com

Bi Skis

Milty's Bi Ski Skistar Technologies
Post Office Box 7461
Tahoe City, CA 96145
Phone: 916-581-2441
Fax: 916-581-2441

http://www.northtahoe.com/skistar/
  contcnt/aboutus.htm

Mountain Man Bi Ski
FFS Dual Ski
720 Front Street
Bozeman, MT 59715
Phone: 406-587-0310

Spokes N Motion Bi Ski
2225 South Platte River Drive W
Denver, CO 80223
Phone: 303-922-0605
Fax: 303-922-7943
http://www.spokesnmotion.com
E-mail: info@spokesnmotion.com

Mono-Skis
Grove Innovations
120 West Church, Box 185
Centre Hall, PA 16828
Phone: 814-364-2677

AT's Freedom Factory
Route 5, Box 50734
Winnsboro, TX 75494
Phone: 903-629-3945
Fax: 903-629-3946
http://www.sitski.com/atff.htm
E-mail: freefact@peoplescom.net

Shadow Rehabilitation Equipment Association
8030 South Willow Street, Unit 4
Manchester, NH 03103
Phone: 603-645-5200

Yetti Radventure, Inc.
20755 238th Place SW
Sherwood, OR 97140
Phone: 503-628-2895

Outriggers
LaCome, Inc
Post Office Box 1026
Questa, NM 87556
Phone: 505-586-0356

Spokes N Motion
2225 South Platte River Drive W
Denver, CO 80223
Phone: 303-922-0605

Fax: 303-922-7943
http://www.spokcsnmotion.com/
E-mail: info@spokesnmotion.com

Ski Doctor: Shockshaft
609 Munroe Street
Sacramento, CA 95825
Phone: 916-488-5398

Tip Retention, Ski Bras
Ski Eze
4401 Devonshire
Lansing, MI 48910
Phone: 517-882-4608

Nordic Sit-Ski
XC Glider
Hall's Wheels
Post Office Box 784
Cambridge, MA 02238
Phone: 617-628-7955,
          800-628-7956

Handcycles
American Wheel Sports
721 North Taft Hill
Ft. Collins, CO 80521
Phone: 800-800-5828

Angletech
318 North Highway 67
Post Office Box 1893
Woodland Park, CO 80866-1893
Phone: 719-687-7475
http://www.angletechcycles.com/
  index.html
E-mail: anglezoom@aol.com

AT's Freedom Factory
Route 5, Box 50734
Winnsboro, TX 75494
Phone: 903-629-3945
Fax: 903-629-3946
http://www.sitski.com/atff.htm
E-mail: freefact@peoplescom.net

Lightning Handcycles
360 Sepulveda Boulevard, Suite 1030
El Segundo, CA 80245
Phone: 888-426-3292
Fax: 310-821-0259
http://www.handcycle.com
E-mail: information@handcycle.com

Sportaid
78 Bay Creek Road
Loganville, GA 30052
Phone: 800-743-7203
Fax: 770-554-5944
http://www.sportaid.com/
   index.htm
E-mail: Stuff@sportaid.com

Tennis Wheelchairs
Spokes N Motion Bi Ski
2225 South Platte River Drive W
Denver, CO 80223
Phone: 303-922-0605
Fax: 303-922-7943
http://www.spokesnmotion.com
E-mail: info@spokesnmotion.com

Texas Assistive Devices, LLC
Route 3, Box 3866, CR
Brazoria, TX 77422
Phone: 409-798-8809,
   409-297-5447
Fax: 409-297-1142,
   409-798-0414
http://www.txad.com
E-mail: hps@tgn.net

Hockey/Klondike Sleds
Spokes N Motion Bi Ski
2225 South Platte River Drive W
Denver, CO 80223
Phone: 303-922-0605
Fax: 303-922-7943
http://www.spokesnmotion.com
E-mail: info@spokesnmotion.com

Groups on Specific Disabilities

Amputees
Amputee Treatment Center
8388 Lewiston Road
Batavia, NY 14020
Phone: 716-343-4154
Fax: 716-343-8101
http://amputee-center.com
E-mail: amputee@iinc.com

Attention-Deficit/ Hyperactivity Disorder
Children and Adults with Attention-
   Deficit/Hyperactivity Disorder
   (CHADD)
8181 Professional Place, Suite 201
Landover, MD 20785
Phone: 800-233-4050,
      301-306-7070
Fax: 301-306-7090
http://www.chadd.org
E-mail: webmaster@chadd.org

National Attention Deficit Disorder
   Association (ADDA)
1788 Second Street, Suite 200
Highland Park, IL 60035
Phone: 847-432-ADDA
Fax: 847-432-5874
http://www.add.org
E-mail: mail@add.org

Autism, Asperger's Syndrome, Fragile X Syndrome, Hyperlexia
American Hyperlexia Association
195 West Spangler, Suite B
Elmhurst, IL 60126
Phone: 630-415-2212
Fax: 630-530-5909
http://www.hyperlexia.org
E-mail: info@hyperlexia.org

Autism Research Institute
4182 Adams Avenue
San Diego, CA 92116
Fax: 619-563-6840
http://www.autism.org
E-mail: samr7@netcom.com

Autism Society of America
7910 Woodmont Avenue, Suite 300
Bethesda, MD 20814-3015
Phone: 800-3AUTISM, ext. 150,
      301-657-0881
Fax: 301-657-0869
http://www.autism-society.org
E-mail: asa@smart.net

Fragile X Research Foundation
45 Pleasant Street
Newburyport, MA 01950

Phone: 978-462-1866
Fax: 978-463-9985
http://www.fraxa.org
E-mail: kclapp@fraxa.org

National Autistic Society
393 City Road
London EC1V 1NG
UNITED KINGDOM
Phone: +44 (0)20 7833 2299
Fax: +44 (0)20 7833 9666
http://www.oneworld.org/
    autism_uk/
E-mail: nas@nas.org.uk

Blind and Visual Impairments
American Council of the Blind
1155 15th Street NW, Suite 1004
Washington, DC 20005
Phone: 202-467-5081,
        800-424-8666
Fax: 202-467-5085
http://www.acb.org
E-mail: info@acb.org

American Foundation for the Blind
    (AFB)
11 Penn Plaza, Suite 300
New York, NY 10001
Phone: 212-502-7600
http://www.afb.org/afb
E-mail: afbinfo@afb.net

Canadian National Institute for the
    Blind (CNIB)
1929 Bayview Avenue
Toronto, Ontario M4G 3E8
CANADA
Phone: 416-480-7520,
        800-268-8818
Fax: 416-480-7700
http://www.cnib.ca
E-mail: webmaster@cnib.ca

National Federation of the Blind
    (NFB)
1800 Johnson Street
Baltimore, MD 21230
Phone: 410-659-9314
http://www.nfb.org/default.htm
E-mail: epc@roudley.com

Brain Injury (TBI/ABI)
American Academy for Cerebral Palsy
    and Developmental Medicine
    (AACPDM)
6300 North River Road, Suite 727
Rosemont, IL 60018
Phone: 708-698-1635
http://149.142.183.10/new/
    site_content/members/index.htm

American Cerebral Palsy Information
    Center
http://www.cerebralpalsy.org
E-mail: ACPIC@cerebralpalsy.org
        stern4hope@aol.com

Centre for Neuro Skills (CNS)
2658 Mt. Vernon Avenue
Bakersfield, CA 93306
Phone: 800-922-4994,
        661-872-3408
Fax: 661-872-5150
http://www.neuroskills.com
E-mail: bakersfield@neuroskills.com

Traumatic Brain Injury Project
University of Kansas Medical Center
Department of Special Education
4001 H.C. Miller Building
3901 Rainbow Boulevard
Kansas City, KS 66160-7335
Phone: 913-588-5943
Fax: 913-588-5942
http://www.sped.ukans.edu/spedpro-
    jects/tbi/TBIHomePage.html
E-mail: lwilkers@kumc.edu
        jtyler@kumc.edu

Cerebral Palsy
United Cerebral Palsy Associations
    (UCPA)
UCPA National
1660 L Street NW, Suite 700,
Washington, DC 20036
Phone: 800-872-5827,
        202-776-0406
TTY: 202-973-7197
Fax: 202-776-0414
http://www.ucpa.org
E-mail: tking@ucpa.org

Deaf and Hearing Impairments

American Speech-Language-
  Hearing Association (ASHA)
10801 Rockville Pike
Rockville, MD 20852
Phone: 888-321-ASHA,
        800-498-2071
TTY: 301-571-0457
Fax: 877-541-5035
http://www.asha.org
E-mail: actioncenter@asha.org

National Association of the Deaf
  (NAD)
814 Thayer Avenue
Silver Spring, MD 20910-4500
Phone: 301-587-1788
TTY: 301-587-1789
Fax: 301-587-1791
http://www.nad.org
E-mail: NADinfo@nad.org

National Institute on Deafness and
  Other Communication Disorders
  (NIDCD)
31 Center Drive, MSC 2320
Bethesda, MD 20892-2320
Phone: 301-496-7243
TTY: 301-402-0252
Fax: 301-402-0018
http://www.nih.gov/nidcd
E-mail: webmaster@nidcd.nih.gov

Dwarfism

Asociación Nacional Para Problemos de
  Crecimeinto (CRECER)
Cuartel de Artiller'a, 12 - bajo
Murcia E-30002
SPAIN
Phone: +34 968 34 62 18
Fax: +34 968 34 62 02
http://www.crecimiento.org
E-mail: crecer@crecimiento.org

Belgian Association of Little People
(Association Belge des Personnes de
  Petite Taille)
Clos des Merisiers, 608 Bte 2
Tubize 1480
BELGIUM
Phone: +32 2 355 79 64

http://www.geocities.com/
  CapeCanaveral/Launchpad/3459
E-mail: jose.leblanc@village.uunet.be

Dutch Organization of Little People
Belangenvereniging Van Kleine
  Mensen (BVKM)
Wevelaan 75
Utrecht 3571
THE NETHERLANDS
Phone: +31 (0)30-27-111 98
Fax: +31 (0)30-27-111 98
http://www.bvkm.nl
E-mail: tlvv@westbrabant.net

The Quebec Association of Persons of
  Short Stature
(Association québécoise des personnes
  de petite taille)
2177, rue Masson, Suite 205
Montreal, Québec H2H 1B1
CANADA
Phone: 514-521-9671
Fax: 514-521-3369
http://www.aqppt.org
E-mail: aqppt@total.net

Down Syndrome

Association for Children with Down
  Syndrome (ACDS)
4 Fern Place
Plainview, NY 11803
Phone: 516-993-4700
Fax: 516-933-9524
http://www.acds.org/index2.html
E-mail: info@acds.org

National Association for Down Syn-
  drome (NADS)
Post Office Box 4542
Oak Brook, IL 60522
Phone: 630-325-9112
http://www.nads.org
E-mail: webmaster@nads.org

National Down Syndrome Congress
  (NDSC)
7000 Peachtree-Dunwoody Road NE
Lake Ridge 400 Office Park
Building #5, Suite 100
Atlanta, GA 30328

Phone: 800-232-NDSC,
       770-604-9500
http://www.ndsccenter.org
E-mail: NDSCcenter@aol.com

National Down Syndrome Society
   (NDSS)
666 Broadway
New York, NY 10012
Phone: 212-460-9330,
       800-221-4602
Fax: 212-979-2873
http://www.ndss.org
E-mail: jschell@ndss.org

Fetal Alcohol Syndrome/ Effects (FAS/FAE)

Fetal Alcohol Syndrome Consultation,
   Education and Training Services
   (FASCETS)
Post Office Box 83175
Portland, OR 97283
Phone: 503-621-1271
http://www.fascets.org
E-mail: dmalbin@oregonvos.net

National Organization on Fetal
   Alcohol Syndrome (NOFAS)
418 C Street NE
Washington, DC 20002
Phone: 202-785-4585
Fax: 202-466-6456
http://www.nofas.org
E-mail: nofas@erols.com

Hydrocephalus and Spina Bifida

Association for Spina Bifida and
   Hydrocephalus
42 Park Road
Peterborough PE1 2UQ
UNITED KINGDOM
Phone: +44 (0)1733 555988
Fax: +44 (0)1733 555985
http://www.asbah.demon.co.uk
E-mail: postmaster@asbah.demon.
   co.uk

Hydrocephalus Association
870 Market Street, Suite 705
San Francisco, CA 94102
Phone: 415-732-7040

Fax: 415-732-7044
http://www.HydroAssoc.org
E-mail: hydroassoc@aol.com

The Spina Bifida Association of
   America
4590 MacArthur Boulevard NW, Suite
   250
Washington, DC 20007-4226
Phone: 800-621-3141,
       202-944-3285
Fax: 202-944-3295
http://www.sbaa.org
E-mail: sbaa@sbaa.org

Spina Bifida and Hydrocephalus
   Association of South Australia
Post Office Box 16
North Adelaide SA 5006
AUSTRALIA
Phone: +61 (08) 8267 2508
http://www.span.com.au/
   spinabif_sa/index.html

Language/Speech Disorders

American Speech-Language-Hearing
   Association (ASHA)
10801 Rockville Pike
Rockville, MD 20852
Phone: 888-321-ASHA,
       800-498-2071
TTY: 301-571-0457
Fax: 877-541-5035
http://www.asha.org
E-mail: actioncenter@asha.org

National Aphasia Association
156 Fifth Avenue, Suite 707
New York, NY 10010
Phone: 800-922-4622
http://www.aphasia.org
E-mail: naa@aphasia.org

Learning Disabilities

International Dyslexia Association
   (IDA)
International Office
8600 LaSalle Road, Suite 382
Baltimore, MD 21286-2044
Phone: 410-296-0232
Messages: 800-ABCD123
Fax: 410-321-5069
http://www.interdys.org

E-mail: http://www.interdys.org/
e-mail_o.stm

Learning Disabilities Association of
America (LDA)
4156 Library Road
Pittsburgh, PA 15234-1349
Phone: 412-341-1515
Fax: 412-344-0224
http://www.ldanatl.org
E-mail: ldanatl@usaor.net

National Center for Learning
Disabilities (NCLD)
381 Park Avenue South, Suite 1401
New York, NY 10016
Phone: 212-545-7510,
888-575-7373
Fax: 212-545-9665
http://www.ncld.org

Mental Retardation
American Association on Mental Re-
tardation (AAMR)
444 North Capitol Street NW,
Suite 846
Washington, DC 20001-1512
Phone: 202-387-1968,
800-424-3688
Fax: 202-387-2193
http://www.aamr.org
E-mail: fttal@uaf.edu

The Arc of the United States
National Headquarters
1010 Wayne Avenue, Suite 650
Silver Spring, MD 20910
Phone: 301-565-3842,
800-433-5255
Fax: 301-565-5342
http://www.thearc.org/
State and local chapters: http://
www.thearc.org/chapters.htm
E-mail: info@thearc.org

The Arc of the United States
Publications Desk
3300-C Pleasant Valley Lane
Arlington, TX 76015
Phone: 888-368-8009
http://www.thearcpub.com

Developmental Disabilities
Center
1400 Dixon Avenue
Lafayette, CO 80026
Phone: 303-665-7789
Fax: 303-665-2648
http://ddcboulder.com/
E-mail: caroline@ddcboulder.com

Muscular Dystrophy
Muscular Dystrophy Association
of Australia
GPO Box 9932
Melbourne 3001
AUSTRALIA
Phone: +61 3 9370 0477,
800 656 MDA
Fax: +61 3 9370 0393
http://www.mda.org.au
E-mail: bms@mda.org.au

Muscular Dystrophy Association
of Canada
2345 Yonge Street,
Suite 900
Toronto, Ontario M4P 2E5
CANADA
Phone: 416-488-0030,
800-567-CURE
Fax: 416-488-7523
http://www.mdac.ca
E-mail: info@mdac.ca

Muscular Dystrophy Association of
United States of America
National Headquarters
3300 East Sunrise Drive
Tucson, AZ 85718
Phone: 800-572-1717
http://www.mdausa.org
E-mail: mda@mdausa.org

Muscular Dystrophy Family
Foundation
615 North Alabama Street,
Suite 330
Indianapolis, IN 46204
Phone: 317-632-8255,
800-544-1213
http://www.mdff.org
E-mail: mdff@prodigy.net

Paralysis and Spinal Cord Injury

American Paralysis Association
500 Morris Avenue
Springfield, NJ 07081
Phone: 800-225-0292
http://www.apacure.com
E-mail: webmaster@apacure.org

Foundation for Spinal Cord Injury
    Prevention (FSCIP)
1310 Ford Building
Detroit, MI 48226-3901
Phone: 800-342-0330
http://www.fscip.org
E-mail: info@fscip.org

National Spinal Cord Injury
    Association (NSCIA)
Network of Metropolitan
    Washington
Plaza West 9
51 Monroe Street
Rockville, MD 20850
Phone: 301-424-8335
Fax: 301-424-8858
http://www.erols.com/nscia
E-mail: steventowle@compuserve.com

Rett Syndrome

International Rett Syndrome
    Association (IRSA)
9121 Piscataway Road
Clinton, MD 20735

Phone: 800-818-RETT,
    301-856-3334
Fax: 301-856-3336
http://www.rettsyndrome.org
E-mail: irsa@rettsyndrome.org

Rett Syndrome Association UK
13 Friern Barnet Road
London N11 3EU
UNITED KINGDOM
Phone: +44 (0) 20 8361 5161
Fax: +44 (0) 20 8368 6123
http://www.rettsyndrome.org.uk
E-mail: info@rettsyndrome.org.uk

Seizure Disorders

Epilepsy Foundation of America
4351 Garden City Drive
Landover, MD 20785
Phone: 301-459-3700,
    800-EFA-1000
Fax: 301-577-4941
http://www.efa.org
E-mail: info@efa.org

Tourette Syndrome

National Tourette Syndrome
    Association
42-40 Bell Boulevard
Bayside, NY 11361-2820
Phone: 718-224-2999
Fax: 718-279-9596
http://tsa.mgh.harvard.edu
E-mail: tourette@ix.netcom.com

Professional Associations for Physical Educators

Adapted Physical Activity Council
    (AAHPERD)
1900 Association Drive
Reston, VA 20191-1599
Phone: 800-213-7193,
    703-476-3430
Fax: 703-476-9527
http://www.aahperd.org/aaalf.html
E-mail: aaalf@aahperd.org

Adapted Physical Education
    National Standards
    (APENS)
Post Office Box 425647
Texas Woman's University
Denton, TX 76204-5647
Phone: 888-APENS-Exam
http://www.twu.edu/apens
E-mail: APENS@venus.twu.edu

American Association for
   Active Lifestyles and Fitness
   (AAALF)
1900 Association Drive
Reston, VA 20191
Phone: 800-213-7193,
      703-476-3430
Fax: 703-476-9527
http://www.healthfinder.gov/text/orgs
   /HR2831.htm
E-mail: aaalf@aahperd.org

American College of Sports Medicine
   (ACSM)
Post Office Box 1440
Indianapolis, IN 46206-1440
Phone: 317-637-9200
Fax: 317-634-7817
http://www.acsm.org
E-mail: twest@acsm.org

American Dance Therapy
   Association
2000 Century Plaza, Suite 108
Columbia, MD 21044
Phone: 410-997-4040
Fax: 410-997-4048
http://www.adta.org
E-mail: info@adta.org

American Kinesiotherapy Association
Post Office Box 614
Wheeling, IL 60090-0614
Phone: 800-296-AKTA
http://www.akta.org
E-mail: lhedrick@aapmr.org

American Occupational Therapy
   Association
4720 Montgomery Lane,
Post Office Box 31220
Bethesda, MD 20824-1220
Phone: 301-652-2682,
      800-377-8555
Fax: 301-652-7711
http://www.aota.org
E-mail: helpdesk@aota.org

American Physical Therapy
   Association
111 North Fairfax Street

Alexandria, VA 22314
Phone: 800-999-2782
Fax: 800-999-2782
http://www.apta.org/Home
E-mail: components@apta.org

American Psychological
   Association
750 First Street NE
Washington, DC 20002
Phone: 800-374-2721,
      202-336-5500
Fax: 202-336-5500
http://www.apa.org
E-mail: webmaster@apa.org

American Therapeutic Recreation
   Association
ATRA National Office
1414 Prince Street, Suite 204
Alexandria, VA 22314-4664
Phone: 703-683-9420
Fax: 703-683-9431
http://www.atra-tr.org
E-mail: membership@atra-tr.org

Canadian Association for Health,
   Physical Education, and
   Recreation
1600 James Naismith Drive,
   Suite 606
Gloucester, Ontario K1B 5N4
CANADA

Canadian Association of Sport
   Sciences
1600 James Naismith Drive,
   Suite 311
Gloucester, Ontario K1B 5N4
CANADA

Canadian Fitness and Lifestyle
   Research Institute
201-185 Somerset Street W,
   Suite 313
Ottawa, Ontario K2P 0J2
CANADA
Phone: 613-233-5528
Fax: 613-233-5536
http://www.cflri.ca
E-mail: info@cflri.ca

Council for Exceptional Children
  (CEC)
1920 Association Drive
Reston, VA 20191-1589
Phone: 888-CEC-SPED,
      703-620-3660
TTY: 703-264-9446
Fax: 703-264-9494
http://www.cec.sped.org
E-mail: service@cec.sped.org

International Federation of Adapted
  Physical Activity (IFAPA)
11168 Windjammer Drive
Frisco, TX 75034

National Association of State Directors
  of Special Education
1800 Diagonal Road, Suite 320
Alexandria, VA 22314
Phone: 703-519-3800

National Consortium for Physical Edu-
  cation and Recreation for
  Individuals with Disabilities
  (NCPERID)
State University of New York—
  Cortland
Department of Physical Education
Post Office Box 2000
Cortland, NY 13045
Phone: 607-753-4908
Fax: 607-753-4929
http://ncperid.usf.edu
E-mail: craft@snycorva.cortland.edu
      ellery@coedu.usf.edu

National Information Center for Chil-
  dren and Youth with Disabilities
  (NICHCY)
Post Office Box 1492
Washington, DC 20013-1492

Phone/TTY: 800-695-0285,
        202-884-8200
Fax: 202-884-8441
http://www.nichcy.org
E-mail: nichcy@aed.org

National Rehabilitation Association
633 South Washington Street
Alexandria, VA 22314
Phone: 703-836-0850
Fax: 703-836-0848
http://www.nationalrehab.org/
  website/index.html
E-mail: info@nationalrehab.org

National Rehabilitation Information
  Center (NARIC)
1010 Wayne Avenue, Suite 800
Silver Spring, MD 20910
Phone: 301-562-2400
Fax: 301-562-2401
http://www.naric.com/index.html
E-mail: http://www.naric.com/
  guestform.html

National Therapeutic Recreation Society
22377 Belmont Ridge Road
Ashburn, VA 20148
Phone: 703-858-0784
Fax: 703-858-0794
http://www.nrpa.org/branches/
  ntrs.htm
E-mail: ntrsnrpa@aol.com

Rehabilitation International USA
25 East 21st Street
New York, NY 10010
Phone: 212-420-1500
Fax: 212-505-0871
http://www.rehabinternational.org
E-mail: rehabintl@aol.com

Sports and Recreation
Organizations for People with Disabilities

Active Living Alliance for Canadians
   with a Disability
Alliance de Vie Active pour les
   Canadiens/Canadiennes ayant un
   handicap
720 Belfast Road, Suite 104
Ottawa, Ontario K1G 0Z5
CANADA
Phone: 613-244-0052,
        800-771-0663
Fax: 613-244-4857
http://www.ala.ca
E-mail: info@ala.ca

Adaptive Sports Center
Post Office Box 1639
Crested Butte, CO 81224
Phone: 970-349-2296
Fax: 970-349-4950
http://www.adaptivesports.org
E-mail: ascl@rmi.net

Australian Deaf Sports Federation
01-117 Wellington Parade South,
East Melbourne, Victoria 3002
AUSTRALIA
TTY: +61 (03) 9650 2524
Fax: +61 (03) 9654 2868
http://www.deafsports.org.au/
   main.htm
E-mail: adsf@deafsports.org.au

British Wheelchair Sports
   Foundation
Guttmann Road, Stoke Mandeville
Buckinghamshire HP21 9PP
UNITED KINGDOM
Phone: +(44) 1296 484848,
        +(44) 1296 395995
Fax: +(44) 1296 424171
http://www.lboro.ac.uk/research/
   paad/wheelpower/home.htm
E-mail: wheelpower@dial.pipex.com

Canadian Amputee Sports Association
217 Holmes Avenue
Willowdale, Ontario M2N 4M9
CANADA

Phone: 416-222-8625
Fax: 416-229-6547
http://www.interlog.com/
   ~ampsport/can_amputee.html
E-mail: ampsport@interlog.com

Canadian Wheelchair Sports
   Association
1600 James Naismith Drive
Gloucester, Ontario K1B 5N4
CANADA
Phone: 613-748-5685
Fax: 613-748-5722
http://indie.ca/cwsa
E-mail: cwsa@bpg.ca

Cerebral Palsy International Sport and
   Recreation Association
   (CP-ISRA)
Post Office Box 16
HETEREN 6666 ZG
THE NETHERLANDS
Phone: +31 26 47 22 593
Fax: +31 26 47 23 914
http://surf.to/cpisra
E-mail: cpisra_nl@hotmail.com

Cerebral Palsy Sports Association of
   British Columbia
6225A—136th Street
Surrey, British Columbia V3X1H3
CANADA
Phone: 604-599-5240
Fax: 604-599-5241
http://www.cpsports.com
E-mail: info@cpsports.com

Disabled Sports USA
451 Hungerford Drive, Suite 100
Rockville, MD 20850
Phone: 301-217-0960
Fax: 301-217-0968
http://www.dsusa.org
E-mail: dsusa@dsusa.org

Dwarf Athletic Association of
   America
418 Willow Way
Lewisville, TX 75077

Phone: 972-317-8299
Fax: 972-966-0184
http://www.daaa.org
E-mail: jfbda3@aol.com

International Blind Sport Association
   (IBSA)
c/ Quevedo, 1-1
Madrid 28014
SPAIN
Phone: +34 91 589 45 33,
         +34 91 589 45 34,
         +34 91 589 45 36
Fax: +34 91 589 45 37
http://www.ibsa.es
E-mail: ibsa@ibsa.es

International Paralympic Committee
Adenauerallee 212-214
Bonn 53113
GERMANY
Phone: +49-228-2097-200
Fax: +49-228-2097-209
http://www.paralympic.org
E-mail: info@paralympic.org

International Sports Organization of
   the Deaf (CISS)
16117 Orchard Grove Road
North Potomac, MD 20878
Phone: 301-990-4151
Fax: 301-990-4151
http://www.ciss.org
E-mail: Ammons@ciss.org

Leisure Education for Exceptional
   People
929 North 4th Street
Mankato, MN 56001
Phone: 507-387-5122
http://www.gotocrystal.net/~leep
Email: leep@mctcnet.net

National Sports Center for the
   Disabled
Post Office Box 1290
Winter Park, CO 80482
Phone: 970-762-1540
Fax: 970-762-4112
http://www.nscd.org/
Program locations:

http://www.nscd.org/
   nearyou/index.html
E-mail: info@nscd.org

Special Olympics International
1325 G Street NW, Suite 500
Washington, DC 20005
Phone: 202-628-3630
Fax: 202-824-0200
http://www.specialolympics.org
Program locations: http://www.
   specialolympics.org/
   programlocations/index.html
E-mail: specialolympics@msn.com

Super Sports Program
3800 Ridgeway Drive
Birmingham, AL 35209
Phone: 888-868-2303,
         205-868-2281
Fax: 205-868-2283
http://www.mindspring.com/
   ~bassanglr/super.htm
E-mail: supersports@mindspring.
   com

U.S. Cerebral Palsy Athletic
   Association
25 West Independence Way
Kingston, RI 02881
Phone: 401-874-7465
Fax: 401-874-7468
http://www.uscpaa.org
E-mail: uscpaa@mail.bbsnet.com

U.S. Association of Blind Athletes
33 North Institute
Colorado Springs, CO 80903
Phone: 719-630-0422
Fax: 719-630-0616
http://www.usaba.org
E-mail: USABA@iex.net

USA Deaf Sports Federation
3607 Washington Boulevard,
   Suite 4
Ogden, UT 84403-1737
Phone: 801-393-7916
Fax: 801-393-2263
http://www.usadsf.org
E-mail: usadsf@aol.com

Committee on Sports for Disabled
(COSD)
U.S. Olympic Committee
1750 East Boulder Street
Colorado Springs, CO 80909-5760
Phone: 719-578-4818
http://www.olympic-
usa.org/inside/disabled.html
E-mail: mark.shepherd@usoc.org

Wheelchair Sports and Recreation
Association
2001 Marina Drive, Suite 113W
North Quincy, MA 02171
Phone: 617-773-7251
Fax: 617-376-0343
http://www.wheelchairsportsinc.com
E-mail: wheerus@aol.com

Wheelchair Sports USA
3595 East Fountain Boulevard,
Suite L-1
Colorado Springs, CO 80910
Phone: 719-574-1150
Fax: 719-574-9840
http://www.wsusa.org
E-mail: wsusa@aol.com

Wheelchair Sports Worldwide
Olympic Village
Guttmann Road, Aylesbury
Bucks HP21 9PP
UNITED KINGDOM
Phone: +44 (0) 01296 436179
Fax: +44 (0) 01296 436484
http://www.wsw.org.uk
E-mail: ismwsfl@aol.com

Organization by Sports

Billiards
National Wheelchair Billiards
Association
http://www.bca-pool.com/nwba

Boccia
International Paralympic Committee
8 Parr Parade Narraweena
Sydney NSW 2099
AUSTRALIA

Phone: +61-2-99-814857
Fax: +61-2-99-814857
http://info.lut.ac.uk/research/paad/
ipc/boccia/boccia.html

Bowling
American Blind Bowling
Association
411 Sheriff
Mercer, PA 16137
Phone: 412-662-5748

American Wheelchair Bowling
Association
6264 North Andrews Avenue
Ft. Lauderdale, FL 33309
Phone: 954-491-2886
Fax: 954-491-2886
http://members.aol.com/
bowlerweb/awba.htm
E-mail: bowlawba@juno.com

Independent Disabled Bowlers of the
Australian Capital Territory
http://www.geocities.com/
Colosseum/Arena/4160
E-mail: mecooke@yahoo.com

Golf
Association of Disabled American
Golfers
Post Office Box 280649
Lakewood, CO 80228-0649
Phone: 303-922-5228
Fax: 303-969-0447
http://www.discovercolorado.com/
golf/adag
E-mail: adag@usga.org

Australian Blind Golfers Association
http://www.blindgolf.org.au
E-mail: judipo@melbpc.org.au

Equestrian/Horseback
Riding
National Center for Equine Facilitated
Therapy (NCEFT)
5001 Woodside Road
Woodside, CA 94062
Phone: 650-851-2271
Fax: 650-851-3480

http://www.nceft.com
E-mail: webmaster@nceft.com

North American Riding for the
 Handicapped Association
 (NARHA)
Post Office Box 33150
Denver, CO 80233
Phone: 800-369-7433
FAX: 800-252-4610
http://narha.org
E-mail: narha@narha.org

Fencing
British Paraplegic Fencing
 Association
20 Preston New Road
Blackpool, Lancs. FY4 4HQ
UNITED KINGDOM
Phone: +44 1253-312180
http://www.lboro.ac.uk/research/
 paad/wheelpower/fencing.htm
E-mail: fencer@enterprise.net

Goalball
International Paralympic
 Committee
1212 Buttenwood Drive
Friendswood, TX 77546
Phone: 713-644-1601
Fax: 713-644-9565
http://www.lboro.ac.uk/research/
 paad/ipc/goalball.html
E-mail: jimleask@vwr-inc.com

Handcycling
United States Handcycling
 Federation
Phone: 831-457-7747
http://www.ushf.org
E-mail: info@ushf.org

Quad Rugby
United States Quad Rugby
 Association
309 Stoney Ford Road
Holland, PA 18966
Phone: 215-504-0443
Fax: 215-504-0445
http://www.quadrugby.com/toc.htm
E-mail: jbishop@quadrugby.com

Tennis
National Capital Wheelchair Tennis
 Association
http://www.magma.ca/~ncwta
E-mail: ncwta@magma.ca
National Foundation of Wheelchair
 Tennis
940 Calle Amanecer, Suite B
San Clemente, CA 92672
Phone: 714-361-3663
Fax: 714-361-6003
http://www.nfwt.org

Racquetball
National Wheelchair Racquetball As-
 sociation
2380 McGinley Road
Monroeville, PA 15146
Phone: 412-856-2468

Road Racing
International Wheelchair Road Racers
 Club, Inc.
30 Myano Lane
Stamford, CT 06902
Phone: 203-967-2231

Shooting
NRA Disabled Shooting Services
11250 Waples Mill Road
Fairfax, VA 22030
Phone: 703-267-1495

Winter Sports
Adaptive Ski & Sport Programs
Tom Cannalonga
504 Brett Place
South Plainfield, NJ 07080
Phone: 908-313-5590
Fax: 908-668-1634
http://www.sitski.com
Program locations:
 http://www.sitski.com/pg3.htm
E-mail: Tom@sitski.com

Disabled Sports/USA
451 Hunderford Drive,
 Suite 100
Rockville, MD 20850
Phone: 301-217-0960
http://www.dsusa.org

Disabled WinterSport Australia
15 Beverly Street
Merimbula NSW 2548
AUSTRALIA
Phone: +61 (02) 6495 2082
Fax: +61 (02) 6495 2034
http://www.acr.net.au/~skidisabled
E-mail: finsko@acr.net.au

The Skating Association for the Blind
   and Handicapped
548 Elmwood Avenue
Buffalo, NY 14222
Phone: 716-883-9728
http://www.sabahinc.org
E-mail: sabah@sabahinc.org

U.S. Deaf Ski & Snowboard
   Association
2202 Cypress Point East
Austin, TX 78746-7223
Fax: 512-328-6457
http://www.usdssa.org
E-mail: President@usdssa.org

U.S. Disabled Ski Team
Post Office Box 100
Park City, UT 84060
Phone: 801-649-9090
http://www.usskiteam.com/
   disabled/disabled.htm

Sledge Hockey
American Sledge Hockey
   Association
10933 Johnson Avenue S
Bloomington, MN 55437
Phone: 612-644-2666
http://www.SledHockey.org
E-mail: info@sledhockey.org

Soccer
American Amputee Soccer
   Association
http://www.ampsoccer.org
E-mail: rgh@ampsoccer.org
lameraven@aol.com

Swimming/Aquatics
Aquatics Council
American Association of Health,
   Physical Education, Recreation and
   Dance (AAHPERD)
7252 Wabash Avenue
Milwaukee, WI 53223
Phone: 414-354-8717
http://www.aahperd.org/index.html
E-mail: webmaster@aahperd.org

Handicapped Scuba Association
   International
HSA International
1104 El Prado
San Clemente, CA 92672
Phone: 949-498-6128
Fax: 949-498-6128
http://www.hsascuba.com
E-mail: hsa@hsascuba.com

United States Aquatic Association of
   the Deaf
http://members.tripod.com/
   USAAD/
E-mail: USAAD@hotmail.com

Softball/Baseball
Challenger Baseball
Little League Baseball Headquarters
Post Office Box 3485
Williamsport, PA 17701

National Beep Baseball Association
2231 West 1st Street
Topeka, KS 66606-1304
Phone: 913-234-2156
http://www.nbba.org
E-mail: info@nbba.org

National Wheelchair Softball Association
1616 Todd Court
Hastings, MN 55033
Phone: 612-437-1792

Volleyball
U.S. Disabled Volleyball Team (USDVT)
Disabled Sports USA
451 Hungerford Drive, Suite 100
Rockville, MD 20850
Phone: 301-217-0960

Fax: 301-217-0968
http://www.volleyball.org/usdvt.html

Waterskiing
International Water Ski Federation
    Disabled Council
http://members.aol.com/IWSF/
    disabled/report1.htm

Wheelchair Basketball
Canadian Wheelchair Basketball
    Association
1600 James Naismith Drive
Gloucester, Ontario K1B 5N4
CANADA
Phone: 613-748-5888
Fax: 613-748-5889

National Wheelchair Basketball
    Association
Charlotte Institute for Rehabilitation
1100 Blythe Boulevard
Charlotte, NC 28203
Phone: 704-355-1064
Fax: 704-446-4999
http://www.nwba.org/index2.html
E-mail: cesar@nwba.org

Wheelchair Hockey
U.S. Electric Wheelchair Hockey
    Association
7216 39th Avenue N

Minneapolis, MN 55427
Phone: 763-535-4736
http://www.usewha.org
E-mail: hockey@usewha.org

Weightlifting/Powerlifting
International Paralympic
    Committee
Powerlifting
Elzenstraat 12
Brugge 8000
BELGIUM
Phone: +32-50-312634
Fax: +32-50-390119
http://info.lut.ac.uk/research/paad/
    ipc/powerlifting/class.html

United States Cerebral Palsy Athletic
    Association (USCPAA)
Powerlifting
8420 West Chester Pike
Upper Derby, PA 19082
Phone: 610-356-1910
http://www.uscpaa.org/
    paranom.htm

U.S. Wheelchair Weightlifting
    Federation
39 Michael Place
Levittown, PA 19057
Phone: 215-945-1964

Index

Page numbers followed by "f" indicate figures; numbers followed by "t" indicate tables.